WORKS ISSUED BY

THE HAKLUYT SOCIETY

BYRON'S JOURNAL OF
HIS CIRCUMNAVIGATION
1764–1766

SECOND SERIES
No. CXXII

ISSUED FOR 1962

Portrait of the Hon. John Byron

by Joshua Reynolds [?]

Byron's Journal
of his Circumnavigation
1764-1766

★

Edited by

ROBERT E. GALLAGHER

CAMBRIDGE
Published for the Hakluyt Society
AT THE UNIVERSITY PRESS
1964

PUBLISHED BY
THE SYNDICS OF THE CAMBRIDGE UNIVERSITY PRESS
Bentley House, 200 Euston Road, London, N.W.1
American Branch: 32 East 57th Street, New York 22, N.Y.
©
THE HAKLUYT SOCIETY
1964

Printed in Great Britain
by Robert MacLehose and Company Limited
at the University Press, Glasgow

PREFACE

SINCE the manuscript of this Byron journal is owned by the National Maritime Museum, it is only fitting that my thanks, and those of the Hakluyt Society, be given first of all to the Museum for their permission to publish this work. I am also indebted to the Public Record Office, London, the Archives of the Department of Foreign Affairs, Paris, the Dixson Library, Sydney, the British Museum, the Hydrographic Department of the Admiralty, and the Hydrographic Office of the U.S. Navy, for the use of their facilities and the permission either to draw upon or to reproduce materials in their files. The copyright in such materials remains their property.

I believe that one owes more thanks to individuals than to institutions. The 'making of a book' is not the result of collecting material, evaluating, and finally presenting it. It is the result of a human relationship in which individuals go out of their way to give the author or editor assistance, encouragement, and advice.

Since it would be impossible for me to name all those to whom I owe a debt of gratitude, I should like to mention specifically Professor Geoffrey Tillotson of Birkbeck College in the University of London, Dr Helen Wallis of the Map Room of the British Museum, Mr R. A. Skelton, the honorary Secretary of the Hakluyt Society and the Superintendent of the Map Room of the British Museum, Mr G. P. B. Naish of the National Maritime Museum, Miss Katherine Lindsay-MacDougall, who was on the staff of the National Maritime Museum when I was working there, and Mr E. K. Timings, Assistant Keeper in the Public Record Office. The help which each of these people gave me was so extensive and was given over such a long period of time that it would be impossible to state just what this volume owes to each of them.

I should also like to thank Mr Peter J. J. Kosiba for reading the early drafts of my Introduction and for making many valuable suggestions, Mrs Vera S. Thale for assisting in the arduous chore of checking the typescript against the photostats of the original manuscript, Mr Walter J. Fromm for helping to prepare the typescript for the printer, Miss Janet D. Hine for making the arrangements regarding the illustrations from the Dixson Library, and Mr James A. Friberg for changing my rough sketches into maps worthy of reproduction.

Finally, I would like to thank Dr Helen Wallis for her permission to include in this volume her excellent article 'The Patagonian Giants'.

R. E. G.

University of Illinois, Chicago
April 1962

CONTENTS

Appendix III: THE PATAGONIANS

ILLUSTRATIONS AND MAPS

Plates

ix

Maps

Acknowledgements

Reproductions have been made by courtesy of the Trustees
of the British Museum, the Trustees of the National
Maritime Museum, the Trustees of the Dixson Library
and the Director of the Hydrographic Department of the
Admiralty.

BIBLIOGRAPHY

I. *Manuscript Material*

PUBLIC RECORD OFFICE

Admiralty—Secretary

PRO Adm 1/162   In-Letters; East Indies   1757–66
(Admirals Stevens and Cornish,
Commodore Byron)

PRO Adm 1/4126   In-Letters; Letters from   1763–5
Secretaries of State

PRO Adm 1/1494   In-Letters; Captains'   1764–7
Letters

PRO Adm 2/92   Orders and Instructions   May 1764–July 1765

PRO Adm 2/234   Lords' Letters   Mar.–Dec. 1764

PRO Adm 2/235   Lords' Letter   1765

PRO Adm 2/537   Secretary's Letters; To   1 Mar.–7 Nov. 1764
Public Offices and Admirals

PRO Adm 2/724   Secretary's Common   Jan.–15 Nov. 1764
Letters

PRO Adm. 2/726   Secretary's Common   27 Nov. 1765–10 Mar.
Letters   1767

PRO Adm 2/1332   Secret Orders and Letters   1762–78

PRO Adm 3/74   Board Minutes   Apr.–Dec. 1766

PRO Adm 3/253   Minutes (Special Minutes)   1761–5

PRO Adm 6/20   Registers, Returns, and   1764–73
Certificates (Various)

PRO Adm 8/40   List Books   1764

PRO Adm 8/41   List Books   1765

PRO Adm 8/42   List Books   1766

Treasurers' Pay Books, Series I

PRO Adm 33/441   *Dolphin*   26 Mar. 1764–3 June
1766

Ships' Logs, Supplementary

PRO Adm 55/34   Logs and Journals of Ships   5 May 1764–5 May
on Exploration; *Dolphin*   1766

PRO Adm 55/35   Logs and Journals of Ships   17 June 1766–13 May
on Exploration; *Dolphin*   1768
PRO Adm 55/131   Logs and Journals of   30 Mar. 1764–27 Apr.
Ships on Exploration; *Tamar*   1765

Admiralty—Navy Board
PRO Adm 106/1132   In-Letters;   1764
Miscellaneous B
PRO Adm 106/1135   In-Letters;   1764
Miscellaneous P
PRO Adm 106/1137   In-Letters;   1764
Miscellaneous W
PRO Adm 106/2197   Out-Letters; To the   1765–6
Admiralty

State Papers
PRO SP 94/253   Spain; Supplementary   1761–70

Chatham Papers
PRO 30/8/94   Papers relating to Minorca,
Gibraltar, Corsica, Malta and the Falkland
Isles

NATIONAL MARITIME MUSEUM

Navy Board
NMM Adm/A/2557   In-Letters from the   Mar. 1764
Admiralty
NMM Adm/A/2558   In-Letters from the   Apr. 1764
Admiralty
NMM Adm/A/2559   In-Letters from the   May 1764
Admiralty
NMM Adm/A/2584   In-Letters from the   June 1764
Admiralty

Admiralty
NMM Adm/B/174   In-Letters from the   Mar.–Aug. 1764
Navy Board
NMM Adm/B/178   In-Letters from the   Jan.–Sept. 1766
Navy Board

Victualling Board

NMM Adm/C/574	In-Letters from the Admiralty	Apr.–June 1764
NMM Adm/C/583	In-Letters from the Admiralty	July–Sept. 1766

Commissioners for Sick and Wounded Seamen

NMM Adm/E/40	In-Letters from the Admiralty	Mar. 1765–Dec. 1769
NMM Adm/F/13	Out-Letters to the Admiralty	Feb. 2–Sept. 1756
NMM Adm/F/14	Out-Letters to the Admiralty	Oct. 1756–Dec. 1757
NMM Adm/F/24	Out-Letters to the Admiralty	Jan. 1763–Dec. 1764
NMM Adm/FP/9	Out-Letters to the Admiralty	Jan.–Dec. 1766

Miscellaneous

NMM Adm/K/13   *Dolphin*'s Ticket Book
NMM 35 MS 0081

MINISTÈRE DES AFFAIRES ÉTRANGÈRES, PARIS

Affaires Étrangères Angleterre, 470.

II. *Printed Material*

Africa Pilot. Pt. I, 9th ed. London, 1930.

AMHERST OF HACKNEY, LORD, and THOMSON, BASIL (eds.). *The Discovery of the Solomon Islands*. (Hakluyt Society, ser. II, nos. 7, 8.) London, 1901.

APRÈS DE MANNEVILLETTE, JEAN BAPTISTE NICOLAS DENISD'. *Le Neptune Oriental*. . . . Paris, 1745.

BEAGLEHOLE, J. C. *The Exploration of the Pacific*. London, 1947.

BEAGLEHOLE, J. C. (ed.). *The Journals of Captain James Cook on his Voyages of Discovery*, I: *The Voyage of the Endeavour, 1768–1771*. (Hakluyt Society, extra series no. XXXIV.) Cambridge, 1955. II: *The Voyage of the Resolution and Adventure, 1772–1775*. (Hakluyt Society, extra series no. XXXV.) Cambridge, 1961.

BRIGHAM, WILLIAM T. *An Index to the Islands of the Pacific Ocean*. Honolulu, 1900. In *Memoirs of the Bernice Pauahi Bishop Museum*, I. Honolulu, 1899–1903.

[BULKELEY, JOHN, and CUMMINS, JOHN] *A Voyage to the South-Seas By His Majesty's Ship Wager.* London, 1743.

BYRON, HON. JOHN. *Narrative of the Hon. John Byron; being an account of the Shipwreck of the Wager. . . .* Edinburgh, 1812.

—— *The Narrative of the Honourable John Byron Containing an Account of the Great Distresses Suffered by Himself and His Companions on the Coast of Patagonia. . . .* London, 1768.

[CAMPBELL, JOHN (ed.)] John Harris, *Navigantium atque Itinerantium Bibliotheca. or, a Complete Collection of Voyages and Travels.* London, 1744.

CARRINGTON, HUGH (ed.). *The Discovery of Tahiti, A Journal . . . of H.M.S. Dolphin . . . written by her master George Robertson.* (Hakluyt Society, ser. II, no. 98.) London, 1948.

CHARNOCK, JOHN. *Biographia Navalis*, v. London, 1797.

CLOWES, G. S. LAIRD (ed.). *Anson's Voyage round the World, by Richard Walter.* London, 1928.

CLOWES, SIR WILLIAM LAIRD, et al. *The Royal Navy.* London, 1898.

COQUELLE, PIERRE. 'Le Comte de Guerchy, Ambassadeur de France à Londres (1763–1767)', *Revue des Études Historiques*, LXIV (Septembre-Octobre, 1908), 417–72.

COWLEY, AMBROSE. 'Capt. Cowley's Voyage round the Globe', *A Collection of Original Voyages*, ed. William Hacke. London, 1699.

COX, EDWARD GODFREY. *A Reference Guide to the Literature of Travel*, II. Seattle, 1938.

DAMPIER, WILLIAM. 'A Supplement to the Voyage round the World,' *A Collection of Voyages*, II. London, 1729.

The English Pilot: The Third Book. Oriental Navigation. London, 1734.

GOEBEL, JULIUS, JR. *The Struggle for the Falkland Islands.* New Haven, 1927.

GREEN, JOHN. *Charts of North and South America . . . 1753*, Chart VI. [London], 1753.

HALLEY, EDMUND. 'A New and Correct Chart, shewing the Variations of the Compass in the Western and Southern Oceans . . .', *The English Pilot: The Fourth Book. . . .* London, 1753.

HARLOW, VINCENT T. *The Founding of the Second British Empire, 1763–1793*, I. London, 1952.

HAWKESWORTH, JOHN (ed.). *An Account of the Voyages . . . by Commodore Byron, Captain Wallis, Captain Carteret, and Captain Cook. . . .* I. London, 1773.

HERBERT, WILLIAM. *A New Directory for the East-Indies.* . . . 4th ed. London, 1775.

HORSBURGH, JAMES. *Directions for Sailing to and from the East Indies, China, New Holland, Cape of Good Hope, and the interjacent ports,* I. London, 1809.

L'Hydrographie Françoise. . . . [Paris], 1756.

KEIR, SIR DAVID LINDSAY. *The Constitutional History of Modern Britain since 1485.* 6th ed. London, 1960.

MAYR, ERNST. *Birds of the Southwest Pacific.* New York, 1945.

Monthly Meteorological Charts of the Eastern Pacific Ocean. London, 1950.

NARBOROUGH, SIR JOHN. 'Sir John Narborough to Magellanica, in 1670,' *Terra Australis Cognita: or, Voyages to the Terra Australis, or Southern Hemisphere.* . . ed., John Callander. Edinburgh, 1768.

NARBROUGH [NARBOROUGH], SIR JOHN. *Voyage to the South-Sea.* London, 1711.

Regulations and Instructions Relating to His Majesty's Service at Sea. 11th ed. London, 1772.

ROSE, REV. HUGH JAMES. *A New General Biographical Dictionary,* v. London, 1848.

Sailing Directions for the Pacific Islands, III, 'Eastern Groups.' H. O. Pub. 80. Washington, D.C., 1952 [corrected to 1961].

SENEX, JOHN. *South America Corrected from the Observations communicated to the Royal Societys of London & Paris.* London, [? 1710].

SHARP, ANDREW. *The Discovery of the Pacific Islands.* London, 1960.

A Voyage round the World, In His Majesty's Ship the Dolphin, Commanded by the Honourable Commodore Byron. . . . By an Officer on Board the said Ship. London, 1767.

WALLIS, HELEN. 'The Exploration of the South Seas, 1519 to 1644. A study of the influence of physical factors, with a reconstruction of the routes of the explorers' (unpublished thesis for the degree of D.Phil., University of Oxford, 1953; copies deposited in the British Museum and the Bodleian Library.)

WALTER, RICHARD (compiler). *A Voyage Round the World . . . by George Anson.* 14th ed. London, 1769.

WOOD, JOHN. 'Capt. Wood's Voyage thro' the Streights of Magellan,' *A Collection of Original Voyages,* ed. William Hacke. London, 1699, pp. 56–100.

B xvii

INTRODUCTION

I. *The Fitting Out*

ON 7 March 1764, the Secretary of the Admiralty, Philip Stephens, wrote to the Navy Board requesting them 'to propose a Ship of Twenty four Guns to be sheathed with Copper, & fitted for a voyage to the West Indies . . . to cause some further Experiments to be made of the efficacy of Copper-Sheathing'.[1] On the 8th, the Navy Board proposed that the *Dolphin*, a frigate built by Fellowes at Woolwich and launched in 1751,[2] be used for the experiment and that she be moved by yachtsmen from Chatham to the yard at Woolwich which had the docking facilities needed for both fitting out and sheathing a ship; and on the 9th, the Lords High Admiral and Commissioners for Executing that Office sent to the Navy Board formal orders to carry out their proposal.[3]

Approximately two weeks later, the Hon. John Byron was commissioned captain of the *Dolphin* and James Cumming, her lieutenant.[4] She was to have a complement of one hundred and thirty men and to be victualled with six months' supply of beef and pork and four months' of all other provisions, with the exception of beer. Her beer allowance was to be cut down because of stowage limitations, and a supply of brandy was to be substituted. Finally, Byron was ordered to use dispatch in getting her ready for sea.[5] Consequently, on the 28th, Byron assumed command of the *Dolphin*, and he, together with Cumming, John Crosier, the ship's surgeon, the warrant and petty officers needed for the fitting out and a handful of able seamen and personal servants, went aboard.[6]

Byron had served in the navy for thirty-three years before he assumed command of the *Dolphin*. The second son of William, the

---

[1] National Maritime Museum (NMM) Adm/A/2557.
[2] Sir William Laird Clowes et al., *The Royal Navy*, III (London, 1898), 12.
[3] NMM Adm/A/2557.
[4] Public Record Office (PRO) Adm 6/20.
[5] Ibid.
[6] See *Dolphin*'s Crew, Appendix I, pp. 143–9.

fourth Lord Byron, he was born on 8 November 1723.[1] His naval career began about the year 1731, when he became a midshipman, and he was still a midshipman when he sailed in the *Wager*, one of Anson's squadron, in September 1740. The *Wager*, an old Indiaman fitted out as a man-of-war and used as a supply ship for the fleet and by all accounts the poorest sailing vessel in the squadron, became separated from the rest of the ships while going round Cape Horn. On 14 May 1741, while Captain Cheap, who had assumed command of the *Wager* upon the transfer of its previous captain, was attempting to keep a rendezvous with Anson, the *Wager* went on the rocks on an island about ninety leagues north of the entrance to the Strait of Magellan and four or five leagues off the mainland, under the shadow of the Cordilleras. There then began one of the most harrowing experiences recorded in English naval history. Byron's own account, *The Narrative of the Honourable John Byron Containing an Account of the Great Distresses Suffered by Himself and His Companions on the Coast of Patagonia*, was published in London in 1768. It was an account of pillaging, treachery, and murder by the crew, most of whom claimed that since their pay ceased the moment the ship was lost they were no longer subject to military discipline and that it was every man for himself. It told of Byron's own living off the sea, without shelter and clothing, on the 'most unprofitable spot on the globe of the earth'; of his going without a full meal for thirteen months; of his living three years in the lands of the Spaniards until he was sent back to Europe in a French ship in 1745; and of his eventual return to England in February 1746, almost five years after the shipwreck.

After his return to England, Byron's rise in the navy was rapid. He was immediately given command of a sloop-of-war. In December 1746, he was made captain of the *Syren* frigate. In January 1753, he assumed command of the *Augusta*, 50 guns, which had been ordered to be fitted out as a guardship at Plymouth. Before the usual tour of duty on a ship of this type was over, he was appointed to the *Vanguard*, 70 guns, in the beginning of 1755. In 1757 he assumed command of the *America*, 60 guns, which took

---

[1] The fullest contemporary biography of Byron is that in John Charnock's *Biographia Navalis*, v (London, 1797), 423–39.

part in the expedition against Rochfort under Sir Edward Hawke. By the close of that year he was senior officer of a small squadron consisting of the *America* and the *Brilliant* and *Coventry* frigates which was ordered to cruise the coast of France. The English squadron met a group of French ships. The *America* had the misfortune to have her adversary, a ship from Quebec laden with furs, burn during the fight. The *Coventry*, though, captured a privateer from Bayonne, the *Dragon*; and the *Brilliant* sank the *Intrépide* another privateer.

In 1760, Byron was in command of the *Fame*, 74 guns, which was ordered to Louisburg with some transports. At Louisburg he was informed by the governor that a French force carrying troops, provisions, and stores had taken refuge in Chaleur Bay. The French had hoped to relieve the garrison at Montreal, but Lord Colville had reached the St Lawrence River with a British squadron before the French could reach the river. Consequently, they went into Chaleur Bay and hoped to land the troops and send them and the provisions and stores overland. Byron attacked the French force with his own ship, the *Fame*, the *Repulse*, and the *Scarborough* and destroyed all the French ships: three frigates, the *Marchault*, 32 guns, the *Bienfaisant*, 22 guns, the *Marquis Marlose*, 18 guns; and the twenty schooners, sloops, and small privateers that were carrying the men and equipment. Byron remained in command of the *Fame* until the end of the war, when he went on half-pay. He remained on half-pay until he was appointed captain of the *Dolphin*.

Byron had known that he would soon be putting to sea even before March 7 when Stephens sent the Admiralty's request for a ship to the Navy Board. For on the 4th he had written to the sister of Lieutenant Philip Carteret, who was to sail on the *Tamar*, the *Dolphin*'s consort, and was to move to the *Dolphin* as one of her lieutenants in April 1765, asking her to let him know where he could reach him. On the 12th, he wrote Carteret: 'If you should chose to go to Sea with me, make all the Haste you can to Town as not a Moments time must be lost.'[1] There is no evidence that at this early date Byron was aware of what would be the exact nature of his mission; unless, of course, one wishes to read this meaning

[1] NMM 35 MS 0081.

into the words 'make all the Haste you can to Town as not a Moments time must be lost'.

The *Dolphin* was a sixth-rate ship, carrying twenty-four guns. Her gun deck measured 113′ 0″, her keel 93′ 4″, her beam 32′ 1″, and she had a depth of 11′ 0″. Her 'burthen in tons' was 511.[1] 'She was one of the earlier types of the "true frigates", without guns on the lower deck, and constructed with the old square forward bulkhead instead of the rounded bow of the later ships of her class. She was rigged normally for the period with foremast, main and mizen, with topsails and top-gallant sails; royals had not then come into fashion.'[2]

When her fitting out began, the Navy Board discovered that the *Dolphin* was in no condition to stand a long sea journey, for 'the Worm has got into the plank of the Dolphin to such a degree, that it is necessary to take the old Plank wholly off her bottom, to put the Ship into a condition more to be depended upon'; but the Admiralty was in such haste to ready the ship for sea that it immediately authorized the Navy Board to have the civilian employees at the Woolwich Yard work overtime on her.[3] So great was the hurry that in order to expedite the repairs the yard used on one Sunday, for example, a foreman, a quartermaster, thirty-six shipwrights, and one team of horses from six in the morning until six at night.[4]

Parenthetically—there seems to be a great mystery about the history of the experimentation with copper sheathing, a device to prevent the worm from eating away a ship's bottom and, at the same time, a means of keeping the bottom from becoming fouled as rapidly as a wooden sheathed bottom would. Clowes, in his edition of *Anson's Voyage*, claimed that the *Alarm* was the first ship to be sheathed with copper and that this was done because of a direct order by Anson in 1761.[5] Sir John Knox Laughton gave the honour of being the first ship so sheathed to the *Dolphin*,[6] but

---

[1] Clowes (et al.), 12.

[2] Hugh Carrington (ed.), *The Discovery of Tahiti, A Journal written by her master George Robertson of H.M.S. Dolphin* . . . (London, 1948), xxx. Carrington gives a plank by plank, compartment by compartment, description (xxx–xxxv).

[3] NMM Adm/A/2557.   [4] PRO Adm 106/1137.

[5] G. S. L. Clowes (ed.), *Anson's Voyage round the World* by Richard Walter (London, 1928), xxi.

[6] In the *Dictionary of National Biography*.

Carrington called her the second.[1] Actually, according to Navy Office records, the order to copper-sheath the *Alarm* was given on 1 September 1763, after Anson had died.[2] Also, on 6 March 1764, before the Navy Board received its letter from the Admiralty asking that it select a vessel for the forthcoming voyage, the *Tartar* was taken into dock, after she had gone aground, in order that her copper sheathing might be examined for possible damage.[3] Thus the *Dolphin* would seem to be at least the third ship to have been given a copper bottom.

The fitting out of both the *Dolphin* and the *Tamar*, the ship selected to accompany her, continued through the months of April and May.[4] Fresh provisions were provided for the crews while the ships were in the yards during May,[5] and some special equipment needed for an extended voyage was placed aboard. When Byron had commanded the *Fame*,[6] 'he found by experience that a Cutter he had in her of twenty six feet, and that rowed double-bank'd, was of infinite use', and such a cutter was put aboard the *Dolphin* in place of the usual captain's barge.[7] Both ships were furnished with portable ovens,[8] and the Woolwich Yard was ordered to supply them with machines for sweetening 'stale and noxious water'.[9] Unfortunately, the yard had only the machine that it was using for experimental purposes, but it was

---

[1] Carrington, XXXI.   [2] NMM Adm/B/178.
[3] NMM Adm/B/174.
[4] The fitting out of the *Tamar* at Deptford was begun at the end of March. NMM Adm/A/2557.
[5] This may have been an unusual procedure, for the Admiralty Board's order to the Commissioners of Victualling reads: 'Notwithstanding any orders to the contrary, You are hereby required and directed to cause the Companies of His Majesty's Ship the Dolphin at Woolwich, & Frigate the Tamar at Deptford, which are under orders to be fitted for foreign service, to be supplied with fresh provisions until they proceed to sea. Given under our hands the 2nd of May 1764' (NMM Adm/C/574).
[6] 'In 1760 he was sent in command of the *Fame* and a small squadron to superintend the demolition of the fortifications of Louisbourg, and while the work was in progress had the opportunity of destroying a quantity of French shipping and stores in the bay of Chaleur, including three small men-of-war. He returned to England in November, but continued in command of the *Fame* until the peace, being for the most part attached to the squadron before Brest' (D.N.B.).
[7] NMM Adm/A/2558. The cutter was twelve-oared, built at Deal, and covered with an awning (PRO Adm 106/1132).
[8] PRO Adm 2/537.
[9] PRO Adm 106/1137.

able to construct a second one before the ships sailed.[1] Incidentally, Lieutenant Orsbridge, the inventor of the machine, received a reward of £100 in November 1765,[2] and on her second trip the *Dolphin* carried a still for 'rendering sea water fresh at sea'.[3]

The first indication that there might be something unusual about the voyage of the *Dolphin* and *Tamar* occurred on June 5 when orders were issued raising the *Dolphin*'s complement to one hundred and fifty men and the *Tamar*'s to one hundred.[4] Needless to say, all the boards and offices involved in the fitting out had to be informed of this change. It could have been coincidental, but on the same day, June 5, the Lords of the Admiralty cautioned the Navy Board 'to direct . . . that no Foreigner of any Rank or Character whatever be admitted, upon any pretence, to visit His Majesty's said Yards, Docks, or Magazines, as they will answer the Contrary at their Peril'.[5] Although this order was to be a standing order and it merely repeated previously issued instructions, the fact that the Admiralty Board would once again warn the Navy Board of the need for security precautions on the very day that the first extraordinary step in the fitting out took place seems to indicate that there was a connection between the two orders and that the Admiralty wanted to forestall the possibility that a foreigner would become suspicious about the true nature of the voyage.

On June 11, Byron reported to Philip Stephens, the Secretary of the Admiralty, that the *Dolphin* was ready for sea. He also requested three or four days' liberty in town and asked the Admiralty Board permission to allow Lieutenant Cumming, 'a very careful man', to take charge of the ship on its trip to the Downs;[6] permission was granted. On the 14th, the *Dolphin* and *Tamar* sailed from

---

[1] NMM Adm/A/2559. The yard at Woolwich had orders to experiment with the machines but had been unable to complete its experiments. Stinking water had been used, 'but the Stench it had imbibed being from the foulness of the Cask and not from Corruption, by its being kept close and confined they did not consider this as a proper trial tho. they allow the water was not quite so bad as when the tryal began' (PRO Adm 106/2197).

'By the 26th, our water was become foul, and stunk intolerably, but we purified it with a machine, which had been put on board for that purpose: it was a kind of ventilator, by which air was forced through the water in a continued stream, as long as it was necessary.' [John Hawkesworth (ed.), *An Account of the Voyages . . . by Commodore Byron, Captain Wallis, Captain Carteret, and Captain Cook . . .* (London, 1773), I, 4. Cited hereafter as Hawkesworth Text.]

[2] PRO Adm 2/235. [3] NMM Adm/C/583. [4] PRO Adm 2/234.
[5] PRO Adm 2/234. [6] PRO Adm 1/1494.

Longreach.[1] And, as ill-luck would have it, while her commanding officer was on leave, the *Dolphin* ran aground. When she arrived at Plymouth, it was necessary to take her into dock and inspect her bottom, but no damage had been done.[2]

On the 17th, Byron, who had rejoined the ship, was ordered to take the Dolphin from the Downs to Plymouth Sound, there to take under his command the *Tamar*, to pay the crew two months' wages in advance, then to sail at 'the first opportunity of wind and weather', then 'to open the inclosed sealed Packet and follow such Instructions as are therein contained for your further proceedings'.[3] A second letter instructed him 'to cause all the Commission and Warrant Officers Servants belonging to the Ship you command, as also those belonging to the *Tamar* Frigate to be discharged and set ashore before you sail from Plymouth'.[4] An allowance equal to the pay of the servants was to be paid at the end of the voyage.

On the 18th, the ostensible destination of the *Dolphin* and *Tamar* was officially changed from the West Indies to the East Indies, when, by order of the Lords of the Admiralty, Byron was 'appointed Commander in Chief of His Majesty's Ships and Vessels employed & to be employed in the East Indies'.[5] His formal appointment also gave him permission to fly his broad pennant as soon as he was clear of the Channel.

The appointment of Byron as Commander-in-Chief in the East Indies was an astute move by the Admiralty Board, for it enabled Byron to 'top off' his supplies and provisions at Plymouth without going through the normal channels and without regard to the quantities normally carried by ships of the size of the *Dolphin* and *Tamar*. Orders went out to the Navy Board to see that he got what he wanted and at his own request.[6] This change in destination to the East Indies would also enable him to refresh his crews and to

---

[1] PRO Adm 106/1132. [2] PRO Adm 106/1135.
[3] PRO Adm 2/1332.
[4] Ibid. 'There is allowed to the Captain of every Ship, Four Servants in every Hundred Men of the Complement. To the Lieutenant, Master, Second Master, Purser, Surgeon, Chaplain, and Cook, in all Ships down to 60 Men inclusive, each one Servant. To the Boatswain, Gunner, and Carpenter, in all Ships down to 100 Men inclusive, each two Servants; and from 100 to 60 Men, one Servant.' [*Regulations and Instructions Relating to His Majesty's Service at Sea*, 11th ed. (London, 1772), 151–2. This edition is identical with the 9th ed. of 1757, that in effect when Byron sailed.]
[5] PRO Adm 6/20. [6] PRO Adm 2/234.

repair the ships at Rio de Janeiro without arousing the suspicions of the Portuguese and the Spaniards, since India-bound ships often had to touch on the coast of Brazil if they had sailed from England during the month of June.[1]

Nevertheless, the subterfuge caused the Admiralty some moments of embarrassment, moments which showed how correct it had been in taking precautions against 'security leaks'. Byron had been appointed Commander-in-Chief of the fleet in the East Indies on June 18. The very next day, Robert James of India House wrote Stephens, asking him to send certain documents to India on the ships. Stephens' reply was a perfect example of how to grant such a request without giving the show away. In part, he wrote:

but as he [Captain Byron] is to call at Plymouth for the latter [the *Tamar*] the Advices which the Gentlemen in the Direction are desirous of sending to the Company's Presidencys may probably be in time; And if you will please to send them to me by tomorrow afternoon I will take care that no time will be lost in forwarding them.

As it is late in the year for Ships to sail from Europe to the East Indies, my Lords Commrs. of the Admty cannot but be under apprehension that the Frigates above mentioned may probably lose their Passage; And as their Lordships take it for granted that the Gentlemen in the Direction may find some Opportunity of sending Duplicates of their Advices over land, if that should be the Case, I must beg the favour of you to give me a few days notice of it, that their Lordships may avail themselves of the same opportunity of sending Duplicates of their Dispatches to their Officers in the East Indies.[2]

The company was to continue to be an embarrassment. A month later, the Secret Committee of the East India Company, 'presuming that the intention of sending the Dolphin & Tamar Frigates of War to the East Indies . . . was with a View to be of Service to the Company in those Parts,' by-passed the Admiralty and wrote directly to the Earl of Halifax at St James's, asking for confirmation.[3] The following day the Secretary of State for the

---

[1] James Horsburgh, *Directions for Sailing to and from the East Indies, China, New Holland, Cape of Good Hope, and the interjacent ports* (London, 1809), 1, 23–6.
[2] PRO Adm 2/537.   [3] PRO Adm 1/4126.

North (Lord Stanhope) passed on the letter to the Admiralty with the following letter:

> By Directions of the Earl of Halifax, I send You inclosed the Copy of a Letter from the Secret Committee of the East India company; and I am to desire You will please to furnish me with the Information therein desired, that his Lordship may be enabled to return an answer to the Secret Committee of the East India Company.[1]

This correspondence does more than illuminate a minor incident in the preparations for the voyage. If one takes Stanhope's letter at its face value—and there is no reason for not doing so—it would seem that at this date, July 20, almost three weeks after Byron had sailed from Plymouth, the Secretary of State for the North was unacquainted with the ostensible details of the voyage, much less with the true objectives, the search for Pepys's Island and the Falkland Islands, the cruising of the South Atlantic, and finally the search for the north-west passage. This fact, in turn, would lead one to believe that the decision to send Byron on his exploration was an Admiralty decision made in consultation with the king and that the Admiralty had not felt it necessary—nor possibly even wise—to take the cabinet into its confidences. Admittedly, the evidence is slender; but, if these deductions are true, it is probable that no one outside the Admiralty, other than the king, was aware of what was taking place until late in July 1765 when the First Lord of the Admiralty, the Earl of Egmont, sent to the Duke of Grafton a letter from Byron telling of the re-discovery of the Falkland Islands.[2]

The fact that the First Lord of the Admiralty was able to keep all information regarding the Byron voyage from his fellow ministers for more than a year and that he chose to do so is not surprising. In the eighteenth century, more often than not, the cabinet was large, loosely-knit, and ill-organized; and the individual ministers 'considered themselves servants of the King rather than colleagues in a united ministry, whose members, agreeing on a common policy and giving one another mutual support, accepted

---

[1] Ibid. I have found no answer from Stephens, and there is no trace of the correspondence in the India Office Library.
[2] See Document No. 1, p. 153.

the leadership of a parliamentary chief'.[1] As a result, Egmont was able to deal directly with the king without having to consult with his fellow ministers. From the Admiralty's point of view, keeping the rest of the cabinet in the dark was the prudent thing to do; for, as we shall see, in 1749 when Anson, then a Lord of the Admiralty, made preparations for a voyage of discovery similar to Byron's, the cabinet, as the result of pressure from Spain, forced the Admiralty to cancel the voyage. In 1764 the Admiralty was taking no chances that the events of 1749 would be repeated.[2]

The Admiralty carried out the pretence that the *Dolphin* and *Tamar* were destined for the East Indies and that Byron was to assume command in that part of the world until the ships returned in early spring 1766. The time for carrying out this 'cover story' was most opportune, for in September 1764 nine ships of the East Indies fleet were recalled and the *Dolphin* and *Tamar* could have been replacements. Also, the commander in the East Indies, Vice-Admiral Cornish, had been recalled in the summer of 1764. In the *List Book*, 'East Indies Command',[3] the *Dolphin* and *Tamar* are listed as having gone to the East Indies in July 1764. On 1 August 1765, the *List Book* showed Byron in the East Indies actually exercising command over the *York*, 60 guns, the *Argo*, 28, the *Dolphin*, 24, and the *Tamar*, 16. In January 1766, Byron was still supposedly in the East Indies, at this time in command of the *Dolphin*, the *Tamar*, and the *Argo*. It was only after the ships returned to England that they were not carried as part of the East Indies command and that Byron was not officially listed as being in charge.

The same concern for security was shown when it became necessary in August 1764, to purchase and fit out the store ship that would meet Byron at either Pepys's Island or Port Desire. The Admiralty directed the Navy Board to purchase the *Gloucester*, 299 tons, to carry stores and provisions to the 'Gulph of Mexico & coast of Florida'. The *Gloucester*, with a complement of twenty-four men, was to be 'Put on the List of the Royal Navy, as a Storeship by the name of the *Florida*'.[4]

---

[1] Sir David Lindsay Keir, *The Constitutional History of Modern Britain since 1485*, 6th ed. (London, 1960), 319.
[2] See below, pp. xxxvii–xxxviii.   [3] PRO Adm 8/40.   [4] PRO Adm 2/234.

On June 29, Byron reported to Stephens that the *Dolphin* had been docked, no damage had been found, that the ship was once again in the Sound, and that he could proceed to sea 'the moment the men has received their advance money'.[1] On 3 July 1764, he sent to London the formal document regarding the 'State and Conditions of Dolphin & Tamar', the post-script of which reads: 'The Wind being favorable, the two Ships are Unmooring.'[2]

The *Dolphin* sailed under the command of the Hon. John Byron. She bore one hundred and twenty-nine seamen, of whom one hundred and twenty-eight were mustered and one was a 'widow's man'.[3] She also carried fourteen marines, under the command of Captain Thomas Parslow. Strangely, the *Dolphin*'s muster sheet does not list a master, although she carried one. Three lieutenants were aboard, rather than the one normally carried by a ship of the sixth rate. Also, her allowance of master's mates had been raised from two to three, of midshipmen from four to twelve, of quartermasters from two to four, of boatswain's mates from one to two, and of yeomen of the sheets from one to two.[4] The *Tamar* was served by an extra lieutenant, and her quota of petty officers included two master's mates, six midshipmen, four quartermasters and two boatswain's mates.[5]

---

[1] PRO Adm 1/1494.   [2] Ibid.

[3] 'There being allowed, by Act of Parliament, to be constantly borne upon the Books of every Ship of War in Sea-Pay, a Man in every hundred Men, that the Complement of such Ship shall consist of; and two Men in every hundred, for such time as the Number of Men employed in the Service of the Royal-Navy, shall not exceed Twenty Thousand: And it being enacted, That the Produce of the Wages of such Seamen, and Value of their Victuals, shall be given and applied to the Relief of the Poor Widows of Commission and Warrant Officers of the Royal Navy; Every Commander is to enter and bear upon the Books of the Ship or Vessel he commands, as Part of her Complement, (till he receives Orders to the contrary) so many fictitious Names of Men, under the Appellation of Widows Men, with the Number of 1, 2, 3, &c. annexed, as two in every hundred of her Complement shall amount to; observing, if the Complement, or broken Number of the Complement, amounts to Twenty-five or upwards, but less than Seventy-five, to allow one Name for such broken Number; but if it amounts to Seventy-five or more, then to allow two for it. The said Names are to be rated able Seamen, and always mustered for Wages, (but not for Victuals) as if the Men were actually on Board; and when Pay-Books shall at any Time be made out for the Payment of the Ship, the said Names are to be entered therein, as if real Seamen, with able Seamen's Pay, free from any Deduction whatsoever' (*Regulations and Instructions*, 220).

[4] For normal complements of ships of all rates, see *Regulations and Instructions*, 146–7.

[5] PRO Adm 2/1332.

Although most of these additional officers and petty officers reported aboard before the Admiralty order authorizing their being carried on the ships was sent to Byron on June 17,[1] there is no real discrepancy between the Admiralty records and what actually took place. For on June 5, the complement of the *Dolphin* had been raised from one hundred and thirty men to one hundred and fifty and that of the *Tamar* to one hundred. No doubt the exact details of the increases were worked out at this earlier date.

This order of the 17th, which authorized the increase in officer and petty officer personnel, also specified that the warrant and petty officers should receive third-rate pay rather than sixth rate and 'that all such of the officers (as well Commission as Warrant Officers) Petty officers, Seamen and Marines, as shall exert themselves in their several Stations, and behave themselves to your [Byron's] satisfaction, Shall be allowed and paid double Wages during the said Voyage . . .'.[2]

The most extraordinary departure from the normal Admiralty procedure was not the bonus pay offered, but the verbal authorization given by Lord Egmont to Byron 'to purchase Vegetables at all such places as your Lordships Memorialist [Byron] might touch at during the said Voyage' and 'to cause the Ships Companys to be served any quantity of Provisions, beyond the established Allowance as your Lordships Memorialist might judge necessary, the better to enable them to undergo the fatigues & Hardships of the Voyage'.[3]

Byron was to take full advantage of this humane privilege. At Madeira, he

[1] Ibid. For example, Lt Cumming reported aboard the *Dolphin* on 28 March 1764 and Lt John Marshall and Lt George Robertson on the 12th. Lt Philip Carteret replaced Cumming when the latter was transferred to the *Tamar* in April, 1765 (see *Dolphin*'s Crew, Appendix 1, pp. 143–9). 'Friday Nov[r] 2[d] Wind NNW a pleasant Gale & very fine weather. *This day after swearing the Lieutenants of both Ships I* [Byron] *delivered them their Commissions for the Dolphin tho' but a 20 Gun Ship bears three lieu[ts] for this Voyage and the Tamar two.* They had only acting Orders from me before, & thought they were not to receive their proper Commissions til after their arrival in India, where they imagined we were bound' (p. 27).

[2] Actually, this is not as generous as it first seems. The pay differential between sixth rate and third rate was not considerable, and in many cases petty officers in a sixth-rate ship received the same pay as those in a third ('Wages in each Rate', *Regulations and Instructions*, 146). Byron did not inform his men of this wage bounty until after the ships left Rio de Janeiro.

[3] See *Byron's Memorial*, Document No. 6, p. 180.

directed Mr Henry Stacy Purser of the Dolphin, to furnish that Ship and the Tamer with Onions . . . at the rate of twenty pounds in weight to each Person on board them for a Sea Store, and at the Cape of Good Hope a quantity of Pumpkins for the same purpose; . . . at Rio de Janero, Batavia and the Cape . . . finding that the Pursers quotas of Vegetables, which they furnished the Ships with, (being as much as they could afford) were not near sufficient, [he] directed Mr Stacy to purchase Vegetables, to Boil with the fresh Beef every Day for Dinner, limitting him to the Prices, which he was not to exceed, and to draw Bills on the Victualling Board for the same.

And when his men were undergoing the rigours of the South Atlantic climate,

observing that the established Allowance of Provisions was not sufficient for the Officers and People, (who had nothing else to Eat or Drink for a great part of the time,) he order'd Breakfasts to be given them, every Day in the Week in the Straits of Magellan and the Coast of Patagonia, also as much Pease above their Allowance as they could eat in the Voyage; the Beef and Pork being very small when Boiled he frequently gave them double Allowance, he also gave them as much Bread as they could eat, with double Allowance of Sugar, and Spirits as often as necessary.

II. *The Historical Background*

The opening of the preamble to Byron's secret instructions,[1]

Whereas nothing can redound more to the honor of this Nation as a Maritime Power, to the dignity of the Crown of Great Britain, and to the advancement of the Trade and Navigation thereof, than to make Discoveries of Countries hitherto unknown, and to attain a perfect Knowledge of the distant Parts of the British Empire . . .

clearly stated what was the long-range objective of his voyage: 'the advancement of the Trade' of Great Britain. And it was advancement of trade—particularly in the Pacific—not discovery for the sake of adding to human knowledge, that was behind not only this voyage in 1764, but also that of Wallis and Carteret in 1766. For England hoped to find new markets for the products of English manufacturers by 'creating a network of commercial exchange extending through the Pacific and Indian Oceans. By

[1] See p. 3.

opening up vast new markets in these regions, a diversity of exotic commodities, earned by home production, would flow back into British ports. The surplus could be sold to Europe, and incidentally the disadvantage of having to spend hard cash in buying China tea and the products of India would be overcome.'[1] Although these voyages began immediately after the Treaty of Paris was signed in 1763 at the end of the Seven Years War,[2] they did not represent a series of steps to put into practice a new policy of empirical advancement by England. The voyages of these Georgian navigators 'represented a conscious revival of an ambition to open up new fields of commerce in the Pacific and the South China Seas which had been in the forefront of national policy under Elizabeth'.[3]

When the voyages of Columbus and Vasco da Gama resulted in rising new empires for Spain and Portugal and England was effectively frozen out of the new territory by these countries, she turned to Cathay and the golden continent of Locach for potential customers who would help her build her own empire; and until Drake, in his voyage of 1577–80, showed that plundering Spanish wealth in the New World was more profitable than establishing an English commercial empire to counterbalance the Spanish and Portuguese, her navigators persistently searched for a north-east and a north-west passage that would bring her into direct contact with the wealth of the Orient. Nevertheless while this was going on there arose the belief that climatic conditions precluded the use of the northern passage into the Pacific, and penetration into the Pacific by way of the Strait of Magellan was urged; this was the route taken by Drake, who was followed by Cavendish in 1586 and by Hawkins in 1593, all plunderers rather than explorers.[4]

The same spirit of mercantilism that motivated the Elizabethan voyages was in operation in the mid-eighteenth century, and its foremost spokesman was John Campbell, who in 1744 published his edition of John Harris's *Navigantium atque Itinerantium*

---

[1] V. T. Harlow, *The Founding of the Second British Empire 1763–1793*, I (London, 1952), 3–4.

[2] The end of this war saw the French empire in collapse, Manila lost by Spain, and England supreme upon the seas in the North Atlantic and in the Indian Ocean.

[3] Harlow, I, 3.

[4] For the roles played by John Dee, his work *Synopsis Republicae Britannicae*, 1569, and the maps of Ortelius and Mercator, see Harlow, I, 13 ff.

Bibliotheca. or, a Complete Collection of Voyages and Travels.[1] Although his 'Dedication' was appropriately addressed 'To the Merchants of Great-Britain', it was in his 'Introduction' that Campbell 'discoursed of the great Importance of new Discoveries, and the Advantages which a Trading Nation may derive from the opening fresh Channels of Communication with the Inhabitants of distant Countries, and consequently of disposing of their Commodities and Manufactures, in Places, where, perhaps, they were never seen or heard of before'.[2] In order that the passionate quality of his appeal to his countrymen may be seen, the last seven paragraphs of the 'Introduction' are set out below:

We are not, however, to hope this until such Time as the Minds of Men are, in some measure, cured of certain Prejudices which prevail but too generally at present. For Instance, while it is possible for any Nation possessed of, or vested with the Power of improving Commerce and Maritime Force, to be induced to imagine that any Thing else is more worthy her Study and Regard: For with respect to extensive Commerce, we may safely venture to assert, it is the one Thing necessary in Politicks; and if we study and pursue this, all Things else will be added unto us. It is a ridiculous Thing for such a Nation to complain, that her Commodities lie upon her Hands, that her Manufactures decay, that Numbers of her People are idle, that Multitudes are poor, and that her Condition grows daily worse and worse. I say, such Complaints are ridiculous, because it is in her own Power to redress all these Evils, by minding her own Interest, and applying herself to that Thing which alone well minded, must certainly and absolutely cure them all: But the most ridiculous Complaint that can be made in a Trading Nation is, against Smuggling; for that plainly proves that she has minded her Business so little, that her Neighbors have got the Start of her, since it is impossible that foreign Commodities should be bought cheaper in one Country than another, unless the Laws of that other Country are so framed, as to oppress and discourage Trade.

The Remedy of all these Evils, is very soon found, and very easily applied, if once Mens Eyes are opened, and their Hearts enlarged; for if the Understanding be clear, and the Will right, a Nation, like a private Family, soon alters its Condition, and recovers, by a prudent Management, what was lost through want of Attention. The great Engine in both Cases is, Industry, and Industry rightly applied. By

---

[1] 2 vols. (London, 1744). [2] Preface to vol. II.

Industry, with respect to a Nation, we must mean Application to Trade, as in private Life, we mean Application to Business; for, both in publick, and in private Life, Men may be industrious, that is to say, may be active, eager and diligent, not only to no Purpose, but to bad Purpose; for Instance, the Gamester takes as much Pains to acquire Money, as the Tradesman, but with this Difference, that the more he labours, the worse he deserves, and the richer he grows, the greater his Infamy. Yet why is he infamous? Not surely because he seeks Wealth, but because he seeks it in a dishonest Way, in a Way which, though useful to himself, is destructive to his Neighbours, in a Way inconsistent with Society, and which truly renders him an Enemy to Mankind. But after all, is not Usury, or the Art of making Money beget Money, of the same Prejudice in Publick, as Gaming in private Life and ought not the Maxims in Government which encourage the one, to be as universally condemned, as those that tolerate the other.

Let any Man, who considers the Consequences of both, speak what his Heart dictates, and he must say they ought; for if the bare Possession of Money, will produce Money; and if by watching the Necessities of the Publick, Men can grow as soon, and as certainly rich, as by applying themselves to Trade, it follows, that where-ever this happens, the Idle will eat the Bread of the Industrious, and those Men be at the Head of a Society, who are Enemies to Society, in Practice at least, if not in Principle. And now let me have Leave to ask, Wherein the Man who betters his private Fortune, without advancing the Stock of the Publick is better than a Gamester?

But Examples are better understood, and move more than Precepts. Let us look Abroad then for one, since it might be inconvenient to look at Home. The State of *Genoa* was once a most rich and powerful Republick, possessing large foreign Dominions, and prodigious Wealth in her own Coffers; it was this, that enabled her Subjects to build and plant, so as to establish, in the most barren Part of *Italy*, a City, which is still deservedly stiled *Genoa* the Proud. But how did she acquire her Fleets, her Dominions, and her Riches? If we look into her History, we shall find, by the very same Method, that these Blessings were acquired, and may be acquired in other Countries, that is to say, by Industry and Trade. But is she now possessed of them? Alas! No; from being the greatest, she is of late become the most contemptible State in *Europe*. And how has this Change been wrought? By forgetting her true Interest by suffering the Wealth her Trade had produced, to corrupt the Manners of her People, by running into Luxury and Idleness, by entering into endless Negotiations, and fruitless Alliances; and finally, by these two fatal Steps, dealing in Money instead of Goods; her Merchants becoming Bankers, and preferring Funds and negotiable Debts to Manufactures and staple Commodities; by neglecting her natural naval Strength, and depending upon her Allies; by engaging in other Peoples Quarrels, and thereby wasting her own Strength, and by preferring the pernicious Arts of Politicks to the noble and generous Arts of Commerce: Such have been the Causes of her Fall; and may her Fall prove a Warning, not a Precedent!

I call the Arts of Commerce noble and generous, because they extend to all Mankind. If we draw Gold and Spices from warmer Climates, we carry them Things more valuable, because more useful. What is it that constitutes the Splendor and Luxury of *Mexico* and *Lima*, but the richest Commodities, and the finest Manufactures of *Europe*; and what renders opulent those Countries which furnish these Commodities and Manufactures, but the Silver of *Mexico*, and the Gold of *Peru*? Does not that Change in Point of Cultivation, Magnificence in Building, and great Increase in Shipping, which, within these two last Ages, has happened in the old World, arise from the Discovery of the new? Why then do we not pursue this Track? Why not prosecute new Discoveries, at least, why not enlarge our Commerce by the Invention of new Branches? The common Answer is, because the Thing is impossible. Idle, ridiculous, and impious Assertion! Have we not Wool; have we not Cloth; are there not naked Nations enough in the World, who would gladly be covered; and was there ever a Nation yet found, that wanted Cloaths, and at the same Time wanted wherewithal to pay for them.

The Negroes on the burning Coast of *Africa*, have Ivory and Gold; the Inhabitants of the frozen Coasts of *Hudson's* Bay, send us Furs and Skins. The very *Laplanders* pay for what they want, and consequently, the more Wants any People have, the more it concerns us to find them out; besides, is not this falling back to the Errors of the Antients? Did not they fancy the same Thing, and were not they mistaken? Should not this put us upon a different Conduct, surely it ought. We have Commodities, we have Manufactures, we have Shipping, we have Seamen, we have Merchants, what can we possibly want, if we have the Will to employ those as we ought? Methinks I hear some modern Sceptick cry, This is very fine, indeed; but where, which Way shall we search; would you have us Freight and Man our Ships, and then turn then [*sic*] a-drift, in Hopes that Chance may bring them to some new World? No, the following Sheets will shew, that the Means of Finding are very well known; that the Methods of extending Commerce are natural and easy, and which is more, in a Manner certain; so that there is no need of employing Chance, the very Skill we have, will do the Business. It may, indeed, be requisite to remove ill-judged Prohibitions, and to break down illegal Exclusions, illegal, because the Terms upon which they were granted, have not been complied with; these may be, and indeed will be requisite, and therefore they ought to be done.

We see in a Time of War, what Encouragement for Privateering has produced, and can any reasonable Man doubt, that in Time of Peace, like Encouragements would not produce as strong a Spirit of Discovery; most certainly they would. Let us maintain Trade, and there is no doubt, that Trade will maintain us. Let our past Mistakes teach us to be wise, let our present Wants and Difficulties revive our antient Industry. Let the Perusal of this Collection excite our Hopes, and dispel our Fears, and then the present Age may become as much the Admiration, as it is now in Danger of becoming the Scorn of Posterity. We want not Capacity, we want not Power; but we want Will, and therefore we want Vigour; let us supply this Deficiency, and all will be well. In fine, let us deserve, and we shall certainly succeed; for that divine Maxim will be found true in worldly as well as spiritual Affairs, *If we search, we shall find; if we knock, it will be opened.*[1]

'*If we search, we shall find; if we knock, it will be opened,*' was Campbell's cry to his countrymen. The fate of England need not be that of Genoa. England had the manufactures, the shipping, the seamen, the merchants. All that she needed was the will—and the foreign markets; and the way to obtain these new foreign markets was clear: through discovery.

In the following year, 1745, a similar awareness of the commercial potentialities of voyages of discovery was placed before the public by the publication of Richard Walter's account of Lord Anson's voyage.[2] Although one tends to associate Anson's name with circumnavigation, plundering, and building up the strength of the navy in the 1750s, the ideas which he expressed in Chapter IX of his *Voyage* were quite visionary and more typical of a state minister than of a sea captain. In this chapter, he first recommended that British cruisers make use of the Island of Juan Fernandez off the south-west coast of Patagonia as a place of refreshment on their voyages into the South Seas. He further recommended that:

[1] Pp. xv–xvi.
[2] As Julius Goebel, Jr., pointed out in *The Struggle for the Falkland Islands* (New Haven, 1927), 195, the words may be Walter's, but the views expressed were obviously those of Anson, not those of his chaplain.

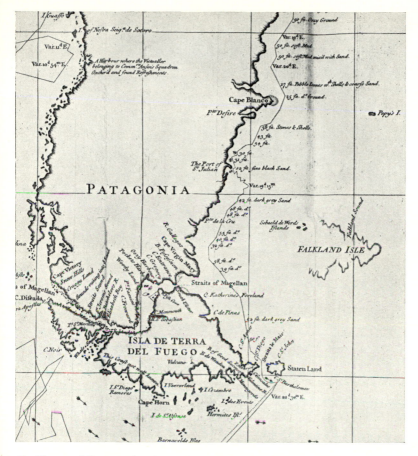

I. Chart of Patagonia showing supposed locations of Pepy's Island,
Sebaeld de Werds Islands and the Falkland Isle

From *Anson's Voyage round the World* (London, 1748)

As therefore it appears that all our future expeditions to the *South Seas* must run a considerable risque of proving abortive, whilst in our passage thither, we are under the necessity of touching at *Brazil*; the discovery of some place more to the southward, where ships might refresh and supply themselves with the necessary sea-stock for their voyage round Cape *Horn*, would be an expedient which would relieve us from this embarrassment, and would surely be a matter worthy of the attention of the public.[1]

Two localities were ideally situated to serve as places of refreshment for ships about to round the Cape: 'One of them is *Pepys's* Island, in the latitude of 47° South, and laid down by Dr. *Halley*, about eighty leagues to the eastward of Cape *Blanco*, on the coast of *Patagonia*; the other is *Falkland's* Isles, in the latitude of $51°\frac{1}{2}$, lying nearly South of *Pepys's* Island'.[2] Anson believed that a voyage from the Falkland Islands to Juan Fernandez and back again would take only two months and that the possession of those islands would make the British the 'masters of those seas' in time of war. Yet, in his mind, the economic advantages to be enjoyed by the nation controlling these islands were as important as the military, a point which he made three times in three pages.[3] And he pointed out that the motive behind Sir John Narborough's voyage in the reign of Charles II was not only to separate the Chilean Indians from the control of Spain but also to bind them with commercial ties to England. In fact, it was by means of the latter that the former was to be accomplished.

Unlike Campbell, who could only exhort his countrymen to action, Anson was soon in a position to put his theories into practice, for in 1745 the Duke of Bedford, the new First Lord of the Admiralty, asked him to join the Admiralty with the rank of rear-admiral of the white.

In the spring of 1749 the Admiralty, with the permission of the king, began to carry out Anson's scheme by making preparations for a voyage of discovery, the ostensible purpose of which was to make discoveries in American waters in order to improve trade in that area. Unfortunately, before the ships could get under way, the

---

[1] Richard Walter (comp.), *A Voyage Round the World . . . by George Anson*, 14th ed. (London, 1769), 125.
[2] Ibid.   [3] Pp. 127–9.

Spanish ambassador at the Court of St James, Richard Wall, an Irishman in the service of Spain, heard of the proposed expedition and immediately protested that the voyage would be, in modern diplomatic terms, inimicable to the best interests of both England and Spain. Therefore, the English laid the plan before the Spanish ministry for its approval, and it came out in the discussions that followed that the specific aims of the expedition were threefold: firstly the discovering, or 'rediscovering', of Pepys's Island, secondly the gaining of full knowledge of the Falkland Islands, and finally the exploring of the South Seas. The last of these objectives would have necessitated refreshing the ships at the Island of Juan Fernandez. It is easy to see Anson's plans for British expansion moving from the blueprint stage to actuality.[1]

The Spanish had also read Anson's *Voyage*, and they immediately realized how vulnerable their position in the New World would be if the English gained a foothold outside both entrances of the Strait of Magellan; and they were very sceptical, also, of the English claims that the expedition was incapable of injuring the navigation, trade, or possessions of Spain. Since, at this time, England was anxious to establish harmonious relations with Spain, she yielded to the Spanish protests and called off the expedition, although she maintained that she had the right to carry out the explorations if she so wished. Not until after the close of the Seven Years War did she have the opportunity of putting her plans into operation, and when she did, there began the series of voyages which commenced with that of Byron and which culminated in the magnificent achievement of Cook.

The Falkland Islands controversy

The accuracy of Anson's estimate of the military and economic importance of the Falkland Islands, with its position commanding the eastern approach to both the Strait of Magellan and Cape Horn, is borne out by the attempts of England and also of France, in the guise of Louise-Antoine de Bougainville, to form establishments upon the islands.

On 12 January 1765, Byron made a landfall on the north-west corner of the Falklands.[2] After anchoring in Port Egmont on the

[1] See Goebel, 195–202.   [2] See p. 56.

15th, he formally took possession of the islands in the name of King George III on the 22nd. He then sailed along the northern coast of both West Falkland Island and East Falkland Island and around the north-east corner of the latter. However, when adverse weather conditions prevented him from circling the two islands, he returned westward along the same northern coast and returned to Port Desire, on the coast of Patagonia just north of the Strait, where he was to meet the *Florida* Storeship bringing him provisions and news from England. Part of the news was that on August 3, about six weeks after Byron had sailed from England, the French had publicly announced that they had occupied the islands.[1]

While Byron was passing through the Strait and crossing the Pacific, the *Florida* Storeship returned to England; and, on the evening of 22 June 1765, Mr Robert Deans, the *Florida*'s master, delivered to Lord Egmont a letter which Byron had written at Port Egmont on February 24,[2] telling of his rediscovery of the Falkland Islands. Egmont circulated the letter to the cabinet and, on July 20, he sent the Duke of Grafton, the Secretary of State for the North, the charts and surveys which Byron had made, together with 'full Extracts of all such accounts as have hitherto come to our Knowledge concerning Falkland's Island from its first Discovery to this day . . .'.[3]

'The perusal of these Papers will', wrote Egmont, 'completely prove his Mtys. Title.' He asked Grafton, 'please to lay them before his Mty^s & those of his principal Servants whose opinion can alone be taken on a Subject of this very great Moment & of the most secret nature'.

The Admiralty believed that the Falkland Islands were '*the Key to the whole Pacifick Ocean*'. The Falklands

must command the Ports & Trade of Chili, Peru, Panama, Acapulco, & in one word all the Spanish Territory upon that Sea. It will render all our Expeditions to those parts most lucrative to ourselves, most fatal to Spain, & no longer formidable, tedious, or uncertain in a future war. . . . What farther advantages may be derived from Discoverys in all that Southern Tract of Ocean both to the East & West of the magellanick

---

[1] Goebel, 232.
[2] See Document No. 1, p. 153.
[3] See Document No. 2, p. 160.

Streights, it is not possible at present to forsee, but those Ports (now almost entirely unknown) will from such a Settlement be soon & easily explor'd. . . .

The Admiralty also believed that Spain could not legitimately claim title to the islands 'lying 80 or 100 Leagues in the Atlantick Ocean Eastward of ye Continent of South America, to which it cannot be deem'd appurtenant'. Furthermore, 'the attempt of France to settle there seems to confirm this argument against all that can be urg'd hereafter by either of those Powers to that Effect'.[1] Any future French claims to the Falklands, argued the Admiralty, would be without merit.

With respect to France—the 1st & 2nd Discoverys of this Island were both made by the Subjects, & under the authority of the Crown of G. Britain in the reigns of Q. Elizabeth & Charles the Second, & the French never saw them till in the reign of Q. Anne. Their present Projector Frezier[2] owns that they were first discover'd by the English.

The Admiralty were content to leave the problem of 'how far & in what Manner this Project may commit G. Britain either with the Spaniards or the French' to Grafton and 'the rest of the King's Servants'.

Since the Admiralty had received intelligence 'that 3 or 4 French Frigates were to be employ'd this summer to make the Settlement' on the islands, their recommendation was that 'the King's Ministers sho^d immediately take this matter under Consideration & come to a very speedy Resolution upon it that the Admiralty may receive his Mty's orders if anything is to be done witho^t delay'.

But the decision to send another expedition to the Falkland Islands—this time, a frigate, a sloop, and a storeship, under the command of Captain John McBride, together with a company of marines—had already been made, for on the very day that Egmont

---

[1] The Admiralty was well aware that the French had preceded Byron to the Falkland Islands. In his letter to Egmont, Byron wrote: 'Mr Stephens informs me the French have been lately at the Isles Malouins so Falkland Islands are call'd in some Charts.' Therefore, the English claim that the Malouins and the Falklands were not the same was made for propaganda purposes.

[2] Amédée François Frezier, whose travels were related in his *Relation du voyage de la Mer du Sud aux côtes du Chily et du Perou, fait pendant les années 1712, 1713 & 1714* (Paris, 1716; trans. into English in 1717), was the Engineer in Ordinary to the French king. See E. G. Cox, *A Reference Guide to the Literature of Travel* (Seattle, 1938), II, 267.

wrote to Grafton, Henry Conway, the Secretary of State for the South, informed the Admiralty that the king had approved the scheme to form a settlement there.[1] Specifically, McBride was ordered to complete the settlement which Byron had started; in reality, all that Byron had done was to plant a garden at Port Egmont.[2] McBride was to erect the portable blockhouse which his ships carried; and marines were to guard the installation, with one of the ships constantly on guard. If any subjects of a foreign power were to be found on the Falkland Islands, they were to be visited and informed that the islands belonged to the king of Great Britain and that they had no right to be there except with the king's permission. McBride was to offer them transportation to a port under the rule of their own nation. If they refused to leave, he was under strict orders not to resort to violence, except in self-defence. And all questions of right to be on the islands should be referred back to Europe.

As the Admiralty had feared, however, the English were too late. Nine months before Byron landed on the Falklands, Bougainville, who had equipped two vessels at his own expense and had sailed from the port of St Malo in September 1763, had taken formal possession of the islands for France and formed a settlement at the head of Berkeley Sound on the eastern tip of East Falkland Island.[3] He went back to France but returned to the settlement in 1765, and it was Bougainville's ship that Byron met in the Strait.[4]

Because she feared that the presence of a French settlement in the South Atlantic would force the English to move in this area, Spain was deeply concerned about this action of her ally, France. Consequently, after personally negotiating the terms of the transfer with the Spanish court, in 1767 Bougainville delivered the settlement to the Spanish. A Spanish governor was appointed

[1] See Goebel, 234. Why did the left hand not know what the right hand was doing? I have no explanation of why the First Lord of the Admiralty was not in attendance at the cabinet discussions of the problem. For an exhaustive account of the Falkland Island affair, see Goebel; for a shorter version, see Harlow, I, ch. 11. Since this matter has been so thoroughly investigated and discussed, I shall merely summarize the developments.

[2] See p. 60.

[3] Byron missed the French settlement because it lay some twenty miles from the mouth of the Sound.

[4] See p. 67.

and placed under the authority of the captain-general, Don Francisco Bucareli.

McBride landed on West Falkland Island in January 1766, and a settlement was made at Port Egmont. In September, he resumed making a survey of all the islands, a survey which he had tried to make immediately after his arrival; and, on 2 December 1766, he discovered the French settlement in Berkeley Sound. Both McBride and the French governor, M. de Nerville, claimed that only nationals from his own country had a right to be on the islands. Not long after this, Bougainville relinquished his claim to the islands, and Spain became the European power contesting with England her right to the islands.[1]

The situation on the islands remained static until the spring of 1770, when, after two encounters between the English and the Spanish, the latter landed on West Falkland Island and opened fire upon the English blockhouse. Its surrender soon followed. This unprovoked attack brought England and Spain close to war, and by the autumn of 1770 public opinion in Europe was infected with war fever. However, the Spanish realized the foolishness of fighting the English without the assistance of the French. France, though, was unwilling to go to war with England. Consequently, a compromise that would save the honour of both England and Spain was sought.

On 22 January 1771, the Spanish ambassador to the Court of St James formally signed a declaration disavowing the offensive action against the British blockhouse on West Falkland Island and orders were sent to Buenos Aires to restore the settlement with all its effects. Thus, British honour was assuaged. At the same time, secret and verbal assurance was given Spain that the settlement would be abandoned, and so Spanish honour was also preserved. On September 15, the British returned to West Falkland Island and took formal possession of it; but because of the intensity of the anti-Spanish public opinion in the country, England was unable to carry out at once its part of the bargain. Finally, in May 1774, the settlement was abandoned and this phase of the Falkland Island controversy came to a close.

[1] See pp. lxvi–lxxi for the diplomatic controversy over England's attempt in 1766 to provision and further fortify its establishment at Port Egmont.

INTRODUCTION

III. *Byron's Instructions and Voyage*

The Instructions

An examination of Byron's sealed instructions shows that the first objective of his voyage was to carry out Anson's plans for exploration in the South Atlantic and that the second was to return to the Tudor and Stuart desire to find a north-west passage.

After making his way to Rio de Janeiro where he was to water his ships and take on what additional provisions might be needed, Byron was to 'stretch over to the Cape of Good Hope' where he was to water and provision his ships for a second time; he was then

to proceed Westward to His Majesty's Island called Pepyss Island, which was first discovered by Cowley between the Latitude of 47°, and the Latitude of 48° South, about Eighty Leagues from the Continent of South America, stretching occasionally in your way thither as far as to the Southward as the Latitude of 53°, and searching diligently yourself, and directing the Captain of the Tamar to search diligently also, for any Land or Islands that may be situated between the Cape of Good Hope and Pepy'ss Island within the Latitudes of 33° and 53° South.[1]

If any land or islands should be discovered, he was 'to endeavour by all proper means to cultivate a Friendship with the Inhabitants —and take possession of convenient Situations in the Country, in the Name of the King of Great Britain: But if no Inhabitants shall be found on such Lands or Islands', he was then to 'take possession of them for His Majesty, by setting up proper Marks and Inscriptions as first Discoverers & Possessors'. If, on the other hand, Byron felt that he could more easily accomplish his mission by not sailing to the Cape of Good Hope and searching the South Atlantic from an east to west direction, he was to leave Rio de Janeiro, search for Pepys's Island, 'then proceed Southward to His Majesty's Islands called Falklands Islands, which are described to be between the Latitudes of 50°00' and 53°00' South, about the same distance from the Continent as Pepys's Island'. He was then to 'proceed Three Hundred Leagues to the Eastward, between the Latitudes of 33°00' and 53°00' South, in order to make discovery of any Land or Islands that may be situated between those

[1] See p. 4.

xliii

Latitudes, and within that distance from Pepys's & Falkland Islands'. Needless to say, if any discoveries were to be made in this region of the South Atlantic, he was to take possession of them in the name of the king.

The second phase of the mission was to be a search for 'a Passage from the said Coast of New Albion to the Eastern Side of North America through Hudson's Bay'. However, before Byron could pass through the Strait of Magellan it would be necessary to re-provision the two ships and spend the winter at either Pepys's Island or some convenient harbour on the mainland of South America. After this was done, he was 'to put to sea with the Ship and Frigate, and proceed to New Albion, on the Western Coast of North America, endeavouring to fall in with the said Coast in the Latitude of 38°, or 38°30′ North, where Sir Francis Drake, who was the first Discoverer of that Country, found a convenient Harbour for his Ship, and Refreshment for his People'. He was then to explore the north-west coast of North America as far as he should 'find it practicable'. If a passage should be found, he was 'most diligently to pursue it, and return to England that way, touching at such Place, or Places, in North America for the Refreshment of your Men, and for supplying the Ship and Frigate with Provisions, Wood & Water'. If, on the other hand, no passage were to be found, while he still had provisions enough for an arduous voyage, he was 'to proceed to the Coast of Asia, China, or the Dutch Settlements in the East Indies'. At the East Indies he was to put the *Dolphin* and the *Tamar* into a proper condition to return to England; he was then to return by way of the Cape of Good Hope, to land at Spithead, and to send the Secretary of the Admiralty an account of his arrival and proceedings.

Byron's reputation as a discoverer

On Wednesday, 7 May 1766, Byron 'made the Islands of Scilly, having been just nine weeks from the Cape of Good Hope, & a little more than Twenty two months upon the Voyage', and what was then the fastest circumnavigation of the globe came to a close. Historians, however, have never been overly impressed by speed records, particularly when the record holder's instructions called for detailed exploration and provided for the well-being of the

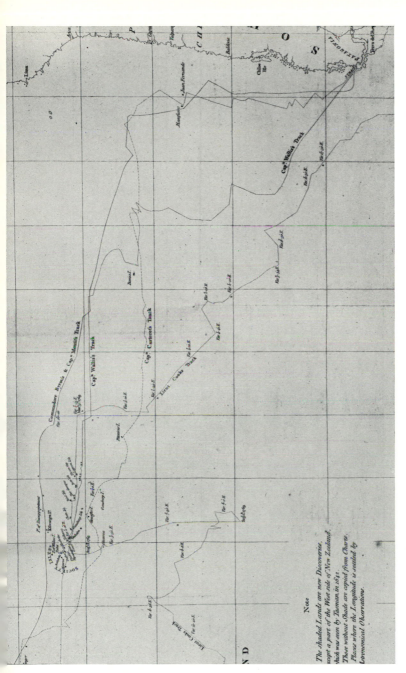

III. Tracks of Byron, Wallis, Carteret, and Cook (on his first voyage) from the Strait of Magellan past the Society Islands

From John Hawkesworth, *Voyages, I* (1773)

ships' crews for an extended period of time; and they, certainly those writing in this century, have dealt harshly with Byron. Hugh Carrington, for example, dismissed Byron's voyage with the statement that, 'half-a-dozen tiny islands were sighted; nothing useful was added to human knowledge';[1] J. C. Beaglehole remarked that 'Byron seems to have ignored his orders as thoroughly as possible . . .';[2] and V. T. Harlow described Byron as being 'deficient in the driving initiative and stern persistence that are essential for a successful explorer'. The latter has also written that 'In his voyage round the world he [Byron] substantially ignored his instructions and for the most part took the line of least resistance'.[3] The most critical account of Byron was that written by Sir John Knox Laughton. In regard to Byron's performance in the Pacific, he wrote:

From the Straits of Magellan the Dolphin and Tamar proceeded westward across the Pacific, skirting the northern side of the Low Archipelago and discovering some few of the northernmost islands. It now seems almost wonderful how these ships could have sailed through this part of the ocean without making grander discoveries; but they appear to have held a straight course westward, intent only in getting the voyage over. Not only the Low Archipelago but the Society Islands must have been discovered had the ships, on making the Islands of Disappointment, zigzagged, or quartered over the ground, as exploring ships ought to have done. And the necessary inference is that Byron was wanting in the instinct and hound-like perseverance which go to make up the great discoverer. Having passed these islands, the ships fell in with nothing new; they seem indeed to have gone out of the way to avoid the possibility of doing so, and to have crossed the line solely to get into the track which Anson had described.[4]

Understandably, though, the author of the 'Life' which was prefixed to Byron's own book, *Narrative of the Hon. John Byron; being an account of the Shipwreck of the Wager* . . . , was quite sympathetic toward Byron and felt that he had been 'completely successful'.[5] In the main, this opinion was repeated by the Rev.

---

[1] Carrington, xxii.
[2] J. C. Beaglehole, *The Exploration of the Pacific* (London, 1947), 239.
[3] Harlow, I, 25.
[4] *D.N.B.*
[5] *Narrative* (Edinburgh, 1812), xxi.

Hugh James Rose many years later in a short biography of Byron,[1] but one suspects that he was merely accepting the opinion of the earlier biographer. Significantly, both of these men pointed out that the purpose of Byron's voyage was 'to ascertain whether there were not several islands lying in the track crossing the Pacific Ocean, between the Southern Tropic and the Equator',[2] which was not at all the case. In his relatively long, sixteen-page, 'official' biography of Byron, John Charnock maintained a non-commital attitude, neither praising nor damning Byron.[3]

Byron's failure to carry out his instructions

Many of the charges made against Byron by the historians are justified, for he did seem to 'throw his instructions overboard' before his mission was half completed and, from the published accounts of his voyage—and from his journal itself—he did seem to take 'the line of least resistance'. After leaving Rio de Janeiro on October 22, he chose not to sail to the Cape of Good Hope and instead cruised along the south-east coast of Patagonia to Port Desire where he took on water and ballast and a supply of fresh meat and fish. He then searched for the non-existent Pepys's Island and returned westward, sailing a short way into the Strait of Magellan. Leaving the Strait on 8 January 1765, he sailed eastward, again searching for islands off the coast of Patagonia, and on the 12th made a landfall on the north-west corner of the Falkland Islands; on the 15th he anchored in Port Egmont, and on the 22nd

went on shore & took Possession of Falklands Island in the Name of His Majesty George the Third on which I [Captain Mouat of the *Tamar*] & his Officers Was present with him he was Saluted wth three Pieces of Ordnance from his Own Ship On which every Man was Serv'd half Allow[ce] of brandy to drink his Majesty's health.

He then sailed along the northern shore and around the north-east corner of the Falkland Islands, missing the French settlement in

---

[1] *A New General Biographical Dictionary* (London, 1848), v, 348.
[2] This is a misinterpretation of the anonymous version of the voyage — *A Voyage round the World. In His Majesty's Ship the Dolphin, Commanded by the Honourable Commodore Byron* . . . By an Officer on Board the said Ship (London, 1767) — which, on p. 151, reads: 'For as we had now finished the business on which we were sent, by the discovery of those islands in the South Seas, according to our original destination. . . '. [3] Charnock, v, 423–39.

Berkeley Sound, and back-tracking to the west when he found that the east coast of the Falklands was a lee-shore. It was now necessary for him to return to the continent in order to keep an appointment with the *Florida* Storeship, which had secretly been sent out from England with a cargo of provisions for the *Dolphin* and the *Tamar*. The rendezvous with the *Florida* Storeship was kept at Port Desire and the provisioning was carried out at Port Famine, in the Strait. Byron's instructions then called for him to 'proceed Three Hundred Leagues to the Eastward between the Latitudes of 33°00′ and 53°00′ South, in order to make discovery of any Land or Islands that may be situated between those Latitudes, and within that distance from Pepys's & Falkland Islands'. Instead of carrying out these instructions, he began to pass through the Strait of Magellan. The passage, which took from February 29 to April 9, was long and hard; but the two ships made it and their crews were in good health. If he had wanted to, at this time, he could have begun to carry out the second half of his mission, which was to 'proceed to New Albion, on the Western Coast of North America', replenish his provisions, and begin his search for a passage across North America to Hudson's Bay. But once again he ignored his instructions. Instead of setting his course for New Albion, he headed for Mas Afuera, a tiny island some four hundred miles off the coast of Chile, where he again took on refreshments. It was still not too late for him to swing northward to New Albion, but, even before he had finished transferring stores from the *Florida* to the *Dolphin* and *Tamar* at Port Famine, he had made up his mind 'to run over for India by a new Track'.

Byron, then, deliberately ignored his instructions twice: He failed to search the South Atlantic eastward from the Falkland Islands, and, after discovering these islands and returning to the Strait of Magellan, he had no intention of even trying to seek out a north-west passage.

Nevertheless, to describe Byron as 'deficient in the driving initiative and stern persistence that are essential for a successful explorer', to say that he 'seems to have ignored his orders as thoroughly as possible', and to dismiss his voyage with the words 'nothing useful was added to human knowledge', is to ignore the problem of why he chose to go counter to his instructions and is to

pass over the intriguing puzzle of what was going on in his mind
when he chose to begin his passage through the Strait of Magellan
rather than to explore the South Atlantic.

Fortunately, we have Byron's own reasons why he failed to carry
out his instructions.[1] When the *Florida* Storeship left the Strait of
Magellan on her return trip to England, her captain had with him
a long letter from Byron to Lord Egmont, giving an account of
what had so far transpired on the voyage and containing also a
detailed explanation of why Byron felt that he could neither search
the South Atlantic nor search for a north-west passage. The date
was February 24, the beginning of the winter season in those
extreme southern latitudes. He informed Egmont that he would
immediately 'push thro' the Straits before the Season is too far
advanced'. It would be impossible for him to winter in the Strait
because, if he did, when the southern spring came he would 'not
have enough Provisions (but especially Brandy) to proceed any
where afterwards', for he had 'been obliged to keep the People all
along upon whole Allowance or they would never have been able
to have gone thro' half the fatigues they have already . . . '. 'As
to running, 200 or 300 Leagues to the Eastward from the Falkland
Islands', he gave the cryptic excuse that 'it is an utter impossibility
to do it without One was to proceed on to the Coast of Africa
afterwards, for their is no getting back to the Westward, as the
Easterly Winds blowing with the utmost Fury constantly prevail
here & there runs such a Mountanous Sea that there is not the
least Chance of gaining any thing to Windward'. After devoting all
of one sentence to informing Egmont of what his future actions
would be—'I intend now to run over for India by a new Track
which if I succeed in I hope Your Lrdship will approve of'—he
used all of another sentence to explain why he was not going to sail
to New Albion after his passage through the Strait: 'Our Ships are
too much disabled for the California Voyage'. This statement
regarding the ships' condition, however, was immediately followed
by this one:

If Your Ldship should ever get my Journal You will see that We have
gone thro' already an infinite deal of Fatigue & many dangers the
natural Consequence of such an Undertaking but I protest for my self

[1] See Document No. 1, p. 159.

that I have gone thro' them with the greatest Chearfulness and I can safely say that in either Ship no man has had so large a Share of them as I have.

And one wonders if the Captain might not have been feeling just a little bit sorry for himself.

Fortunate as we may be in having Byron's own explanation of his actions, when one scrutinizes his excuses, one by one, the inescapable conclusion is that the explanation is unsatisfactory, so unsatisfactory, in fact, that one wonders if the reasons were not given to hoodwink Egmont.

Although an examination of the first stages of his voyage shows that the hardships undergone by the crews of the *Dolphin* and *Tamar* were not unusual for a voyage of exploration, Byron probably cannot be criticized for not husbanding his provisions in a better fashion. He had been given permission by Egmont to take extraordinary measures in feeding his men. Consequently, his reason for not wintering in the Strait should be taken at face value.

However, if one keeps in mind the fact that he had no intention of sailing northward along the coast of the Americas, his reason for failing to cruise the South Atlantic is unacceptable. Even if he would have had to proceed to the coast of Africa with no chance of returning to the Strait, it would not have mattered. He was not going to carry out the latter half of his instructions anyway.

His reason for not carrying them out—'Our Ships are too much disabled for the California Voyage'—is obviously contrary to fact. It is true that at the time Byron wrote to Egmont the *Tamar*'s rudder was 'Sprung or rather split all to pieces' and that the *Dolphin*'s main mast was sprung. The ships' bottoms, however, were in excellent condition: Byron could inform Egmont that his 'Opinion of Copper Bottoms is that it is the finest Invention in the world'. And the timber needed for the repairs on the ships was readily available at Port Famine, where they were anchored. Furthermore, the fact that the ships were able to withstand the battering they took during their extended passage through the Strait and that they were then able to make the crossing of the Pacific, attests to the good condition they were in when Byron wrote to Egmont, 'Our Ships are too much disabled for the California Voyage'. To argue that the *Dolphin* and *Tamar* might

D

not have been in a condition to withstand an exploration along the far northern coast of North America after their rough trip through the Strait is to confuse the issue: In the first place, Byron was describing the ships as they were before they went through the Strait, and he had no way of knowing that the passage would be as difficult as it turned out to be. In the second place, the ships came within a hairbreadth of reaching the Pacific on March 23, two and a half weeks earlier than April 9, when they did pass through the Strait. If they had reached the Pacific on the earlier date, they would have been spared the worst of the weather that they endured.

Could Byron have been deceiving himself as well as Egmont? And could the self-pity underlying the words, 'but I protest for my self that I have gone thro' them [fatigues and dangers] with the greatest Chearfulness and I can safely say that in either Ship no man has had so large a Share of them as I have', indicate a deeper desire to call a halt to the voyage? It is possible! If so, then his plan 'to run over for India by a new Track which if I succeed in I hope Your Lrdship will approve of' could have been a face-saving attempt to compensate for not carrying out instructions.[1]

The answer to the question—why did Byron choose not to carry out his instructions?—is to be found not in his explanations to Egmont, but in an examination of his actions on the Pacific leg of his voyage. Also, this examination will explain how he 'could have sailed through this part of the ocean without making grander discoveries' and why he appeared 'to have held a straight course westward, intent only in getting the voyage over'.

Upon leaving Mas Afuera on 30 April 1765, Byron sailed due west in search of the non-existent Davis's Land. Finding that he could make little headway westward in those high latitudes (below 30° S), on May 9 he changed his base course from west to

---

[1] It is interesting to recall the comment of the *Paris Gazette*, reproduced in the *Scots Magazine*, 28 (Edinburgh, 1766), 329, under *Affairs in England* — 'London, June 3': 'Capt. Byron, who formerly made the tour of the world with Adm. Anson, has been making the same voyage a second time. About two years ago he sailed from England, with the Dolphin and Tamar frigates, the former of 26, the other of 16 guns, and to these were added two smaller vessels laden with provisions. This little fleet has crossed the southern ocean; and it is reported, that the object of the expedition was the discovery of a passage northward of America to China. This project, however, could not be carried into execution, by reason of the ice and mists and a number of islands with which the seas in that part of the globe abound.'

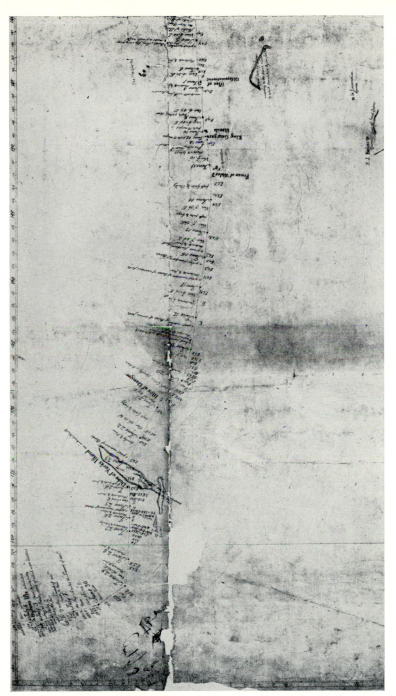

IV. Portion of Byron's track across the Pacific showing positions of the 'Land seen by Quiros' and the Solomon Islands 'according to the French Chart'

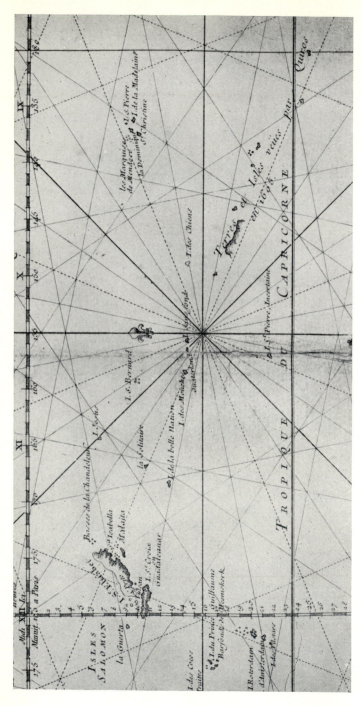

V. French chart of 1756 showing supposed portions of 'Terres et Isles veües par Quiros' and 'Isles Salomon'.

north-west in an attempt to get the true trade winds. And it is now that one gets a hint as to what he was really up to: 'I intend if possible to make a NW Course to the W^tward in hopes of falling in with Solomon's Islands if there are such, or else to make some new Discovery,' he wrote in his journal. On May 16, he thought that he had passed some land or islands to the southward. Actually, the ships were from two hundred to two hundred and fifty miles north of Sala-y-Gomez, a tiny island midway between the South American coast and the Tuamotu or Low Archipelago and the Society Islands. By now his base course had shifted back to west, and he held this course until May 22, when he swung more to the northward, sailing for the most part on a course between 280° T and 300° T, with his base course closer to 300° T than to 280° T.[1] This was a fateful change of course, because on the 22nd his position was due east of the lower portion of the Tuamotu Archipelago, and the western course that he had been sailing—even when the southern swell is allowed for—would have taken him through the centre of the chain of islands. As it turned out, he almost missed the Archipelago entirely, since his landfall on June 7 was of a small island on the extreme north-eastern tip of the chain. Because no landing was possible on this island or on any of its equally small companions, Byron called them the Islands of Disappointment. After sailing due west on the 9th, he made another landfall on the 10th, this time at the islands he named the King George Islands. Although he was still unable to find an anchorage, a great deal of refreshment was procured; and on the 13th he continued to the westward. The next day a large island forty miles in length was sighted. Once again, no anchorage could be found, and this, the Prince of Wales's Island (Rangiroa), and the Archipelago were left behind. On the 16th, Byron made a significant observation in his journal:

For a day or two before we made the Islands of Disappointment til this day we had entirely lost that great Swell & for some time before we first made the Land we saw vast Flocks of Birds which we observed towards

[1] Byron changed course for two reasons: 'Wind from ESE to EbN a faint breeze & cloudy with so great a Swell from the S°ward that we were in danger of rowling our Masts over the side, so that I was obliged to haul more to the N°ward to ease the Ship, & at the same time by so doing was in hopes of getting the true trade. . .'.

Evening always flew away to the S°ward. This is convincing proof to me that there is Land that way, & had not the Winds failed me in the higher Latitudes as mentioned before, I make no doubt but I should have fell in with it, & in all probability made the discovery of the S° Continent.

On the 21st, some thousand miles to westward of the Archipelago, he discovered three islands, in regard to which he wrote: 'I take these to be part of Solomon's Islands & am in hopes I shall fall in with some others of them that may possibly have harbours, tho' I take this to be as dangerous a navigation as any in the World.' The islands were appropriately named the Isles of Danger. Instead of the Solomon Isles, though, on the 24th he found only the Island of Atafu, or, as he called it, the Duke of York's Island, a small island due north of Samoa and east of the Ellice Islands. At first he was unwilling to name the island, 'not being certain but it might be that called Maluita in the Neptune Francois, & laid down about a Degree to the E^tward of the Great Island of St. Elizabeth one of Solomon's Islands'. But later he recorded, 'Finding there is no such Land as laid down in the Neptune Francois for Solomon's Islands, tho' I have run down to the W^tward of them as laid down in that Chart, I intend to have to the N°ward to cross the Equinoctial, & afterwards shape my Course for the Ladrone Islands.' On the way, he discovered one of the Gilbert Islands, Nukunau, or Byron's Island as he called it.

In summary, Byron, in sailing along the north of the Tuamotu Archipelago, discovered the Isles of Disappointment, refreshed at King George's Islands, which were possibly discovered in 1616 by Le Maire and Schouten and one of which was probably seen by Roggeveen in 1722, touched at the Prince of Wales's Island, an earlier Dutch discovery; he then discovered the Isles of Danger, probably the Duke of York's Island, and the one named after him. And, all the while, the rest of the huge Archipelago and the Society Islands, with its prize of Tahiti, lay just to the south of his track.

Why was Byron's accomplishment so slight? Because his driving ambition was to rediscover the Solomon Islands. When one reads his journal, the significance of his references to the islands is not at once perceived. He first mentioned them on May 9 and the next reference to them was not until June 21, when he thought that the Duke of York's Island might be one of the Solomons. Furthermore, his reference on the 25th and that on the 29th were phrased in a doubtful or negative fashion: 'not being certain but it might be that called Maluita . . . and laid down about a degree to the E^{t}ward of the Great Island of Elizabeth one of Solomon's Islands' and 'Finding there is no such Land as laid down in the Neptune Francois for Solomon's Islands . . .'. The tone of these entries is that of disappointment and failure.

The other side of the coin, hope and expectation of success, however, is seen in the entries made by Captain Mouat in his journal.[1] Mouat had been transferred from the *Tamar*, which he commanded, to the *Dolphin* as its commanding officer on 30 April 1765, the day that the ships left Mas Afuera. Of the Isles of Danger, the three small islands about one thousand miles west of the Tuamotu Archipelago, Mouat wrote: 'And the Islands bear from the Prince of Whales Isle^d WbN 370 L^{gs} and agree in Lat^d with one laid down in the Neptune Francois by the Name of I Solitaire, wch Isle^d is laid down by them 160 L^{gs} to the Eastw^d of the Islands of Solomon.'[2] When the Duke of York's Island was discovered some four hundred miles to the north-west, 'We', that is, Byron and Mouat, 'now look'd upon ourselves not to be more than 30 or 40 L^{gs} dist from the Isle^d of *Solomon*, and that this Island is what is called in the Draughts and Acc^{ts} the Isle^d *Melita* it agreeing in Lat^d wch Isl^d is said to be but 24 L^{gs} to the East of the Largest Isle^d of Solomon'.[3] So hopeful were the men that they 'therefore expected to make it the next Day'.[4] Even when it became obvious that they were not going to find the Solomons, Mouat could write: 'whoever finds it [the Solomons] must seek it to the East^d of 170°0' W^t of London'.[5]

Mouat's corroborative testimony on this point is of great importance, for, compared to Byron, he was a most matter-of-fact and, if anything, reticent chronicler. For example, when the ships encountered a violent storm off the coast of Patagonia on 13 November 1764, Byron wrote:

At 4 PM from the weather being extremely fine the wind shifted at once to SW, began to blow fresh and looked very black to Windward. We all

[1] 'Remarks on Board his Majesty's Frigate Tamer', 1–129, and 'Remarks from Cape Pillar across the South Sea to the Bashie Islands, on the Coast of China', 130–7, PRO Adm 55/131.
[2] P. 134. [3] P. 134. [4] P. 135. [5] P. 135.

upon Deck heard a very unusual noise, it seemed like the breaking of the Sea upon the Shore. . . . I was sure if it had taken us with any Sail out we must either have overset or lost all the Masts. . . . I never remember to have seen anything more dreadful than this Squall, nor anything came on with so little warning, if it had happened in the night I think the Ship must have been lost.

Mouat, on the other hand, merely commented that the *Tamar* met with 'a Violent Squall'.[1] Again, when the ships were sailing for a safe anchorage after their arrival at the Falkland Islands Byron wrote: 'I bore down to her & found it to be the Tamar's boat with Mr Hindman in her the 2^d Lieut. He had ventured off in all that Sea & bad weather to inform me he had found a very fine Harbour. . . .'

Mouat only mentioned that 'At ½ past 5 the Cutter return'd with the Lieut. & found a good Harbour for Ships to lie in 10 fathoms Water he went on board the Commodore to carry him in'.[2] One gets the impression that, because of his matter-of-factness and reticence, Mouat's journal is a more trustworthy document than Byron's.[3] To cite only one of many possible examples: Byron described his crew's encounter with the natives on King George's Island,

Our Boats followed them close in when the Savages began the attack with Clubs & Stones, & wounded two of our People; Upon which our Men fired & killed 5 or 6 of them. One of them that had three Balls through him took up a large Stone to heave at one of our Men just before he died—Those that remained unhurt amongst them carried off all their dead. . . .

'All their dead,' according to Mouat, were two men killed.[4] Therefore, when he recorded, 'We now look'd upon our selves not to be more than 30 or 40 L^gs dist. from the Isl^d of Solomon . . .

---

[1] P. 23. [2] P. 33A.

[3] This raises the question: why not print Mouat's account of the voyage rather than Byron's? The Mouat journal is incomplete. While in command of the *Tamar*, Mouat kept an official log, but after he moved to the *Dolphin*, he kept only a sketchy narrative of the voyage. See p. lxii, n. 3. Whenever a significant difference occurs between the two accounts, I have included Mouat's as a gloss. Also, since the early portion of Mouat's journal is an official log and, therefore, contains details missing from Byron's, which was in the form of a journal to be submitted to Lord Egmont, I have given these details in footnotes.

[4] P. 133.

& we therefore expected to make it the next Day', one can be sure that the commodore and his captain did expect to make a landfall in the Solomons the next day.

The lure of the Solomon Islands

Byron was not the first to be obsessed with a desire to find the Solomons, discovered by the Spaniard Alvaro de Mendaña on 7 February 1568. But in order to understand the hold that these islands had over men's imaginations one has to turn to Inca myth.[1] An Inca, Tupac Yapanqui, so the story goes, discovered the islands in the Pacific and brought back to the mainland gold, silver, a throne made of copper, a multitude of black slaves, and the skin of an animal like a horse.[2] Stirred by the tradition, in the second quarter of the sixteenth century, Cortes sent out many expeditions in search of the islands, and, in 1537, Grijalva and Alvarado sailed the Pacific in hopes of finding 'islands believed to abound in gold . . .'.[3] In 1567, as a direct result of the theorizing of Pedro Sarmiento de Gamboa, 'whose studies in Inca tradition and history led him to the conviction that these islands were the outposts of a great continent stretching from Tierra del Fuego northwards to within fifteen degrees of the equator, where it was about 600 leagues from Peru', another voyage was undertaken, this time under the command of Alvaro de Mendaña, the twenty-five year old nephew of the Viceroy of Peru. To his disappointment, Sarmiento was appointed only the captain of the *capitana*, *Los Reyes*, the flagship of the two-ship fleet. On 7 February 1568, the Solomon Islands were discovered. Instead of finding islands populated by a people anxious to become Spanish slaves, Mendaña encountered cannibals who met force with force; and instead of an abundance of gold and silver, he found only native clubs, whose heavy knob-like ends glittered because of the iron pyrites that were mixed with the stone. Nevertheless, in spite of the sickness that

[1] See Beaglehole, *Pacific*, ch. III, 'Mendaña and the Solomon Islands', and ch. IV, 'Mendaña and Quiros'; and Lord Amherst of Hackney and Basil Thomson (eds.), *The Discovery of the Solomon Islands*, 2 vols. (London, 1901).

[2] Amherst and Thomson, I, iv, n. 2, cite Sir Clements Markham's suggestion that the islands might have been two of the Galapagos Islands, about 600 miles off the coast of Peru.

[3] Beaglehole, *Pacific*, 47. One result of this voyage may have been the discovery of the Gilbert group.

struck his crew, when he decided to leave the islands some of the soldiers with him were in favour of establishing a settlement, so convinced were they of the presence of precious metals in the islands. From the time when Mendaña drew out of visual range of them on 11 August 1568, 'for two centuries the Solomon Islands remained lost to the sight of men'.[1]

It was upon Mendaña's return to the mainland that fact and myth became inter-mixed. The official reaction to the voyage was realistic and far from encouraging to Mendaña. An official of New Spain wrote to the king:

In my opinion, according to the report that I have received, they [the islands] were of little importance, although they [the discoverers] say that they heard of better lands; for in the course of those discoveries they found no specimens of spices, nor of gold and silver, nor of merchandise, nor of any other source of profit, and all the people were naked savages. . . . The advantage that might be derived from exploring these islands would be to make slaves of the people, or to found a settlement in some port in one of them, where provisions could be collected for the discovery of the mainland [of the southern continent], where it is reported there is gold and silver, and that the people are clothed.[2]

The popular reaction, however, was the opposite. The waterfronts were swept with the rumour that the voyagers had returned with 40,000 pesos of gold.[3] As Beaglehole wrote:

Tupac Yupanqui, it seemed, was a legend justified. And no one knows how the distant abode of headhunters and cannibals was transformed to the land of Ophir, for it was not the work of Mendaña or his journal-keepers on the voyage; and what Gallego the chief pilot knew as the Western Islands became to imaginative minds in vivid detail the Isles of Solomon. And so in history they remained, rich like those fabled treasures and as inaccessible.[4]

---

[1] Beaglehole, *Pacific*, 63.
[2] Cited by Beaglehole, *Pacific*, 67, 68.
[3] Actually Mendaña and Gallego, the chief pilot, had to pledge their own resources in order to have the ships repaired in Mexico after their return. (See Amherst and Thomson, I, lviii–lxiii, for a detailed discussion of the presence of precious minerals in the Solomons and how the belief in the wealth of the islands came about.)
[4] Beaglehole, *Pacific*, 68.

Between the time of their discovery in 1568 and Byron's unsuccessful search for them in 1765 and their eventual rediscovery by Carteret in August 1767, these half-historical, half-mythical islands were continually being searched for. In 1595 Mendaña sought to return to them in a voyage led by a fellow Spaniard, Quiros. While they did discover the Marquesas, they just missed finding the Solomons on their journey from Santa Cruz (which they discovered also) to Guam and the Philippines. Ten years later, Quiros sailed once more in search of the Solomons, discovering instead Espirito Santo. The next to look for the Solomons were an Amsterdam merchant, Isaac le Maire, and his Dutch East India Company pilot, Willem Schouten. Sailing independently of the company, in 1616 they searched for Vera Cruz and Quiros's Terra Australis, which was, in reality, Espirito Santo and which had been thought to be the Solomon Islands.[1] When the company sent Tasman on his first voyage, 1642–3, his instructions contained the note that the Solomons might be a possible base for finding the southern continent;[2] and during his second voyage, 1644, he had on board a vocabulary which was purported to be of the Solomon Islands language.[3] In 1721, Roggeveen, who sailed under the auspices of the Dutch West India Company in search of the continent of Quiros,[4] was convinced that whoever should settle Juan Fernandez would 'become in a few years master of a country as rich as Mexico and Peru, or Brazil'.[5]

[1] See Helen Wallis, 'The Exploration of the South Sea, 1519 to 1644. A study of the influence of physical factors, with a reconstruction of the routes of the explorers' (University of Oxford, unpublished thesis for the degree of D.Phil., 1953), 337–8.
[2] Ibid., 370–1.   [3] Ibid., 412–13.
[4] Campbell's edition of Harris's *Voyages*, 'The Voyages of . . . Quiros, for the Discovery of the Southern Continent and Islands', 1, 63–4: 'This Gentleman Don *Pedro* made a Voyage to *Spain*, where, in the Year 1609, he presented several Memorials to the Court, desiring Assistance for the Conquest and Settlement of these new-found Countries. . . . In this Memorial, he first represents to his Catholic Majesty, that the Continent he desired to settle was equal in Bigness to *Europe* and the *Lesser Asia* taken together, lying all in the Torid Zone, and therefore, in his Opinion, like to be extremely rich. He says, that it ought to be esteemed the Fourth-part of the Globe; but, in this respect, his Meaning is not very clear. The best Interpretation, that I have met with, is this; That he reckons *Europe*, *Asia* and *Africa* the First Part; the *East Indies* the Second; *America* the Third; and this new-found Country the Fourth. As for the Extent of it, he speaks partly from his own Knowledge, but mostly from Conjecture, having discovered only that Part, which lay in or near 15° South Latitude.'   [5] Beaglehole, *Pacific*, 217.

Since Byron's actions on the Pacific were determined by his desire to find the Solomon Islands—recall that immediately upon leaving Mas Afuera he recorded in his journal: 'I intend if possible to make a NW course to the W^tward in hopes of falling in with Solomons Islands if there are such, or else to make some new Discovery'[1]—and since his reasons for not carrying out his instructions after meeting the *Florida* Storeship were so obviously weak, it is probable that this desire was his real reason for not carrying out his instructions.

Admittedly, this explanation in no way exculpates him from the charges of wilful disobedience, for his duty was clear and he deliberately went counter to it. Nevertheless, in defence of Byron, it was not until the days of Cook—a professional sailor up from the ranks, as it were, and one chosen because of his competence and training—that the Admiralty could be certain that its orders would be carried out by an explorer. Nor does this explanation completely remove the stigma of a lack of courage and determination from Byron, for in electing to search for the Solomons rather than to carry out his orders he was choosing the easier of two alternatives. Nevertheless, it does show that he was a victim of the intellectual climate of the day and that he was responding to a romantic call to discover the lost land of riches.

Byron's failure to discover Tahiti

In spite of his shortcomings, Byron came close to winning a place among the most famous Pacific discoverers. And a comparison of his trip from the Island of Mas Afuera to the Tuamotu Archipelago with that made by Captain Wallis from the Strait of Magellan to his landfall in the Archipelago will show that, were it not for his decision on May 22 to change course to the northward, Byron rather than Wallis would have been the discoverer of Tahiti. In other words, why was Wallis in April, May, and the first part of June 1767 able to battle the winds and southern swell and reach Tahiti, when Byron in May and the first part of June 1765 was not? [2]

[1] Recall also the tentativeness with which he always wrote of the islands, in contrast to Mouat's definiteness.
[2] Wallis needed fifty-seven days, Byron thirty-seven. I have used Wallis's own log, PRO Adm 55/35.

lis

It is true that Wallis knew approximately where to look for his islands.[1] As Byron was swinging along the northern rim of the Archipelago, he recorded his conviction that just to the south of his position lay the southern continent. Also, later in the voyage, Mouat wrote in his journal that whoever finds the Solomon Islands 'must seek it to the East^d of 170°0′ W^t of London'. Consequently, when Wallis changed his base course from north and north-west to due west, his projected track—when the southern swell was allowed for—would carry him through the area indicated by Byron and Mouat. And there lay Tahiti, waiting to be discovered. One question remains—to what extent did the meteorological conditions favour Wallis and work against Byron?

Neither man could make much westing against the strong Pacific seas until he was almost at the twentieth parallel. During the entire voyage, Byron's winds were predominantly from the north and east.[2] During April and the first half of May, Wallis's winds were from the north-west quadrant; from May 18 on, from the east (shifting from south-east for the 18th to 26th to north-east from then on). If anything, Byron's wind conditions were more favourable than Wallis's. For his entire trip, Byron recorded only eleven days of gale-force winds, while Wallis recorded nineteen, eighteen of which were in the first part of his voyage, a time when he was undergoing heavy thunderstorms.

It was on the crucial leg of the voyage, though, that Wallis seems to have been favoured by the weather, for twenty of his last twenty-two days were excellent for sailing and all that he had to do was maintain his course. On the other hand, a reading of Byron's journal for this phase of his voyage leaves one with the impression that he was constantly battling the heavy sea swell and that the *Dolphin* was fortunate in not sinking.

A closer look at the journal shows that Byron's problem with the swell was not as bad as he made it out to be and that, if

---

[1] His instructions read: '. . . Whereas there is reason to believe that Land or Islands of Great extent, hitherto unvisited by any European Power may be found in the Southern Hemisphere between Cape Horn and New Zeeland . . .' and 'You are then to proceed with the *Dolphin* and the *Swallow* round Cape Horn or through the Strait of Magellan, as you shall find most convenient; and stretch to the Westward about One Hundred or One Hundred and Twenty degrees of Longitude from Cape Horn, losing as little Southing as possible' (cited by Carrington, xxii–xxiii). [2] See pp. 88–94.

anything, the swell that he encountered was at worst no greater than that met by Wallis.

On Byron's voyage, the swell was present from May 6 to 17, with the exception of the 15th. On the 18th the sea conditions suddenly changed. For four consecutive days the swell was absent. Then on the 22nd, the swell returned. On this day, Byron wrote: 'Wind from ESE to EbN a faint breeze & cloudy with so great a Swell from the S° that we were in danger of rowling our Masts over the side, so that I was obliged to haul more to the N°ward to ease the Ship, & at the same time by so doing was in hopes of getting the true Trade, which we certainly have not had as yet. . . .' It was at this time that Byron was due east of the lower portion of the Tuamotu Archipelago and that his course of 275°T would have taken him directly through the centre of the island group. Although his new base course of 285°T was only ten degrees to the north, this change was enough to cause him almost to miss the islands altogether. Ironically, on the 23rd the sea calmed and remained quiet for four days. On the 27th, Byron wrote: 'I had flatter'd myself that before we had run 6 Degrees to the N°ward Masa fuera we should have found a settled Trade at SE. but we have generally had the winds from the N°ern Quarter, tho' at the same time we have always had a mountainous Swell from the SW.' The swell made its last appearance the next day, the 28th, and the final ten days of sailing were without swell.

In summary, notwithstanding Byron's statement that 'we have always had a mountainous Swell from the SW', there was little or no swell on eighteen of the last twenty-one days.

The degree of similarity between the sea conditions on this leg of Byron's voyage and those on Wallis's was remarkable.

Why, then, did Byron fail to make the significant discovery that Wallis did? When Byron met the south-west swell on the 22nd after enjoying four days of smooth sailing, he turned ten degrees to the northward. When Wallis encountered 'great swell'[1] on the 28th and on June 2 and 3, he held his course at these crucial moments. If Byron had not made his change of course, or if he had resumed sailing on his previous course when the sea quieted the next day, he, rather than Wallis, would have discovered Tahiti.

[1] 'Great swell' is strong language for Wallis.

	Byron		Wallis	
	Swell	*No Swell*	*Swell*	*No Swell*
May 6	6		6	
7	7		7	
8	8		8	
9	9			9
10	10		10	
11		11	11	
12		12	12	
13		13		13
14	14			14
15		15		15
16	16		16	
17	17			17
18		18		18
19		19		19
20		20		20
21		21		21
22	22			22
23		23		23
24		24		24
25		25		25
26		26		26
27	27			27
28	28		28	
29		29		29
30		30		30
31		31		31
June 1		1		1
2		2	2	
3		3	3	
4		4		4
5		5		5
6		6		6
7		7		7

And why, then, does Byron's journal give the false impression that his sea conditions were so bad? The only answer that one can offer is that Byron was writing in an exaggerated fashion that distorted the true facts. Once again we are fortunate in being able to compare Byron's account with that of Mouat. On May 22, for example, Byron wrote: 'Some of my best Men (to my great sorrow) begin to complain of the Scurvy'; on the 31st: '. . . my People fall down daily in the Scurvy'; on June 5: '. . . My people fall down daily in the Scurvy, & several of my best Men already so bad in it, that they are confined to their Hammocks'; on the 8th, after the ships left the Isles of Disappointment: 'Bore away & made Sail to the W^tward greatly grieved I could procure no Refreshment for our Sick here, who are now most of them in a very desponding way'.

On the 10th refreshments were found on the King George Islands, and Mouat wrote in his journal: 'We sent our Boats on Shore for Refreshments, they found a great Quantity of Cocoa Nutts, and Pepper Grass, wch were of infinite Service to our people a few of which were down with the Scurvy. . . .'[1]

IV. *The Paying Off*

At 8 o'clock on the morning of 7 May 1766, the *Dolphin* 'made the Islands of Scilly, having been just nine weeks from the Cape of Good Hope, & a little more than Twenty two months upon the Voyage'. On the ninth, she was in the Downs. The *Tamar*, however, was not to reach England for another two months, her rudder having been severely damaged on the run from the Cape.[2]

Because the Navy Board and the Commissioners for Victualling had no previous knowledge of the bonus pay offered to the men of the *Dolphin* and *Tamar* nor of the verbal agreement between Egmont and Byron allowing him to supplement the diet of his men, plus the fact that the Admiralty Board, in order to keep secret the details of the voyage, took from the officers and petty officers the journals and log books that they normally would present in order to receive their pay,[3] the paying off of the *Dolphin* and the

---

[1] P. 133.

[2] Byron sent her to Antigua for repairs. The Admiralty endorsement of Byron's letter of the 9th states that they 'approve of his sending the Tamar to Antigua for the reasons he gives' (PRO Adm 1/162).

[3] The only official record of the Admiralty's confiscation of the journals and logs from the personnel of the *Dolphin* is an entry, No. 11, 410, in the *Dolphin*'s Ticket Book, NMM Adm/k/13, 'Directing His Majesty's Bounty to be paid to the Officers & Seamen & Marines & the Officers Journals & Logg Books dispenced with'. That this took place can be shown also by inference from other documents. On July 18, Stephens wrote Mouat that he was 'ordered to be paid for the Tamar, & the want of his Journals dispensed with, but [he] must

settling of the purser's accounts was a complicated and tedious process, but after much correspondence between the Admiralty Board and other offices and after many memorials by Byron, most of the problems which arose were solved.

One problem which a memorial could not solve was that presented by John Crosier, the *Dolphin*'s surgeon. Before the *Dolphin* sailed from England, Byron had informed Crosier that he was going to command a squadron of ships in India. Consequently, the surgeon 'purchased such a quantity of Medicines, Instruments and Utensils necessary for an Hospital, as he supposed a Squadron in that sickly Climate about to require; by which' he 'incurred an expense of upwards of ninety Pounds'.[1] When he returned to England, he still had 'the greater part of these Medicines . . . by him, but so damaged by variety of Climates and accidents as to be of very little value'. Byron brought the question of reimbursing Crosier to the attention of Egmont; but, as the surgeon noted in the memorial he presented to the Admiralty Board, 'the great hurry of Business, and the short time his Lordship remained afterwards at the Admiralty prevented its taking place'. Seven months later, in answer to a letter from Philip Stephens, the Controller of the Navy and the Surveyors rejected Crosier's plea on the grounds that they found no instance of making allowances to surgeons in cases similar to his and that they were not competent

pass an Account for the Dolphin' (PRO Adm 2/726). Also, on July 31, he wrote Capt. Cumming of the *Tamar*: 'My Lord Commiss^{rs}. of the Admty having given directions to the Navy Board to dispense with the officers & Petty Officers of the Sloop under your Command not producing Journals or Log Books of the proceedings of the said Sloop during her late Voyage; I am commanded by their Lordships to acquaint you therewith, & to signify their directions to you to collect all their said Journals & Log Books & transmit them to me for their Lordships perusal' (PRO Adm 2/726).

According to de Guerchy, the crew of the *Dolphin* was taken before a judge of the Navy and sworn to secrecy and the officers took a vow of secrecy before the Treasurer of the Admiralty (*Affaires Étrangères Angleterre*, devise 83.019, de Guerchy to Choiseul, 4 July 1766, 470 ff. 157).

In spite of the security measures which the English took, the French were still able to buy information from informers with surprising ease. Durand wrote to Choiseul (20 July 1766) that two Englishmen, one a volunteer and the other Byron's draughtsman or artist, who were to sail with Wallis, had agreed to give him information regarding where the English would establish bases. They wanted 150 guineas as salary and a guarantee that if they fell into the hands of either the French or the Spanish they would be freed with all their effects (Ibid., ff. 318).

[1] Crosier's memorial is in NMM Adm/E/40. All correspondence relative to this matter is in this same volume.

judges of the 'quantity of Medicines, Instruments and Utensils, if any were necessary to be provided by him in case of such a Voyage, or what may be a suitable compensation to be made him on account thereof'. The last we see of the case is Stephens writing to the Commissioners for Sick and Hurt in March 1767, ten months after Crosier landed in England, asking them 'to consider and report whether it may be reasonable to make any, and if any, what allowance in compensation for the Extra Expence he was put to'. The Commissioners' answer is lost.

The *Dolphin* returned from the circumnavigation in excellent condition. After the Admiralty Board had instructed the Navy Board to put the *Dolphin*, which was laid up at Deptford, into proper condition for further foreign service,[1] the master shipwright at Deptford inspected the bottom of the ship and, on June 16, reported to the Navy Board:

Pursuant to Your Warrant of the 6th instant, we have viewed and inspected the Bottom of his Majesty's Ship Dolphin Sheathed with Copper Plates, and find on each side of the Bows three plates rubb'd off by the Anchors, and one abreast of the Main Mast by the Buoy, and have likewise taken off at different places six Plates to inspect into the Plank and Caulking Work of the Bottom, all which we find to be good and firm, and don't perceive where the Copper is rubb'd off, the Planks to be touched with the Worm; all the rest of the Copper Plates are whole and entire, and set well and close on the Surface of the Bottom, and are in our opinion fit for further Service; the Ship has not been hove down, Clean'd, nor the Bottom had any Repair since her Sailing from England in July 1764 to this time, and the Surface of Copper is very clean. We have cut out several pieces in the Plates that cover'd the Heads & Points of the Bolts, Dovetailed & Horseshoe Plates, and likewise drove out of the Breast hooks Eight Bolts, Lower Deck Hanging Knees Eight, Transom Knees Two, Crotches two, Butts end Four, Keelson Bolt Five, and find the said Iron Work, and Bo[lts] which was covered on the Starboard Side with Flannel and Larboard side with Canv[as] to be in a good State and but little corroded with rust, more than we usually find in Ships that is not Copper'd; We have also drove out the Bolts of the Scarphs of the Keel & Boxing of the Stern which is found much corroded and Eaten, and on examin[ing] the Four pair of Copper

---

[1] 5 June 1766. NMM Adm/A/2584. This order marked the beginning of the fitting out of the ship for Wallis's voyage.

Pintles & Braces find the Lower Pintle worn 3/4 of an inch the Second half an Inch the third $\frac{1}{4}$, & the fourth very little to be perceived, the Shoulder Crown & Straps of them and the Copper Strap are in a very good Condition.

And humbly acquaint you that the Stern at the Surface above the Copper is much worm Eaten, and obliged to be taken out to have a New one we have Open'd the Starboard Bon to perform the said Work and shall give all the Dispatch that lay in our power to complete her in all Respects for Foreign Service.

V. *The Aftermath*

The first result of Byron's voyage was the sending of Captain McBride's expedition to the Falkland Islands in 1765. The second was the shifting of the area of immediate English exploration from the South Atlantic and North Pacific to the South Pacific.[1]

To review briefly: After Byron sailed across the Tuamotu Archipelago, he recorded in his journal his conviction that the long sought after southern continent lay due south of the small islands that he had discovered. Also, after Byron and Mouat became convinced that Quiros's Solomon Islands were not in the position indicated on the chart that they carried, Mouat wrote that, in his opinion, these islands were east of 170° West of London.[2] Consequently, when the *Dolphin* and *Swallow* sailed from England on 21 August 1766, the objective of Captain Wallis and Lieutenant Carteret was to find 'Land or Islands of Great extent, hitherto unvisited by any European Power . . . in the Southern Hemisphere between Cape Horn and New Zeeland, in Latitudes convenient for Navigation, and in Climates adapted to the produce of Commodities useful in Commerce . . .' .[3]

There are many documents which explicitly bring out the relationship between Byron's voyage and McBride's, but few records were kept of the discussions among the king, the cabinet, and the Admiralty about Wallis's. However, from the documents

---

[1] In 1769, the Hudson's Bay Company began to search for a north-east passage. For details of these expeditions and other attempts to find the passage, see Harlow, I, 56–7.
[2] We have seen how this information influenced Wallis's actions in the Pacific. See p. lx.
[3] From Wallis's orders as cited in Carrington, xxii.

that there are, it is possible to show how Byron's opinion about the location of the southern continent and Mouat's about the Solomons did influence the course of subsequent English exploration.

It would appear that, originally in the eyes of the Admiralty, the primary objective of the Wallis expedition was the strengthening of the English establishment on the Falkland Islands. McBride had landed there on January 8, 1766, and, in May, England had been advised of the cession of the islands to Spain by Bougainville. Egmont, who wanted to consolidate the English position there regardless of the claim of Spain to sovereignty over the Falklands, worked from June through most of August to obtain the cabinet's approval of the Admiralty scheme of sending ships to Port Egmont. Although the actual fitting out of the fleet had begun on June 5, it was not until August 15 that the situation came to a head.[1]

At the cabinet meeting held on this date, Egmont urged that orders to sail be issued to the fleet. The Duke of Grafton, however, had been informed that the Spanish and French had increased their strength in the Falklands and that their force would be superior to the English. For this reason and because he believed that sending the ships would cause a complete break in relations between England and France and Spain, he opposed the plan. According to the French chargé d'affaires in London, whose report is the only extant record of the meeting, both the Lord Chancellor, Lord Camden, and General Conway agreed with Grafton, who wanted to postpone having to make a decision for at least a week. Egmont now argued that Chatham, who had recently rejoined the ministry, had previously approved the plan.[2] At this time, Chatham remained silent. Within a few days of this rebuff by the cabinet,

---

[1] Unfortunately, the only record of the cabinet meeting of this date is the report of Durand, the French chargé d'affaires in London. Because of the paucity of English records, all the corroborative evidence we have comes from other Durand reports and those of the Comte de Guerchy, the Ambassador. See Goebel, 238–43; and Pierre Coquelle, 'Le Comte de Guerchy, Ambassadeur de France à Londres (1763–1767)', *Revue des Études Historiques*, LXIV (Septembre–Octobre, 1908), 417–72.

[2] Durand to Choiseul, London, 17 July 1766: Marginal note reads that Egmont had informed Pitt (Chatham) of the expedition and that he had approved of the voyage because he did not want the execution of the plans delayed. (*Affaires Étrangères Angleterre*, devise 83.019, f. 233. This French document and others to be cited are in the archives of the French Foreign Office, Quai d'Orsay.)

Egmont resigned. Strangely, after Egmont's resignation, which was followed by those of Saunders and Keppel, junior Lords of the Admiralty, Chatham reversed his position; and the decision was made to send the fleet to the Falklands within a week unless the Spanish and French should continue to press their objections to the plan. However, when Captain Wallis—whose ship, the *Dolphin*, together with the *Swallow* and the *Prince Frederick* Storeship, was by now riding at anchor in Plymouth Sound—received his sailing orders on August 20, they did not call for him to sail to the Falkland Islands.[1] And much to our regret, there is no record, either English or French, of what specifically occurred to cause the cabinet to change its collective mind again, after Chatham had agreed to send Wallis to the Falklands.

The scanty records of the planning on the Admiralty and cabinet levels for Wallis's voyage show that, from the beginning, Egmont saw the expedition as having two objectives: support for the Falkland Island settlement and 'Discoveries in the Southern Parts of the World'. (And it was in regard to the latter that the influence of Byron, recently returned from the Pacific, came into play.) One can argue that if the Admiralty were sending ships to the mouth of the Strait of Magellan these ships might just as well pass through the Strait or sail around the Cape and search the Pacific; and this argument certainly reduces the exploratory phase of the voyage to a role quite subsidiary to that of fortifying the Falklands;[2] but the minute of a cabinet meeting on June 3[3] shows the importance which, even at this early date, Egmont placed upon the plans for southern exploration. The minute reads:

Referr'd, Draft of the Kings Speech read & approved. At the same time Lord Egmont desir'd the Sense of the Lords concerning the consideration of the Expedition to Falklands Islands and for Discoveries in the Southern Parts of the World. Advis'd that if His Majesty thinks

---

[1] Carrington, 6. After provisioning the *Dolphin* and the *Swallow* in the Strait of Magellan, the *Prince Frederick* sailed to the Falklands. Ibid., 42–3.

[2] In the case of Byron's voyage, there is no doubt that locating the Falklands was the primary objective and that the other aims were secondary.

[3] This minute, written at General Conway's office and headed: 'Present, Lord Chancellor, Lord President, Lord Privy Seal, Marquis of Rockingham, Earl of Dartmouth, Earl of Hardwicke, Earl of Egmont', is the one extant English document dealing with the forthcoming Wallis voyage on the cabinet-Admiralty level (PRO 30/8/94, p. 219, Chatham Papers).

fit, the said Discoveries be maintained, and further pursu'd with the addition of one or two Sloops at the discretion of the Lords of the Admiralty and agreeable to former Orders.[1]

Furthermore, while the *Dolphin* was being fitted out at Deptford for her second voyage, George Robertson, her master for this trip, wrote in his log sometime between June 24 and July 8, 'The Lords of the Admiralty has ordered her to be got ready with the Greatest Expedition, to prevent her losing the proper Season for going Round the world by the Streights of Magellan;'[2] and, on August 6, he wrote, 'Here I was Informed that there is no Broad pendant to be Hoisted On b^d the *Dolphin* this Voyage, and by same authority am toald our Incoragement will Intirely Depend on our Success in Discovering a Place of Concequence in the South Seas.'[3] The gossip in the yard and aboard the *Dolphin*, then, was about the ship's forthcoming voyage around the world, not about an expedition to the Falkland Islands.

Finally, on the front leaf of the journal kept by Robert Molyneux, master's mate of the *Dolphin* on her second trip, there is this note, which reads in part:

N.B. After the return of Commodore Biron from the expedition upon wch he was sent by the Earl of Egmont then first Lord of the Admiralty, and his discovery of Falklands Islands, together with other islands in his track through the Pacific Ocean; upon representation of the said earl to the King, that the knowledge of the ports in Falklands Islands, & of the Streights of Magellan would greatly facilitate farther discoveries in the Pacific Ocean, south of the line, if pursued, before a war with France or Spain, or the jealousy of those two powers should oblige Great Britain to part with the possession of Falklands Islands or otherwise interrupt the attempts of Great Britain in that part of the world, His Majesty was graciously pleased to authorize this second expedition to be undertaken,

---

[1] A public announcement which appears to reflect Egmont's ideas on the Falkland Islands appeared in the *Scots Magazine*, 28 (Edinburgh, 1766), 329, under '*Affairs in England* — London, June 24': 'It is said, that Com. Byron settled a colony at the isles of the Malonines, or Falkland islands, almost opposite to the mouth of the streight of Magellan, in the Atlantic, about five degrees from the continent. This island was first discovered in 1706, and may be of great use to Britain in any future rupture with Spain, as ships may sail from that island to the South Seas in a few days.'
[2] Carrington, 3.
[3] Ibid., 4.

in hopes of finding a continent of great extent never yet explored or seen between the Streights of Magellan and New Zealand. . . .[1]

This evidence—the minute of the cabinet meeting of June 3, Robertson's record of the navy yard and shipboard gossip, and finally the note in Molyneux's journal—points to the fact that the Admiralty, or at least Egmont, felt that the exploratory phase of Wallis's voyage was of great importance. It would probably be a mistake to argue that it was of greater importance than the Falkland Island phase, for, after all, it was the cabinet's refusal to approve Egmont's plan to send the fleet to the islands at once that brought about his resignation. At the same time, though, to relegate the Pacific phase of the voyage to minor significance is to go counter to the evidence that we do have.

Byron's role in planning the Wallis–Carteret voyage

And what role did Byron play? As we have seen, the area of English exploration shifted from the South Atlantic and the North Pacific to the South Pacific with the exact objective of Wallis's voyage being 'Land or Islands of Great Extent . . . between Cape Horn and New Zeeland'. Because the planning for this voyage was done in such complete secrecy, it is necessary to fall back upon second-hand English information and intelligence which the French were able to buy from English informers. Fortunately, Robertson had an 'Old Friend' who kept him informed of events at the Admiralty. Although this 'Old Friend' has never been identified, his information was reliable. For instance, on August 19, four days after the cabinet decided to postpone the fleet's departure for the Falklands, Robertson wrote in his journal: 'This day I rec^d advice from my Old Friend that our Voyage is likely to be stopt If we do not sail soon. . . .'[2] The next day Wallis received his orders. Previously, on August 6, this same informant had told him of Byron's discoveries in the Pacific and that 'its Capt. Byron's posative oppinion that the Southern Continent is not far to the Southward of what He calls King George's Islands . . .' . When it is taken by itself, the significance

---

[1] Cited in full by Carrington, xxvii–xxviii. It is believed that this note is in Egmont's own hand.
[2] Carrington, 5–6.

of this statement in Robertson's journal is not at once apparent. But, when it is viewed in the light of the information gathered by the French, one can see that the words 'its Capt. Byron's posative oppinion . . .' are not merely a statement of Byron's belief in the location of the southern continent but that they hint at the fact that Byron was in reality one of the chief planners of Wallis's voyage.

The first indication of the importance of the role played by Byron is contained in the dispatch from Durand to Choisseul, dated 17 July 1766, which told of Egmont's having informed Chatham of the intended voyage by Wallis and of Chatham's approval. While the relevant portion of the text reads: 'On m'assure que l'expedition projettee de s'emparer des decouvertes par le capitaine Byron a ete communiquee par milord Egmond à Mr Pitt . . . ', the marginal comment reads: 'l'expedition projette par le Cap^{ne} Byron a ête communiquée à M. Pitt par milord Egmond'.[1]

It is possible that this marginal gloss is the result of a mis-reading of the letter. However, in his dispatch of 23 July 1766, Durand himself wrote: '. . . que de l'expedition projettée par Le Capit^e Byron. . . .'[2] Two days later Durand informed his superiors of what was then the first destination of the *Dolphin*, the Falkland Islands. Two weeks later, on August 8, Durand was able to send to Versailles more information about Byron's plan:

Par differents discourse des gens de l'amirauté on a scu [su] que Le Capit^e Byron avois d'abord engagé le Bureau a preferer l'establishment a former aux Isles Byron situees prés des Philippines à cause de la beauté et de la grandeur du port qu'il a trouvé, mais que tout considere on etois decidé a se fixer dans les Isles falkland à present qu'on a decouvert une route sure pour traverser le Detroit de Magellan. . . .[3]

Obviously this intelligence was inaccurate, and the French spy in the Admiralty had garbled his details. 'De la beauté et de la grandeur du port qu'il a trouvé' probably describes Port Egmont in the Falkland Islands.[4] And it is doubtful if Byron would have

---

[1] *Affaires Étrangères Angleterre*, devise 83.019, de Guerchy to Durand, 470 f. 233.
[2] Ibid., f. 324.   [3] Ibid., 4 Livre a, 471 f. 23.
[4] See p. 58, and Document No. 1, p. 156.

recommended settling on Byron's Island: his eyes were on the southern continent. Nevertheless, Durand's information did indicate accurately the area of the world in which Byron had the most interest, the South Pacific, and it is at this point that the passage in Robertson's journal and the French intelligence coincide. Although one must take into account the inevitable inaccuracies in information obtained from paid informers, the persistent recurrence in the French dispatches of the idea that Byron was involved in the planning of Wallis's voyage, with the fact that from the beginning the Admiralty intended to send its ships in search of 'Land or Islands of Great extent . . . in the Southern Hemisphere between Cape Horn and New Zeeland . . .' leads one to conclude that it was extremely probable that Byron was instrumental in sending Wallis into the Pacific.

Final appraisal of Byron and his voyage

Historians have not granted Byron an enviable position in the history of exploration. Over the centuries three charges have been placed against him: he lacked the qualities of a great discoverer; he did not follow his orders; and, although he did locate the Falkland Islands—but only after Bougainville had beaten him to them—his discoveries in the Pacific could be dismissed with a scratch of a pen. In short, Byron was a dilettante.

There is no denying that the man lacked the qualities of a great discoverer; these have been aptly described by John Beaglehole: 'In every great discoverer there is a dual passion—the passion to see, the passion to report; and in the greatest this duality is fused into one—a passion to see and to report truly.'[1] A reading of his journal will show that Byron was no Cook. Nor can one deny that Byron failed to carry out his orders. But, until the days of Cook, a professional sailor up from the ranks, was it not the experience of the Admiralty that orders were more likely to be ignored than observed? Neither can one claim that Byron's discoveries in the Pacific in any way justified his not following his instructions. The islands he found could just as well have been left unfound.

Nevertheless, his voyage should not be viewed as a failure, nor should his position in history be expressed only in negative terms.

[1] Beaglehole, *Pacific*, 3.

To do so would be to over-simplify the case. The historical significance of his finding the Falkland Islands and accurately positioning them is obvious. In regard to the Pacific phase of his voyage, the Admiralty did not consider his performance disappointing. The information which he had gathered was the basis for sending a second expedition into the Pacific. And Byron himself was probably one of the chief planners of this second voyage, a voyage which might not have been undertaken had it not been for Byron. The real significance of his voyage lay not in the discoveries made but in the fact that it was the first step in the eventual discovery of a great territory and potential market for English products in the Pacific, and the Admiralty recognized this.

The remaining days of Byron's career bear out this contention. Rather than being assigned to the limbo of unsuccessful naval officers, in January 1769 he was appointed governor of Newfoundland, an office which he held for three years. In 1775, he was promoted to the rank of rear-admiral; and, in 1778, when England was again at war with France, he was made vice-admiral of the white, a rank which he held at his death.

VI. *The Text*

In the letter which he ordered the captain of the *Florida* Storeship to deliver to Lord Egmont, Byron wrote:

I have kept a Journal of this Voyage which, in Case any thing happens to me and the Ships ever return home I shall desire may be deliver'd to Your Ldship.—No Soul has ever seen it besides myself and in it I have been as particular as possible.—I wish'd much to have sent it now but I was afraid to trust it to the Storeship and I have no time to copy it, & I don't chuse any body else should.

The text of the journal printed in this volume is, within the limits of modern typography, that of a bound, two hundred and thirty-one page fair copy, which the National Maritime Museum purchased on 10 July 1957, at a sale at Messrs Hodgson & Co, Chancery Lane, London. This copy came from the library at Hinchingbrooke. There is no evidence showing exactly when or by whom it was made from the original journal referred to in the letter to Egmont. But, since it is not in Byron's own hand and since he told Egmont that he did not 'chuse any body else should . . . copy it', one can infer that this copy was made at the Admiralty. The marginal annotations on it and on a log of Captain Wallis's voyage[1] in the Public Record Office show that it was the Admiralty's copy. When John Hawkesworth was commissioned to compile an 'official' account of the voyages of Byron, Wallis and Carteret and of Cook's first voyage, he received from the Admiralty the journals, logs, and notebooks which had been taken from the naval personnel when the ships returned. On page 83r of the Wallis log there are about twenty-five textual and page references in Hawkesworth's hand which refer to the bound Byron journal, and the journal itself is sprinkled with notes, queries, and underscorings made by Hawkesworth while he was using the journal in compiling his account of the Byron voyage. The actual work of using these markings to determine the authenticity of this bound Byron journal was done by Miss Katherine Lindsay-MacDougall, before the National Maritime Museum purchased it.

Until the summer of 1957, when the National Maritime Museum made its purchase, the main detailed source materials for a study of Byron's voyage were two eighteenth-century works: an unauthorized 1767 account, *A Voyage Round the World, In His Majesty's Ship the Dolphin, Commanded by the Honourable Commodore Byron* . . . By an Officer on Board the said Ship. London: Printed for J. Newbery, in St Paul's Church-Yard; and F. Newbery, in Pater-noster Row, MDCCLXVII;[2] and the authorized account in the compilation of John Hawkesworth, *An Account of the Voyages undertaken by the Order of his Present Majesty for making Discoveries in the Southern Hemisphere, and successively performed by Commodore Byron, Captain Wallis, Captain Carteret, and Captain Cook; In the Dolphin, the Swallow, and the Endeavour: Drawn Up From the Journals which were kept by the several Commanders, And from the Papers of Joseph Banks, Esq; By John Hawkesworth, LL.D., In Three Volumes, London: Printed for W. Strahan; and T. Cadell in the Strand, MDCCLXXIII.*

[1] PRO Adm 55/35.
[2] The degree of international interest in Byron's voyage is shown by the fact that in 1767 a French translation appeared; in 1768, an Italian; and in 1769, two Spanish and a German.

A third eighteenth-century account, though of much less significance than the above two, was a short 1767 pirated version of the better-known 1767 account: *A Journal Of a Voyage round the World In His Majesty's Ship the Dolphin, Commanded by the Honourable Commodore Byron.* . . . By a Midshipman on Board the said Ship. London: Printed for M. Cooper, in Pater-noster Row. MDCCLXVII.[1]

The first 1767 account, 'By an Officer on Board,' is obviously the work of a Grub Street hack who referred to himself in the text as the 'editor' (p. 52). The style is highly melodramatic. For example, when Byron's boat approached the Patagonian shores, the editor began his narration of the event: 'Evident signs of fear appeared among those in the boat, on seeing men of such enormous size, while some, perhaps to encourage the rest, observed that these gigantic people were as much surprised at the sight of our muskets, as we were at seeing them . . .' (p. 43). And, when an old Indian offered to the sailors his daughter who had 'tolerable features, and an English face', the editor wrote: 'Various were the conjectures we formed in regard to this circumstances, though we generally agreed, that their signs plainly showed that they offered her to us, as being of the same country' (pp. 92–3).

Not only is the narration melodramatic, but the work reads like a travelogue, with a three-page description of St Jago (pp. 10–12), a twelve-page one of Rio de Janeiro (pp. 15–27), and a six-page one of Port Desire (pp. 31–7), to cite only three of many possible examples. Also catering to the public's hunger for the melodramatic and the strange was the 'Appendix on Patagonians' (pp. 182–6) which claimed that the voyage had put an end to the dispute over whether or not a race of giants existed. Byron's voyage had proved 'what is recorded in scripture, and even in heathen authors, that there was, (and still is) a race of giants'.

The so-called author's avowed intention in writing the work was 'to remove the Doubts of his Countrymen concerning some

---

[1] I am indebted to John Parker, Curator of the James Ford Bell Collection, University Libraries, University of Minnesota, for calling my attention to this work and for furnishing me a copy of it.

Matters which have lately occasioned much Altercation' ('Preface', also p. 180). Nevertheless, one feels that it was written, not from this noteworthy motivation nor from a desire to 'pay this Tribute of grateful Acknowledgement' to Byron, but from a desire to capitalize upon the public controversy over the Falkland Island issue.

Mercenary as the author's, or editor's, motives may have been, the work is highly patriotic. For instance, it pointed out that six or seven men of the line could knock out the batteries at Rio de Janeiro (p. 15), and it assumed that the Pacific islands that Byron discovered would soon be in the possession of the English (p. 123).

When one discounts the work's flamboyant style and exceedingly colourful descriptions of ports-of-call, it is surprisingly accurate. There are details which are incorrect. For example, the expedition's 'original destination', or primary objective, was reported to have been the discovery of islands in the South Seas, in context the Pacific (p. 151). This discrepancy can be accounted for by noting that there is no evidence that Byron informed either his officers or his crew of the exact nature of his mission. But on the whole, a day by day comparison of this account with Byron's own journal will show that the two are in agreement on almost all essential points and on most minor ones. This fact leads one to conjecture that this 1767 *Account* was probably based upon a journal or log kept by an officer on board and not turned in to the Admiralty at the end of the voyage.

This work, together with the journal kept by Captain Mouat when he was aboard the *Tamar* and the *Dolphin*, serves not only as a source against which the Byron journal may be checked, but also as a source of additional information. To cite one important example: Byron's journal gives neither the date nor a description of the ceremony marking his taking possession of the Falkland Islands. The 1767 *Account* and Mouat's journal both do.

On the other hand, the other 1767 account, that 'By a Midshipman on Board the said Ship', affords the reader nothing but a further example of the art of literary piracy. Ironically, in this case the piracy was of a work which should never have been published in the first place. Essentially, this 'Midshipman' account is a short paraphrase of the earlier work. For example, the first forty-three pages cover the material in the first one hundred and eight of the 'Officer' account. At first the publisher was careful to disguise from the reader the relationship between the two works. Only a close examination would bring out that almost every phrase in the first page of the 'Midshipman' was stolen from the 'Officer'. Within a few pages, though, whole sentences were borrowed with only slight alteration. 'Nothing worthy of observation happened on our passage to Madera, which we made on the 14th of July' ('Officer', p. 5) became 'Nothing remarkable happened on our voyage to Madeira, where we arrived the fourteenth of July' ('Midshipman', pp. 6–7). One should note that the pirated version scrupulously corrected possible misprints, changing 'the Dolphin striking the bottom, swung round on her heel', to 'the Dolphin . . . swung round on her keel', and mis-spellings, as in the case of Madeira. Eventually, the publisher of the 'Midshipman' became bolder and lifted whole pages from the 'Officer'. For example, the long quotation from Magellan (pp. 25–6) comes from the 'Officer's' Appendix (pp. 182–4). By this time, however, the unsuspecting reader would already have bought the book.

Unlike the 1767 accounts of Byron's voyage, Hawkesworth's edition was an authorized publication of the voyages of Byron, Wallis, and Carteret, and of the first voyage of Cook. Lord Sandwich, the First Lord of the Admiralty, commissioned Hawkesworth to do the work. Although the unreliability of this account was recognized at once, over the years it has been the only readily available version of Byron's voyage.

Basically, the Hawkesworth text is a printing of the bound holograph journal, now in the possession of the National Maritime Museum. The holograph bears the same relationship to the Hawkesworth version as a realistic preliminary pencil sketch does to the finished impressionistic portrait; and, in this case, the portrait bears a closer resemblance to the artist, Hawkesworth, than it does to the sitter, Byron; for, in his role as editor of the journal, Hawkesworth did not confine himself to the task of giving to the public a readable version, but he altered the journal to the point of distortion and to the point of falsification.

Some of the changes which Hawkesworth made can be justified. For instance, he did not print whole portions of the journal which were nothing more than statistical accounts of the daily runs. Other changes were not important and could be justified on the grounds of creating dramatic interest or creating suspense, though they do tend slightly to distort the original. To cite one example: while sailing down the coast of Patagonia, Byron continually referred to the natives as 'indians' or 'wild indians'; Hawkesworth, on the other hand, reserved the term 'Indian' until Byron actually met them.

Most of the changes, however, cannot be justified, either upon aesthetic grounds or upon those of economy. In the first place, Hawkesworth took Byron's educated prose—and a reading of the journal and of Byron's book dealing with his adventures after the *Wager* was sunk will show that they were not bad writing—and turned it into a polished, over-refined, and at times flowery prose. Byron's description of a bird, 'black as Jet & shined like the finest Silk' became 'as black as jet, and as bright as the finest polish could render the mineral' (I, 15); his 'The flesh of the Hares here are as white as Veal' became 'The flesh of the Hares here is as white as snow' (I, 19). Scores of other minor alterations which Hawkesworth made contributed to this 'softening' of Byron's style.

More serious were the changes made by Hawkesworth when he started acting as a self-appointed expert in anthropology. Byron described his first encounter with the Patagonians in the following manner:

I drew up my people on the Beach with my Officers at their Head with Orders for none of them to move till I either called or beckoned to them. I then went up alone to these People but they retired as I advanced; I made Signs for one of them to come near which it seems they understood. This person was a Chief amongst them & was one of the most extraordinary Men for size I had ever seen till then. We mutter'd something to one another by way of Salutation & I walked a little farther with him to the rest. I made signs for them to sit down which they complied with, but I never was more astonished to see such a Set of People. The Stoutest of our Grenadiers would appear nothing to these. They were painted in the most frightful manner imaginable, some of them had a large circle of white paint round one Eye, & about the other a circle of white or red; Others had their faces streaked all over with different colour'd paint. Nothing in Nature could appear more frightful than these People did both Men & Women. Many of the oldest

People kept singing a most doleful tune & seem'd extremely earnest all the time. they were all cloathed in Skins of wild Beasts of different kinds which they wore as a Highlander wears his Plaid, many of these Skins were very curious & very large, as indeed they ought to be to cover these People who in size come to the nearest to Giants I believe of any People in the World, excepting the Skins which they wear loose about them with the hair inwards they were most of them Naked. Some few of them had a kind of boot with two sharp sticks fastened to their heels which served for Spurs. Their Horses were very poor & not large but were very nimble & appeared to be well broke; Both Men & Women came galloping over the Spit we landed upon which was covered with large loose round slippery Stones, their Bridles were a leather Thong with a bit of wood for the Bitt, & the Saddles was something like the Pads our Country People use in England without Stirrups. Both Men & Women had teeth as white as snow, very even & well set.

Hawkesworth rendered this passage thus:

I drew up my people upon the beach, with my officers at their head, and gave orders that none of them should move from that station, till I should either call or beckon to them. I then went forward alone, towards the Indians, but perceiving that they retired as I advanced, I made signs that one of them should come near: as it happened, my signals were understood, and one of them, who afterwards appeared to be a Chief, came towards me: *he was of gigantic stature, and seemed to realize the tales of monsters in a human shape:* he had the skin of some wild beast thrown over his shoulders, as a Scotch Highlander wears his plaid, and was painted so as to make the most hideous appearance I ever beheld: round one eye was a large circle of white, a circle of black surrounded the other, and the rest of his face was streaked with paint of different colours; *I did not measure him, but if I may judge of his height by the proportion of his stature to my own, it could not be much less than seven feet. When this frightful Colossus* came up, we muttered somewhat to each other as a salutation, and I then walked with him towards his companions, to whom, as I advanced, I made signs that they should sit down, and they all readily complied: there were among them many women, who seemed to be proportionably large; and few of the men were less than the Chief who had come forward to meet me. I had heard their voices very loud at a distance, and when I came near, I perceived a good number of very old men, who were chanting some unintelligible words in the most doleful cadence I have ever heard, with an air of serious solemnity, *which inclined me to think that it was a religious ceremony*: they were all painted and clothed nearly in the same manner; the circles round the two eyes were in no instance of one colour, but they were not universally black and white, some being white and red, and some red and black; their teeth were as white as ivory, remarkably even and well set; but except the skins, which they wore with the hair inwards, most of them were naked, a few only having upon their legs a kind of boot, with a short pointed stick fastened to each heel, which served as a spur. *Having looked round upon these enormous goblins with no small astonishment*, and with some difficulty made those that were still galloping up sit down with the rest, . . .[1] [I. 28–9].

Although Hawkesworth, as one might expect from a finicky man of letters, rearranged many details Byron gave and although he frequently used two words in place of one, the actual additions made in this passage were not numerous; but their significance in determining both the tone and the content was great. That the chief was seven feet tall and a 'frightful Colossus', that he 'seemed to realize the tales of monsters in a human shape', that the Patagonians were 'enormous goblins', and that a religious ceremony was taking place, was pure Hawkesworth, not Byron.

Even more distasteful is Hawkesworth's version of Byron's account of his giving beads and ribbons to the Patagonians. The original was graphic simplicity at its best:

I then took out a quantity of yellow & white Beads & distributed them amongst them, with which they seem'd mightily pleased. I then took out a whole piece of green Silk Ribbon & giving the end of it into the hands of one of them I made those that were next to him take hold of it & so on as far as it would reach. They sat very quiet without offering to pull it from one another, tho' I saw it pleased them of all things. I took out a pair of Scissars & cut every one of them about a Yard as far as it would go, & then tied it about their heads which they every one kept on without offering to touch it as long as I was with them.

After expanding this description to twice its length, Hawkesworth gratuitously added:

It would be very natural for those who have read Gay's fables, if they form an idea of an Indian almost naked, returning to his fellows in the woods adorned with European trinkets, to think of the monkey that had

---

[1] The italics in the Hawkesworth citations are mine (ed.).

seen the world; yet before we despise their fondness for glass, beads, ribands and other things, which among us are held in no estimation, we should consider that, in themselves, the ornaments of a savage and civil life are equal, and that those who live in a state of nature, having nothing that resembles glass, so much as glass resembles a diamond; the value which we set upon a diamond, therefore, is more capricious than the value which they set upon glass [1, 29–30].

This dissertation upon ornamentation and human vanity continues for another two hundred and fifty words. Since all the voyages in Hawkesworth's compilation were written in the first person, one can only imagine the Admiral's feelings when he saw attributed to him this and many similar passages comparing the natives 'who live nearly in a state of nature' and the overly civilized European. Such passages may be good Hawkesworth, or even poor Samuel Johnson, but they are not Byron.

Hawkesworth seems to have tried deliberately to change Byron's character. Byron was a humane person: his treatment of the crews of the *Dolphin* and *Tamar* attests to that. But his compassion did not extend to either the French or the natives of the Pacific islands. Yet, if one read only Hawkesworth's account of the voyage, one would believe that Byron was a great friend to all humanity. Hawkesworth was able to give this false view of Byron by omitting remarks made in the journal and by adding comments which, in their context, though misleading were not totally inappropriate. As an example of a serious omission, one can cite Byron's feelings when the French ship followed the English ships into the Strait of Magellan. Byron wrote: 'I was in great hopes she would have run ashore upon one of the Banks between Point Possession & the first Narrow, for the Navigation is extremely difficult to those who are not well acquainted.' This is the normal reaction of a sea captain whose mission was secret and who would need to avoid having to take any defensive action which might compromise his mission. Yet Hawkesworth deleted the passage. No mariner should desire to see fellow sailors run aground. Two examples should be sufficient to show how the subtle addition by Hawkesworth of a few words or a clause could misrepresent Byron's character. The first is a portion of Byron's description of the first encounter with the Pacific natives:

Our people would gladly have saluted them with a few Balls, but as they had no Orders from me they desisted. However if it had been possible for us, for if we could not have made these Savages our friends, we should presently have driven them off, & as the Island was so small, I could easily have guarded every part of it, so that I should have been under no apprehension of being molested from the Savages of the Great Island.

Hawkesworth changed this passage to read:

The people on board her . . . would fain have fired upon them; but the officer on board, having no permission from me to committ any hostilities, restrained them. I should indeed have thought myself at liberty to have obtained by force the refreshments, for want of which our people were dying, if it had been possible to have come to an anchor, supposing we could not make these *poor* savages our friends; *but nothing could justify the taking away their lives for a mere imaginary or intentional injury without procuring the least advantage to ourselves* [1, 94–5].

The second example is the description of a clash between the sailors and the natives which actually took place when Byron once again wanted to attempt a landing; he described the incident thus:

In the Evening I saw a great Number of the Savages upon the Point near the Spot we had left them in the morning, they seemed to be very busy in loading a number of large Canoes that lay upon the Point, I fired a Shot over their heads & they all disappeared in a moment.

Hawkesworth changed the final portion of this passage to read:

As I thought they might be troublesome, *and was unwilling that they should suffer by another unequal contest with our people*, I fired a shot over their heads which produced the effect I intended, for they all disappeared in a moment [1, 100–1].

Ironically, the chief cause of the outbreak of public furore which took place in 1773 over the Hawkesworth compilation was not the additions he made to Byron's journal and the other source materials but rather his open-faced use of the materials to propagate his own religious views. In his 'General Introduction', he wrote: 'I have now only to request of such of my Readers as may be disposed to censure me for not having attributed any of the critical escapes from danger that I have recorded, to the particular interposition of

F

Providence, that they would, in this particular, allow me the right of private judgement' (I, xix). In the case of the Byron journal, Hawkesworth exercised this right of private judgement five times (I, 46, 71, 74, 83, and twice on 84), in each case omitting Byron's references to God.

THE SECRET INSTRUCTIONS

Byron's Secret Instructions

Whereas nothing can redound more to the honor of this Nation as a Maritime Power, to the dignity of the Crown of Great Britain, and to the advancement of the Trade and Navigation thereof, than to make Discoveries of Countries hitherto unknown, and to attain a perfect Knowledge of the distant Parts of the British Empire, which though formerly discovered by His Majesty's Subjects have been as yet but imperfectly explored; And Whereas there is reason to believe that Lands and Islands of great extent hitherto unvisited by any European Power may be found in the Atlantick Ocean between the Cape of Good Hope and the Magellanick Streight, within Latitudes convenient for Navigation, as likewise His Majesty's Islands called Falkland's Islands, lying within the said Tract, notwithstanding the first discovery and possession thereof taken by Cowley in 1686, and notwithstanding the visitation thereof by Dampier and other British Navigators, have never yet been so sufficiently surveyed, as that an accurate judgement may be formed of their Coasts or Product; And more over as the Countrey of New Albion in North America first discovered and taken possession of by Sir Francis Drake in the Year 1579, has never been examined with that care which it deserves, notwithstanding frequent recommendations of that Undertaking by the said Sir Frans Drake, / Dampier, & many other Mariners of great Experience, who have thought it probable that a passage might be found between the Latitude of 38° and 54° from that Coast into Hudson's Bay: His Majesty taking the Premisses into His Royal Consideration, and conceiving no Conjuncture so proper for an Enterprise of this Nature as a Time of profound Peace which His Kingdoms at present happyly enjoy, has thought fit to make those Attempts which are specified in the following Instructions; and confiding in the Skill and Prudence of you the Honorable Captain John Byron, has signified His Pleasure that you shall be employed therein, with full Powers to undertake, prosecute and conduct the same.

3

You are in consequence thereof hereby required and directed to proceed with the Ship you command, together with the Tamar Frigate (whose Captain is directed to follow your Orders) to the Island of Madiera, & having taken on board such a Quantity of Wine as may be sufficient for the use of the Companies of the said Ship and Frigate, you are to make the best of your way to Rio Janeiro, on the Coast of Brazil, where you are to compleat your Water, and take in such a Supply of Provisions as you shall judge necessary, and may be able to procure.

You are then to put to Sea without loss of time, and stretch over to the Cape of Good Hope; and having compleated your Provisions & Water there also, and given such Refreshment as you shall have judged / necessary to the Companies of the said Ship & Frigate, you are to proceed Westward to His Majesty's Island called Pepys's Island, which was first discovered by Cowley between the Latitude of 47°, and the Latitude of 48° South, about Eighty Leagues from the Continent of South America, stretching occasionally in your way thither as far to the Southward as the Latitude of 53°, and searching diligently yourself, and directing the Captain of the Tamar to search diligently also, for any Land or Islands that may be situated between the Cape of Good Hope and Pepy'ss Island within the Latitudes of 33° and 53° South.

In case you shall discover any Land or Islands in your passage from the Cape of Good Hope to Pepys's Island which have not already been discovered or taken notice of by former Navigators, You are to endeavour by all proper means to cultivate a Friendship with the Inhabitants, if you shall find any, presenting them with such Trifles as they may value, and shewing them all possible civility and respect, taking caution however if they be numerous not to be surprised, but to be constantly on your guard against any Accidents: You are also to make purchases, with the consent of such Inhabitants, and take possession of convenient Situations in the Country, in the Name of the King of Great Britain: But if no Inhabitants shall be found on such Lands or Islands, You must then take possession of them for His / Majesty, by setting up proper Marks and Inscriptions as first Discoverers & Possessors.

You are to ascertain the Latitude and Longitude in which such Land or Islands are situated, and to observe the height direction &

4

course of the Tydes and Currents, the depth & soundings of the Sea; the Shoals & Rocks; the Bearings of Head Lands, and variation of the Needle; and also to survey and make Plans and Charts of such of the Coasts, Bays, and Harbours as you shall judge necessary.

But if you shall be of opinion, upon your departure from Rio Janeiro, that from the Season being too far advanced, or from any other Circumstance which cannot now be foreseen, you shall be better able to perform the Service upon which you are employed, by shaping your Course directly to Pepys's Island, and proceeding from thence upon discoveries to the Eastward, than by going to the Cape of Good Hope and proceeding upon Discoveries from thence to the Westward, you are at liberty to proceed to Pepys's Island without touching at the Cape of Good Hope accordingly; And upon your arrival there, you are to investigate the said Island and explore with great diligence & care its Coasts, Harbours, & Bays, and to survey and make Charts & Plans thereof in the best manner you can, ascertaining also the Latitude & Longitude in which it is situated, and making proper Observations of the Head Lands, Tydes, Cur/rents, Soundings, Shoals & Rocks, variation of the Needle, and whatever else may be either usefull or curious.

Having so done you are to proceed Southward to His Majesty's Islands called Falklands Islands, which are described to lie between the Latitudes of 50°00′ and 53°00′ South, about the same distance from the Continent as Pepys's Island: And having made the like Surveys and Observations at those Islands as you are above directed to make at Pepys's Island, You are to proceed Three Hundred Leagues to the Eastward, between the Latitudes of 33°00′ and 53°00′ South, in order to make discovery of any Land or Islands that may be situated between those Latitudes, and within that distance from Pepys's & Falkland Islands: And upon falling in with any such Land or Islands, which have not been hitherto discovered or taken notice of, You are to take possession of them for His Majesty in the manner before mentioned.

You are to cruize for that purpose until you shall judge it necessary to return to Pepys's Island with the Ship & Frigate under your Command in order to lay them up during the Winter Season, it being our intention to send a Storeship thither, laden with a sufficient quantity of Provisions & Necessaries to enable

5

you to proceed in the ensuing Season upon farther Discoveries.

But if contrary to our expectation / you shall not be able to find at Pepys's Island a convenient Harbour for the Ship & Frigate during the Winter Season, You are to proceed to Port Desire, or such other Place on the Continent, as you shall judge more proper for securing them, & refreshing their Companies, during the said Season, leaving, in such case, Directions at Pepys's Island, for the Master of the Storeship to follow you; which Directions may be inclosed in a Bottle, and buried Two feet deep, at the distance of Six feet on the South Side of a large Cross which you are to erect as a Mark of your having been there, and as a Guide to him to find the said Directions.

But as the Master of the Storeship may perhaps be unable to find Pepys's Island, We shall direct him, in such case, after having searched a reasonable time for it, to proceed to Port Desire in order to join, or get Intelligence of you; And you are therefore, (whether you winter at Pepys's Island, or not) to go to Port Desire, or send the Tamar thither, to leave such Directions, buried Six feet South behind a Cross as before mentioned, as may enable the Master of the Storeship to find you—And to the end that You may know each other, we shall direct him, upon discovering the Ship & Frigate under your Command, to make the Signals hereunto annexed, which are to / be answered on your part in the manner there in mentioned.

When the Storeship shall have joined you, you are to take out the Provisions and Necessaries with which she will be laden, and distribute them to the Ship and Frigate under your Command, and then discharge the Vessel and leave her Master to pursue such Orders as he shall have received from us, giving him a Certificate of the time of his being discharged; unless you shall judge that it may be for the good of the Service on which you are employed that you should Keep the Vessel with you; in which case you are at liberty to detain her so long as she may be useful to you.

When the Season will admit, you are again to put to Sea with the Ship and Frigate, and proceed to New Albion, on the Western Coast of North America, endeavouring to fall in with the said Coast in the Latitude of 38°, or 38°30′ North, where Sir Francis Drake, who was the first Discoverer of that Country, found a convenient Harbour for his Ship, and Refreshment for his People.

You are to search the said Coast with great care and diligence, from the Latitude above mentioned, as far to the Northward as you shall find / it practicable, making all such Observations of the Head Lands, Harbours, Bays, Inlets &c^a as may be useful to Navigation, and endeavouring by all proper means to cultivate friendship & alliance with the Inhabitants, where there are any, by presenting them with Trifles &c^a as mentioned in the former part of these Instructions. And in case you shall find any probability of exploring a Passage from the said Coast of New Albion to the Eastern Side of North America through Hudson's Bay, you are most diligently to pursue it, and return to England that way, touching at such Place, or Places, in North America for the Refreshment of your Men, and for supplying the Ship and Frigate with Provisions, Wood & Water, as you shall judge proper.—But on the other hand, if you shall see no probability of finding a passage from the Coast of New Albion into Hudson's Bay, you are to leave that Coast while you have a sufficient quantity of Provisions left to enable you to proceed to the Coast of Asia, China, or the Dutch Settlements in the East Indies, And you are to proceed to the Coast of Asia, China, or the Dutch Settlements accordingly, touching or not touching at Bengal, or any of the English Settlements as you / shall judge most convenient; And having put the Ship and Frigate into a proper condition to return to Europe, you are to make the best of your way with them to England around the Cape of Good Hope, repairing to Spithead, and sending to our Secretary an Account of your arrival & proceedings.

If you shall find it necessary, in your passage from Pepys's Island to the Coast of New Albion, to touch upon the Coast of Patagonia, or Terre Magellanique, either to obtain Refreshments for your Men, or from any unforeseen Accident, You are to make enquiry after the People who were Shipwrecked in His Majesty's Ship the Wager and left upon that Coast, and use your best endeavours to bring them home with you, taking all possible care to avoid giving any Kind of Umbrage of Offence to the Spaniards, and continuing no longer there than shall be absolutely necessary.

But for as much as in an Undertaking of this important Nature several Emergencies may arise, not to be foreseen, and therefore not to be provided for by Instructions before hand, You are, in all such Cases, to proceed as you shall judge may be most advantageous to the Service on which you are employed. Given under our hands the 17th of June 1764.

To   Egmont
   The Honorable   Carysfort
John Byron, Captain   Howe.
of His Maj'ˢ Ship the
Dolphin.
           By &cᵃ
              PS.

Signals.

The Storeship upon discovering the Dolphin & Tamar, or either of them, shall make herself known by hoisting a Dutch Ensign at her Foretopgallant Mast-head; which shall be answered by the Dolphin, or Tamar, by a Dutch Ensign at the Main Top Gallant Masthead.

The Storeship shall then haul down the Dutch Ensign from the Fore Top Gallant Mast-head, & hoist an English Ensign at her Main Topgallant Mast head; And the Dolphin or Tamar shall farther answer by hauling down the Dutch Ensign from the Main top gallant Mast-head, and hoisting an English Ensign at the Foretop gallant Mast-head.

Letter to the Master of the Florida Storeship Covering his Instructions.

                                        By &cᵃ
Notwithstanding any Orders which you have received, or may receive, from the Navy Board or from the Commissioners for Victualling His Majesty's Navy, You are hereby required & directed to make the best of your way to Sᵗ Jago, one of the Cape de Verd Islands, and use the utmost dispatch in completing the Water, and taking on board such Refreshments as may be needful for the Company of the Storeship you command, And having so done you are to put to Sea again without a moments loss of time, and proceed to the Southward until you have lost sight of the

Island of St Jago, And then (and upon no account sooner) you are to open the enclosed Sealed Packet and follow such Instructions as you will find therein for your farther proceedings.

If thro' sickness, or by any other accident, you shall be unable to carry these, and the inclosed Sealed Instructions into execution, You are to be very careful to leave them with your Mate, or the next person in command to you, who is, in such case, hereby enjoined to observe & execute them strictly, that the Service may not suffer by any inability on your part; And as an Inducement to him so to do, / he will be sure to meet with such Encouragement and Reward as may be suitable to his diligence and Services. Given &c^a the 11th of September 1764.

To
Mr Robert Deans,
Master of the Florida
Storeship

Egmont
Carysfort
Howe.

[PRO, Adm 2/1332]

THE JOURNAL

THE JOURNAL

Sailed from the Downs His Majestys Ship Dolphin and Tamar Frigate June 21st 1764.—The Dolphin having got a ground in coming down the River,[1] we put into Plymouth where we docked her but found she had received no damage. Changed some few of our Men there[2] and sailed again Tuesday July 3d (our People having first received two Months Advance) with the Wind at NNW.—Wednesday 4th at Noon off the Lizard with a very little air of Wind. Thursday 5th a fine breeze at NE having sprung up yesterday afternoon, we found ourselves in the Latitude of 48°48' No Longde made 1°52' West, M. Dist 74 M W from the Lizard, and the Lizard No 43 Et. Dist 36 Leagues. Friday 6th. Having for the most part since yesterday noon had a fine breeze we made the best of it, tho' the Tamar sailing much heavier than the Dolphin we cannot crowd all that sail we could wish. Have got our Ship into some little order having terribly lumber'd upon first coming out with Beer, Provisions &ca. Our Course since yesterday So 36° Wt. Dist 111 Miles. Lat. in 47 17 No. Longde made 3°28'. M. Dist 139 Ms. Lizard No 40°13' Et. Dist 71 Leagues. Saturday 7th a Pleasant gale at NE. The Officer of the first Watch last night either saw an extraordinary Phenomenon or it was some Ship on fire at some / distance from us, which continued to blaze near half an hour.[3] Our Course since Yesterday Noon So 28° Wt. Dist 156 Miles.

[1] Byron was not aboard. See Introduction, p. xxv. According to one of the anonymous 1767 versions of the voyage, *A Voyage round the World, In His Majesty's Ship the Dolphin* .... By an Officer on Board the said Ship (London, 1767), 2–3, the *Dolphin*, whose draft was 15'6" forward, 14'6" aft, went aground at 7 a.m. on the 14th, in muddy ground, and was aground for about two hours.

Henceforth, this version will be referred to as the 1767 Officer *Account*. See Introduction, pp. lxxiv–v, for a discussion of this work and its reliability as a source, and for a comparison of it and the other anonymous 1767 version.

[2] Byron had been ordered 'to cause all the Commission and Warrant Officers Servants belonging to the Ship you command, as also those belonging to the Tamar Frigate to be discharged and set ashore before you sail from Plymouth' (PRO Adm 2/1332).

[3] Capt. Mouat of the *Tamar* made no mention of this phenomenon in his log (PRO Adm 55/131).

Lat. in 44°59′ N°. Long^de made 5°12′ W^t. M^n Dist 212 M W^t. Lizard N° 34°59′ E^t. Dist 122 Leagues.—Sunday July 8th a brisk Gale with a large Sea, Course S° 27° W^t. Dist 186 M^s. Lat. 42°13′ N°. Long^de made 7°06′ W^t.—M^n Dist 297 M W^t. Lizard N° 32°15′ E^t. Dist 184 Leagues.—Monday July 9th. A fresh gale with hazey weather & a large Sea, shipp'd a great deal of Water which I am afraid has done some damage to our Slops & Portable Soup, of which we have a great quantity,[1] & no place to stow them but in mine & the Officers Cabbins.—The Tamar sails so heavy that she has hinder'd us much way. Course S° 17° W^t. Dist 190 M^s. Lat in 39°10′ N°. Long^de made 8°17′ W^t. M^n Dist 352 M^s.—Lizard N° 28°29′ E^t. Dist 246 Leg^s.—Thursday 10th. A fine Gale, the Wind has not varied three Points these six days. Course S° 16° W^t. Dist 178 M^s. Lat in 36°18′ N°. Long^de made 9°19′ W^t. M^n Dist 402 M^s. Lizard N° 26°15′ E^t. Dist 305 Leag^s.—Wednesday 11th. A fine steady Gale, expect to see Porte Sancto before night. Course S° 18° W^t. Dist 156 M^s. Lat in 33°52′ N°. Long^de made 10°17′ W^t. M^n Dist 450 M^s. Madeira S° 49°34′ W^t. Dist 42 Leag^s.—Thursday July 12th. A steady Gale not seeing the Land as expected imagined ourselves too far to the Eastward, being in the Latitude of the Island we hauled up to the Westward & at Night saw the Desertos.

p. 3 The Island of Madeira in / most Charts is laid down in 17° Long^de, but by all our Reckonings we find it near 19°. Course S° 54 W^t. Dist 134 M^s. Lat 32°34′ N°. Long^de 12°23′ W^t. M^n Dist 556 M^s. Lizard N° 27°51′ E^t. Dist 394 Leag^s.—Friday July 13th. This morning close in with the Desertos, hauled round the outer one, & stood in for the Road of Fonchial, but were much baffled

---

[1] Portable soup, or portable broth, the equivalent of present day bouillon cakes, was first used as a curative for scurvy cases late in 1756 or early in 1757. In 1763 the Commissioners for Sick and Hurt Seamen decided that it should be used as a preventative medicine to be served twice a week, on Banyon (meatless) Days. On one day it was to be mixed with oatmeal; on the other, with peas. The directions for serving portable soup are as follows:

'On the Day when it is served with Pease. A Pint of Water to each four Ounces of Pease with one Ounce of the Soup.

'When the Pease are boiled soft, then the Soup is to be dissolved in them, and in a quarter of an Hour it will be fit for use. After the Soup is put in, it should be kept stirring to prevent its burning to the Copper.

'On the Day when it is served with Oatmeal A Quart of Water to each Two Ounces of Oatmeal with one Ounce of the Soup.

'The Oatmeal and the Water to be boiled about Twenty Minutes, then put in the Soup, and when well dissolved, (which will be in about a quarter of an Hour) it is fit for use.'

VI. Two views of the *Dolphin*. A sketch by Captain Samuel Wallis,
1766, from the Wallis Journal now in the Mitchell Library

with the Winds coming off from the high land of Madeira,[1] Anchored about 3 PM. the Loo Rock NWBN, the Great Church NNE, Brazen head SE½E in 30 fᵐ Water, & about ¾ of a Mile from the Shore. The next day I waited upon the Governor who received me with great politeness & saluted me with 11 Guns, which I returned from the Ship.—The day after he returned my visit at the Consul's House, upon which I saluted him with 11 Guns from the Ship, & he returned the same number from the Fort. His Majᵗˢ Ship Crown & Ferret Sloop whom I found here likewise saluted the Broad Pendant, which I ought to have mentioned I hoisted the day after I left Plymouth.[2] Employed our time in watering &cᵃ.—I procured all the Refreshments I was able for the two Ships Companies, they had fresh Meat every day, & every Man had 20ˡᵇ weight of Onions for his Sea Stock.[3]—Thursday July 19th. Having finished our business here made the Signal to unmoor; At 6 PM weighed & had but very little wind all night & that / frequently all round the Compass in less than five Minutes. About 7 AM July 20th got into a fresh Gale at NE which generally blows here every day at this time of the Year, at about 3 Leagˢ from the Island, Run off about 2 Leagˢ & then brought too for the Tamar, who for some hours after lay becalm'd under the high Land,[4] but at last got into the breeze when we made Sail again, & at Noon were about 11 Leagˢ from the Island. Saturday July 21ˢᵗ. A fresh Gale

p. 4

The correspondence dealing with the experiments with portable soup is in NMM Adm/F/13, /14, /24, and /FP/9. In *Medicine and the Navy 1200–1900*, Volume III—1714–1815 (Edinburgh and London, 1961), 87, 93, 314–415, although they say that portable soup was the most important of all innovations, Christopher Lloyd and J. L. S. Coulter have an ambiguous attitude toward the preventative efficacy of portable soup.

[1] Azores: 'The prevailing winds are from between south and west in winter and from the north and northeast in summer, but the direction is much affected by local topography' [*Africa Pilot*, 9th ed. (London, 1930), Pt. I, 37]. Byron expected north-east winds, not north-west.

[2] 'The broad pendant was flown to distinguish a commodore's ship in a squadron' (Carrington, 4, n. 2). In 1766, Capt. Wallis was not given this distinction.

[3] 1767 Officer *Account*, 9: 'very indifferent of the kind', as they are 'both lean and under the common size'.

[4] 'In the summer Madeira comes under the influence of the north-east trade. In the principal bays there are regular land and sea breezes, but the former never extends far from the shore; it commences about 2200 and dies away about 0900 or 1000, when there is a calm interval until the sea breeze sets in. In the middle of the channels between the islands the prevailing north or north-east wind continues both night and day' (*Africa Pilot*, Pt. I, 37).

about Noon made the Island of Palma, one of the Canaries. The Tamar hinders us much way, she sails so heavy we could run her out of sight in a few hours. Course S⁰ 12° Wᵗ. Dist 216 Mˢ. Lat. in 29°18′ N⁰. Longᵈᵉ made 0 55′ Wᵗ from Madeira. M. Dist 47 Mˢ. Madeira N⁰ 12° Eᵗ 72 Leagues.[1] Sunday July 22ᵈ. A fresh Gale with a great Sea. Course S⁰ 32° Wᵗ. Dist 144 Mˢ. Lat in 26°30′ N⁰. Longᵈᵉ made 1°26′ Wᵗ from Palma. Mⁿ Dist 77 Mˢ.—Palma N⁰ 32° Eᵗ. Dist 48 Leagˢ.—Monday July 23ᵈ. A large Sea still continues which occasions the Ship to rowl very much. Upon examining into the quantity of Water on board, find it will be necessary to touch at one of the Cape de Verd Islands for a fresh Supply,[2] without puting the Men to a small Allowance, which I held by no means good when it possibly / can be prevented. Served the Men this day a Quarter of a Pound of Mustard each. Course S⁰ 12° Wᵗ. Dist 166 Mˢ. Lat in 23°49′ N⁰. Longᵈᵉ made 2°05 Wᵗ. M. Dist 112 Mˢ from Palma which bears N⁰ 21°18′ Eᵗ. Dist 103 Leagˢ. Variation allowed 12°00 Wᵗ.—Tuesday July 24ᵗʰ. Moderate & hazey Course S⁰ 12° Wt. Dist 130 Mˢ. Lat in 21°43′ N⁰. Longᵈᵉ made 2°34′ Wᵗ. Mⁿ Dist 139 Mˢ Wᵗ from Palma which bears N⁰ 18°26′ Eᵗ. Dist 146 Leagˢ.—Wednesday July 25ᵗʰ. A pleasant Trade. *We have remarked that no fish follows our bottom which we suppose is owing to our being sheathed with Copper.* Mixed a quantity of *Portable Soup* with the Pease which our People seem to like much, this is the first time we have tried it. I have a great deal on board & intend to serve it once or twice a week to them, in the same manner which will be as good as a fresh Meal. Course S⁰ 17° Wᵗ. Dist 124 Mˢ. Lat in 19°45′ N⁰. Longᵈᵉ made 3°12′ Wᵗ. Mⁿ Dist 175 Mˢ. Wᵗ from Palma which Island bears N⁰ 18°05′ Eᵗ. Dist 187 Leagˢ. Variation allowed 10° Wᵗ. Thursday July 26ᵗʰ. Little wind for these last 24 hours & hazey; is extremely hot. *Made use of a new invented Machine for Purifying Stinking Water & found it answer very well.*[3] Course S⁰ 21° Wᵗ. Dist 104 Mˢ. Lat in 18°08′ N⁰. Longᵈᵉ made 3°50′ Wᵗ. Mⁿ Dist 212 Mˢ Wᵗ from Palma / which Island bears N⁰ 14°30′ Eᵗ. Dist 218 Leagˢ. Variation allowed 10° Wᵗ.—Friday July 27ᵗʰ. Little wind & hazey. This Morning

p. 5

p. 6

[1] 'M. Dist' signifies 'Meridian Distance', the distance made due east or due west during the day's run.
[2] This was not his original intention (see Byron's Instructions, p. 4).
[3] Lt Orsbridge's water sweetener. See Introduction, p. xxiv.

made the Island of Sal.[1] *Saw several Turtle upon the Water.* hoisted our Jolly Boat out to attempt to strike them, but they all went down before the Boat could get near them.—Saturday July 28th. Little wind & some times calm. This Morning very near the Island of Bona Vista. A great Swell from the Soward. Sunday July 29th. Off the Isle of May in the morning. Steered close in for the Island of St Jago, but were some time at a loss for Port Praga Bay, which after some hours search we found to lay close round the SWt point of the Island.—Monday July 30th. Came to an Anchor in Porto Praga Bay. The extreme Points of the Bay from EBS to WSW & the Fort NWbN in 9 fathom water, about a quarter of a Mile from the Shore.—The Rainy Season was already set in, which makes this Place very unsafe to remain in at present.[2] A large Swell from the Soward tumbles in which makes a prodigious Surf upon the Shore, and we are under hourly apprehensions of a Tornado which / might prove of fatal consequence to Ships in this Bay, as they are extremely violent & blow directly in. No Ships ever offer to come in here after the 15th of Augt til the rainy Season is over, which is generally in November; For these reasons I made all the haste possible to fill our Water & to get away. We found the Watering very inconvenient from the great Surf upon the Shore, as well as being obliged to rowl our Cask at some distance from the Beach to a dirty muddy Well, which is the only Water here even for the use of the Natives. I procured three Bullocks here for the People, but they were little better than Carrion, & the weather so excessively hot that Meat stunk in a few hours after being killed.— Thursday Augt 2d.—Having completed our Water we weighed with a small breeze off the Land, our Ships full of fowls, lean Goats & Monkeys, which our People contrived to get by exchanging old Shirts, Jackets &ca.—Friday Augt 3d. Calm Yesterday Evening, & all night, this Morning saw the Island of St Jago at about 10 Leagues distance; Caught several large Sharks which our People eat tho' they have plenty / of other Provision as mentioned above.

p. 7

p. 8

[1] North-easternmost of the Cape de Verde Islands.
[2] Port Praga Bay (Porto da Praia): 'The anchorage is safe in the dry season, from December to June inclusive, for vessels of any size, but during the rainy season the wind occasionally sets in strongly from the southward, with a heavy swell and short sea, which render it unsafe for sailing vessels' (*Africa Pilot*, Pt. 1, 134). Modern anchorage: 'Sailing vessels, during the rainy season, July to September, should anchor well outside in 17 fathoms' (Ibid., 135).

Course S^o. Dist 52 M^s. Lat in 14°09′ N^o. St Jago N^o. Dist 17 Leag^s. Variation 8°15′ W^t.—Saturday Augt 4th. The first & latter part light Airs of Wind, the middle Calm & the Weather most extreamly hot with a great Swell from the S^{o}ward & some rain. Course S^o 12° E^t. Dist 33 M^s. Lat in 13°36′ N^o Long^{de} made 0°2′ E^t. M^n Dist 2 M^s E^t from St Jago, Variation allowed 8°30′ W^t. St Jago N° 2°0′ W^t Dist 28 Leag^s.—Sunday Augt 5th. Light airs of wind & calm for the first & middle part, the latter dark cloudy weather & much rain, with very strong Squalls from the S^{o}ward with a very great Sea, which obliged us to hand the Topsails. Saw a Sail in the SE Quarter standing to the Westward. Course S^o 13° E^t. Dist 37 M^s. Lat in 13°00′ N^o. Long^{de} made 0°11′ E^t. M^n Dist 10 M^s E^t from St Jago. Variation 8°2′ W^t. St Jago N° 5°06′ W^t. Dis 40 Leag^s.——Monday Augt 6th. Much Rain with heavy Squalls the wind to the S^{o}ward with a very great Sea, at any other time of the Year we might have expected a brisk NE Trade in these Latitudes, but as this is the rainy Season upon the Coast of Africa when the Southerly Winds prevail, we have great reason to dread a long passage, the Sun so near as makes it excessively hot & the

p. 9 continual Rains must make / these Climates very unhealthy.[1]—My People begin now to fall down in Fevers, tho' we take all the care we can to make them shift themselves when wet. Course S^o 41° E^t. Dist 80 M^s. Lat. in 12°0′ N^o. Long^{de} made 1 04 E^t. M^n Dist 62 M^s

[1] 'There are many journals which tend to prove that the north-east trade-wind is deflected by the projection of Cape Verd to the westward, and that ships which keep near the coast of Africa lose the trade sooner than others which are at a greater distance from the coast. To guard against this, it is recommended by many commanders to keep well to the westward at the time the north-east trade fails, with a view to continue it longer, to have fewer calms and baffling winds in the variable space, and to meet the south-east trade-wind sooner than if more eastward. By adhering to this precept, several ships have crossed the equator far westward, and then meeting with the south-east trade, hanging far to the southward, and strong westerly currents, have made the Brazil coast, obliged to tack to the eastward, which occasioned considerable delay.

'In the summer months, particularly when the sun is in the northern hemisphere, it is imprudent for outward-bound ships to run too far to the westward; for in this season it has sometimes happened that the north-east winds have continued longer with ships in longitude 19° to 23° W., than with others which had been separated from them, and lost the trade in 26° and 27° west longitude' (Horsburgh, I, 23–4). Horsburgh then cites nine instances of ships set either near or on the coast of Brazil from May 5 to Oct. 16. He hints that the best place to hit the coast is slightly to the southward of Cape St Augustine. However, ships coming upon it as far north as 7° or 8° S have no difficulty in making their way south (Ibid., 26).

E^t from St Jago. Variation 8°0′ W^t. St Jago N° 19°05′ W^t. Dist 63 Leag^s.—Thursday Augt 7th. Much rain & hard squalls the Wind to the Westward. Course S^o 8° E^t. Dist 85 M^s. Lat in 10°36′ N^o. Long^{de} made 1°17′ E^t. M^n Dist 74 M^s E^t from St Jago. Variation allowed 7°0′ W^t. St Jago N° 15°55′ W^t. Dist 91 Leag^s. Wednesday Augt 8th. The wind from W^t to SW^t blowing strong with thick rainy weather. At ½ past 12 last night in a Squall the *Tamar fired a Gun upon which we shorten'd Sail til she came up,* when Capt Mouat informed me he had carried away his Man topsail Yard. We made an easy sail til he had got another *across by which unfortunately we lost a good deal of way as the* wind seems inclinable to come to the S^{o}ward again. Course S^o 3°0′ E^t. Dist 126 M^s. Lat in 8°31′ N^o. —Long^{de} made 1°24′ E^t. M^n Dist 81 M^s E^t from St Jago. Variation 8°19′ W^t. St Jago N° 11°55′ W^t. Dist 131 Leag^s.—Thursday Augt 9th. Hard Squalls with much rain; the wind for the most part from SW to SSW with / a very great Sea. Course S^o 35 E^t. Dist 96 M^s. *p. 10* Lat in 7°13′ N^o. Long^{de} made 2°20′ E^t M Dist 137 M^s E^t from St Jago. Variation allowed 8°0′ W^t. St Jago N° 16°23′ W^t. Dist 162 Leag^s.—Friday Augt 10th. The wind from SW to S^o.—Saw a Sail Yesterday afternoon who shewed us French Colours, suppose her to be a Guinea Man bound off the Coast to the West Indies by the Course she steered. This is a most unfortunate wind for us & at present see no likelihood of a change. At Noon I tacked & stood to the Westward as we have been obliged by these winds to make more Easting than I could have wished. Course S^o 73° E^t. Dist 76 M^s. Lat in 6°50′ N^o. Long^{de} made 3°32′ E^t.—M^n Dist 209 M^s E^t from St Jago. Variation allowed 8°0′ Wt. St Jago N° 23°7′ W^t. Dist 177 Leag^s. Saturday Augt 11th. The wind from S^o to SSW & fine weather. Course S^o 74 W^t. Dist 102 M^s. Lat^{de} in 6°22′ N^o. Long^{de} made 1°54′ E^t. M^n Dist 111 M^s E^t from St Jago, D^o bears N° 12°12′ W^t. Dist 177 Leag^s.—Sunday Augt 12th. The wind for the most part at S^o & no appearance as yet of a change, the weather most extremely hot. Course S^o 67° W^t. Dist 87 M^s. Lat in 5°48′ N^o. Long^{de} made 0 04 E^t. M^n Dist 31 M^s E^t from St Jago. Variation allowed 8°0′ W^t. St Jago N° 3°30′ W^t. Dist 184 Leag^s. Monday Augt 13th. The wind continuing / in the same Quarter I yesterday *p. 11* at Noon tacked & stood to the E^{t}ward. Course S^o 76° E^t. Dist 75 M^s. Lat in 5°30′ N^o. Long^{de} made 1°47′ E^t. M^n Dist 104 M^s E^t

from St Jago. Variation 8°10′ W^t St Jago. N° 10°27′ W^t. Dist 193 Leag^s.—Tuesday Augt 14th. The wind from S^o to SbE tacked yesterday at Noon & stood to the W^{t}ward against an ugly head Sea, to all appearance it seems a settled Trade here at this time as the wind is almost fixed to a Point. Course S^o 72° W^t. Dist 98 M^s. Lat in 5°0′ N^o. Long^{de} made 0°14′ E^t. M^n Dist 11 M^s E^t from St Jago. Variation 8°0′ W^t. St Jago N° 1°19′ W^t. Dist. 200 Leag^s.— Wednesday Augt 15th. Wind from S^o to SSE & fine clear weather. Course S^o 65° W^t. Dist 90 M^s. Lat in 4°20′ N^o. Long^{de} made 1°15′ W^t. M^n Dist 75 W^t from St Jago which Island bears N° 6°40′ E^t. Dist 213 Leag^s.—Thursday Augt 16th. Tacked yesterday at Noon & stood to the E^{t}ward fine Weather & little wind at S^o.—Course N° 85 E^t. Dist 53 M^s. Lat in 4°25′ N^o. Long^{de} made 0°22′ W^t. M Dist 22 M^s from St Jago. Variation 7°0′ W^t. St Jago N° 1°0′ E^t. Dist 212 Leag^s.—Friday Augt 17th. Tacked last night at 8. the Wind coming something to the E^{t}ward tho' but little of it all night. This Morning it came to SE a pretty fresh breeze & am in great

p. 12 hopes it may continue, we see abundance of Fish but / none comes near enough to strike. Course S^o 27° W^t. Dist 29 M^s. Lat in 4°0′ N^o. Long^{de} made 0°35′ W^t. M^n Dist 35 M^s W^t from St Jago. Variation 6°30′ W^t. St Jago N° 2°49′ E^t. Dist 220 Leag^s.—— Saturday Augt 18th. Little wind for the most part at SE. Course S^o 30°. W^t. Dist 35 M^s. Lat in 3°13′ N^o. Long^{de} made 1°12′ W^t. M^n Dist 62 M^s W^t from St Jago, which bears N° 5°1′ E^t Dist 237 Leag^s.—Sunday Augt 19th. Little Wind for the first part, about Sun set saw a Sail in the SE Quarter & about 9 at night spoke with His Maj^{ts} Ship Liverpool from the East Indies, she had touched at the Cape & had been but three weeks from thence. The wind coming to the S^{o}ward again I tacked at 2 in the morning & stood to the E^{t}ward. Course S^o 63° E^t. Dist 5 M^s. Lat in 3°11′ N^o. Long^{de} made 0 57′ W^t M^n Dist 57 M^s W^t from St Jago. Variation 6°30 M^s. St Jago N° 5°0′ E^t. Dist 236 Leag^s.—Monday Augt 20th. Wind at S^o fair weather. Course S^o 87° E^t. Dist 84 M^s. Lat in 3°7′ N^o. Long^{de} made 0°27′ E^t. M^n Dist 27 M^s E^t from St Jago. Variation 6°10′ W^t. St Jago N° 2°10′ W^t. Dist 238 Leag^s.—Thursday Augt 21st. Wind at S^o & fine weather. Course S^o 83° E^t. Dist 80 M^s. Lat in 2°58′ N^o. Long^{de} made 1°46′ E^t. M^n Dist 106 M^s E^t from St Jago Variation 6°20′ W^t. St Jago N° 8°21′ W^t. Dist 243 Leag^s.—

Wednesday Augt 22d. Wind from S to SbW with a great Swell / from the Soward. Course So 74° Et. Dist 78 Ms. Lat in 2°36′ No. *p. 13* Longde made 3°01′ Et. Mn Dist 181 Ms Et from St Jago. Variation 7°0′ Wt. St Jago No 13°40′ Wt. Dist 255 Leags. Thursday Augt 23d. Wind from SbE to SbW tacked last night at 7 & again this morning at 7. Course So 6° Wt. Dist 29 Ms. Lat in 2°08′ No. Longde made 2°58′ Et. Mn Dist 178 Ms Et from St Jago. Variation 7°15′ Wt. St Jago No 12°59′ Wt. Dist 264 Leags.—Friday Augt 24th. At 5 Yesterday afternoon tacked, the wind shifting to SEbE, this morning it came to SE so that we are in hopes we have now the true Trade. Course So 23° Wt. Dist 57 Ms. Lat in 1°16′ No Longde made 2°35′ Et. Mn Dist 155 Ms Et from St Jago. Variation 7°0′ Wt. St Jago No 10°39′ Wt. Dist 279 Leags.—Saturday Augt 25th. Little wind from SE to SbE. Course So 53° Wt. Dist 66 Ms. Lat in 0 36′ No. No Longde 1°42′ Et. Mn Dist 102 Ms Et from St Jago. Variation 7°30′ Wt. St Jago No 6°44′ Wt. Dist 290 Leags.— Sunday Augt 26th. Wind from SE to So with a very great Swell. Course So 55° Wt. Dist 102 Ms. Lat in 0°23′ So Longde. made 0°19′ Et. M. Dist 19′ Et from St Jago. Variation 7°0′ Wt. St Jago No 1°11′ Wt. Dist 308 Leags.[1]—Monday Augt 27th. Wind from SbE to SE with a great Swell from the Soward. Course So 43 Wt. Dist 116 Ms. Lat in 1°49′ So. Longde made 1°0′ Wt. Mn Dist 60 Ms Wt from / St Jago. Variation 6°36′ Wt. St Jago No 3°24′ Et. *p. 14* Dist 337 Leags.—Tuesday Augt 28th. Wind for the most part at SE. Have found for these three days past a strong Currant seting to the Soward. Course So 30° Wt. Dist 92 Ms. Lat in 3°8′ So. Longde made 1°46′ Wt. Mn Dist 106 Ms Wt from St Jago. Variation 5°30′ Wt. St Jago No 5°34′ Et. Dist 364 Leags. Wednesday Augt 29th. Wind for the most part at SE with some small Showers of Rain. Course So 29° Wt. Dist 102 Ms. Lat in 4°37′ So. Longde made 2°36′ Wt. Mn Dist 156 Ms Wt from St Jago Variation 5°30′ Wt. St Jago No 7°33′ Et Dist 396 Leags.—Thursday Augt 30th. A fine gale for these last 24 hours. Wind from SE to ESE. Course So 12 Wt. Dis 122 Ms. Lat in 6°37′ So.—Longde made 3°2′ Wt. Mn Dist 182 Ms from St Jago, Variation 5°0′ Wt. St Jago No 8°20′ Et. Dist 437 Leags.—Friday Augt 31st. A fine brisk Trade being near the

[1] Mouat: Aug. 26, at 2 a.m. crossed the 'Equnoxial Line into South Latitude' (PRO Adm 55/131, p. 13).

Latitude of Cape Augustine, alter'd our Course & steered SSW½W. Course S^o 12° W^t. Dist 116 M^s. Lat in 8°29′ S^o. Long^{de} made 3°27′ W^t. M Dist 207 M^s W^t from St Jago. Variation 4°0′ W^t. St Jago N° 8°20′ E^t. Dist 477 Leag^s.—Saturday Septem^r 1st. A fine steady gale. Course S^o 22° W^t. Dist 173 M^s. Lat in 11°3′ S^o. Long^{de} made 4°50′ W^t. M^n Dist 288 M^s W^t from St Jago. Variation 3°20′ W^t. St Jago N° 10°25′ E^t. Dist 530 Leag^s.—Sunday Sepr 2^d. Wind EbS a brisk gale *The Tamar sails (if possible) worse than ever, we are* *p. 15* *obliged to spare more than | half our Sail, tho' we are far from a good sailing Ship.* Course S^o 30° W^t. Dist 175 M^s. Lat in 13°34′ S^o. Long^{de} made 6°20′ W^t. M Dist. 376 M^s W^t from St Jago. Variation 2°20′ W^t. St Jago N° 12°22′ E^t. Dist 585 Leagues. Monday Sepr 3^d. Wind EbS. a fine pleasant gale. *Excepting Sharks in all this Run we have not got one single fish (tho' we have such abundance at some distance from us) which must be owing to our being sheathed with Copper that prevents their coming near. This is great distress to us, as it is common for all other Ships in these hot Latitudes to take them in great plenty. I thank God at present our Ship's Company are very healthy.*[1] Course S^o 29° W^t. Dist 157 M^s. Lat in 15°30′ S^o. Long^{de} made 7°39′ W^t. M^n Dist 452 M^s W^t from St Jago. Variation 0°30′ W^t. St Jago N° 13 46 E^t. Dist 635 Leag^s.—Tuesday Sepr 4th. Wind from E^t to NNE a pleasant gale & fine clear weather Course S^o 29° W^t. Dist 107 M^s. Lat in 17°22′ S^o. Long^{de} made 8°33′ W^t. M. Dist 504 M^s W^t from St Jago. No variation St Jago N° 14°36′ E^t Dist 669 Leag^s. Cape Frio S^o 61°0′ W^t. Dist 268 Leag^s.—Wednesday Sepr 5th. For the first & middle part wind at NE a pleasant gale, the latter part very little wind & sometimes calm. Course S^o 30° W^t. Dist 98 M^s. Lat in 18 46 S^o. Long^{de} made 9°25′ W^t. M^n Dist 553 *p. 16* M^s W^t from St Jago. Variation | 1°30′ E^t. St Jago N° 15°22′ E^t. Dist 700 Leag^s. Cape Frio S^o 65°35′ W^t. Dist 205 Leag^s.— Thursday Sepr 6th. A fine pleasant gale at NE. Yesterday at noon being abreast of the Shoals called the Abrollos,[2] alter'd our Course & steered SW^t. I could never meet with any particular description

---

[1] See p. 16. No cooler than July 25, but drier.

[2] Abrollos (Abrollios): Admiralty Chart 2203 shows their position to be 18° S 38°37′ W, extending 50 miles from the coast. But the entire system of shoals, including Rodgers Bank and Hotspur Bank down through the Victoria Banks, runs from about 17° S 35° W to 21° S 34°50′ W and extends into the Atlantic for about 330 miles.

of the Coast of Brazil.—Some Charts lay these Shoals down at
Seventy Leag^s from the Land & others still farther, but how far
they extend to the S^{o}ward I never heard, they must certainly be
very dangerous therefore the only safe way for a Ship is to keep
well to the E^{t}ward of them. We have now the comfort to find the
weather something cooler, for many days between St Jago & the
Equinoctial, *a Thermometer we have on board stood at 79°* so that it
will be easily imagined the heat was very intense. Course S^o 46 W^t.
Dist 118 M^s. Lat in 20°9′ S^o. Long^{de} made 10°55 W^t. M^n Dist
637 M^s W^t from St Jago. Variation 3°50′ E^t. St Jago N° 16°59′ E^t.
Dist 735 Leag^s. Cape Frio S^o 70°8′ W^t. Dist 170 Leag^s. Friday
Sepr 7th. Wind from NE to NbW a fresh gale. Course S^o 65° W^t.
Dist 147 M^s. Lat in 21°12′ S^o. Long^{de} made 13°17′ W^t. M^n Dist
770 M^s W^t from St Jago. Variation 4°38 E^t. St Jago N° 19°49′ E^t.
Dist 770 Leag^s. Cape Frio S^o 72°19′ W^t. Dist 121 Leag^s.—
Saturday Sepr 8th. For the most part dark / cloudy weather with *p. 17*
much rain. Wind from NNW to SSW. saw a vast number of Birds
about the Ship of a dark brown colour upon the back, with a streak
of white upon the tail, from which we imagine we are not far from
the Land. Course S^o 79° W^t. Dist 104 M^s. Lat in 21°31′ S^o.
Long^{de} made 15°07′ W^t. M Dist 873 M^s from St Jago. Cape Frio
S^o 70°50′ W^t. Dist 90 Leag^s. Sunday Sepr 9th. Wind from SW to
SSE for the most part a hard gale with a great Sea. Course S^o 47°
E^t. Dist 50 M^s. Lat in 22°5′ S^o. Long^{de} made 14°27′ W^t. M^n Dist
836 M^s W^t from St Jago. Cape Frio S^o 78°35′ W^t. Dist 93 Leag^s.—
Monday Sepr 10th. I spoke with a Portugueze Snow from Rio
Janeiro to Bahia, who told us Cape Frio bore WSW 70 Leag^s which
agrees pretty much with our Reckoning. Wind from SEbS to N^o
the latter part a very hard gale with a prodigious great Swell from
the S^{o}ward. Saw Birds innumerable about a Grampus[1] that was
wounded, one of the latter passed close by us attacked by a
Thousand.—Course S^o 63° W^t. Dist 108 M^s. Lat in 22°54′ S^o.
Long^{de} made 16°13′ W^t. M^n Dist 932 M^s. W^t from St Jago.
Variation 6°0′ E^t. Cape Frio S^o 87°54′ W^t. Dist 59 Leag^s.—
Tuesday Sepr 11th. Course to the time we saw the Land N° 87°
W^t. Dist 33 M^s. Lat in 22°56′ S^o. Long^{de} made 16°48′ W^t. M^n Dist
965 M^s W^t.—At ½ past 3 PM saw the Land, At 4 Cape Frio bore

---

[1] A type of blackfish; also, the common killer whale.

p. 18 WbN Dist 14 or 15 Leag^s. / At 8 d^o Cape Frio WbS dist 5 or 6 Leag^s.—Soundings 45 f^m black mud.—Wednesday Sepr 12th. At 4 PM the remarkable Sugar Loaf Peek at Rio Janeiro Wt½S^o. dist 6 or 7 Leagues. At 6 sounded 30 f^m grey sand & pieces of broken Shells. At 3 PM Soundings 35 f^m black sand, the entrance of Rio Janeiro NW Dist 2 Leag^s.—At 7 AM the City of Janeiro NWbN dist 3 Leag^s, sounded 30 f^m.—At Noon anchored in 18 f^m in the Great Road of Rio Janeiro, Fort St Cruz, the first Fort on the Starboard side coming in, SE½S, the Sugar Loaf Peek SbE, & the Island of Eobra at the N^o end of the City W½N about half a Mile. The City of Janeiro makes a a very handsome appearance, is very large & governed by the Vice Roy of all the Brazils, who is as absolute as any Prince in the Universe; Several Instances of which he shewed whilst we were here.—*When I visited him he received me with great form,* above 60 Officers were drawn up before the Palace as well as a Captain's Guard, all extremely well clothed & very well looking Men. The Vice King with a number of Persons of the first distinction belonging to the Place received me at the head of the Stairs, upon which 15 Guns were fired from the nearest Fort, we *p. 19* then enterd into / his Room of State & after conversing about a quarter of an hour in French, I took my leave & went out with the same forms I had come in with:—*Some time after he returned my visit on board,* but offer'd first to do it at *a house I had on Shore which I did not* chuse. The Tamar came in here very sickly, I procured a place on Shore for her People where they soon recovered.[1] My Ship's Company were all very healthy, they had fresh meat with as much greens as they could eat every day.[2] As our

---

[1] This took five days. Mouat, Sept. 17: Sick 'sent on Shore to the Hospital on a Small Island that stands on the Starboard side coming into the Harbour, there being but one Fisherman & his Family Resides there' (p. 16).
[2]   By &c^a
'Whereas you have represented to us, by your Letter of the 15th Instant. "That the Honble Capt Byron has acquainted you, by his Letter dated at Rio de Janeiro the 16th of Octr last, that, as the Voyage on which His Majesty's Ship Dolphin and the Tamar Frigate are bound may run them short of Bread, he had, in order to prevent it as much as possible & to make the Bread, then on board, last them to India, ordered the Purser of the former to purchase a quantity of Yams, and to serve them in lieu of Bread; That the People had likewise been served with fresh Beef, from the time of their arrival at the said place, & as the quantity of Greens & Vegetables which he had thought necessary to have boiled with the Beef, must have greatly injured the two Pursers to pay for out of their pockets, he had also ordered Mr Stacey, Purser of the former, in addition to the

Ships were quite open I hired a number of Portugueze Caulkers, at which work they were employed for some time.[1] Whilst we lay here Lord Clive put in, in the Kent India Man who had sailed from England a Month before us & had touched no where, & now came in here just a Month after us, they had many of their people down in the Scurvy——Sunday Octo^r 21st we put to Sea again, glad to leave Rio Janeiro where the heat was intollerable, we lay 4 or 5 days above the Bar without having the Land breeze to carry us out, for their is no turning out with the Sea breeze, the entrance between the two first Forts is so narrow, & a vast / Sea breaks upon them, it *p. 20* was with the utmost difficulty we got out when we did, & that attended with a great deal of danger, for if we had followed the Portugueze Pilot's advice, who was frightened out of his Senses we had lost the Ship. Another great inconvenience attending this Place is the risque you run of loosing your people, for as the Portugueze carry on a great Trade from hence, they make it their business to attend every Boats landing in order to entice away some of the Crew, by this means I lost five Seamen, who were made drunk & immediately sent away into the Country, & care enough taken they should not return til after I sailed.[2]——The Tamar had lost 8 or 9 of her People, but by great good luck heard where they was detained, & in the night sent & surprized them & got them

quantity furnished by him to purchase Vegetables of different Kinds for the two Ships to the Amount of seven Shillings a Sixpence a day, which he had found of the greatest Efficacy in restoring the Sick people, and that Mr Stacey had drawn upon you for those Articles & for Watering the said Ships, in favour of Scott & Pringle, or Order, for One hundred & Twenty four pounds. Eleven shillings & Sixpence. And Whereas you have desired to receive our directions touching the Acceptance of the said Bill; You are hereby required and directed to accept & pay the same Charging the amount as Imprest to the said Mr Stacey.
 'Given &c^a the 20th March 1765.   Egmont
 To   Carysfort
 The Commiss^{rs} for Victualling   Howe'
  His Majestys Navy—
   By & PS   [PRO Adm 2/92]
The imprest was removed upon the ships' return to England.
 The *Tamar* received 100 lb. of fresh beef daily, according to Mouat's log. Also, on Sept. 30, she received 2,804 lb. of yams (pp. 13 ff.).
 [1] The Minutes of the Admiralty Board for 13 March 1765 show that Byron spent £200 for his contingent expenses at Rio de Janeiro. This was in addition to the cost of provisions and water (PRO Adm 3/253).
 [2] The Muster Sheet lists eight 'run men': Joseph Brown, William Chalmer, Thomas Darvell, Thomas Kennedy, Thomas Nicholas, Daniel Robinson, William Ranter, and John Symonds; and one 'Straggler': Thomas Lake. All were ABs (PRO Adm 33/441).

every one back.—Monday *Octr 22^d*. Being now at Sea again I called all Hands upon Deck & informed them I was not immediately bound to the East Indies as was imagined, but upon some certain Discoveries which was thought might be of great importance to our Country, and that the Lords Commissioners of

p. 21 the Admiralty / were pleased *to promise them double Pay with several other advantages* if they behaved themselves to my satisfaction.[1] They all expressed the greatest Joy imaginable upon the occasion & assured me there was no Difficulties they would not go through with the greatest chearfulness to—serve their Country & obey every Order I should give them. Course S^o Dist 142 M^s. Lat in 25°22′ S^o. Rio Janeiro bore N^o. Dist 47 Leagues. Variation 6°0′ E^t. Tuesday Octo^r 23^d. Came on last night about 9 a very hard gale of wind at SW with a very great Sea, Struck our Top gallant Masts & got our Stumps up. Course S^o 43 E^t. Dist 43 M^s. Lat in 25°53 S^o. M Dist 29 M^s E^t. Long^{de} made 32° E^t. Rio Janeiro N° 10° W^t. Dist 59 Leag^s.—Wednesday Octo^r 24th. The Gale continued til about 4 this morning, tacked & stood to the W^{t}ward. Course S^o 39° E^t. Dist 31 M^s. Lat in 26°19′ S^o. Long ^{de} made 0 50 E^t. M Dist 45 M^s E^t. Variation ¾ points E^t. Rio Janeiro N° 13°10′ W^t. Dist 67 Leagues.—Thursday Octo^r 25th. Wind from ESE to ENE a great Swell continues but the weather moderate. Course S^o 20 W^t. Dist 90 M^s. Lat in 27°43′ S^o. Long^{de} made 16 M^s E^t. M Dist 15′ E^t from R. Janeiro. The Island of St Catharine W^t. Dist 96 Leag^s. Rio Janeiro N° 2°0′ W^t. Dist 94 Leagues. Friday Octo^r 26th. Wind /

p. 22 between the NE & E^t a fine moderate Gale. Course S^o 21° W^t. Dist 120 M^s. Lat in 29°42′ S^o. Long^{de} made 0°38′ W^t. M^n Dist 32 M^s W^t. Variation 7°30′ E^t. Rio Janeiro N° 5°30′ E^t. Dist. 136 Leag^s.— Saturday Octo^r 27th. Wind from NE to N^o a pleasant gale. Course S^o 22 W^t. Dist 146 M^s. Lat in 31°57′ S^o. Long^{de} made 1°42′ W^t. M Dist 86 M^s W^t from Rio Janeiro.—Rio Grande W^t. Dist 108 Leag^s. Rio Janeiro N° 9°34′ E^t. Dist 181 Leag^s. Variation 9°0′ E^t. —Sunday Octo^r 28th. Wind NbE hazey weather Course S^o 21 W^t. Dist 132 M^s. Lat in 33°59′ S^o. Long^{de} made 2°39′ W^t. M Dist 133 M^s W^t from Rio Janeiro. The entrance of Rio de Plata S^o 79°28′ W^t. Dist 184 Leag^s. Rio Janeiro N° 11°57′ E^t. Dist 225 Leag^s. Variation 10° E^t.—*Monday Octo^r 29th. PM. Wind NbE at 8* am

---

[1] See Introduction, p. xxx, for details.

shifted to the NW & blew a perfect Storm with a most terrible Sea.
at 11 shifted again to WSW still blowing as hard as ever, the Ship
laboured much, to ease her in some measure *I ordered the two fore
most & two aftermost Guns to be thrown over board.* Course S⁰ 2°
Wᵗ. dist 142 Mˢ. Lat in 36°11′ S⁰. Longᵈᵉ made 3°41′ Wᵗ. M Dist
183 Mˢ Wᵗ. Variation 11° Eᵗ. Cape Sᵗ Anthony the entrance of Rio
Plata N⁰ 86°17′ Wᵗ. 159 Leagˢ. Rio Janeiro N⁰ 13°36′ Eᵗ. Dist 271
Leagˢ.—Tuesday Octʳ 30ᵗʰ. Wind PM SW blowing very hard till
night, at 7 AM—shifted to SbW we had lain too from the time the
gale came on till 9 AM under a / double reefed Mainsail, then made *p. 23*
sail & stood to the Wᵗward. Course N⁰ 44° Eᵗ. Dist 30 Mˢ. Lat in
35°50′ S⁰. Longᵈᵉ made 3°16′ Wᵗ. M Dist 163 Mˢ Wᵗ. Variation
10° Eᵗ. The entrance of Rio Plata Wᵗ 74 N⁰. Dist 155 Leagˢ. Rio
Janeiro N⁰ 12°28′ Eᵗ. Dist 262 Leagˢ.—Wednesday Octoʳ 31ˢᵗ.
Little wind & variable for these last 24 hours, having been at SW.
WbN & SbE. Bent a new Mainsail. *The weather is now as cold here
as it is at this time of the Year in England, a great change to us who
but a week since found the heat intolerable. The Men have all applied
for Slops as they thought they were to continue the whole Voyage in a
hot Climate, warm Clothes were unnecessary, so they contrived to sell
all theirs as well as their Bedding at the different Ports we have
touched at; they are now all well provided again & in all probability
will not have an opportunity of selling these for some time to come.*
Course S⁰ 34° Wᵗ. Dist 35 Mˢ. Lat in 36°19′. S⁰. Longᵈᵉ made
3°41′ Wᵗ. M Dist 183 Mˢ Wᵗ. Cape Sᵗ Anthony N⁰ 83° Wᵗ Dist
150 Leagˢ. Rio Janeiro N⁰ 12°33′ Eᵗ 273 Leagˢ. Variation 12° Eᵗ.—
Thursday *Novemʳ 1ˢᵗ*. Wind from SE to NWbW fine moderate
weather. Course S⁰ 52 Wᵗ. Dist 38 Mˢ. Lat in 36°42′ S⁰. Longᵈᵉ
made 4°18′ Wᵗ. M Dist 213 Mˢ Wᵗ. Variation 12°52′ Eᵗ. Rio
Janeiro N⁰ 15°10′ Eᵗ. Dist 284 Leagˢ. Point de Leones S⁰ 66°51′
Wᵗ. 371 Leagˢ.—Friday Novʳ 2ᵈ. Wind NNW a pleasant Gale &
very / fine weather. *This day after swearing the Lieutenants of both* *p. 24*
*Ships I delivered them their Commissions for the Dolphin tho' but a
20 Gun Ship bears three Lieuᵗˢ for this Voyage & the Tamar two.*[1]
They had only acting Orders from me before, & thought they were
not to receive their proper Commissions til after their arrival in
India, where they imagined we were bound. Course S⁰ 60° Wᵗ.

[1] See Introduction, p. xxx.

Dist 100 M^s. Lat in 37°32′ S^o. Long^{de} made 6°08′ W^t. M^n Dist 300 M^s W^t. Porto de Leones S^o 67°30′ W^t. Dist 338 Leag^s. Variation 13°1′ E^t.—Saturday Novr 3^d. Fine moderate weather. Course S^o 72 W^t. Dist 110 M^s. Lat in 38°6′ S^o. Long^{de} made 8°18′ W^t. M Dist 402 M^s W^t. Variation 13° E^t. Porto de Leones S^o 67°1′ W^t. Dist 302 Leag^s. Sunday Novr 4th. Wind NW. the Water having changed it's colour, sounded but had no Ground with 150 f^m of Line.—*Abundance of Birds about the Ship for these four days past some of an immense size brown & white, others as large quite black, & a great many Pentados which are something larger than a Pidgeon black & white spotted, we see a great deal of Rock weed with several Seals playing about it, so that I imagine we are nearer the Land than we expect,* for I do not remember when I was upon this Coast before to have seen Seals at any great distance *from the Land.* Course S^o 56° W^t.

p. 25 Dist 84 M^s. Latt in / 38°53′ S^o. Long^{de} made 9°48′ W^t. M Dist 472 M^s W^t. Variation 13° E^t. Porto de Leones S^o 68°2′ W^t. Dist 274 Leag^s. Cape St Andrew N° 88°16′ W^t. Dist 143 Leag^s.—Monday Novem^r 5th. Wind from NWbN to WbN for the most part a very thick Fog attended with a cold damp rain. A very great Swell from the NW. Many Seals playing about the Ship with much Rock weed floating. about. Course S^o 67° W^t. Dist 79 M^s. Latt—39°24′ S^o. Long^{de} made 11°21′ W^t. M^n Dist. 544 M^s W^t from Rio Janeiro. Porto de Leones S^o 68°10′ W^t. 247 Leagues. Cape Blanco S^o 68°49′ W^t. 287 Leagues.—Tuesday Novr 6th. The first part calm, a thick Fog, with a very ugly Swell running in heaps, the certain forerunner of a Gale. Hoisted the Boat out & tried the Current, & found it to set NW 5 f^m. At 6 PM a breeze sprung up at S^o & presently after flew round to SW blowing excessively hard with a great Sea. At 3 AM brought too under the Mainsail, Many hard Squalls with hail & the weather as cold as it is at Christmas in England. The prevailing winds here are W^{t}erly, & as we are continually drove by them to the Eastward, I am afraid we shall find it a difficult matter to get in with the Coast of Patagonia.[1] Course S^o 58° E^t. Dist 21 M^s. Latt in 39°35′ S^o.—Long^{de} made 10°57′ W^t. M^n Dist 526 M^s W^t from Rio Janeiro. Variation 14° E^t.

p. 26 Cape Blanco / S^o 60°0′ W^t. Dist 290 Leag^s.—Wednesday Novem^r 7th. Continued blowing very hard til night when it abated

---

[1] See citation from Horsburgh, I, 26, p. 18, n. 1, above.

something, but the Swell kept up, made Sail again. Course S^o 30° E^t. Dist 41 M^s. Latt in 40°10' S^o. Long^{de} made 10°31' W^t. M Dist 506 M^s W^t. Variation 14° E^t. Cape Blanco S^o 62°30' W^t. Dist 287 Leag^s.—Thursday Novr 8th. Wind from NNW to SWbS the weather extremely cold. Amongst many other sort of Birds there are constantly a number of Peterells about us, which of all other kinds are so much disliked by Seamen, & that not without great reason. At $\frac{1}{2}$ past 11 AM tacked & stood to the W^{t}ward. Course S^o 23° W^t. Dist 66 M^s. Latt in 41°10' S^o. Long^{de} made 11°5' W^t from Rio Janeiro. M Dist 531 M^s W^t. Cape Blanco S^o 65°16' W^t. Dist 271—Leag^s.—Friday Novem^r 9. Wind from SW to SE & fine weather. Course S^o 77° W^t. Dist 71 M^s. Latt in 41°26' S^o. Long^{de} made 12°35' W^t. M. Dist. 600 M^s W^t from Rio Janeiro. Variation 14°30' E^t.—Cape Blanco S^o 64°12' W^t. Dist 248 Leag^s.—Saturday Novr 10th. Wind from SEbE to NW^t. the latter part a fine gale. We have steered by the Compass WSW these last 24 hours, yet find by a good observation we have made 10 Miles Northing, so that we must have had a strong Current setting to the N^{o}ward.—We have run through several strong Ripplings both last / night & this p. 27 morning, & the water has changed its colour three or four times, & we have as often sounded but have found no Ground with 140 f^m of Line. Course N° 84 W^t. Dist 92 M^s. Latt in 41°16' S^o. Long^{de} made 14°57'. M^n Dist 691 M^s W^t from Rio Janeiro. Variation 18°20' E^t. Porto de Leones S^o 72°30' W^t. Dist 182 Leag^s. Cape Blanco S^o 59°50' W^t. 222 Leag^s.—Sunday Novr 11th. Wind NW a fine fresh gale. Stood in for the Land till 8 PM then Sounded & had Ground at 45 f^m red Sand, Steered SWbS til Morning & after SW. at Noon Sounded & had 52 f^m much the same Ground. The Tamar sails so very heavy that I look upon it as a great misfortune our having her with us, as I verily believe I could make the passage in half the time if it was not for her. Course S^o 62 W^t. Dist 168 M^s. Latt in 42°34' S^o. Long^{de} made 17°57' W^t. M^n Dist 840 M^s W^t from Rio Janeiro. Variation 1 point $\frac{3}{4}$ East. Porto de Leones S^o 77°24' W^t. Dist 131 Leag^s.—Cape Blanco S^o 59°39' W^t 169 Leag^s. —Monday Novr 12th. At 4 PM It thunder'd & Lightened very much, & looked very black almost round the Horizon, I was then walking the Quarter Deck when all the People upon the Forecastle called out at once Land right a head, I looked under the Foresail &

p. 28 upon the Lee Bow, & saw / it to all appearance as plain as ever I saw Land in my life,[1] It made at first like an Island with two very scraggy Hammocks upon it, but looking to Leeward we saw the Land joining it & running along way to the SE, we were then steering SW. I sent Officers to the Mast head to look out upon the weather Beam & they called out immediately they saw the Land a great way to Windward. I brought too & sounded & had 52 f^m—I now thought I was embay'd & as it looked very wild all round I wished myself out before night. We made Sail & steered ESE. All this time the appearance of the Land did not alter in the least, the Hills looked very Blue as they generally do at some little distance in dark rainy weather, & many of the People said they saw the Sea break upon the Sandy Beaches. After steering out for about an hour, what we took for Land all at once disappeared to our great astonishment, & certainly must have been nothing but a Fog Bank. Tho' I have been at Sea now 27 Years & never saw such a Deception before, & I question much if the oldest Seaman breathing ever did, except it was some in that Ship when the

p. 29 Master made Oath of seeing an Island between / the West End of Ireland & Newfoundland, & even distinguishing the Trees upon it, & which since has never been heard of tho' Ships have been sent out on purpose to look for it. And had the weather come on very thick after the sight we had for some time of this Imaginary Land so that we could not have seen it disappear as we did, I dare say there is not a Man on board but would have freely made Oath of the certainty of it's being Land. Course S° 47° W^t. Dist 108 M^s Latt in 43°46′ S°. Long^de made 19°47′ W^t. M^n Dist 920 M^s W^t.— Variation 19°30′ E^t. Porto de Leones W¼S Dist 98 Leag^s.—Cape Blanco S° 62°35′ W^t. 133 Leag^s.—Tuesday Novr 13th. At 4 PM from the weather being extremely fine the wind shifted at once to SW. began to blow fresh & looked very black to Windward.[2]

We all upon Deck heard a very unusual noise, it seemed like the breaking of the Sea upon the Shore. I ordered the Topsails to be handed but before that could be done we saw the Sea from some distance approaching us all in a foaming Breach, I called to them immediately to hawl the Foresail up, & to let go the Main Sheet, for

---

[1] Mouat, 23, made no mention of this spurious landfall.
[2] Mouat, 23, called this 'a Violent Squall'.

by what I saw I was sure if it had taken us with any Sail out we must either have / overset or lost all the Masts, before we could rise *p. 30* the Main Tack it reached us & laid us upon our Beam ends, we cut the Main Tack, for it was then impossible to cast it off; the Main Sheet struck the first Lieu^t down bruised him terribly & broke three of his teeth. The Main topsail was not quite handed so was split to pieces. I never remember to have seen any thing more dreadful than this Squall, nor any thing come on with so little warning, if it had happened in the night I think the Ship must have been lost. It lasted about 20 Minutes & then lull'd, what was very remarkable was that there was hundreds of Birds flying before it & Shrieking terribly. The Tamar split her Mainsail but as she was to Leeward of us she had more time to prepare for it. It presently began to blow very hard again, we reefed the Main sail & lay too under it all night, towards morning it grew more moderate but a great Sea kept up, the wind shifted to SbW we stood to the W^tward under our Courses. The Sea was as red as blood being covered with a small Shell fish / something like our Crawfish but smaller, we took *p. 31* up great Quantities of them in Baskets.

Course S^o 63° W^t. Dist 14 M^s. Latt in 43°52′ S^o. Long^de made 20°4′ W^t. M Dist 932 M^s W^t. Variation 19°40′ E^t. Porto de Leones W¼S Dist 96 Leag^s. Cape Blanco S^o 62°36′ W^t. 128 Leagues. Wednesday Novr 14th. Wind from WbN to SW & back again to W^t. at 4 PM it was at NW & blew very fresh. I take every opportunity it allows of getting in with the Land. This day at Noon Sounded & had 45 f^m black ozey Ground & abundance of Sea weed about us & many Birds & Seals. For these last 24 Hours we have had a prodigious great Swell from the S^oward. Course S^o 71° W^t. Dist 57 M^s. Latt in 44°8′ S^o. Long^de made 21°11′ W^t. M Dist 980 M^s W^t from Rio Janeiro, Variation 19°41′ E^t. Porto de Leones N° 88°25′ W^t. Dist 80 Leag^s. Cape Blanco S^o 61°15′ W^t. Dist 112 Leag^s. Thursday Novr 15th. Wind variable from WbS to NW & back at Noon to SW. Stood in for the Land til night, then steered SSW til day break, when we hauled in again; At ½ past 4 AM saw the Land, it appeared to us to be an Island of 8 or 9 Leag^s length, as we could see no other land joining to it either to the Northward / or Southward, but by the Charts it should be Cape St Helena *p. 32* which projects out some way from the other Land & forms two

Bays to the N^{o}ward & S^{o}ward, as it was very fine weather I tacked at 10 & stood in for it to make it plain, but as there are many dangerous sunken Rocks at above 2 Leagues from it, upon which the Sea broke very high & falling little wind I tacked again & stood off, the Land appeared very barren & rocky without either Tree or Bush. I sounded when nearest & had 45 f^m black muddy Ground. —I have the misfortune at this time to have my three Lieutenants & Master sick when they are most wanted, the rest of my Ships Company are very healthy. Course S^o 50° W^t. Dist 112 M^s. Latt in 45°21′ S^o. Long^{de} made 23°13′ W^t. M Dist 1066 M^s. Variation 19°41′ E^t. Cape Blanco S^o 66 19 W^t. Dist 75 Leag^s.—Friday Novr 16th. Shaped our Course for Cape Blanco by the Chart in Lord Anson's Voyage. In the Evening it came on to blow extremely hard at SWbS, at 12 at Night brought too under the Mainsail & at day light made sail again, there run a very great Sea which broke *p. 33* very much. We imagined at Noon we were not / above 7 or 8 Leagues from the Cape. This may be called the Summer here but the weather is much worse than it is in the depth of Winter in the Bay of Biscay;[1] It is certainly the most disagreable sailing in the world, forever blowing & that with such violance that nothing can withstand it, & the Sea runs so high that it works & tears a Ship to pieces. Course S^o 8° E^t. Dist 72 M^s. Latt in 46°32′ S^o. Long^{de} in 66°28′ W^t. Cape Blanco S^o 27 W^t. Dist 23 M^s.—Saturday Novr 17th. It continued to blow very hard till between 4 & 5 PM when the wind in a minute or two went once or twice all round the Compass, & then fell flat calm for about half an hour, the Sea running very high all in heaps. As I wanted to make the Land before night I carried as much Sail as possible; but it blew so hard between 12 & 4 that we set & handed the Foretopsails five or six different times. About 6 we made the Land bearing about SSW which we took for Cape Blanco as we had a good observation of the Sun, It then began to blow harder than ever and continued so all night with a Sea that broke over us continually & the Ship worked *p. 34* & laboured very much. At 4 / AM Sounded 40 f^m rocky Ground. Wore Ship & stood in again blowing all this time a storm of wind attended with hail & snow. At 6 Saw the Land again bearing about SWbW. Our Ship is now so light that she drives bodily to Leeward

[1] Mouat, 24, agreed.

when it blows. I want if possible to get into Port Desire to get her Hold into order & to take in more Ballast, for in the trim she is in at present it would be very dangerous to be caught upon a Lee Shore with her. Sunday Novr 18th. The wind shifted to NE steered in for the Land & made it plain to be Cape Blanco before Sun set.— Brought too but the wind coming to the W^{t}ward we were drove some way off again—before morning. At 7 AM standing in again & steering. SWbS by the Compass we perceived the Sea to break pretty much right a head of us when we suddenly shoaled our water from 13 to 7 f^m & presently after deeped our water from 17. to 42 f^m so that we went over the end of a Shoal that a little farther to the N^{o}ward might have been very dangerous, Cape Blanco at that time bore WSW$\frac{1}{2}$S^o. Dist 4 Leag^s.—We were now at a loss for Port Desire for certainly nothing was ever so confused as Sir John Narborough's description / of that Harbour,[1] I stood into a Bay to *p. 35* the S^{o}ward of the Cape as directed by him, but could find no such place; So I stood along shore to the S^{o}ward the wind off the Land blowing excessively hard, we saw at different times very great Smokes upon the Shore which we supposed were made by the wild Indians, no tree nor Bush to be seen but the appearance of the Land is something like some of our barren Downs in England. The water is very shoal at 7 or 8 Miles from the Shore frequently not having above 10 f^m.—Monday Novr 19th. The first part a hard Gale at SWbS. kept along shore as near as possible, towards night it fell little wind when we saw an Island about 6 Leagues from us. In the morning we had a small breeze at WNW we stood in for the Island which proved to be Penguin Island by Sir John Narborough's description. I sent my Boat in Shore to look for Port Desire which is said to lay about 3 Leagues NW from this Island;

[1] Narborough is viewing Port Desire from Penguin Island. Port Desire is NNW about three leagues: '. . . to the Northward of these Islands is a Bay, four Leagues long, and a League and half deep; in the Northwest thereof lies the Harbour of *Port Desier*, which we could see from *Penguin Islands*, bearing North-north-west from *Penguin Island*, distant about 3 Leagues: About the middle of this Bay are steep white Cliffs, near two miles long; the upper part of the Cliff has black streaks down a fourth part, caused by the Water draining down on it: the Land is plain on the top of these Cliffs, but further into the Country high rounding Hills and Downs, and towards the Waterside low. On the South part of the Bay are craggy Rocks on the Main like great Walls; near the Sea there's a sandy Cove, to hale a Boat up in foul weather: the Cove is just under these Wall-like Rocks' [Sir John Narbrough (Narborough), *Voyage to the South-Sea* (London, 1711), 25–6].

towards Noon it fell calm. Thousands of Seals & Penguins about
p. 36 us. There lays several small Islands or rather Rocks—/ about
Penguin Island. Latt Observed this day is 48° S⁰.—Tuesday
Novr 20th. stood in for the Land, towards evening we saw a
remarkable Rock spired like a Steeple[1] which stands in the S⁰ side
of the Entrance of Port Desire, & is an excellent mark to know that
Harbour by, which otherwise would be difficult to find. At night
being little wind we anchored at 4 or 5 Miles from the Shore. In
the morning the wind being off Shore we turned up to the Harbours
mouth, which appeared very narrow with several Rocks & Shoals
about it, & the most rapid Tide runs here I ever saw in my life. I
came to an Anchor off the Harbour; The entrance of the River
open WSW. Penguin Island SE½E about 3 Leagues Distance. The
remarkable Rock mentioned before to be on the S⁰ side of the
Harbour SWbW; The Northermost Land NNW. Two Rocks
covered at half Tide at the S⁰most extremity of a Reef running
from the same Land bearing NEBN & in depth of Water 9 f^m.—
I have been the more particular in mentioning all these Bearings
p. 37 as I am in hopes it may be of Service hereafter to / any of my
Countrymen that may be ordered this way, & as I think that those
very few that have been here before have been too deficient in.
It blew very hard the best part of the day & there run an ugly Sea
where we lay, however I ordered two boats in to sound the Harbour
& went in myself in my own Boat. We found it very narrow for near
2 Miles & the Tides run at the rate of 8 Miles an hour, there are
many Rocks & Shoals, but all the danger shews itself at low water.
I landed & walked a little way into the Country which is all Downs
as far as I could see without a single Tree to be seen. We saw the
dung of many Beasts. Saw four that fled as soon as they saw us, but
of what kind they were we did not know, two of them appeared to
be Guaniers or Peruvian Sheep,[2] since that we have seen many
come down to the water side, they resemble our Deer but are much
larger, they seem to be not less than 12 or 13 hands high, are very
shy & run vastly swift. I returned to my Boat & went further up
the Harbour, & landed upon an Island that was covered
with Seals, we killed above fifty, some of them larger than a

---

[1] Not mentioned by Narborough.
[2] See Narborough (1711), 32.

Bullock,[1] we had half loaded our Boat before with different kinds / of *p. 38*
Birds, of which & Seals there are enough to supply the Navy of
England. One Bird in particular we got this afternoon was the most
surprizing one I ever saw, he measured *twelve feet from wing to wing*,
his head was like that of an Eagle, only with a large Comb upon it,
round his neck was a white Ruff exactly like a fine Tippet, his feathers
upon his back were as black as Jet & shined like the finest Silk, his
Legs were immensely strong & large & had Claws like an Eagle but
not so sharp, Nobody dare approach him he bites so hard, but he is
so much wounded I am afraid we shall not keep him alive much
longer.[2]—Wednesday Nov[r] 21st. The Tamar upon the Tide of
Flood worked into the Harbour this morning, but I thought it too
great a risque for the Dolphin, so lay fast til we might have a
leading wind, but that shifting to the Eastward soon after, I
intended going up upon the Evenings flood, accordingly we weighed
about 5, but before we got under sail the wind shifted again to
NWbN. It being low water & the Ship barely laying into the
Harbour & having no tide to assist us, was obliged to anchor near
the S[o] shore. The wind coming off from the Land in very hard
flaws the Anchor / came home & the Ship tailed ashore against a *p. 39*
steep gravelly Beach. It is to be observed that the Anchoring
Ground as far as we had Sounded was but bad, as it is extremely
hard; it is ten to one if it blows fresh but your anchor comes home
before you can bring up. It now began to blow very hard & the tide
running like a Sluce it was with the utmost difficulty that we could
carry an Anchor out to heave her off by; however after above 4
hours work that was effected, & we got her out in the Stream w[th]out
(I hope) any damage for there was only about 6 or 7 feet of the after
part of her that touched the Ground. If any part has suffered I
imagine it must be the Rudder, for which reason I intend to unhang
it that we may be certain.—Thursday Nov[r] 22[d]. All last night &
this morning it blew a perfect fnt of wind, we lay in a very
unpleasant situation our small Bower Anchor came home again,
our best Bower we had let go before when we was near the Shore in
hopes it would have brought us up & have not since been able to

---

[1] The original text reads 'Peacock'. 'Peacock' is scratched out and 'Bullock'
written above it. The correction is in Hawkesworth's hand.
[2] A condor.

weigh it, so we got a hawser out to the Tamar who lay in the
p. 40 Stream & after weighing the small Bower hove out by her & let / it
go again. We are now ardently wishing for fair weather that we may
get our Ship properly moored.—Friday Novr 23^d. Sounded the
Harbour higher up & found the Ground softer than where we are
at present & the water not so deep; Intend therefore going up the
moment we can. It has blown a Storm of Wind almost *the whole
time we have been here. we have found a small Spring of Water* about
half a Mile in Land upon the N^o Side it is but very indifferent
having a brackish taste, & I believe will give but very little in a day
of that.[1] We intend to dig some depth & then sink a Cask there, in
order to make a kind of Well. I have been several Miles into the
Country, It is all barren Downs (the Soil Gravelly) as far as the
Eye can see. We have seen many large Deer at a distance, but they
will not let us come near enough to get a Shot at them. I found a
Nest of Ostriches Eggs which were very good. We found the print
of many Beasts feet near to a Salt Pond & amongst the rest one of a
very large Tyger. I imagine all these Animals must drink the Salt
water of these Ponds, for there is not a drop of fresh to be met with
p. 41 any / where, except we call that so I mentioned on the N^o Side, &
that we found by seeing only a little moisture upon the Earth, so
judged there might be a Spring thereabouts, & was obliged to dig
some time before we found any water. Saturday Novr 24th. This
day upon Slack water carried both Ships up higher & moored
them. The extreme Points of the Harbour's Mouth at low water
from EbS¼S to E^t.—The Steeple Rock on the S^o Side SE¼E. we
have but 6 fath^m where we are at low water, but never hardly did I
see such a Tide as runs here. It rises above four f^m & a half upon
Spring Tides. We had a Man fell over board who swam extremely
well, but before we could send the Boats after him, tho' they were
all along side, he was almost out of sight the tide run so strong,
however we luckily saved him. I this day walked above 6 Miles in
Land, we saw several Hares as large as some of our Deer, we shot
one & *if I had a good Greyhound I dare say the Ships Companies
might live upon Hare two days in the week.*[2] We are employed in

---

[1] Narborough (1711), 28, 'found 2 Springs of fresh Water, one in a Valley
close by the Water side, in a gully above the Ship, half a mile up the River; the
other . . .'.
[2] Narborough (1711), 30, had a greyhound.

clearing the Hold, have got our Cables all upon Deck in order take in a quantity of Ballast & to strike the most of our Guns into / the *p. 42* Hold.—Sunday Novr 25th. This day I went up in the Boat a good way up the Harbour, we found an old Oar of a very odd make, & the Barrel of a Musquet with the King's broad Arrow upon it, You might crumble it to pieces with your fingers. I imagine it must have been left here by the Wager's People, or possibly by Sir John Narborough.[1] No kind of Vegetables as yet found, but a kind of wild Pease. We have seen some Places where the Indians have made their Fires but does not appear to be lately. We shot some wild Ducks & a Hare, the latter ran near 2 Mile after being shot through the body with a Ball. At night it blew hard, our Decks being so lumber'd we could not hoist our Boats in, we moor'd them a stern. About Midnight our Six Oar'd Cutter, from the Boatkeeper's neglect filled & broke adrift, the fellow narrowly escaped drowning. This will be an imparable loss if we do not find her again, as it was the Tide of Flood when this happened she must have drove up the Harbour. I have sent this morning to look after her, but have heard nothing of her as yet.—Monday Novem^r 26th. We have had the good luck to find our Cutter again which was drove many Miles / up the Harbour. The Serjeant of Marines & some *p. 43* others went ashore the night before last to try to shoot some of the Deer of this Country, they killed three, two old ones & a Fawn. I was obliged to send a Number of Men 6 Miles off to bring them down, tho' they are but half the weight Sr John Narborough mentions, but some I have seen here I believe may be upwards of 300 wt.[2] I was yesterday along way up in the Country, we got very near to a very large Deer, he neigh'd just like a Horse & gave us a long run after him, for he would stop every now & then & look at us till we came pretty near him, & then set out again. My Dog would not run him being tired, or else he would not have escaped. We killed a Hare & a little ugly Animal that stunk so we could not any of us go near him. The flesh of the Hares here are as white as

---

[1] The *Wager*, one of Anson's squadron, was wrecked off the west coast of Patagonia. Part of the crew made their way through the Strait of Magellan in a small boat. For the full story of the rest of the crew, see Byron, *Narrative of the Hon. John Byron; being an account of the Shipwreck of the Wager . . .* (London, 1768).

[2] I could find no mention of weight in any edition of Narborough.

Veal & nothing can be better tasted than they are. Some of our People have been above 15 Miles in the Country, but saw no signs of a drop of fresh water any where, they saw the Deer drink at the Salt Ponds.[1]—The Weather is certainly cold here & not a day passes but it blows very hard. Tuesday / Novem^r 27th. A very hard gale at SW^t. our People found nothing but a few Bones of two of the Deer they had shot, for whilst they returned to the Ship in order to get assistance to bring them down the Tygers had eat them, & had even cracked the largest bones to pieces. I was yesterday at the Wells which we had dug as deep as possible, but they yield not above 30 Gallons in the 24 hours, So that I wish now to be gone from hence, for the little water we have now on board goes away very fast, many of our Casks we found quite leaked out. We have hauled our Six Oar'd Cutter on the Beach & our Carpenters are all employed in repairing her, as soon as that is done & our Ship is in a little Order again I intend leaving this for Pepy's Island, where I hope to find water; some of our people yesterday found the Skull & bones of a Man on the North Side which they brought off with them. No Signs of any Indians as yet tho' we are every day straggling many Miles in the Country;[2] Six or eight of our Men went away yesterday Evening to try for more Deer but they are not yet returned. Wednesday Novem^r 28th. Yesterday for the whole afternoon it blew as hard a Gale as I almost ever saw. We kept hands continually by the Sheet Anchor / fearing our Cables would part. At night it grew something more moderate. Some *of our People discovered two more Springs of tolerable water about 2 Miles directly in Land from where we lay on the S^o Side.*[3]—I had sent twenty hands a shore this morning to get water from them with Barricas,[4] & in making several turns we have already got about one Tun on board which is a great help to us.—I shall keep the People continually employed in fetching water whilst we remain here. The Men that went out for Deer, returned with only one young one alive, which is as beautiful a Creature as can be seen.—Thursday Novr 29th. Yesterday I went up the River in my boat about 12

p. 44

p. 45

---

[1] Narborough (1711), 40: water scarce in summer time.
[2] Narborough did not see them either.
[3] All Narborough springs were on the north side [Narborough (1711), 40.]
[4] 'Barecas' in Hawkesworth Text, I, 20 (see Introduction for a comparison of this text with the journal).

Miles, & it then beginning to be bad weather I landed; Still as far as I could see up it, It appeared very broad with a number of large Islands.—I make no doubt but it runs some hundred of Miles. I landed upon one of the Islands, where there was such an incredible number of Birds that they absolutely darkened the Sky as they rose, & we could not walk a step without treading on their Eggs, they kept hovering over our heads that the Men knock'd many of them down with Stones & sticks & carried off many hundreds of Eggs most of them with young ones in them which they / eat *p. 46* immediately after our landing upon the Main.[1]—I saw no signs of any Indians any where, but a vast number of Deer on each side the River, often 60 or 70 together which would stand looking at us from the Hills.—Our Doctor who was with me shot a Tyger Cat, a very fierce little Animal for tho' much wounded he held a tight battle with my Dog before he was killed outright. We have now got almost all the Ballast I intend taking in here. It has been a troublesome piece of work wth one small Boat only, when the tides are so strong & such constant gales of wind. Friday Nov[r] 30th. Got off near another Tun of water yesterday Evening. This morning the weather has been so bad we have not as yet been able to send a Boat a shore. Employed in setting up our Rigging. Two of the Men going to the Well on the S[o] side this morning, saw a large Tyger there & having no fire Arms with them they threw Stones at him, but he did not move till more of the Men came up when he walked leisurely away.[2] Saturday December 1st. Very cold, blowing, rainy weather. Have our Cutter off again well repaired & have got all the Ballast off & the Hold stow'd, but was not able to get any water off the weather was so bad. Sunday Decem[r] 2[d]. Struck our Tents at the / watering Place & are getting all ready for the Sea *p. 47* again. I have fixed a mark near the two Wells on the S[o] side that they may be easily found, tho' it is sufficient to say they bear of the

---

[1] Probably terns.
[2] Hawkesworth's flowery and melodramatic version: 'The two men who first came up to the well found there a large tyger lying upon the ground; having gazed at each other some time, the men who had no fire-arms, seeing the beast treat them with as much comtemptuous neglect as the lion did the knight of La Mancha, began to throw stones at him: of this insult however he did not deign to take the least notice, but continued stretched upon the ground in great tranquillity till the rest of the party came up, and then he leisurely rose and walked away' (Hawkesworth Text, I, 21–2).

Steeple Rock about SSE 2 Miles & a half—Monday Decem^r 3^d. We have Sounded every part of this Harbour as far as a Ship can go up with great care, & as I have mentioned before there is no danger but what may be seen at low water. If it were not for the rapid Tides it might be a very convenient place for Ships to touch at upon any particular occasion, especially since *we have found out fresh water tho' at some distance in Land*.[1] Here are great plenty of Deer & wild fowl in abundance, such as Ducks, Geese, Widgeon, Sea Pyes & many other kinds which we know no names for.[2] The Muscles here are very good & you may load your Boats with them every low water. Wood is scarce, however in case of necessity the large Bushes here would supply one well enough with fuel. Tuesday Decem^r 4th. Unmoored this Morning in order to go out, but the best Bower coming up foul, before we could heave short upon the small Bower, the Tide of Ebb was made strong, for at this

p. 48 Place slack water does not hardly ten / minutes, however I am in hopes we shall get out at low water if the wind stands.—This has been a remarkable fine warm day, so that we begin to flatter ourselves there may be a chance of having some little Summer weather in this part of the world.—*Wednesday Decr 5th*. Between 5 & 6 PM weighed with a fresh gale at NNW steered out ENE & afterwards shaped a Course for *Pepy's Island* supposing it to lay in about the Latt of 47° S^o. Course N° 66° E^t. Dist 69 M^s. Latt in 47°22' S^o. Long^{de} made 1°32'. M Dist 63 M^s E^t from Port Desire. Variation 19° E^t. Pepys's Island according to Halley's Chart E$\frac{3}{4}$N^o.[3] Dist 34 Leag^s. Port Desire S^o 66 W^t 23 Leagues. Thursday Decem^r 6th. A pleasant gale at W^t & very fine weather Course N° 79° E^t. Dist 93 M^s. Latt in 47°5' S^o. Long^{de} made 2°13' E^t. M Dist 154 M^s. Variation 18°34' E^t. Port Desire S^o 74° W^t. Dist 54 Leag^s. Pepy's Island E^t. Dist 24 Leag^s.—Friday Decr 7th. The first a fresh gale at WSW, the latter part calm. I found myself this day by our Observation much to the N^{o}ward of what I expected, supposing it must be owing to the Current setting that way. I have

[1] The *Tamar* had only 34 tuns of water on board (Mouat, 28).

[2] Mouat, 28, Dec. 5, mentioned killing an ostrich 'of Considerable Size & 10 or 12 Young Ones which Appeared to Us as large as Turkeys'.

[3] Edmund Halley, 'A new and correct chart, shewing the Variations of the Compass in the Western and Southern Oceans . . .', *The English Pilot: The Fourth Book* . . . (London, 1753).

now made 80 Leagues Easting,[1] which is the Distance from the Main that Pepys's Island is laid down in by Dr Halley, but the great misfortune is that we have no certain Accounts at all of this Island. Cowley was the only person that pretends to / have seen it,   *p. 49* & all he says of it (for I have now his Voyage before me) is that it lays in the Latt of 47° but mentions nothing of the Longitude he was in at the time, & at the same time he tells us it has a fine Harbour &c^a, he says it blew so hard he could not get into it but stood away to the S^{o}ward.[2] I am now Steering S^o for as this day was very fine I could see a long way to the N^{o}ward of what it is laid down in, & If I do not see it before night I take it for granted if there is such an Island it must still be some way to the E^{t}ward of us. Course N° 79 E^t. Dist 67 M^s. Latt in 46°33' S^o. Long^{de} made 5°21' E^t. M Dist 220 M^s E^t. Variation 18°30' E^t. Port Desire S^o 75°10' W^t. Dist 76 Leag^s. Saturday Decem^r 8th. Wind from NNE to NW. Yesterday PM I made the Tamar's Signal to spread, & as the afternoon was very fine we could see between us at least 20 Leag^s. We steer'd SE by the Compass, at night brought too, when I imagined I was about the Latt of 47°18'. This morning it blew hard at NWbN & as we have seen no Island yet imagine if there is any it must lay further to the E^{t}ward, so intend standing 20 or 30 Leag^s that way, & then to return into 47° again. Course S^o 26° E^t. Dist 45 M^s. Latt in 47°33' S^o. Long^{de} made / 5°50' E^t. M Dist   *p. 50* 240 M^s E^t. Variation 18°0' E^t. Port Desire S^o 86°0' W^t. Dist 81 Leag^s. Cape Blanco W$^t\frac{1}{2}$N° 80 Leag^s.—Sunday Decr 9th. Wind from NNW to WSW a hard gale & a great Sea. at about 6 PM brought too under the Main sail, at 8 AM the wind being at WSW made sail again under our Courses to the Northward. I judg'd myself to be about 16 Leag^s. to the E^{t}ward of the Tract I had run

---

[1] The 80 leagues are 'Common French Leagues' as shown on Halley's chart. According to the chart, one common French league equals 3.6 British nautical miles.

[2] Dec. 1683} Jan. 1684} Cowley came upon the island, 47° S: 'a very commodious place for Ships to water at and take in Wood, and it has a very good Harbour, where a thousand sail of Ships may safely ride: Here is a great plenty of Fowls, and we judge, abundance of Fish, by reason of the Grounds being nothing but Rocks and Sands . . . the Wind was so extraordinary high that we could not get into it to water, we stood to the Southward, shaping our Course S.S.W. till that we came into the lat. of 50 deg. South . . . we came into the lat. of 53 deg. where making the Land of Terra del Fuogo . . .' [Ambrose Cowley, 'Voyage', *A Collection of Original Voyages*, ed. William Hacke (London, 1699), 6].

before. Saw a vast quantity of Rock weed & many Birds. Course N° 54 E^t. Dist 46 M^s. Latt in 47°6' S^o. Long^{de} made 6°45' E^t. M Dist 278 M^s E^t. Variation 18°0' E^t. Port Desire S^o 80°53' W^t. Dist 94 Leag^s. Monday Decr 10th. Wind from SW to NW. The first part blowing hard with a very great Sea, I stood to the N^{o}ward under Courses & at night being in the Latt of about 46°50' I wore Ship & stood in to the Westward again. The Tamar & we have every day spread as far as we could well see one another & this day at Noon being certain there can be no Island as mentioned by Cowley & laid down by Halley, I resolved to stand in for the Main to look out for Wood & Water wch both Ships are in want of, & the Season advances fast, so that we have no more time to lose here. Course S^o 80 W^t. Dist 36 M^s. Latt in 47 12 S^o. Long^{de} made 5°53' E^t. M Dist 243 M^s E^t. Variation 18° E^t. Port Desire S^o 80°50' W^t. Dist 79 Leag^s.—Tuesday Decr 11th. Wind from NW to W^t. very fine weather; Many Birds about / the Ship & some large Whales which are in great Numbers upon this Coast. We haul in for the Land as the Wind permits. Course S^o. 61° W^t. Dist 92 M^s. Latt in 47°57' S^o. Long^{de} made 3°53' E^t. M Dist 163 M^s E^t. Variation 18°30' E^t. Port Desire W^t$\frac{1}{2}$N^o. Dist. 55 Leag^s.— Wednesday Decr 12th. Wind from NNW to WSW fine weather but very cold. Many Whales seen & variety of Birds. Course S^o 50° W^t. Dist 71 M^s. Latt in 48°42' S^o. Long^{de} made 2°30' E^t. M Dist 109 M^s E^t. Variation 18°30' E^t Port Desire N° 62°32' W^t. Dist 37 Leag^s.—Thursday Decr 13th. Wind between W & SW fine pleasant weather. Course S^o 9° W^t. Dist 64 M^s. Latt in 49°45' S^o. Long^{de} made 2°16' E^t. M Dist 100 M^s E^t. Variation 18°20' E^t. Port Desire N° 38° W^t. Dist 48 Leag^s. River St Julian N° 70°40' W^t. 65 Leag^s. —Friday Decem^r 14th. Wind for the first part at WbN, it afterwards shifted to NW & from that to SW & back again to W^t all the time blowing very hard with a very ugly breaking Sea. We kept a constant look out for Sebald De Werts Islands which by the different Charts we have on board we can not be far from.[1] Course S^o 52° W^t. Dist 79 M^s. Latt in 50°33' S^o. Long^{de} made 0°40' E^t.

p. 51

---

[1] Shown on John Senex's chart *South America corrected from the Observations communicated to the Royal Societys of London & Paris* [London, (?1710)]: 'Sebald de Weerts Is. so Named when he discover'd them in the Year 1599'. The position of the centre of the group of three islands: 50°30' S, 59° W. De Weerts Islands may have been the Jason Islands of West Falkland Island (see Goebel, 45 ff.).

M Dist 38 M^s E^t. Variation 19°0′ E^t. Port Desire N° 11°26′ W^t. Dist 55 Leag^s. St Julian N° 47°3′ W^t. 54 Leag^s.—Saturday Decem^r 15th.—About 6 PM came on as hard a Gale as ever I remember to have been in all my life it was at SW. I double / reefed the Mainsail $p.\ 52$ but it blew much too strong to set him afterwards. The Sea run full as high as ever I saw it in going round Cape Horn with Lord Anson.[1] I dreaded every Minute its filling us, as our Ship is much too deep waisted for such a Voyage, therefore should have put before it under bare poles had I had a sufficient quantity of fresh water on board, but as that was not the case I was afraid of being drove off the Land irrecoverably, so lay too under a ballanced Mizen. We ship'd several very heavy Seas & now found our Screen Bulkheads of infinite Service to us. The Gale continued til about 8 this morning. At 10 I made Sail again under Courses to the W^{t}ward as the Wind was at S^o, but am afraid I shall find it a difficult matter to get in with the Land as the winds generally hang here. Course N° 6° W^t. Dist 18 M^s. Latt in 50°15′ S^o. Long^{de} made 0°37′ E^t. M Dist 36 M^s E^t. Variation 19° E^t. Port Desire N° 14° W^t. Dist 50 Leag^s. St Julians N° 50°57′ W^t. 50 Leagues.— Sunday Decr 16th. Wind from S^o to NNW the latter part a hard gale & a great Sea with cold hazey weather.—*The only difference between Midsum^r here & the depth of Winter in England is that we have long days.* I have steered in WbS$\frac{1}{2}$S^o for the Land & am in hopes if it clears up I shall make it before night. Course N° 84 W^t. Dist 82 M^s. Latt in 50°6′ S^o. Long^{de} made 1°28′ W^t. M Dist 45 M^s. / Variation 19°30′ E^t. Port Desire N° 23°2′ E^t. Dist 49 Leag^s. $p.\ 53$ St Julian N° 24°26′ W^t. 32 Leag^s.—Monday Decem^r 17th. Yesterday afternoon the wind shifted from NWbN to SW & blew very strong with a great Sea. At night we Sounded & had 52 f^m so that we reckon ourselves not above 12 or 14 Leag^s from the Land. I stood all night to the S^{o}ward as near as the wind would permit. Course S^o 32 W^t. Dist 50 M^s. Latt in 50°48′ S^o. Long^{de} made 20°9′ W^t. M Dis 76 M^s W^t. Variation 19° E^t. River St Julian N° 5°0′ W^t. Dist 43 Leag^s. Cape Virgin Mary the N^o Entrance of the Streights of Magellan S^o 34°30′ W^t. Dist 30 Leagues.—Tuesday Decem^r 18th. The first part the wind variable the latter calm. This morning at 4 made the Land from the Masthead, but having had

[1] In the *Wager* in 1741 (see Introduction, p. xx).

little or no wind since, have not been able to get in with it. Course S° 59° W^t. Dist 40 M^s. Latt in 51°8' S°. Long^{de} made 3°3' W^t.— M Dist 110 M^s W^t. Variation 19°0' E^t. St Julians N° 5°57' E^t. Dist 50 Leag^s. Cape Virgin Mary S° 19°50' W^t. Dist 19 Leag^s.— Wednesday Decr 19th. The Wind being to the N°ward I stood this morning into a deep Bay,[1] at the bottom of which there appeared to be a Harbour but it was Barr'd, & the Sea broke from one side of it to the other. At low water I could perceive that it was almost all

p. 54 dry with several Rocks in it, & / the water was shoal at a good distance from it, for I was in 6 f^m before I stood out again. There seemed to be plenty of Fish about this place & many Porpoises after them white as snow with black Spots a very uncommon as well as beautiful Sight. The Land has the same appearance as that about Port Desire. All Downs without a Tree to be seen. I intend if possible keeping the Shore close aboard til I am the length of Cape Virgin Mary Course N° 83 W^t. Dist 35 M^s. Latt in 51°4' S°. Long^{de} made 3°59' W^t. M Dist 145 M^s W^t. Variation 20°15' E^t. Cape Virgin Mary S° 18° E^t. Dist 24 Leag^s.—Thursday Decr 20th. Yesterday Evening we had Thunder & Lightning & Rain with little wind & that all round the Compass. This morning at day break we were off Cape Fair Weather,[2] which bore about West 4 Leag^s Distance, when we had but 13 f^m water, so that it is necessary to give that Cape a good Berth. From thence I ran close in shore to Cape Virgin Mary but we found the Coast to to lay very different from what it is mentioned by Sir John Narborough for we steered SE & SEbS the Coast laying SSE. to the S°ward of the Cape there runs a long Spit of Sand for above a League.[3]—We saw a great

[1] Indicated on Senex's chart with hills and downs shown, about 22 leagues from Cape Virgin Mary, midway between River St Croix on the north and River Gallegas on the South.

[2] Not shown on either Senex's or Anson's chart. However, Narborough, 59, mentioned the cape by name and the chart in his voyage shows it as being at the mouth of the River Gallegas.

[3] Not in the 1711 edition nor in *Histoire des Navigations aux Terres Australes*, ed. President Charles de Brosses (Paris, 1756), II, 29; but, in 'Sir John Narborough to Magellanica, in 1670', *Terra Australis Cognita: or, Voyages to the Terra Australis, or Southern Hemisphere* . . . , ed. John Callander (Edinburgh, 1768), in the section of Narborough's voyage written by Lt Nathaniel Peckett we find: 'Here is very good sounding all the coast along, from this cape [Cape Blanco] to *Cape Virgin-Mary*, which lies in 52 degrees, 15 minutes south. Within five leagues off the main, you will have 25 and 30 fathoms water; it is black oozy sand' (II, 517).

number of Guanicos[1] feeding in the Valleys as we ran along Shore. Just as I got the length of the Cape the / wind shifted to SW & *p. 55* blows excessively hard with a very ugly breaking Sea, which obliges me to carry a prodigious Sail to prevent my being blown off again. Friday Dec[r] 21st. I yesterday Evening worked up close to the Spit of Sand abovementioned & came to an anchor in 15 f[m] water where we lay all night. The Tamar was so far to Leeward that she could not fetch into Anchoring Ground so kept under way all night. All the afternoon we saw a vast smoke about 4 or 5 Leag[s] up the Streights—upon the N[o] Shore. This morning at day break I got under Sail & seeing the same smoke kept up I stood in for it & anchored in 15 f[m] about 2 M[s] from the Shore. This is the same place where the Wager's Crew mention there having seen a number of Horsemen waving to them with white Handkerchiefs to come on shore, & that tho' they were very desirous of knowing what these People were, it blew so hard that they could not come near the Shore & was obliged to stand off to Sea; Bulkeley, Gunner of the Wager says in his Book we could not by any means come to the knowledge of these People; whether they are unfortunate Creatures that have been cast away, or whether they are Inhabitants about the River Gallegoes we can't tell.[2] Just as we came to an anchor I could see very plain / with my Glass a number of Horsemen *p. 56* opposite to the Ship riding backwards & forwards & waving to us to come on shore exactly in the manner Bulkeley mentions to have seen them, as I was very anxious to know what these People were I immediately ordered my 12 Oar'd Boat out, & went towards the Shore in her very well armed. I took M[r] Marshall the 2[d] Lieu[t] with me & M[r] Cumming the first followed in the 6 Oar'd Cutter. When we came near the shore we saw I believe near 500 People some on foot but most on Horseback.[3] The drew up upon a Stony Spit that

Byron was reading Narborough as early as 1741: 'Being at the honourable Mr. B——n's tent, I found him looking in Sir *John Narborough's* voyage to these seas; this book I desired the loan of, he told me it was captain C——p's' [(John Bulkeley and John Cummins), *A Voyage to the South-Seas, By His Majesty's Ship Wager* (London, 1743), 33–4].

[1] A South American mammal related to the llama but larger and more graceful.

[2] Bulkeley and Cummins, 112–13. 'Whether they are unfortunate Creatures that have been cast away, or whether they are Inhabitants about the River Gallegoes we can't tell' is a direct quotation from Bulkeley and Cummins.

[3] When the cutter approached the shore, 'evident signs of fear appeared among those in the boat, on seeing men of such enormous size, while some, perhaps to

ran some way into the Sea where it was very bad landing for the water was very Shoal & the Stones were very large. These People kept waving & hollowing to us to come on Shore as we understood them, I made Signs to them to retire at some little distance which they did, we could not perceive they were armed, but they made a prodigious noise. After some time we landed with a great deal of difficulty my Boats Crew being up to their middle in water. I drew up my people on the Beach with my Officers at their Head with Orders for none of them to move till I either called or beckoned to them. I then went up alone to these People but they retired as I

p. 57 advanced, I made / Signs for one of them to come near which it seems they understood. This person was a Chief amongst them & was one of the most extraordinary Men for size I had ever seen till then. We mutter'd something to one another by way of Salutation & I walked a little farther with him to the rest. I made signs for them to sit down which they complied with, but I never was more astonished than to see such a Set of People.[1] The Stoutest of our Grenadiers would appear nothing to these. They were painted in the most frightful manner imaginable, some of them had a large circle of white paint round one Eye, & about the other a circle of black or red; Others had their faces streaked all over with different colour'd paint. Nothing in Nature could appear more frightful than these People did both Men & Women. Many of the oldest People kept singing a most doleful tune & seem'd extremely earnest all the time. They were all cloathed in Skins of wild Beasts of different kinds which they wore as a Highlander wears his Plaid, many of these Skins were very curious & very large, as indeed they ought to be to cover these People who in size come the nearest to Giants I

p. 58 believe of any People / in the World, excepting the Skins which they wear loose about them with the hair inwards they were most of them Naked. Some few of them had a kind of boot with two

encourage the rest, observed, that those gigantic people were as much surprised at the sight of our muskets, as we were at seeing them, though it is highly probable they did not know their use, and had never heard the report of a gun'. 1767 Officer *Account*, 43. See Appendix II, 'The Patagonians', for material on the Patagonians; in particular, see Helen Wallis's essay, 'The Patagonian Giants', pp. 185–96. Also, see Introduction, pp. lxxvii–lxxx, for the manner in which John Hawkesworth distorted Byron's reports of his encounters with the Patagonians.

[1] 'Their middle stature seemed to be about eight feet; their extreme nine and upwards' (1767 Officer *Account*, 45–6).

VII. Sketch of 'A Sailor giving a Patagonian Woman some Biscuit for her Child'

From *A Voyage round the World in His Majesty's Ship the Dolphin* (1767)

sharp sticks fastened to their heels which served for Spurs. Their Horses were very poor & not large but were very nimble & appeared to be well broke; Both Men & Women came galloping over the Spit we landed upon which was covered with large loose round slippery Stones, their Bridles were a leather Thong with a bit of wood for the Bitt, & the Saddles was something like the Pads our Country People use in England without Stirrups. Both Men & Women had teeth as white as snow, very even & well set. It was some time before I could make them all sit down as there was such Numbers of them & constantly fresh ones coming galloping in, however when they understood me, there was not one of them offered to stir. I then took out a quantity of yellow & white Beads & distributed them amongst them, with which they seem'd mightily pleased. I then took out a whole piece of green Silk Ribbon & giving the end of it into the hands of one of them I made those that were next to him take hold of it & so on as far as it would reach. They / sat very quiet without offering to pull it from one *p. 59* another, tho' I saw it pleased them of all things. I took out a pair of Scissars & cut every one of them about a Yard as far as it would go, & then tied it about their heads which they every one kept on without offering to touch it as long as I was with them. One woman in particular was remarkably fine, she was of a most extraordinary Size,[1] her face was most hideously painted, her hair was parted & hung down before in two long Que's covered all over with a large blue Bead, on her Arms she had a kind of Bracelets either of brass or very pale Gold. I wanted much to know where they got those things but there was no making them understand me. One of the Men shewed me the bowl of a Tobacco pipe made of a kind of red earth but they had no Tobacco amongst them, however he made me understand he wanted some. Upon which I beckoned to our People who remained upon the Beach drawn up as I left them. I could observe the Indians had constantly their Eyes upon them, & when three or four of them offer'd to run up as they imagined I wanted them there was immediately a general clamour amongst them, All rising up & as I supposed a going to run to their Arms

---

[1] 1767 Officer *Account*, 49–53, quotes a ship's officer, unnamed of course, to the effect that the women ranged from 7′ 6″, the men around 9′; Byron, who was 6′ tall, on tip toes could just reach the top of the head of one of the Patagonians.

p. 60 which / they had without doubt left but at a little distance from them. As soon as I saw their uneasiness I ran to meet our People & hollowed to them that I would have but one come up with all the Tobacco he could collect from the rest, which as soon as the Indians saw they were all very quiet again & every man took his place, except a very old man who came up to me & sung a very long Song the meaning of which I understand nothing of. Mr Cumming came up with the Tobacco & was as much astonished at the size & figure of these People as I was, for tho' he is very tall himself he appeared comparatively speaking a mere shrimp to them.[1] Four or five of the Chief Men came up to me & by the Signs they made me, I understood they wanted me to get up upon one of their Horses & go up with them to their Habitations, but I made signs in returns to them that I must go on board, upon which they seem'd to express great concern, & all sat down again. When I left them not one offer'd to follow us, but as long as I could see them after, they all continued seated as I left them. They had some hundreds of Dogs with them with which I suppose they hunt their wild Beasts. An old man often laid his head down upon the Stones & then shut

p. 61 his Eyes, & afterwards pointed / to his mouth & then to the Hills, meaning I imagined that if I would stay to the morning they would procure me some Deer.—Saturday Decr 22^d. Soon after I came on board again yesterday I got under way & worked up the Streights with the Flood, the breadth here is 8 or 9 Leag^s.—At 8 PM the Tide of Ebb begining to make I anchored in 25 f^m Point Possesion NNE dist about 3 Miles & some remarkable Hummocks on the N^o Shore called by Bulkeley the Asses Ears (wch they resemble very much) W$\frac{1}{2}$N.[2] At 3 AM weighed with the wind at East & steered SWbW 12 Miles. We run over a Bank in the fair way which Sr John Narborough nor any body else that has passed these Streights have taken any notice of. We had but 6$\frac{1}{2}$ f^m upon it, but in two or three Casts deepn'd it again to 13 f^m then steerd SWbS 6 Miles to the entrance of the first Narrow & steered thro' SSW 5 or 6 Miles. The Tide here was extremely rapid so that we was through in an Instant almost. We saw a single Indian upon the S^o Shore who kept waving to us as long as he could see us. We saw likewise some

[1] Cumming was 6′ 2″ tall (1767 Officer *Account*, 53).
[2] Bulkeley and Cummins, 111.

Deer upon the Hills, tho in Wood's Voyage he says there is none upon that side.[1] As soon as we were out of the first Narrow we enter'd into a little Sea for we could not see / the Entrance of the Second Narrow til we had run upwards of two Leagues, It is 8 Leag^s over to the Second Narrow, the Course SWbW. The Land on the N^o side is very high, through this last Narrow we steer'd SW$\frac{1}{2}$W about 5 Leag^s the Soundings between 20 & 25 f^m.—At Noon we passed the West End of this Second Narrow & steer'd S^o 3 Leag^s for Elizabeth Island & then the wind heading us we anchored in 7 f^m the said Island bearing SSE about 1 Mile, & Bartholomew's Island bore ESE. In the Evening Six Indians came down to the water side & hollowed & kept waving to us for a long time but as my People wanted rest I did not chuse to hoist a Boat out, so they walked off. In steering from Point Possesion to the first Narrow the Flood set to the S^{o}ward, but in coming in to the first Narrow the Flood set strong over to the North Shore. When on the Shoal between Point Possesion & the first Narrow in 6$\frac{1}{2}$ f^m the Asses Ears bore NWbW$\frac{1}{2}$W 3 Leag^s, & the N^o point of the first Narrow WbS 5 or 6 Miles. It flows here full & change 10 o'Clock. Between the first & second Narrow the Flood sets to the SW, & Ebb NE, when you pass the West End of the Second Narrow the Course with a leading Wind is SbE 3 Leag^s.—Between St Bartholomew's & Elizabeth Islands the Channel is about $\frac{1}{2}$ a Mile over & deep water.—The Flood / set through to the S^{o}ward very strong, & makes a great Ripling, but the Tides round the Islands set many different ways.—Decr 23^d. Wind SbW In the morning weighed & worked between Elizabeth & Bartholomew's Islands, before the Tide was done we got over upon the N^o Shore & anchored in 10 f^m.—The Course from the Islands SSW 4 Leag^s, St George's Island then bore NEbN 3 Leag^s.—A Point of Land which had no name before we called Porpus Point NbW about 5 Miles, and the S^o most Land SbE. about 2 Miles from the Shore, In the Evening weigh'd & steered SbE 5 Miles along the N^o Shore at about 1 Mile distance, & found very regular Soundings between 7 & 13 f^m all along good anchoring Ground. At 10 Anchored in

---

[1] Actually, Wood said that there were no sheep and ostriches on the south shore ['Capt. Wood's Voyage thro' the Streights of Magellan', in William Hacke (ed.), *A Collection of Original Voyages* (London, 1699), 82].

13 f^m Sandy Point bearing SbE 4 Miles, Porpus Point NNW 3 Leag^s & St Georges Island NE 4 Leag^s.—All along this shore the Flood sets to the S^{o}ward, & flows full & change 11 o'Clock. The Tides rise about 15 feet.—Decr 24th. This morning I went in my boat to Sandy Point & then Landed; here is plenty of Wood & very good water, as I came with an intention of finding Fresh Water Bay I order'd my Boat to row along shore, & the Second Lieu^t & I walked it. The Shore here is extremely pleasant, for 4 or 5 Miles,

p. 64 over Sandy Point is a fine level Country, the Soil / mostly good & sweeter than any Garden, being covered with flowers & Berries. The Grass is very good inter mixed with Pea blossoms. Hundreds of painted Geese were feeding here. We gave them that name from their beautiful feathers. We walked above 12 Miles & found plenty of exceeding good fresh water, but not the Bay we looked after, for all along this Shore from Sandy Point no Boat can land but with great hazard as it is shoal & the Sea breaks high. We found a Number of Whigwhams which had been left by the Indians not above a day or two, for in some of them the Fire was hardly out. These Hutts were generally in snug Places in the Woods & always close to fresh water. Here is great plenty of wild Cellery & many Herbs that must be excellent for Seamen after a long Voyage. In the Evening I walked back again & found our Ships anchored in Sandy Point Bay about ½ a Mile from the Shore. Our People were hauling the Seine & had got about sixty large Mullets; Others were shooting, for here are abundance of Ducks, Geese, Teal, Snipes &c^a.—I thank God our Ship's Company are all extremely healthy; this cold Air has given them such voracious Appetites that they could eat three times their Allowance.—Decem^r 25th. Observed by /

p. 65 two Altitudes & find Sandy Point to be in the Latt of 53°10′ S^o.— At 8 AM weighed & steered SbE½E 5 Leag^s from Sandy Point, & anchored in 32 f^m the South Point of Fresh Water Bay bearing NNW about 4 Miles, the S^{o}most Land SEbS. our Distance from the Shore about 1 Mile. In sailing along the shore at 2 Miles distance had no Ground with 60 f^m of Line & about 1 Mile off had from 20 to 32 f^m.—It flows full & change off Fresh water Bay 12 oClock, the Tides run but little tho' it flows very much by the Shore.—The Course from St George's Island to Sandy Point is SSW by the Compass Dist 6 Leag^s.—From Sandy Point to Fresh

Water Bay SbE 5 Leag^s.—Decem^r 26th. At 8 AM weighed, Wind
ENE & steered SSE for Port Famine. At Noon St Ann's Point
bore SbE½E 3 Leag^s. Along this Shore at 2 or 3 Miles distance you
have very deep water, but being within 1 Mile, will have 25 & 30
f^m. About 4 or 5 Miles to the N^oward of St Ann's Point, wch is the
N^omost Point of Port Famine runs off a Reef of Rocks about 2
Miles from the Shore & lie SEbE; In coming near it you will shoal
the water from 65 to 35 & 20 f^m at two Cables length from it. The
Course from Sandy Point to St Ann's Point is SSE 12 Leag^s; about
Midway is Fresh Water Bay. St Ann's Point is very steep & no
Soundings til you come very near it, & if bound into Port Famine
must be very careful in standing in, especially if you should be so
far to the S^oward as Sedgers River, / then you will shoal the water *p. 66*
all at once from 30 to 20. 15. 12 f^m & about two Cables length
further in, is no more than nine feet at low water, which is more
than a Mile from the Shore. If you haul close round St Ann's Point
you will soon get Soundings & shoal them very fast, so that it is not
safe coming nearer in than 7 or 8 f^m very good Anchoring Ground,
the Inner part of the Bay is very shoal. Here the Streights is not
above four Leag^s over.—Decem^r 27th. In the morning had little
wind variable & sometimes calm. At Noon anchored with the best
Bower in 8 f^m at Port Famine, St Ann's Point bearing ENE½E
Dist about ½ a Mile. The River Sedger S^o near 2 Miles & the S^omost
Land which is Cape Forward SbE½E 4 Leag^s.—This is a very
convenient Port, a SE wind is the only one you are exposed to, &
that I believe seldom blows, but suppose a Ship even to be drove
ashore in the bottom of the Bay she could receive no damage, for it
is all fine soft ground. We lay close to the Shore & here is drift
wood enough for a thousand Sail without being at the trouble of
cutting Green if you do not chuse it. Where we are at present there
is not Tide sufficient to thwart a Ship. The water is extremely good
in Sedger's River but your Boats can't get in till about two hours
flood for at low water it is very shoal for ¾ of / a Mile. I went up it *p. 67*
in my Boat above 4 Miles which was as high as I could get for the
fallen Trees, & it is very difficult as well as dangerous for a Boat to
go up as high as that as I experienced; for as the Stream is vastly
rapid & there are many Stumps of Trees hid under Water, a very
large one run through my Boats bottom & in an Instant she was full

of water & we got a shore as well as we could. With great difficulty we hauled her up afterwards upon the side of the River, & contrived to stop the hole in her bottom by which we made a shift to bring her down to the River's Mouth where we hauled her up & had her repaired. Here grows most noble Trees on each Side this River & I make no doubt but some of them would make very good Masts for Ships. Trees are to be found here of an immense length that are above eight feet through. The Pepper Tree or Winter's Bark is very plenty.[1] We get Fish enough every day for both Ships Companies, & those that will take a little pains for it may kill as many Geese & Ducks as they please.[2] I have shot every day enough for my own Table & to spare to several others. In the Woods tho' the Climate is so cold there are abundance of Parrots & many other very

p. 68 beautiful Birds. I / have seen the prints of many wild Beasts feet on the Sand, but have met with none tho I have walked more than any Man here. The Country here abouts is as fine I think as most I have seen, & the Soil is good, & none can be better warter'd, there are no less than three pretty large Rivers between this Port & Cape Forward, wch is something more than 4 Leag^s from it besides several Brooks. We have seen no Indians since we have been here tho' their Whigwhams are to be met every where. I was the other day upon Cape Forward & should have gone farther if the weather had not proved so bad that it made us glad to stop there & make a great fire to dry ourselves. The Indians had been there very lately, the wood was still warm they had left where they had their fires. Upon the Terra del Fuego side they answered our fire by making another directly opposite to it. I walked across the Cape to

---

[1] 'Among the trees are many whose trunks are forty inches in diameter, with large green leaves resembling those of our bay-trees. The rind is grey on the outside and pretty thick. This is the true Winter's bark, a name which it obtained from its being brought in the year 1767, from the streights of Magellan, by Mr. William Winter. This bark, on being taken off the tree and dried, turns to the colour of chocolate. It has an acrid, burning, pungent taste, and is esteemed an excellent remedy against the scurvy. The bark itself is extremely fragrant, and the tree, when standing, has a strong aromatic smell. We frequently made use of the bark on board our ship in pies, instead of spice, and being steeped in water it gives a very agreeable flavour. These trees are likewise found in the woods, in many other places in the streights, and also on the east and west coasts of Patagonia' (1767 Officer *Account*, 64–5).

[2] On Dec. 28, 280 fish were brought aboard the *Tamar*; on the 29th and 30th, 14 cords of wood. Throughout the stay, she stowed away a good supply of wood and water (Mouat, 32 ff.).

see how the Streights run from thence & imagine it is about WNW.
The Hills as far as I could see were immensely high & ragged &
cover'd with Snow to the very bottom of them. I was yesterday
some Miles along shore to the N^{o}ward & found the Country vastly
pleasant as well as beautiful, for some parts of are cover'd with /
Flowers of different kinds which smell as sweet as the finest we   *p. 69*
have in England. In short if it was not for the Cold in Winter I
believe this Country might be made as fine a one as any whatever.
Three of our People that have a little Tent ashore at the bottom of
this Bay where they are washing close to a little Rivulet, & just at
the skirts of the wood, were terribly alarmed last night by the
roaring of some large wild Beasts who approached very near their
Tent & did not leave them till near day break. All they had for it
was making a large fire, which kept them off. One of my Men told
me that in passing over a Hill (which has been cleared of Wood, &
where we suppose the spot to have been where the Spaniards
formerly settled) that in a particular part of it the Ground sounded
very hollow, which made him go over it several times, & that he
imagined something lay buried there, upon which I carried several
with Spades &c^a and dug down pretty deep but could find nothing.
In travelling thro' the Woods we found two large Skulls of wild
Beasts but we could not make out what kind of Beasts they were./
Friday Janry 4th 1765.—Having completed our Wood & Water in   *p. 70*
both Ships, at 4 this morning weighed from Port Famine with little
wind between the N^o & NW & worked to Windward. At Noon S^t
Ann's Point bore S$\frac{1}{2}$W 3 Leag^s & Fresh Water Bay NWbW 4
Leag^s; At 6 in the Afternoon Sandy Point NNW$\frac{1}{2}$W 5 or 6 Leag^s.
—In the night worked to Windward with a fresh Breeze of Wind at
NNE. Janry 5th. Little wind N^{o}therly. At 6 in the Morning Sandy
Point bore SSW 3 Miles, then had 65 f^m water. At Noon S^t
George's Island bore N° 4 or 5 Leag^s. Sandy Point SW$\frac{1}{2}$W 7 Miles,
and Porpus Point W$\frac{1}{2}$N. At 1 in the afternoon the wind shifted to
WSW & blew a fresh gale, Steered NWbN 4 Leag^s then S^t
George's Island bore NNE between 2 & 3 Leag^s. Porpus Point
WNW 2 Leag^s & the East end of Elizabeth Island NbW 3 Leag^s.
Then steer'd N° 3 Leag^s between Elizabeth & St Bartholomew's
Islands, & from the Islands NbE 3 Leag^s to the Second Narrow &
steered thro' NE$\frac{1}{2}$E & continued that Course from the Second

Narrow 8 Leag^s to the first Narrow, the Wind still continuing to blow fresh steered thro' the first narrow against the Flood NNE. At 10 in the Evening it proving very little wind the Flood set us back again into the Entrance of the first Narrow, where we were obliged to anchor with a Bower in 40 f^m not above two Cables *p. 71* length from the / Shore. Here it flows full & change 2 o'Clock & the Tide runs full 6 Knots.

Sunday *Janry 6th*. At 1 in the Morning weighed, little wind N^{o}ly, at 3 passed the first Narrow. I then, having been upon Deck all the day before & all that night went to lay down for an hour or two but *was presently awoke by the Ships thumping upon a Bank*.[1] I ran upon Deck & found her grounded upon *a hard Sand*, luckily for us it was stark calm, I immediately order'd all the Boats out to carry out an Anchor a stern of us where was the deepest water, but before we could begin to heave she went off of herself, for it was just upon low water that she grounded & there was 15 feet forward & six f^m a very little way a stern. The Master told me he had 13 f^m the Cast of the lead before she was a Ground, & the next but 15 feet. This is *a very dangerous Shoal & not mentioned by any person that has ever passed the Streights, tho' it lays directly in the fair way between Cape Virgin Mary and the first Narrow*, it is in the Midway between the S^o & N^o Shores & is of a great length & breadth being more than 2 Leag^s in length & full as much in breadth & in many places steep to, when on it Point Possession bore NE 3 Leag^s. The Entrance of the Narrow SW 2 Leagues. I saw part of it afterwards dry in several *p. 72* places / & in other parts where it was very shoal the Sea broke high upon it. A Ship would have very little chance that should come upon this Shoal when it blows any thing. At 6 AM after getting off of it, anchored in 15 f^m the Shoal bearing NNW$\frac{1}{2}$W half a Mile. At Noon weighed with little wind at NE & worked with the Ebb tide till 2 PM but finding Shoal Water anchored again in 6 f^m & a half on the S^o side of the Shoal. The Asses Ears bearing NWbW 4 Leag^s & the S^o Point of the Entrance of the first Narrow WSW about 3 Leag^s & half a Mile from the S^o side of the Shoal. At this

---

[1] 'The Dolphin being to the Southward of Us about 2 Miles & the Tide of Ebb Running Prodigious Strong the Ship not having Steerage She fell on Shore on a Sand Bank Came too with the Small Bower Veerd to $\frac{1}{2}$ a Cable At $\frac{1}{2}$ past 4 the Comm^{re} got off but driving She fell on another Sandy Shoal D^o weigh'd & Came to sail' (Mouat, 33).

IX. A Mercator Chart of part of the Falkland Is

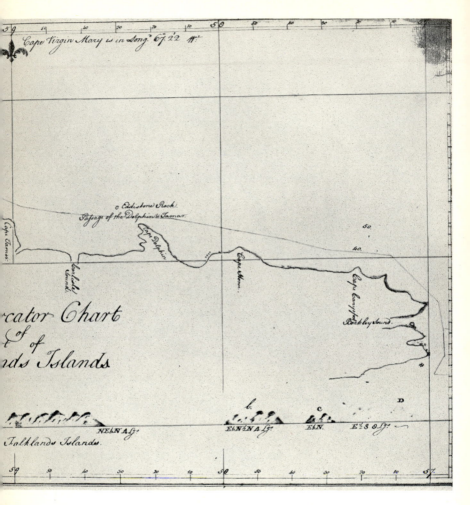

lands showing the track of the *Dolphin* and the *Tamar*

time the Opening of the Narrow was shut in. Sent the Boats a Sounding between the Shoal & the S⁰ Shore, who found a Channel between them. The Tamar had like to have been a shore in attempting to come nearer to us having got into 3 f^m water. She is now at an Anchor in the N⁰ Channel.

January 7th. At 8 AM weighed, little Wind WSW, Steered SEbE ½ a Mile & deepened the water to 13 f^m then steered between the East & ENE along the S⁰ side of the Shoal & 6 or 7 Miles from the S⁰ Shore keeping two Boats at some distance upon each Bow; the Soundings very irregular from 9 to 15 f^m but in hauling nearer the Shoal soon had but 7 f^m.—Between the Shoal & the S⁰ Shore the Boats had Soundings on a Bank of 6 f^m & a half at low water & 13 f^m within it. At noon we were to the E^{t}ward of the Shoal & hauled over to the N⁰ Shore & soon deepen'd the / Water to 20 f^m then *p. 73* Point Possesion bore NNW 4 or 5 Leag^s, and the Asses Ears WNW 6 Leag^s, Cape Virgin Mary NE½E 7 Leag^s. We then steered NEBE for the South End of the Spit, had no Soundings with 25 f^m of Line. At 4 PM Cape Virgin Mary NE & the S⁰ end of the Spit NEbE Dist 3 Leag^s.—At 8 PM Cape Virgin Mary bore NBW Dist 2 Leag^s. Soundings 11 & 12 f^m.—Brought too for the Tamar who came thro' the N⁰ Channel & was some Leagues a Stern of us. *Tuesday Janry 8th.*—This Morning the Officer of the Watch informed me the head of the Main Mast was sprung. I went up immediately to look at it & found it a long Rent almost strait up & down, but could not see how far it might go for the Checks on the Mast. We have clapt on a strong Fish[1] & woolded him well so that I hope the Mast is as strong as he was before. We imagine this to have happened in that very hard gale of wind we had some time since. Course N⁰ 62 E^t. Dist 63 Miles. Latt in 50°50′ S⁰. Long^{de} made 1°30′ E^t. M Dist 55 M^s E^t. Variation 20 E^t. Cape Virgin Mary S⁰ 62° W^t. Dist 21 Leag^s. Wednesday Janry 9th. Wind from SW to NEbN. Course S⁰ 67 E^t. Dist 47 M^s. Latt in 52°8′ S⁰. Long^{de} made 2°40′ E^t. M Dist 98 M^s E^t. Variation 20° E^t. Cape Virgin Mary S⁰ 83 W^t. Dist 33 Leag^s. /

[1] 'FISH, is a long piece of oak, convex on one side, and concave on the other. It is used to fasten upon the outside of the lower masts, as an additional security, to strengthen them when it becomes necessary to carry an extraordinary pressure or sail. The fishes are also employed for the same purpose on any yard, which happens to be sprung or fractured' (Hawkesworth Text, 'An Explanation of the Nautical Terms,' I, xxvi).

p. 74 Thursday Janry 10th. For these last 24 hours very little wind between the N^o & E^t wth thick foggy rainy weather. Course N° 18 W^t. Dist 39 M^s. Latt in 51°31' S^o. Long^{de} made 2°21' E^t. Variation 20° E^t. Cape Virgin Mary S^o 60°0' W^t. Dist 33 Leag^s.

Friday Janry 11th. Wind SW blows strong & a great Sea. Course N° 87 E^t. Dist 99 M^s. Latt in 51°24' S^o. Long^{de} made 5° E^t. M Dist 185 M^s E^t from Cape Virgin Mary. Variation 19° E^t. Cape Virgin Mary S^o 73°8' W^t. Dist 65 Leag^s.—Cape Fair Weather W^t 2°0' S^o 70 Leag^s.

Saturday Janry 12th Wind for the first part at SW & S^o blowing hard with a very great Sea. Made an East Course til 8 yesterday Evening, when the Tamar being some Leagues a stern I wore Ship & made an easy Sail off. Just before we shortened Sail I thought I saw the Land a head of us. This Morning at day break stood in again, the wind had shifted in the night to NW^t at 4 saw the Land a head making like three Islands, we imagined they were *the Sebald de Werts*,[1] but intending to stand between them we found they were joined by very low Land which formed a deep Bay; we tacked & stood out again. At the same time we saw Land a great way to the S^oward. We had no longer any doubt but this was the Land mentioned in the Charts by the name of the New Islands. In

p. 75 hawling out again we saw a long / low Shoal of Rocks stretching out for above a League to N^oward of us, and another of the same kind laying between that & what we took for the Northermost of the Sebald de Werts when we first saw it; This Land is high, ragged barren Rocks something like Staten Land. *I would advise all Ships hereafter to avoid if possible falling in with this part of the Land, for we were quite embay'd* this morning, & if it had come on to blow hard at SW so great a Sea must tumble in here, that it would be almost impossible to claw off the Shore. The Seals & Birds here are innumerable & many large Whales spouting about us. Course S^o 88° E^t. Dist 78 M^s. Latt in 51°27' S^o. Long^{de} made 7°4' E^t. M Dist 262 M^s E^t. Variation 23°30' E^t. Cape Virgin Mary S^o 78°32' W^t. Dist 89 Leag^s. Cape Fair Weather W^t. Dist 95 Leag^s. Sunday Janry 13th. For the first part the Wind at N^o & NE at 2 AM shifted

---

[1] See p. 42, n. 1. Mouat called the land sighted the 'North Part of the Faulklands Island' north-east 4 leagues (33A). 1767 Officer *Account*, 69, has landfall occur on the 13th.

to WSW & at 8 to SE. Last Night bro^t too, & at daybreak stood in for the N^o part of the Island which was the Land we were off last night:[1] when we had got about 4 Miles to the E^{t}ward if [it] fell calm & rained very hard, & at once there rose such a Swell I hardly ever remember to have seen, it came from the W^{t}ward & ran so quick & high that it appeared as if it would break every minute. It set us fast towards the Shore which is as dangerous a one as any in the World. / I could plainly see the Sea break at some distance from *p. 76* it mountains high. It pleased God a fresh Gale sprung up at SE when we stood off from it. *Whoever comes this way hereafter should take particular care to give the N^o part of these Islands a very good Berth.* After I had got some distance from the Land I brought too, the weather being extremely thick & raining very hard. Course N° 27° E^t. Dist 30 M^s. Latt in 51°0′ S^o. Long^{de} made 7°25′ E^t. M Dist 275 M^s E^t from Cape Virgin Mary. Variation 23°30′ E^t. Cape Virgin Mary S^o 73°50′ W^t. Dist 96 Leag^s. Monday Jan^{ry} 14th. The weather clearing up & the Wind shifting to SSW steered along Shore SEbE 4 Leag^s, & saw a low flat Island full of high tufts of Grass bearing S^o between 2 & 3 Leag^s & the N^{o}most Land W^t 6 Leag^s, then had 38 f^m the Ground Comb Rocks. Continued the Course along shore 6 Leag^s & saw a low Rocky Island bearing SEbE about 5 Miles. Brought too & Sounded 40 f^m white Sand. This Island is about 3 Leag^s from the other Land which forms here a very deep Bay. It bears EbN from the Island I mentioned before with the high tufts of Grass like Bushes, & the Sea breaks a good distance off. In the night stood off and on. / Tuesday Jan^{ry} 15th. At 3 in the Morning made Sail & steered in for *p. 77* the Land to look for a Harbour. At 6 the East End of the Rocky Island bore WSW 2 or 3 Miles, Soundings 16 f^m Rocky ground, & when within it had 20 f^m fine white Sand. The Coast from this Rocky Island lays EbS dist 7 or 8 Leag^s to two low Islands which is the Eastermost Land in sight. At 8 saw an opening which has the appearance of a Harbour bearing ESE between 2 or 3 Leag^s. Bro^t too & sent a Boat from each Ship to examine it, but a little after it begining to blow hard with thick dirty rainy Weather we were obliged to stand out to Sea with the two Ships & had much to do

---

[1] Byron and Mouat had held a consultation about what to do (Mouat, 33A). Their frequent conversations are not recorded in Byron's journal.

to clear the two low Rocky Islands to the E^tward of us. Here run a very great Sea & I began to be very uneasy least we might be blown off & so leave our people behind. About 3 in the Afternoon the Weather clearing again I tacked & stood in again & presently after saw a Boat a long way to leeward of us. I bore down to her & found it to be the Tamar's boat with *Mr Hindman in her the 2^d Lieu^t. He had ventured off in all that Sea & bad weather to inform me he had found a very fine Harbour;*[1] We immediately stood in for it & found /

p. 78 it answer far beyond my expectation. The Entrance is about a Mile over & no danger going in, the depth of water from 10 to 7 f^m. Close to the shore. It forms two little Bays on the Starboard side where Ships might anchor with safety, both of them has a fine Rivulet of fresh water, but if you chuse to go into *Port Egmont* (which I so named after the Earl of Egmont) I think it without exception *one of the finest Harbours I ever saw in my Life.* The mouth of this Port is EE Dist 7 Leag^s from the low Rocky Island which is a good mark to know it by. When you are within the Island you will find 17 & 18 f^m within two Miles of the Shore, & about 3 Leag^s to the W^tward of the Harbour will see a remarkable white Sandy Beach, off which a Ship might anchor til an opportunity to run in. In standing in for this Sandy Beach you will see two low Rocky Islands to the E^tward which I mentioned before we had some difficulty to clear when the weather obliged us to stand off. Port Egmont is about 16 Leag^s from the N^o End of the Islands. In the S^o most part of the Harbour is several Islands but no passage out for a Ship. I have been thro' my boat above 7 Leag^s from where our Ships lay which bro^t us into a large Sound too much exposed to a W^terly Wind to be a safe place for Ships, &

p. 79 the Master of the / Tamar who had been round in their Boat to the Entrance of it reports, it as rather a dangerous Place for Ships to go into, many Shoals laying off it. Fresh water is to be found every where in the greatest plenty. Geese, Ducks, Snipes &c^a are in such numbers that our People are grown tired of them. It is a common thing for a Boat to bring off 60 or 70 fine Geese without expending one single charge of Powder or Shot, for the Men knock down as

[1] Mouat, 33A, merely recorded: 'At ½ past 5 the Cutter return'd with the Lieut & found a good Harbour for Ships to lie in 10 fathoms Water he went on Board the Commodore to carry him in.'

many as they please with Stones.[1] *The only thing this Place wants is Wood, however there is almost every where a little Drift Wood along Shore, which we suppose to be drove from the Streights of Magellan.* Here are many excellent refreshments for Seamen; Wild Cellery & Wood Sorrel is to be met with every where, nor is there any want of Mussels, Clams, Cockels & Lympets. The Seals & Penguins are innumerable & at first would not get out of our way without we obliged them to it. The Sea Lion here is rather a dangerous Animal, I was attacked by one when I least expected it, & had much a do to get clear of him; They are of a monstrous size & when Anger'd make a dreadful roaring. We have had many Battles with them, & it has sometimes given a dozen of us above an hours work before we could dispatch one of them. / A fine large Mastiff I have, *p. 80* was almost tore to pieces by the bite of one of them. The Master of the Dolphin in Sounding near the S⁰ Shore had (as he told me) four Wolfs come running up to their Bellies in Water to attack the Boat, they happened to have no Musket with them so was obliged to keep off. The next morning I went upon that Shore & whilst the Boat's Crew was engaged with one of the largest Sea Lions I have seen here, one of these Animals came running down directly amongst us & tho' he was fired at before he could reach us, it did not hinder his coming amongst the thickest of us; he was presently shot tho' I dare say we might easily have taken him alive for it seemed to be curiosity more than any thing else that brought him so near to us. We killed four more that day, for if they saw us at ever so great a distance they would come running to us immediately. Some of our People will still have them to be Wolves, but I think they resemble our Foxes in every thing but their size & Tail, their heads are almost twice as large as an English Fox & they have prodigious long sharp teeth. They are here in great numbers we have seen & killed several since. Our People saw three of them set / upon a large Seal & near their holes I have seen a number of *p. 81* Penguin Skins & peices of Seal. How they came here first will be difficult to account for, as these Islands are 100 Leag⁸ from the Main; At present they will be routed from this part of the Country, as it has been in a blaze as far as one can see for these three days past, Our People having set fire to the grass. I have dug in several

[1] Jan. 17, 80 fine geese brought aboard the *Tamar* (Mouat, 34).

places, the Soil is for about a foot or two down a black mould & then a light Clay. We moored here in 10 f^m water fine holding Ground; The N^{o}most Point on the West shore 2$\frac{1}{2}$ Miles, the Watering Place on d^o WNW$\frac{1}{2}$W $\frac{1}{2}$ Mile. The Islands on the East Side EbS 4 Miles. All the Navy of England might ride here together very safely. We got our Forge a shore with which our Armourer has completed a good deal of Iron Work that was much wanted. Every morning our People has had an excellent breakfast here made with Portable Soup & Wild Cellery thickend with Oatmeal. The Surgeon of the Tamar mad a pritty little Garden near the Watering Place which we surrounded with a Fence of Turf, for the benefit of those that may come next. I took Possession of this Harbour & all these Islands for His Majesty King George

p. 82 the Third / of Great Britain & His Heirs, tho' they had been before taken Possession of by Sr Richd Hawkins in the Year 1593.[1] Sunday Janry 27th. The wind being at SSW at 8 AM sailed from Port Egmont, I was hardly out before it began to blow extremely hard & came on very thick, so that we could not see the Rocky Islands, I wished myself back again, but it fortunately cleared up, tho' it continued to blow very hard the whole day. At 9 the Entrance of the Harbour bore ESE 2 Leagues; the two low Islands to the N^{o}ward EbN 3 or 4 Miles & the Rocky Island W$\frac{1}{2}$N 4 Leag^s. At 10 the two low Islands bore SSE 4 or 5 Miles. Then steered along shore East by the Compass & had run about 5 Leag^s when we saw a remarkable Headland (with a Rock a little distance off it) which I called Cape Tamer bearing ESE$\frac{1}{2}$E 3 Leagues. Continued the same Course 5 Leag^s farther & saw a high Rock 5 Miles from the Main bearing NE 4 or 5 Leag^s.—This Rock I called the Edystone; then steered ENE 5 Leag^s between the Edystone & a remarkable Head land which I named Cape Dolphin, From Cape Tamer to Cape Dolphin the Land forms a deep Sound which I called Carlisle Sound, in the bottom of which we saw an Opening

p. 83 which / has the appearance of a Harbour. The distance between the Capes is 7 or 8 Leagues. From Cape Dolphin steered along shore

---

[1] '. . . the Commo^{re} hoisted his Colours & went on Shore & took Possession of Faulklands Island in the Name of His Majesty George the third on which I & his Officers Was present with him he was Saluted Wth three Pieces of Ordnance from his Own Ship On which every Man was Serv'd half Allow^{ce} of brandy to drink his Majesty's health' (Mouat, 34).

E$\frac{1}{2}$N 16 Leagues to a low flat Cape or Headland & brought too. The Land for the most part in this days run resembles very much the East Side of Patagonia, not a Tree nor a Bush to be seen but all Downs, & here & there those high Tufts of Grass like those at Port Egmont. I frequently sailed within 2 Miles of the Shore that I might discern if there was any Wood. Our Soundings in the Night was 40 f^m rocky ground.

Monday Janry 28th At 4 AM made sail; the low flat Cape bore SEbE 5 Leagues. At $\frac{1}{2}$ past 5 the Cape bore SSW dist two Leagues. From the Cape steered ESE 5 Leagues to three low Rocky Islands which lie about 2 Miles from the Main, then steered SSE 4 Leag^s to two other low Islands which lie about a Mile off. Between these Islands the Land forms a very deep Sound which I named Berkeley's Sound; In the South part of it is an Opening which has the appearance of a Harbour. We had now a prodigious great Swell from the S^{o}ward. About 3 or 4 Miles to the S^{o}ward of the S^o point of Berkeley's Sound lie some Rocks above / water upon *p. 84* which the Sea breaks vastly high & they are 3 or 4 Miles from the Land. When abreast of these Breakers I steered SWbS about 2 Leag^s, then the S^{o}most Land in sight which I take to be the S^{o}most part of Falkland's Islands bore WSW 5 Leag^s. The Coast now began to grow very dangerous being nothing but Rocks & Breakers at a great distance from the Shore. The Hills as far as we could see, were all high scraggy, ragg'd, barren Rocks; In short it has the appearance of that Part of Terra del Fuego near Cape Horn. As the Sea rose every moment I was afraid of being caught here upon a Lee Shore, where one could have little or no chance of getting off, So I tack'd & stood to the N^{o}ward. The S^o most Point we saw lay in about 52°3′ S^o.—*This Island must be of a vast extent for we have run above 70 Leag^s along shore & it is full 63 Leag^s to the E^t most Point. Some former Voyages mention its being 200 Miles round, but I make no doubt it is nearer Seven.*[1] At Noon Janry 28th. Hauld the Wind & stood to the N^{o}ward, at 3 PM the Entrance of Berkeley's Sound bore SWbW 5 or 6 Leag^s. At 8 the Wind shifted to SW stood to the W^{t}ward. The Extreams of the Land bearing from SbW to WNW$\frac{1}{2}$W^t and Berkeley's Sound SW 3 or 4 Leag^s. / January 29th. At 8 AM the Wind NW stood to the W^{t}ward, the *p. 85*

[1] Mouat, 111: Falkland Islands were '50 Leagues in length'.

N⁰ most part of Berkeley's Sound SSE dist^ce 7 Leag^s. Latt observed 51°26′ S⁰ and Longitude in from the Meridian of London 60°19′ W^t. Sounded 55 f^m white sand & pieces of broken Shells 6 Leag^s from the Shore. In the night had violent hard Squalls with rain & a very great Sea. *It is incredible the number of Whales that are here, it makes it dangerous for a Ship*, we were very near striking upon one, & another blew the water in upon the Quarter Deck & they are of the largest kind we ever have seen.

Wednesday Janry 30th. Wind from NbW to SWbS blowing hard & a great Sea. Course N⁰ 8° W^t. Dist 44 M^s. Latt in 50°38′ S⁰. M Dist 87 M^s E^t. Long^de made 2°23′ E^t from Port Egmont, Long^de in from London 60°30′ W^t. Port Egmont S⁰ 63°45′ W^t. Dist 33 Leag^s. Variation of the Compass 23°24′ E^t.

Thursday Janry 31st. Wind SW a hard gale & a great Sea, the weather extremely cold. Course N⁰ 16° E^t. Dist 45 M^s. Latt in 49°53′ S⁰. Long^de made 2°31′ E^t. M Dist 92 Miles E^t from Port Egmont. Long^de in 60°22′ W^t from London. Port Egmont S⁰ *p. 86* 47° / 10′ W^t. Dist 44 Leag^s. The North End of Falklands Islands S⁰ 59°19′ W^t. Dist 53 Leag^s.—Port Desire N⁰ 65°8′ W^t. Dist 100 Leag^s. Friday Febry 1st. Wind from S⁰ to SW. blowing hard with a mountainous Sea. Course N⁰ 26 W^t. Dist 76 M^s. Latt in 48°44′ S⁰. Long^de made 1°40′ E^t. M Dist 39 M^s E^t from Port Egmont, . Long^de in 61°13′ W^t from London. Variation 23 E^t. The N⁰ End of Falklands Islands S⁰ 35° W^t. Dist 61 Leag^s. Port Desire N⁰ 76°50′ W^t. Dist 82 Leag^s.

Saturday Febry 2^d. Wind from S⁰ to NWbW the latter part fine moderate weather. Course N⁰ 38° W^t. Dist 62 M^s. Latt in 47°55′ S⁰. Long^de made 0°40′ E^t M Dist 22 M^s E^t from Port Egmont. Long^de in from London 62°10′ W^t. Variation 23° E^t. Port Egmont S⁰ 7°39′ W^t. Dist 69 Leag^s.—The N⁰ End of Falklands Islands S⁰ 17° W^t. 68 Leag^s. Port Desire N⁰ 88°6′ W^t. Dis^t 70 Leag^s.

Sunday Febry 3^d. Wind variable from NW to SSW & back to WNW fine pleasant weather Course S⁰ 73° W^t. Dist 60 M^s Latt in 48°12′ S⁰. Long^de made 0°43′ W^t. M Dist 32 M^s W^t from Port Egmont. Long^de in 63°36′ W^t from London. Variation 23° E^t. The N⁰ End of Falklands Islands S⁰¼E 61 Leag^s. Port Desire N⁰ 80°48′ W^t. Dist 50 Leag^s.[1]

---

[1] *Tamar*'s weekly expenditure of water: 600 gal. (Mouat, 35).

Monday Feby 4th. Wind from WbN to SW. Course N° 51° W^t. Dist 37 M^s. Latt in 47°48′ S^o Long^{de} made 1°26′ W^t. Long^{de} from London 64°19′ W^t. Port Desire W^t. Dist 39 Leag^s. Variation 20° E^t. /

Tuesday Febry 5th. Wind from WSW to NWbN. Course S^o 84°W^t. *p. 87* Dist 83 M^s. Latt in 47°56′ S^o. Long^{de} made 34°30′ W^t. M Dist 143 M^s from Port Egmont Long^{de} in from London 66°23′ W^t. Variation 19° E^t. Port Desire N° 76°14′ W^t. Dist 11 Leag^s.

Wednesday Feby 6th. At 1 PM saw the Land & stood in for Port Desire, soon after saw the Store Ship we expected from England[1] At 4 came to an Anchor off the Harbour's Mouth.

Thursday Feby 7th. Finding by Mr Deane Master of the Storeship that his Foremast was badly sprung & that his Ship was little better than a Wreck, I determined to go into the Harbour & try to unload her there, tho' it is a most dangerous place from its narrowness & the rapid Tides that run there; Accordingly we weighed & got in this Evening, but in the night it blowing very hard both the Tamar & Storeship drove up the Harbour (tho' moor'd) & had very near been ashore, they made Signals of distress & I sent our boats to assist them, but as it blows here continually with the utmost violence, the next night they were in the same distress driving again.[2] I now found it would be impossible to take the Provisions out of the Storeship, as she was driving about the Harbour & in danger of being lost every hour. I sent all our Carpenters on board her to fish her Foremast & to do many other Jobbs for / them, I likewise sent them our Forge to *p. 88*

[1] According to the 1767 Officer *Account*, 80, Byron feared he would miss connections with the storeship and that he would have to steer to the Cape of Good Hope for supplies and not be able to go into the South Seas: 'as by this delay it would be too late for us to attempt a passage into the South Sea, either by passing the streights of Magellan, or doubling Cape Horn, consequently an end would be put to all our discoveries, and the expence of fitting us out be thrown away.' The author or authors must have been unaware of Byron's instructions.

[2] 'Fresh Gales with Squalls of Wind & Rain at times At 3 PM Veerd away & Moor'd Ship a Cable each way D^o lower'd down the Lower Yards At 7 Rece'd on board by our Boats from the Store ship 38 Puncheons of bread & 13 Casks of Brandy At ½ past 2 PM the Storeship drove on which her Anchor hooked our Cable & came up to our Cut Water [?] We fir'd a Gun as a signal for Assistance from the Commodore before She brought Up damag'd Our Cables & Carried Away a Piece of our Cut Water & I [   ] our Rudder in the Lead D^o got his Anchor Up to our Bower At ½ past 7 have Up the small Bower At 8 hove into [   ] third on the best Bower At 9 Veer'd away to ½ a Cable found one of the Casks which we Rece'd from the store ship to be a Cask of Vinegar Containing 60 Gallons' (Mouat, 36).

compleat what Iron work they wanted, & resolved the moment she was in condition to put to Sea to carry her with us to the Straits of Magellan in order to unload her there, as I saw it was out of the nature of things to do it here. Capt Mouat informed me his Rudder was sprung & split to pieces, I ordered the Carpenter of the Dolphin on board to examine it, who reported to me it was so bad that it was almost impossible she could proceed the Voyage without a new one, but as that was not to be had here, I desired Capt Mouat would get his Forge ashore & secure his Rudder for the present with Iron Clamps &c^a in the best manner they could, which was accordingly done, Possibly in the Straits of Magellan we may find a Piece of Timber that may make him a new one, tho' it will be a difficult Jobb.

Wednesday *Feby 13th.* The Storeship being now ready for the Sea I put on board of her one of our Petty Officers who was well acquainted with the Straits, & 3 or 4 of our Seamen to assist in navigating her; & her boats being stove I spared them two of ours *p. 89* & took her's onboard of us to repair. I then gave / Mr Deane the Master of her, Orders to put to Sea directly & to make the best of his way for Port Famine in the Straits of Magellan, tho' I did not doubt but I should be up with her long before she got that length, as I intended following her the moment the Tamar was in readiness, and Capt Mouat informing me that he could proceed next morning we accordingly sailed & a few hours after being abreast of Penguin Island we saw the Storeship a long way to the E^{t}ward of us. A prodigious high Swell tumbled in upon the Shore.

Thursday Feby 14th. But little wind all night & variable. Course S^o 29$°$ W^t Dist 35 M^s. Latt in 48$°$30' S^o. Long^{de} made 0$°$25' W^t. M Dist 17 M^s W^t from Penguin Island, Long^{de} in from London 67$°$25'W^t. Variation 20$°$ E^t Penguin Island N° 29$°$ E^t. Dist 12 Leag^s. At Noon the Edystone Rock bore SSW Dist 3 Leag^s.—This Rock is 5 Leag^s from the Land & is quite cover'd at high Water. *It is a most dangerous Rock* It is in the Latt of 48$°$36' S^o & Long^{de} from London 67$°$30' W^t & bears from Penguin Island SSW by Compass 14 or 15 Leag^s.

Friday Febr^y 15th. Wind between the NNE & NNW a fresh Gale. *p. 90* Course S^o / 24$°$ W^t. Dist 139 M^s. Latt in 50$°$36' S^o. Long^{de} made 1$°$53' W^t. M Dis 73 M^s W^t from Penguin Island. Long^{de} in 68$°$53'

W^t from London. Variation 20° E^t. Cape Virgin Mary S^o 37°15′ Dist 44 Leag^s. Cape Fair Weather S^o 61°35′ W^t. Dist 37 Leag^s.— The Edystone Rock N° 26° E^t. Dist 44 Leag^s.

Saturday Feby 16th. At 6 AM Saw Cape Fair Weather bearing WSW 5 or 6 Leag^s. At 9 saw a strange Sail to the NW standing after us.[1]

Sunday Feby 17th. At 6 PM Cape Virgin Mary bore SSE 7 or 8 Leag^s. In the night had Soundings each hour with 30 f^m soft ground & found a strong Current sitting to the S^{o}ward. At 6 AM Cape Virgin Mary bore S^o. Dist 5 Miles, we hauld in for the Straits, when Cape Virgin Mary bore NW between 2 & 3 Miles had but 7 f^m water & the appearance of shoal water a little within us, therefore haul'd more out. At 11 the S^o End of the Spit bore NWbW 1 Mile. At Noon Point Possession bore W^t 5 Leag^s a fresh gale at NE. The strange Ship haul'd into the Straits after us.

Monday Febry 18th. Steering for the N^o Channel to the first Narrow, when Point Possession bore N. Dist 1 Mile, steered by the Compass WSW until the Asses Ears bore WNW, then steered SWbW until they bore NWbW, then steered between the SWbS & SSW^t to the Entrance of the first / Narrow & steered thro' SSW. *p. 91*

As I observed the strange Ship had shaped the same Course from the time she first saw us, & shortened or made Sail as we did we could not tell what to make of her. When I had got thro' the first Narrow I brought too for our Storeship who was a great way a Stern, and after having got my Ship in the best Order I could for it, I was resolved if possible to speak with this Stranger & ask him the reason he followed us in the manner he had done for these two days past. I was in great hopes she would have run ashore upon one of the Banks between Point Possession & the first Narrow, for the Navigation is extremely difficult to those who are not well acquainted. But the misfortune was, the Storeship kept so far a Stern that she served as a Pilot to the Stranger. As soon as he had passed the Narrow & saw me laying too, he did the same about 4 M^s to Windward of me. Night came on & the Tide setting me over upon the S^o Shore we came to an Anchor.[2] In the night the

---

[1] Bougainville's ship (see Introduction, p. xli).
[2] 'At 7 [pm] the Commodore made the signal to speak me D^o Wore Ship & bore down to him At ½ past 7 Spoke him the Commodore Acquainted me that

wind shifted to the W^t ward & at daybreak I saw the same Ship at an Anchor about 3 Leag^s to Leeward of me. The Tide of Flood /

p. 92 making I thought of working thro' the Second Narrow, but seeing the Stranger get under way & working up towards us, I run directly over into Gregory Bay & bro^t my Ship to an Anchor with a spring upon our Cable & got all our Guns over on one side, which was eight, & those I got out of the Hold upon the occasion & was all I could get at. In the mean time this Ship worked up to us and various were our conjectures about her. She shewed no Colours nor did we. The Storeship in attempting to come to an Anchor near us run a Ground. The Stranger came to an Anchor some way a Stern of her & hoisted French Colours, and was very officious in sending his Launch with an Anchor & another Boat to assist her. I shewed him no Colours but sent the Tamar's & our Boats to assist the Storeship, & with Orders to the Officer who commanded them not to let the French Boats come on board of her, but to thank them for their intended assistance, which was accordingly done, & the Storeship got off presently after. This French Ship is full of Men & seems to have a great many officers.

Tuesday Feby 19th. Wind from SW to NW at 6 PM made

p. 93 the Signal & weighed / & worked thro' the Second Narrow, at 10 passed the W^t End of it, at 11 Anchor'd in 7 f^m off Elizabeth Island. The French Ship anchor'd to the S^{o}ward of St Bartholomew's Island which shew'd he was not acquainted, for he lay in a very ugly berth. At 6 AM weighed with the Wind at NW & sailed between Elizabeth & Bartholomew's Islands & after steering SSW 5 or 6 Miles cross'd a Bank & had 7 f^m amongst the weeds. This Bank is WSW & between 5 & 6 Miles from the middle of George's Island & by some former Accounts has in many places but 3 f^m upon it & in some less, & therefore may be truly called very dangerous. To avoid which you must mind to keep near Elizabeth Island til you come near the Western Shore, then you may steer to the S^{o}ward clear of all Danger til you come to the Reef which is about 4 Miles to the N^{o}ward of St Ann's Point, & shews itself. At Noon the N^o Point of Fresh water Bay bore WbN & St Ann's

the Ship a Stern he took to be a Spanish Man of War & if She offer'd to Stop Us to Discharge our broadside & to board her as he would do the Same. . . .' Later 'She hoisted french Colours which We took her to be one of the Two Ships that was on Discov'rys on this Coast' (Mouat, 38).

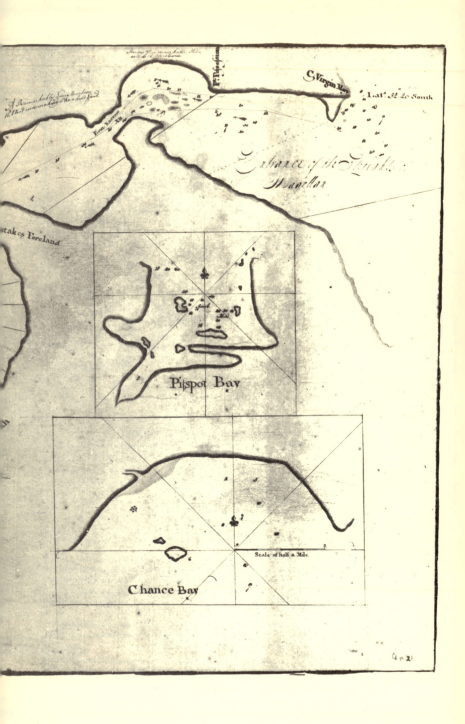

C. Virgin Mary

Lat.º 52.20 South

Entrance of the Straights Magellan

F: Possession

Stakes Foreland

Pitspot Bay

Chance Bay

Scale of half a Mile

G p 21

Point SbE½E 4 Leags. The French Ship steering after us. I imagine she is either from the Malivin Islands (as the French are pleased to call them)[1] to get Wood, or else upon a Survey of these Straits, I should rather think the latter, for / if the first had been his intention it certainly was not necessary for him to come up as high as they are now to procure it.[2] In all probability we shall soon know for I intend if possible to push thro' the Straits before the Season is too far advanced.

p. 94

Wednesday Febry 20th. Light Airs of Wind variable & sometimes calms. at 5 PM hoisted out the Boats & tow'd round St Ann's Point into Port Famine.[3] At 6 anchored with the small Bower in 7 fm & moor'd with the Stream Anchor. The French Ship passed passed by to the Soward.

Monday Febry 25th. Both the Dolphin & Tamar having taken out of the Storeship as much Provisions as they could stow,[4] I gave Mr Dean Master of her, Orders to return to England the instant he could get ready.[5] And we weighed from Port Famine at 5 AM with little wind. At Noon St Ann's Point bore NW Dist 3 Leags & Shut up[6] SSW 3 or 4 Miles. Point Shutup bears from St Anns Point S¼E by the Compass between 4 & 5 Leags. Between these Points is a flat Shoal which runs from Port Famine before the River Sedger, & 3 or 4 Miles to the Soward.

Tuesday Febry 26th. PM Little wind at NW Steering SSW along

[1] 'Mr. Stephens informs me the French have been lately at the Isles Malouins so Falkland Islands are call'd in some Charts: if Your Lordship will please to look over Freziers Voyage You will see that the French themselves acknowledge our Countryman Sir Richd Hawkins to have been the first Discoverer of Falklands Islands.' Byron to Lord Egmont, 24 Feb. 1765 (see Document No. 1, p. 156).

[2] See Feb. 26, p. 68. It was for wood.

[3] 'We saw no remains of the Famous Phillips City, there is a quantity of Ground cleared in the Cod of the Bay, where we suppose it stood; And some clear ground just within the Point of Saint Ann (mentioned before in the description of that point where we suppose the Fort stood)' (Mouat, 118).

[4] On Feb. 21 and 22. The *Tamar* took on board: peas, 13 bar. and 3 gal.; beef, 1,320 pieces; brandy, 817 gal.; wheat, 16 bushels 7 gal.; oatmeal, 28 bushels 9 gal.; mustard, 166 lb.; pork, 2,566 pieces; bread, 6,272 lb.; oil, 145 gal.; vinegar, 60 gal. (Ibid., 38–9).

[5] Henry Blythe, Robert Shaw, James Webster, all ABs, and all marked 'Unsble.' in the *Dolphin's* Muster Sheet, returned to England on the *Florida* Storeship. Pte. Henry Stoneman also returned, but because he was too ill to continue the voyage.

[6] '. . . Point Shut up, which is so called because the Land on the South Shore rounds up so far to the Northward as to make it appear as if there was no farther passage to the West . . .' (Mouat, 119).

p. 95 shore from Point Shutup towards Cape Froward. / At 2 Point Shutup bore NNW 3 Miles. At 3 passed by the French Ship in a little Cove about 2 Leag^s to the S^o ward of Point Shutup, she had hauld her Stern close into the Woods, & we could see large Piles of Wood which they had cut down laying of each side of her, so that I think there can be no doubt but she is here on purpose to get Wood for their New Settlement. From Point Shutup to Cape Froward the Course is SWbS by the Compass Dist 7 Leag^s. At 8 PM Cape Froward bore NW$\frac{1}{2}$W about a Mile. Brought too & lay by all night, Little wind at NE. This part of the Strait is about 7 or 8 Miles over. At 4 AM Cape Froward bore NNW 2 Miles. At 7 Sent a Boat in Shore to sound off the Cape & found 40 f^m within half a Cable's length of the Shore. At 8 Little wind & variable all round the Compass. Cape Froward NEbE 3 or 4 Miles & Cape Holland WNW$\frac{1}{2}$W 5 Leag^s. At 10 fresh Gales at WNW & every now & then most violent hard Squalls, which obliged us every time they came on to clew every thing up. At Noon Cape Froward bore ENE 5 or 6 Miles & Cape Holland NWbW 5 Leag^s.—Working to windward
p. 96 & looking out for an / anchoring place.

Wednesday Febr^y 27th Strong Gales of wind Westerly with dreadful hard Squalls. Working to windward for a Bay about 2 Leag^s to the Westward of Cape Froward. At 5 sent a Boat in with an Officer to Sound & found it a good anchoring place. At 6 stood in & anchored in 9 f^m. Cape Froward bearing E$\frac{1}{2}$S dist 5 Miles; A Small Island (which is in the middle of the Bay & about a Mile from the Shore) WbS $\frac{1}{2}$ a Mile, and a Rivulet of fresh water NWbW $\frac{3}{4}$ of a Mile. In standing in we had very regular Soundings from 17 to 9 f^m.—At 6 AM weighed, wind N^oerly & frequent hard Gusts from the High Scraggy Hills. At 8 Cape Froward bore ENE$\frac{1}{2}$E 3 Leag^s & Cape Holland WbN between 2 & 3 Leag^s.—At 10 Cape Froward E$\frac{1}{2}$N 5 Leag^s & Cape Holland NEbN 2 Leag^s. From Cape Holland the Coast lays W$\frac{1}{2}$S^{o 1} by the Compass, dist^{ce} 8 Leag^{s 2} to Cape Gallant which is a high steep Cape. Between the Capes is English Reach, & is about 3 Leag^s over. South by the Compass dist^{ce} 5 Miles from Cape Gallant is a large Island called Charles's Island which you must keep to the N^o /
p. 97 ward of, we sailed along the North Shore at about 2 Miles distance

---

[1] Slip of the pen; the coast runs W$\frac{1}{2}$N. [2] Actually, 12 n. miles.

& sometimes much less. A Little to the East ward of Cape Holland is a fair Sandy Bay called Wood's Bay where is good Anchoring. At Noon Cape Holland bore E$\frac{1}{2}$N between 3 & 4 Leag^s and Cape Gallant W$\frac{1}{2}$N 5 Leag^s.—The high Mountains on each side the Straits can be surpass'd by nothing but the Cordeliers,[1] either for heigth or dismal appearance, these being like them as ragged & steep as its possible for nature to form them & cover'd with Snow from top to bottom.

Thursday Feby 28th. Fresh Gales N^{o}erly with hard Squalls & rain. At 2 PM Cape Gallant bore ENE 4 or 5 Miles, & Passage Point WNW 2 Leag^s. From Cape Gallant the Coast lies WbN by the Compass Dist^{ce} 3 Leag^s to Passage Point, which is a low Point with a Rock off it, and is the East Point of Elizabeth Bay. Between Cape Gallant & Point Passage lays several Islands, some very small, the largest & E^{t}ermost which is upwards of 2 Leag^s in length is called Charles's Island, the Second, Monmouths, and the W^{t}ermost Ruperts, which lies SbE from Point Passage. These Islands make the Straits narrow here, and you must go to the N^o ward of them all, keeping the N^o Shore on board, we sailed within two Cables / length of it & had no ground with 40 f^m of Line. Between $p.\ 98$ Passage Point & Rupert's Island the Channel is not more than 2 Miles over. At 6 PM the wind shifted to the W^{t}ward, we stood in for Elizabeth Bay & anchored in 10 f^m very good ground, Rupert's Island bearing SbE between 2 & 3 Miles. Passage Point SEbS $\frac{3}{4}$ of a Mile.—The weathermost point of the Bay WbN 2 Miles, and the break of a Reef of Rocks which are just cover'd at high water, & is upwards of a Cable's length from the Shore NWbW $\frac{1}{4}$ of a Mile. We sent a Boat round the Ship to Sound & found but 3 or 4 f^m about a Cables length within us. The best anchoring is in about 13 f^m In this Bay is a good Rivulet of fresh water. AM the wind continued W^{t}erly & very squally with hard Rain. Here we found the Flood Tide set very strong to the Eastward, and as near as we could calculate it flows full & change about 12 ^{o}Clock, And the Compass has about two Points East Variation.

Friday March 1st. In the afternoon fresh Gales between the NW & W^t & very squally with hard rain. At 2 PM made the Signal to

[1] Cordeliers: mountains on the coast of southern Chile, where the *Wager* was shipwrecked. See Introduction, p. xx.

weigh, & when short came on a hard Squall & brought the Anchor home. The Ship drove into shoal Water. We let go the Small

p. 99 Bower in 4 f^m & had but 3 f^m under the Stern, about / two Cables length from the Shore. Carried the Stream Anchor out & hove taught on that, & hove up the Bowers, then slipt the Stream Cable, & with the Jibb & Staysails run out into 10 f^m & anchored with the best Bower, the same Bearings on as before. In the Night wind N^{o}erly, moderate weather. At 5 AM made the Signal & weighed. At 7 passed Mussel Bay which is on the S^o Shore, & about a League to the W^{t}ward of Elizabeth Bay. At 8 came a breast of Batchelors River on the N^o Shore about 2 Leag^s WbN by the Compass from Elizabeth Bay. At 9 passed St Jerom's Sound, the Entrance of which is about a League from Batchelors River. When St Jerom's Sound was open it bore NW. We then steered WSW by the Compass for Cape Quad which is 3 Leag^s from the S^{o}ermost Point of St Jerom's Sound. Between Elizabeth Bay & Cape Quad is Crooked Reach & is about 4 Miles over. At Noon Cape Quad bore WSW$\frac{1}{2}$W 4 or 5 Miles. This morning we saw three or four Fires at the Entrance of St Jerom's Sound upon the N^o Side, & soon after observed two or three Canoes paddling after us.

Saturday March 2^d. Light Airs of wind with Calms. PM drove to

p. 100 the E^{t}ward with the Flood Tide. / One of the Indian Canoes after some time paddling about us had the resolution to come on board. The Canoe was of Bark badly contrived, and the Indians the poorest Wretches I have ever seen, In number they were four Men, two women & a boy; They had nothing to cover them but a stinking Seals Skin over their Shoulders. I made them some little trifling Presents, & in return had their Bows & Arrows. At 5 Anchor'd with the Stream Anchor in 25 f^m to the Eastward of Batchelors River. At 6 weighed and towed abreast of Batchelors River, and Anchored with the best Bower in 14 f^m. The Entrance of the River NBE 1 Mile. The N^{o}ermost Point of St Jerom's Sound WNW 3 Miles. About $\frac{3}{4}$ of a Mile E^{t}ward from Batchelors River is a Shoal, which has not more than 6 feet water on it at low water; It is near $\frac{1}{2}$ a Mile from the Shore & shews itself by the weeds. It flows here full & change about 1 o'Clock. Several Indian Canoes came on board of us, that we might not frighten them by our Numbers, I took our Jolly Boat & went on Shore amongst them, to make us welcome they picked some Berries[1] & brought them to us, which with a few Mussels is all they have to live upon themselves in this Place. At 5 AM weighed & towed with the Tide; but finding at 10 that we were drove to the E^tward again, & having no wind anchor'd with the Stream Anchor / in 15 f^m on a Bank about half a *p. 101* Mile from the N^o Shore, after veering two thirds of a Cable had 45 f^m along side & still deeper water a little way from us. The S^o Point of St Jerom's Sound NNE 2 Miles, and Cape Quad WSW 7 or 8 Miles. From the S^o Point of St Jerom's Sound to Cape Quad is SWbW by the Compass Dist 3 Leag^s.—

Sunday March 3^d. In the afternoon had light Airs of wind variable & sometimes calm. The Tides in this Reach are excessively strong, tho' very irregular. We found them set to the E^tward from 9 o'Clock in the morning till 5 o'Clock the next morning, and then set about four hours to the W^tward. At 12 at Night it came on to blow very hard at WNW. At 2 AM the Ship drove off the Bank. We hove the Anchor up & found both the flukes broke off. We had no Ground till 3, when we drove into 16 f^m water at the Entrance of St Jerom's Sound, it then blowing a Storm of wind, we immediately let go the best Bower & Veered to ½ a Cable, & when brought up had but 5 f^m & that amongst the Breakers. We let go the small Bower under foot. At 5 found the Tide setting to the W^tward & the weather proving more moderate hove up the Anchors, and kept working to Windward. At 10 / found the Tide setting strong again *p. 102* to the E^tward, hoisted out a Boat & sent her to look for an anchoring place, which she found in a Bay on the N^o Shore about 4 Miles to the E^tward of Cape Quad; A little way within some small Island, we endeavoured to get into it, but the Tide made out so strong we found it impossible. At noon bore away for York Road at the Entrance of Batchelors River.

Monday March 4th. Fresh gales Westerly & squally weather. At 1 PM anchored with the small Bower in York Road in 10 f^m & steadied the Ship with the Kedge Anchor & Hawzer. Batchelors River bearing NNE ½ a Mile. At 6 AM weighed & worked wth the Tide which we found set the same as yesterday, but could not gain an anchoring Place. At Noon bore away for York Road again. I

---

[1] Red berries resembling cranberries, the size of hazel nuts (1767, Officer *Account*, 93–4).

went up Batchelors River in our Jolly Boat as high as we could go, which was about 4 Miles. In some Places the River is very wide & deep & the water very good but towards the Mouth of it at Low water it is so shoal that a small Boat can't get in.

Tuesday March 5th. For the first part fresh gales of Wind Westerly & Squally, but towards the Morning had but little wind & that Notherly. At 6 weighed at 8 Calm sent all the Boats ahead to
p. 103 Tow. / at 11 the Tide setting strong from the Westward found we could not gain the Bay I mentioned before on the No Shore, (& which is an exceeding good place for 5 or 6 Sail to lay in) so was obliged to anchor on a Bank in 45 fm with the Stream Anchor, Cape Quad bearing WSW 5 or 6 Miles, the So Point of the Island to the Etward of the Cape just on with the Pitch of it, & a remarkable Stone Patch on the No Shore N½W Dist ½ a Mile, found 75 fm within us close to the Shore. Sent the Boat away with an Officer to the Wtward to look for an Anchoring Place.

Wednesday March 6th.[1] PM Light Airs of Wind Wterly, in the night Calm. The Tide setting to the Etward from the time we anchored to 6 AM: Then weighed & with the Boats towed to the Wtward; At 8 a fresh breeze at WSW & Wt. At Noon Cape Quad bore EBS 4 or 5 Miles. Sent the Boats to look out for an Anchoring Place. At 12 Anchored in a small Bay on the So Shore opposite to Cape Quad in 25 fm very good ground. A Small Rocky Island WbN about 2 Cables length, the Etermost Point E½So & Cape Quad NEbN 3 Miles. Here we got plenty of Shell fish.

Thursday March 7th. Wind NNW moderate & hazey. At 2 the
p. 104 Tamar not being able to work up to us, anchored in / the Bay on the No Shore I mentioned before 5 or 6 Miles to the Etward of Cape Quad. In the night calm, AM light Airs of wind Wterly, at 8 weighed & worked with the Tide. At Noon Cape Quad bore EbS between 2 & 3 Leags, & Cape Monday wch is the Wtermost Land in sight on the So Shore WbN 10 or 11 Leags.[2]—This part of the

---

[1] An Indian family—an old man, his wife, two sons, and a daughter—approached the Englishmen, who could not understand the Indians. The daughter had 'tolerable features, and an English face'. 'Various were the conjectures we formed in regard to this circumstance, though we generally agreed, that their signs plainly shewed that they offered her to us, as being of the same country' (1767, Officer *Account*, 92–3).

[2] The distance from Cape Quad to Cape Monday is approximately 38 n. miles. Byron's 'fix' is very inaccurate.

Straits lays WNW$\frac{1}{2}$W by the Compass & is about 4 Miles over. The high Rocky Mountains on each Side cover'd with Snow make the most dismal appearance in the world: The Tides not very strong; the Ebb sets to the W^t ward, but runs so irregular that without a great deal of time there is no accounting for them.

Friday March 8th. PM Moderate breezes between the WNW & WSW. At 1 PM. The Tamar anchored in the Bay on the S^o Shore opposite to Cape Quad, which we came out of. We continued working to Windward till 7, then Anchored in 15 f^m in a small Bay on the N^o Shore 5 Leag^s to the W^{t}ward of Cape Quad, very good holding ground. This Bay may be known by two large Rocks which shew themselves above water, & the East part of the Bay makes a low Point. The Anchoring Place is between the two Rocks. The E^{t}ermost bearing NE$\frac{1}{2}$E about 2 Cables length, & the / Westermost, *p. 105* which is near the Point WNW$\frac{1}{2}$W about the same distance. A Small Rock that shows itself at Low water amongst the weeds E$\frac{1}{2}$N 2 Cables length; but if more Ships than one they may anchor further out in deeper water. In the Night Calm & foggy weather. At 10 AM The Fog cleared, but continues calm. There is plenty of good fresh water here. I went ashore this morning & found abundance of Shell Fish. No signs of Indians ever having been here.

Saturday March 9th. PM calm, employed in filling our water. I went up this afternoon to the head of a deep Lagoon, which is just round the W^{t}ermost Rock, at the end of it there is a very fine fall of water, & on the East side several snug Coves where Ships of the greatest Draught of Water might lay secure. We filled our boat with very large Mussels. In the Night light Airs of wind variable. At 7 AM weighed & towed out of the Bay. At 8 a moderate breeze of wind at ESE & fair weather. Saw the Tamar a long way a stern steering after us. At 10 Cape Monday bore WbN dist^{ce} 5 Leag^s. At Noon very little wind ENE.

Sunday March 10th. PM Light Airs of wind E^{t}erly. At 5 the wind shifted to WNW a fresh gale & hazey. At 6 / abreast of Cape *p. 106* Monday. In the night very squally & rain. At 6 AM Cape Upright bore EbS 3 Leag^s. From Cape Monday to Cape Upright which are on the S^o Shore the Course is WbN by the Compass Dist^{ce} 4 or 5

Leag^s.[1] The Shore on each side very rocky broken ground. At 7 hard gales WSW & squally with rain, & very thick weather & a great Sea. At ½ past 7 in a very hard Squall & the weather extremely thick, we saw a reef of Rocks close under the Lee Bow on which the Sea broke extremely high. We had but just time to tack clear of them, and had the Ship missed Stays every Soul must have been lost. Never had a Ship a more narrow escape than this was; These Rocks lay at a great distance from the S^o Shore & are about 3 Leag^s to the W^{t}ward of Cape Upright. It pleased God that it cleared for a moment & shew'd us those Breakers just time enough to avoid them, for three or four minutes longer it would have been too late. At 9 by the weather clearing a little saw the Entrance of Long Reach. Bore away & kept nearest to the S^o Shore to look for an anchoring place. At 10 Strong Gales & thick Weather with hard

p. 107 Rain. / At Noon was abreast of Cape Monday but could find no anchoring Place.

Monday March 11th. PM. Strong Gales SW & thick weather, continued steering along the S^o Shore & looking for an anchoring Place. We joined the Tamar again who had been 6 or 7 Leag^s to the E^{t}ward of us all night. At 6 Anchored with the small Bower in a deep Bay about 3 Leag^s to the E^{t}ward of Cape Monday. We let go the Anchor in 25 f^m near an Island in the bottom of the Bay, but before we could bring up the Ship drove off, & the Anchor took the ground in about 50 f^m, veered to a whole Cable & moored with the Stream Anchor. The Extreme Points of the Bay bearing from NW to NEbE & the Island W½S a Cable's length from the Anchor to the nearest Shore. In the Night fresh Gales W^{t}erly & Squally with hard Rain. AM Moderate, wind WNW thick & hard Rain. At the bottom of this Bay is a Bason with but 3 f^m & ½ at Low water in the Entrance, but within it 10 f^m & room enough for six or seven Sail to lay where no wind can hurt them. I remained in this Bay till *the 15th* as we had the most dreadful weather imaginable all that time. It never ceased raining with hard Gales W^{t}erly & very thick. I sent

p. 108 a Boat with / an Officer[2] to look out for Harbours on the S^o Shore; She was absent two days & then returned with an Account of their

---

[1] Byron using land league of 2 miles =1 league. Cape Monday to Cape Upright is about 10 miles.
[2] Lt Hindman of the *Tamar* (Mouat, 43).

having found five Bays between this Place & Cape Upright, where Ships may anchor with safety. Some Hills that had no Snow upon them when we first came in here, are now cover'd with it, & it is grown extremely cold. *The Winter has set in all at once,* It is a terrible time for Seamen for they hardly have ever now a dry thread about them. I distributed two Bales of Fearnought amongst the two Ships Crews (Officers as well) which will make them good warm Jackets, & is very acceptable to them at this time. We had a great Swell setting into this Bay which broke very high upon the Rocks that we lay very near to; this obliged me to heave our Anchors up & warp the Ship to the Bank where the Tamar lay, I then let go our Anchor in 14 f^m & moor'd with the Stream Anchor to the E^{t}ward in 45 f^m whilst our People that went in the Boat were looking for Harbours, *they fell in with a few Indians near Cape Upright, who gave them a Dog & offer'd them a Sucking Child if they would accept of it*; The first they brought off, but the latter / they *p. 109* left to it's tender Parents.

Friday March 15th. Fresh Gales SW & squally with hard Rain & Hail. At 8 weighed & made sail. At Noon Cape Monday bore West Dist^{ce} 2 Leag^s.

Saturday March 16th. PM Fresh Gales & squally with hard rain. At 3 abreast of Cape Monday. At 5 Anchor'd with the small Bower in 16 f^m in a Bay on the E^t side of Cape Monday; The Pitch of the Cape bearing NW ½ a Mile & the Extream Points of the Bay from E^t to NbW & about ½ a Cables length from the nearest Shore which is a low Island between the Ship & Cape. Steadied with the Kedge Anchor to the E^{t}ward in 40 f^m. At 6 AM made the Signal & weighed, found the Palm gone from the small Bower Anchor, Wind WNW with hard rain. Found since 8 o'Clock a strong Tide or Current setting to the E^{t}ward. At Noon Cape Monday bore WNW 2 Miles. The Tamar being to to windward of us fetched into the Bay & anchor'd again.

Sunday March 17th. PM fresh gales W^{t}erly & squally with hard rain. Loosing ground upon every Tack at 2 Anchor'd on the S^o Shore in 16 f^m about 5 Miles to the E^{t}ward of Cape Monday. The Boat in Sounding round the Ship found the ground very rocky, therefore finding it not a safe Place to lay in at 3 weighed, Wind NW / with hard rain, kept working all night, every Soul upon deck *p. 110* with not a dry thread on them, for it never ceased raining or rather pouring, & the weather extremely cold. In the morning found we had lost ground upon every tack, having a strong Current setting to the Eastward. At 8 bore away & at 9 Anchor'd in the same Bay we sailed from the 15th. Fresh gales & hard rain. Have had no Tide to the W^tward since we left Cape Monday.

Wednesday March 20th. For these two days past Wind from W^t to WNW. the Weather extremely bad, hard Squalls & continual rain. Tried the Current several times a day, & found it always setting strong to the E^tward. I sent a Boat with an Officer to sound a Bay on the N^o Shore but he did not find it a convenient Anchoring place. At 6 AM In a hard Squall the Ship drove & brought the anchor off the Bank into 40 f^m carried out the Kedge Anchor, hove up the Bower & got the Ship on the Bank again.

Thursday March 21st. Wind from WNW to SW very bad weather. *p. 111* At 8 AM weighed & stood out the Bay, & at / Noon had gained about 1½ Mile to the W^tward. A Strong Current still setting to the E^tward.

Friday March 22^d. PM Fresh gales and squally, with violent hard rain & hail. wind variable from SW to NW. At 5 the Ship had gained 3 or 4 Miles to the W^tward, but could get no Anchoring place, & falling less wind we drove fast to the E^tward. At 6 we anchor'd in 40 f^m very good ground in a Bay about 2 Miles to the W^tward of that we sailed from in the Morning. Veer'd to a Cable & a half & had 62 f^m along side, a very ugly Swell drove in here all night, Wind at WSW with hard rain. AM blowing very fresh at 9 weighed & made Sail, & at Noon Cape Monday bore W^t 5 or 6 Miles.

Saturday March 23^d. Wind from W^t to WSW & very rainy thick weather, every body continually wet to the Skin, & no opportunity of ever drying their wet cloaths, however I thank God my People are all very healthy, & go through this fatiguing work with great chearfulness. *This day to our infinite Joy we found the Current setting to the W^tward*, & now we gain ground fast. At 6 we anchor'd in the Bay on the E^t Side of Cape Monday (where the Tamar lay) *p. 112* in 18 f^m the Pitch of the Cape bearing / WbN half a Mile. This is a very safe anchoring Place, the Ground being exceeding good & room enough for two or three Line of Battle Ships to moor in. In the night strong gales & squally with hard Rain. AM fresh Gales from WSW to WNW, At 8 weighed & made Sail & as *we now open the South Sea*[1] we have a prodigious great Swell tumbling in. At Noon Cape Monday bore SE½E between 2 & 3 Leag^s & Cape Upright W½S 2 Leag^s.

Sunday March 24th. PM fresh gales WNW & hazey, At 4 anchord with the Small Bower in a very good bay about a League to the E^{t}ward of Cape Upright in 14 f^m veer'd two thirds of a Cable & moored with the Stream Anchor to the Eastward in 54 f^m. The extreme Point of the Bay from NW to NEbE, Cape Upright WNW about a Cable's length to the E^{t}ward of a low Island which makes the Bay. In the night strong Gales NW & squally with Rain. At 2 AM veer'd a whole Cable. At 3 I sent a Boat away with an Officer from each Ship to look for anchoring Places to the W^{t}ward. Fresh Gales from WNW to NW with thick weather & hard rain. This Bay may be easily known by a deep Sound in the bottom. /

Monday March 25th. Hard Gales WNW & very squally with rain. *p. 113* At 4 the boat returned not being able to get round Cape Upright. AM the weather moderate but very thick with hard rain. At 7 I saw the boat to the W^{t}ward again.

Tuesday March 26th. Wind from WNW to WSW. At 7 the boat returned, had been about 4 Leag^s to the W^{t}ward. They found two anchoring places, but neither of them very good. AM fresh gales WNW & squally. At 6 unmoor'd, at 8 weighed & made sail. At Noon Cape Upright bore SSE 2 or 3 Miles.

Wednesday March 27th. PM Fresh Gales NW & NNW hazey weather. At 3 PM Cape Upright bore ESE near 3 Leag^s & a remarkable Cape[2] on the N^o Shore NE 4 or 5 Miles. This Cape is NNW by the Compass from Cape Upright Dist 3 Leag^s & is a high steep Cape. The S^o Shore appears very bad, many sunken Rocks laying a great way from it upon which the Sea breaks vastly high. At 4 the weather came on very thick. At ½ past saw the S^o Shore at about a mile Distance but could get no anchoring Place, tacked & stood over for the North Shore. At ½ past 6 I made the Tamar's Signal to come under our stern, & order'd her to keep a head of us all night

[1] Byron not really reaching open sea: he is merely approaching the Sea Reach, which extends south-east some 45 miles.
[2] Point Tamar.

to shew Lights & fire a Gun at each time of Tacking. At 7 it
p. 114 clearing for a moment saw the Land on the N⁰ Side bearing / WbN,
Tacked at 8 the wind shifted to WNW & blew as hard a gale as ever
Ship was in. Nothing could be more melancholly than our present
situation. The weather extremely thick with the hardest rain, a
long dark night before us; A narrow Channel & that full of sunken
Rocks & Breakers; Before we could clew the Mizen topsail up he
blew all to Rags. I brought too with the Main & Fore topsail close
reefed & on the Cap, the Ships head to the SW. A prodigious great
Sea ran which broke over us often. At 9 we saw the remarkable
Cape on the N⁰ shore, bearing Eᵗ about a Mile distance. Lost sight
of the Tamar. At ½ past 3 we were close to a high Land on the S⁰
Shore, wore Ship & brought too to the N⁰ward the Gale continuing
with the utmost violence & the rain never ceasing. Not a Man of us
with a dry thread on & expecting every moment to be amongst the
Breakers. The long wished for day came at last but could see no
Land till after 6 the weather was so thick, We then saw the S⁰ Shore
at about 2 Miles distᶜᵉ & soon after saw the Tamar. At ½ past 6
Cape Monday bore SE about 4 Mˢ. Bore away the gale if possible
rather increasing. At 7 Anchored in the Bay on the Eᵗ side of Cape
Monday, as did the Tamar, a very ugly Sea tumbles in here,
p. 115 however we were glad to get to / an Anchor any where. I have now
been twice within 3 or 4 Leagˢ of Tuesday Bay at the Wᵗ Entrance
of the Straits & have both times met with the most dreadful hard
gales imaginable, which has drove me back 10 or 12 Leagˢ.—
*Passing these Straits at a proper time of year in my opinion would be
nothing, but now the Season is far advanced it is become a most
dangerous undertaking,* as it never ceases blowing day nor night a
perfect hurricane, with continual rain & thick weather.
Thursday March 28ᵗʰ. Hard Gales WNW with rain & very thick
weather. Cutt our Outer best Bower Cable into Junk it being
entirely worn out, & bent a new one, rounded it with old Rigging
8 fᵐ from the Anchor.
Friday March 29ᵗʰ. Strong gales WNW & Squally with hard rain.
At 1 PM the Tamar parted a new best bower Cable, it being cut
with a Rock, & drove over to the East side of the Bay, where she
brought up, not far from the Rocks on which breaks a very ugly
Sea. AM fresh gales from NNW to WNW with hard rain. At 6

unmoor'd, at 7 weighed & found our small bower Cable very much rub'd having been in foul ground; Cutt 26 f^m off it, & / bent it *p. 116* again. At ½ past 7 the Tamar made the Signal of Distress being near the Rocks & could not purchase her Anchor. At 9 stood into the Bay again & anchor'd with the best Bower in 22 f^m. Sent hawsers on board the Tamar & hove her up whilst they purchas'd the Anchor, then hove her to Windward. At noon she got into a proper Berth & anchor'd again.

Saturday March 30th. Violent hard Gales from W^t to SW. AM wind shifted to WNW & blew so terrible a Gale that it is almost past all description, the Water was tore up all about up & carried much higher than our Mastheads. A most dreadful Sea tumbles in so that we were under constant apprehension of parting our Cables as we knew already by experience that the Ground was foul, and had that been the case the Ship must have gone instantly to Atoms, for never did I see a more frightful Sea than broke upon the Rocks just to Leeward of us.

Sunday March 31st. The Gale continued, or if possible rather encreased, we let go the small Bower & veer'd a Cable & a half on the best Bower, lower'd the main & fore Yards & bent the Sheet Cable & stood by the Anchor all night, at Midnight it fell less wind, tho' the / weather still continued very bad; the Sea sometimes *p. 117* broke up half way our main Shrouds.

Monday Ap^l 1st. PM Hard Gales NNW & Squally. In the night the wind shifted to SW was moderate & clear. AM Calm & sometimes light Airs of wind E^terly with very thick weather & hard rain. A Strong Current setting to the E^tward. At 4 got up the Lower Yards. Unbent the Sheet Cable & weighed the Small Bower. At 8 weighed the best Bower, & found the Cable very much rub'd in several places. This is a great misfortune as it was a fine new Cable never wet before. At 11 hove short on the Stream Anchor.

Tuesday Ap^l 2^d. PM calm & very thick weather with hard rain, veer'd away the Stream Cable & with a Warp to the Tamar hove the Ship on the Bank again. Let go the small Bower in 22 f^m & veer'd 2/3 of a Cable. At 6 strong Gales at WNW with dreadful hard Squalls & rain.

Wednesday Ap^l 3. PM little wind variable & clear weather. In the

L

night calm. AM fresh Gales WNW & hazey wth rain. A Strong
Current setting to the E^tward. Bent a new best bower Cable &
shifted the one that was rub'd for an Inner Cable. I sent the
p. 118 Tamar's Boat / with an Officer from each Ship to the W^tward on
the S^o Shore to look for anchoring Places, & our Cutter with an
Officer on the N^o Shore for the same purpose.

Thursday April 4th. PM Hard Gales WNW & Squally with rain &
snow. AM fresh gales at W & WSW at 4 unmoored & hove short
on the Small Bower. At 6 the Boat returned from the N^o Shore, she
had been about 5 Leag^s to the W^tward & had found two anchoring
places. They fell in with some Indians, who had with them a diff^t
kind of Canoe from any they had seen in the Straits before, she
being of plank sew'd together, those we had seen before were of the
bark of large Trees. These People were very Savage, they eat all
their food raw & that of the worst kind for they had with them a
large piece of the blubber of Whale which stunk abominably, one
of them tore it to bits with his teeth & gave it about to the rest who
devoured it immediately; and notwithstanding the weather is
piercing cold they were all naked except a Scrap of Seals Skin they
had over their Shoulders. They are great Thieves for whilst one of
our People lay a sleep they cut off the hinder part of his Jacket with
p. 119 a sharp flint which they make use of instead of Knives. / At 8
weighed & made sail, found little or no Current. At noon Cape
Upright bore WSW 3 Leag^s.

Friday Ap^l 5th. PM fresh gales from WNW to WSW with frequent
Squalls & hard rain. At 6 anchored with the small Bower in 15 f^m
in the Bay on the S^o Shore about a League to the E^tward of Cape
Upright & moor'd with the Stream Anchor to the E^tward in 40 f^m.

Saturday Ap^l 6th. PM Little wind WSW & hard rain. AM Light
Airs of wind E^terly & calm. At 9 weighed the small Bower Anchor.

Sunday Ap^l 7th. PM Calm & fair weather sent the Boats for wood
& water, moor'd again with the small bower. A Canoe came round
the W^t Point of the Bay with 7 or 8 Indians in her, they landed
opposite the Ship & made a fire but could not be induced to come
on board by all the signs we could make them. Upon which I took
our Jolly Boat & went on shore to them. I made them several little
Presents which they esteemed greatly & we were very intimate in a
few minutes. I staid with them & sent my boat off for some Bread,

which as soon as she returned with I divided amongst them. I observed / if I let a bit of Biscuit fall none of them offer'd to touch *p. 120* it till I gave them leave. As my people were cutting a little Grass for two or three Sheep I had left on board, the Indians perceiving what they were at run immediately & tore up all the weeds & trash they could get & filled my boat with it. When I returned on board they all got into their Canoe & followed me tho' in a great fright when they came near the Ship, however I got 4 or 5 of them to come on board, where we made them so many Presents that they seemed in no hurry to go on shore again. One of our Midshipmen plaid on the Fiddle & some of our people danced to entertain them. In return for our Civilities one of them brought a bag of paint up, & daub'd one of my Officer's faces all over with it, & wanted to pay me the same complement. In the night light airs of wind variable & calm. At 4 AM unmoor'd, at 6 weighed with a moderate breeze at ENE & fine weather. At 7 abreast of Cape Upright. At noon a light Air at East, Cape Upright ESE. 4 Leagues. Try'd the Current & found it set a knot & a half to the E^tward.

Monday Ap^l 8th. PM Calm & fair weather. At 3 Sounded & had 50 f^m continuing calm & finding that the Current drove us back / very fast to the E^tward anchor'd with the Stream Anchor, but be- *p. 121* fore it took the ground was in 120 f^m veer'd two Cables. The Tamar's Boat returned from the Westward, had been within two or three Leagues of Cape Pillar, & found several good anchoring places. At 1 AM fresh gales at W^t & thick weather, weighed & made sail. At 11 it blowing very hard with violent rains & a great Sea found we rather lost ground, so stood in for a Bay on the S^o Shore about 4 Leag^s to the W^tward of Cape Upwright & anchor'd with the small Bower in 20 f^m & moor'd with the Stream Anchor to the E^tward in 35 f^m the ground not good but otherwise as snug a Bay as any I had seen in the Straits, where no wind could hurt you.

Tuesday Ap^l 9th. PM Little wind variable between the S^o & W^t at 2 unmoor'd, at 4 weighed with a moderate breeze at SSE & hazey weather, steer'd to the W^tward 2½ Leag^s.—The night coming on fast we anchored with great difficulty in a very good Bay on the S^o Shore in 20 f^m very heavy Squalls came off the Land before we could let go the Anchor, so that we were very near drove off, which if it had happened we must have passed a dreadful night in the

Straits for it blew till morning a perfect Hurricane of Wind with
p. 122 hard / rain & snow; At 6 AM weighed with a fresh Gale at SSE &
Squally, Steer'd WbN along the S⁰ Shore, at 11 was abreast of
Cape Pillar which is 13 or 14 Leag⁵ W½N by the Compass from
Cape Upright. Cape Pillar may be known by a large Gap on the
top, & when the Cape bears WSW you will see an Island off it,
which makes something like a Hay Stack, & several small Rocks off
it. The Straits to the E^tward of the Cape is 6 or 7 Leag⁵ over. The
Land on each Side of a moderate height, but lowest on the N⁰
Shore & very ragged. Westminster Island is nearest the N⁰ Shore
& is NE by the Compass from Cape Pillar. The S⁰ Shore is by
much the boldest. The Land near the W^t End of the Straits on the
N⁰ Shore makes in many Islands & Rocks & frightful Breakers. The
Land about Cape Victory is NWbN distance 10 or 11 Leag⁵ from
Cape Pillar. From the latter the Coast trenches SSW¼W to Cape
Deseada which is a low Cape with many Rocks & Breakers off it, &
about 4 Leag⁵ WSW by Compass lies some dangerous Rocks which
Sir John Narborough called the Judges upon which the Sea breaks
mountains high. The Islands of Direction which is 4 small Islands
is NWbW by Compass 7 or 8 Leag⁵ from Cape Pillar; When we /
p. 123 were off this Cape it fell calm, & never in my life did I see such a
mountainous Swell as drove in here, & such Breakers on each side
that it is impossible for those who did not see him to form any
Idea of. I now expected every minute that the wind would spring
up from its old Quarter, & that the best that could happen to us
would be to be drove up the Straits many Leagues again, but
contrary to all expectations it pleased God that the Wind sprung
up at SE a fine steady gale, upon which I carried as much Sail as it
was possible for the Ship to bear, & run off from this frightful
desolate Coast at the rate of nine Knots, & by 8 in the evening I
was good 20 Leag⁵ from it. In order to make the Ship as stiff as
possible, I knocked down our after Bulkhead, & got two of our
Boats under the half deck; The Bulkhead was soon up again & my
12 Oar'd Cutter I placed under the Booms, so that we had nothing
left upon the Skids but the Jolly Boat. This made a surprizing
alteration in the Ship, those heavy Boats being always upon the
p. 124 Skids before, made her crank, besides the danger of loosing / them
in a great Sea, but now She goes as upright as any Ship I ever had

82

my foot in. *It is but natural to imagine that whoever reads the Account of the many dangers & difficulties we encounter'd in passing these Straits will say it would certainly be a folly for Ships to attempt it hereafter. But I am far from being of that opinion as I would prefer it twenty times over to the going round Cape Horn, I have been twice round the latter, & therefore speak by experience. I will venture to say that even a large Squadron might pass thro' the Straits at a proper Season in less than three weeks, but then they should contrive to be at the East Entrance sometime in the Month of Decem^r. Notwithstanding all we have gone thro' I have not at this time one Man touched with the Scurvy, and my Ship's Company I thank God are all as healthy as the day they left England. Fish is to be met with in great plenty in many parts, & excellent Shell fish almost every where, wood & water wherever you come to anchor after you are the length of Fresh Water Bay. Wild Cellery, Scurvy Grass, Berries &c^a you have* | *in the* p. 125 *greatest abundance. It was our misfortune to be passing these Straits just as the Sun approach'd the Equator & consequently in these high Latitudes nothing was to be expected but the weather we met with, & indeed dreadful it was beyond any discription; But I say all these difficulties are to be easily avoided by taking the proper Season.*

Wednesday Ap^l 10th. PM fresh Gales SSE. In the night moderate weather Wind SbE. AM little wind & variable from SSW to W^t with a prodigious great western Swell. Course N° 74 W^t. Dist 108 M^s. Latt in 52°26′ S^o. Long^{de} made 2°54′ W^t. M Dist 105 M^s W^t from Cape Pillar. Cape Pillar S^o 74° E^t. Dist 36 Leag^s. Variation 22° E^t.

Thursday Ap^l 11th. PM fresh gales WNW & Squally. AM Little wind NW^t with a very great Swell from the SW. Course S^o 65° W^t. Dist 48 M^s. Latt in 52°46′ S^o. Long^{de} made 4°6′ W^t. M Dist 148 M^s W^t from Cape Pillar. Cape Pillar S^o 86° E^t. Dist 50 Leag^s.

Friday Ap^l 12th. PM little wind NW. In the night fresh gales NNE & NE wth rain, & a great Western Swell. Course N° 37° W^t. Dist 59 M^s. Latt in 52°14′ S^o. Long^{de} made 5°27′. W^t. M Dist 198 M^s W^t / from Cape Pillar. Variation by an Azimuth 21°20′ E^t. p. 126 Cape Pillar S^o 78°5′ E^t. Dist^{ce} 68 Leag^s.

Saturday Ap^l 13th. Wind from N^o to SSE. moderate & cloudy weather. Course N⁰ 7° Wᵗ. Dist 77 Mˢ. Latt in 50°57' S⁰. Long^de made 5°43' Wᵗ. M Dist 208 Mˢ Wᵗ from Cape Pillar. Variation 21° Eᵗ. Cape Pillar S⁰ 60°38' Eᵗ dist^ce 81 Leag^s.

Sunday Ap¹ 14ᵗʰ. Wind from SSW to Wᵗ moderate & hazey weather. Course N⁰. Dist 122 Mˢ. Latt in 48°55' S⁰. Lond^de made 5°43' Wᵗ. M Dist 208 Mˢ Wᵗ from Cape Pillar. Variation by Azimuth 19° Eᵗ. Cape Pillar S⁰ 41 54 Eᵗ. Dist 108 Leag^s.

Monday Ap¹ 15 PM Little wind SW & a great Western Swell. At 2 AM shifted to SSE & at 4 to the SE fresh gales and cloudy. Course N⁰ 4° Wᵗ. Dist 86 Mˢ. Latt in 47°30' S⁰. Long^de made 5°52' Wᵗ. M Dist 214 Mˢ from Cape Pillar. Variation by Azimuth 17°52' Eᵗ. Cape Pillar S⁰ 34°36' Eᵗ. Dist 132 Leag^s. Juan Fernandez N⁰ 5°18' Eᵗ. Dist 278 Leag^s.

Tuesday Ap¹. 16ᵗʰ. PM a fresh gale SE & Cloudy AM Moderate & hazey. Wind from SSE to Eᵗ. Course N⁰. Dist 109 Mˢ. Latt in 45°41' S⁰. Long^de made 5°52'. M Dist 214 Mˢ W from Cape Pillar. D⁰ S⁰ 27°45' Eᵗ Dist 164 Leag^s. Juan Fernandez N⁰ 6°11' Eᵗ. 242 Leag^s.

Wednesday Ap¹ 17. PM Wind Eᵗ & ENE moderate & cloudy
p. 127 weather, D⁰ at 10 / fresh gales & hazey. At Noon hard Gales NEbE & Rain with a great head Sea. Course N⁰ 3° Wᵗ. Dist 137 Mˢ. Latt in 43°25' S⁰. Long^de made 6°1' Wᵗ. M Dist 221 Mˢ from Cape Pillar. Variation 16° Eᵗ. Cape Pillar S⁰ 22°46' Eᵗ. Dist 206 Leag^s. Juan Fernandez N⁰ 8°25' Eᵗ. Dis 197 Leag^s.

Thursday Ap¹ 18ᵗʰ. PM Strong gales ENE & rain with a very great head Sea. Our Ship drove several times forecastle under, so that it put us by our Topsails. Course N⁰ 7° Wᵗ. Dist 65 Mˢ. Latt in 42°21' S⁰. Long^de made 6°11' Wᵗ. M Dist 229 Mˢ Wᵗ from Cape Pillar. Variation 15° Eᵗ. Cape Pillar S⁰ 21°24' Eᵗ. Dist 227 Leag^s Juan Fernandez N⁰ 10°20' Eᵗ. 176 Leag^s.

Friday Ap¹ 19ᵗʰ. Wind from SW to WbN moderate & hazey weather. Course N⁰. Dist 94 Mˢ. Latt in 40°47' S⁰. Long^de made 6°11' Wᵗ. M Dist 229 Mˢ Wᵗ from Cape Pillar. Variation by Azimuth 12°40' Eᵗ. Cape Pillar S⁰ 19°4' Eᵗ. Dist 257 Leag^s. Juan Fernandez N⁰ 12°42' Eᵗ 146 Leag^s.

Saturday Ap¹ 20ᵗʰ. Wind from Wᵗ to SbW fine weather. Course N⁰. Dist 79 Mˢ. Latt in 39°28' S⁰. Long^de made 6°11' Wᵗ. M Dist 229 Mˢ W from Cape Pillar. Variation by Amplitude 12°30' Eᵗ.

Cape Pillar S⁰ 17°30′ E^t. Dist 283 Leag^s. Juan Fernandez N⁰ 15°35′ E^t 120 Leag^s.

Sunday Ap^l 21st. Wind SSE moderate / & cloudy weather with a *p. 128* great Swell from the S⁰ward. Course N⁰ 10 E^t. Dist 112 M^s. Lat in 37°38′ S⁰. Long^{de} made 5°47′ W^t. M Dist 210 M^s W^t from Cape Pillar. Variation 11°12′ E^t. Cape Pillar S⁰ 14°46′ E^t Dist 316 Leag^s.—Juan Fernandez N⁰ 16°32′ E^t 83 Leag^s.

Monday Ap^l 22^d. PM wind SSE moderate & cloudy weather. AM Little wind variable between the N⁰ & W^t & sometimes calm. By observation find the Ship 12 M^s to the N⁰ward of Account. Course N⁰ 10° E^t. Dist 69 M^s. Lat in 36°30′ S⁰. Long^{de} made 5°33′ W^t. M Dist 199 M^s W^t from Cape Pillar. Variation 11° E^t. Cape Pillar S⁰ 13°22′ E^t. Dist 338 Leag^s. Juan Fernandez N⁰ 17°29′ E^t. Dist 60 Leag^s. Masafuera N⁰ 5°38′ W^t. Dist 57 Leag^s.

Tuesday Ap^l 23^d. PM. Little wind N⁰ly & Cloudy weather. AM Wind NE fresh gales & squally, Course N⁰ 36° W^t. Dist 52 M^s. Latt in 35°48′ S⁰. Long^{de} made 6°11′ W^t. M Dist 230 M^s W from Cape Pillar, Variation by Azimuth 10° E^t. Cape Pillar S⁰ 14°19′ E^t. Dist 353 Leag^s. Juan Fernandez N⁰ 34°12′ E^t. Dist 51 Leag^s.— Masafuera N⁰ 7°18′ E^t 43 Leag^s.

Wednesday Ap^l 24th. Wind N⁰erly strong gales & a great head Sea. Course N⁰ 74° W^t. Dist 41 M^s. Latt in 35°37′ S⁰ Long^{de} made 6°58′ W^t. M Dist 269 M^s. Variation 9°30′ E^t. Cape Pillar S⁰ 15° / 43′ E^t. Dist 360 Leag^s. Juan Fernandez N⁰ 46°36′ E^t. 57 *p. 129* Leag^s. Masafuera N⁰ 27°2′ E^t. 44 Leag^s.—Thursday Ap^l 25th. Wind from NNE to ENE fresh gales & cloudy with a great Northern Swell. Course N⁰ 54° W Dist 40 M^s. Latt in 35°13′ S⁰ Long^{de} made 7°37′ W^t. M Dist 301 M^s W^t. Variation by medium 3 Azimuths 9°46′ E^t. Cape Pillar S⁰ 16°59′ E^t. Dist 370 Leag^s. Juan Fernandez N⁰ 59°30′ E^t. Dist 61 Leag^s.—Masafuera N⁰ 44°45′ E^t. 45 Leag^s.—

Friday Ap^l 26th. At Noon we saw the Island of Masafuera bearing WNW½W Dist 16 Leag^s. But being hazey to the N⁰ward could not see Juan Fernandez Course N⁰ 20° E^t. Dist 73 M^s. Latt in 34°5′ S⁰. Long^{de} made 7°6′ W^t. M Dist 275 M^s W^t from Cape Pillar. Variation by Azimuth 9°46′ E^t. Cape Pillar S⁰ 15 5 E^t Dist 390 Leag^s.

Saturday Ap^l 27th Wind SE & ESE moderate & fair weather. At ½ past Noon bore away for the Island of Masafuera, At Sun Sett it bore WNW Dist 7 or 8 Leag^s. At 7 PM brought too & afterwards kept the wind all night. At day light bore away for the Island.[1] I sent a Boat with an Officer from each Ship to sound all the E^t side of the Island. At Noon the middle of the Island bore W^t 3 Miles. Latt observed 33°49′ S°. /

p. 130 Sunday Ap^l 28th. Moderate & Cloudy weather. Wind SEbS. seeing the Boats run along shore & that they could land no where for the great Surf, I run down to the N° part of the Island & brought too for them. I observed a Reef running off this End of the Island for about 2 M^s & a most terrible Sea broke upon it. This Island is very high & mostly cover'd with wood, the only clear Spots I saw upon it were towards the N° End. They appeared very green & pleasant & there were hundreds of Goats feeding there. When the Boats returned the Officer informed me he had found *a Bank where we might anchor a good distance from the Shore nearest the S° Point & opposite to a fall of Water*, but could find no anchoring near the N°ermost Point. They brought off a great quantity of very fine Fish which they had taken with hook & line near the shore.[2] We made Sail & worked to Windward in the night, and at 7 AM anchored with the small Bower in 24 f^m black sandy Ground on the East side the Island, The Extream Points bearing from S° to NW & the fall of water SSW & near a Mile from the Shore. The Soundings are very regular from 24 to 15 f^m within two Cables length of the Shore. This part of the Island lies N° & S° & is about 4 Miles in Length. *I sent the Boats to attempt if possible to get* /

p. 131 *Wood & Water, but the Surf breaking with great violence upon a Rocky Shore, I was afraid they would find it a very difficult matter; accordingly I ordered them all to put on Cork Jackets which were sent with us on purpose to be made use of on such occasions, and we found them of great Service, for these not only assisted them in Swimming ashore, but prevented their being knocked to pieces upon the Rocks.*

Monday Ap^l 29th. Fresh gales S°erly & hazey weather. A very great Surf breaks on the Shore notwithstanding, by the help of our

[1] Called at Masafuera because 'it being rather more secure than the latter [Juan Fernandez], from any discoveries which the Spaniards might make of our designs; in consequence of which our voyage, and all our farther discoveries, might have been prevented' (1767 Officer *Account*, 109).
[2] Rock cod, coal fish, cavallies, and turbot (Mouat, 130).

Cork Jackets we contrived to get off a good deal of water & wood, but what makes this work still more dangerous here is the number of *large Sharks* that come into the very Surf when they see a Man in the water. One of an immense size being upward *of 20 feet long* came close to the Boat that was watering, & got hold of a large Seal which he made but one mouthful of. I saw another of about that size do the same thing a stern of our Ship. Our People killed some Goats & sent them off, they were as good as any Venison. / One of *p. 132* them was marked by having it's Ear slit. As to Fish they are in such plenty that one boat going in Shore for a few hours with hooks & Lines will get sufficient to serve a large Ship's Company for two days. There are great variety & all excellent in their kind, many of them weigh between 20 & 30 Pounds.

Tuesday Ap¹ 30ᵗʰ. PM fresh gales SbE & hazey weather; the boats all employed watering. The watering Place which we find most convenient on account of the Surf which is much higher than it was yesterday, is about a mile & a half to the Nºward of the Ship, & about midway between the Nº & Sº points of the Island; found a Tide setting 12 hours to the Nºward, 12 to the Sºward which proved very convenient to us, for otherwise as the wind was Sºerly blowing fresh & a great Swell, the Boats could not have got on board with the water. We got off 10 Tun this day.[1] The Gunner & one of our Seamen were left on Shore last night at the first watering place, I sent a Boat for them this afternoon but the Surf was so great, the Seaman who could not swim was afraid to venture. I sent another boat to inform them that as it looked likely to blow I was afraid I might be drove off the Bank in the night, the consequence of which would / be their being left behind upon that *p. 133* Island. The Gunner swam thro' the Surf & got safe to the boat, but as to the Seaman he declared he chose to die a Natural death, for he said he was sure he should be drowned if he attempted to get off to the Boat tho' he had a Cork Jacket on. He took a very affectionate leave of the People & said he wished us all happiness, but that he was resolved to remain upon the Island. Upon which one of our midshipman jumped out of the Boat & swam thro' the Surf, carrying an end of a Rope with him, & whilst he was expostualating with the fellow who suspected nothing, he threw the

---

[1] 7 or 8 tuns for the *Tamar* (Mouat, 130).

end of the Rope about him, and called to them in the boat to haul away, they having the other end of the rope in their hands. He was presently draged thro' the Surf into the Boat, but when they got him in he was both speechless & motionless, for he had swallowed such a quantity of Water that he was to all appearance dead; they held him up by the heels till he came to himself & he was perfectly well next day. *I here removed Capt Mouat from the Tamar appointing him Captain of the Dolphin under me; My first Lieu^t Mr Cumming I* p. 134 *appointed Captain | of the Tamar, & her first Lieu^t Mr Carteret I took on board in his room, & gave Mr Kendal one of the Mates of the Dolphin a Commission for Second Lieu^t of the Tamar.*[1] AM fresh gales & squally SSE At 7 made the Signal & weighed. Steered to the N^{o}ward along the E^t & NE side of the Island but could find no anchoring place. Bore away & at Noon the middle of the Island bore SSE dist^{ce} 8 Leagues.

Wednesday May 1st. Fresh gales SE & hazey weather. Course N° 3° W^t. Dist 178 M^s. Lat in 30°52' S^o. Long^{de} made 0°11' W^t. M Dist 9 M^s from Masa fuera. Variation 9°30' E^t. Masa fuera S^o 3° E^t. Dist 39 Leag^s.

Thursday May 2^d. Wind SE fresh gales & Cloudy Course N° 2° W^t. Dist 187 M^s. Lat in 27°45' S^o. Long^{de} made 0°19' W^t. M Dist 15 M^s W^t. Variation 9° E^t. Masa fuera S^o 2°21' E^t Dist 121 Leag^s.

Friday May 3^d. Wind from SSE to ESE I yesterday at noon alter'd my Course Steering W^t, intending if possible to make the Land called Davis's in the Charts, which is laid down in the Latt of 27°30' S^o about 500 Leag^s West from Copiapo in Chili.[2] Course N° 80 W^t. Dist 168 M^s. Lat in 27°16' S^o. Long^{de} made 3°23' W. M Dist 180 M^s W^t. Variation by Azimuth 9°50' E^t. Long^{de} in 88°22' W^t. Masa fuera S^o 23°55' E^t. Dist 144 Leag^s.

---

[1] Byron received 'Rear Admiral's pay and Table Money for the time he had a Captain under him . . . also ten Shillings a day above his wages for the time his broad Pendant was flying on board the Dolphin' (Minutes of the Admiralty Board Meeting, 18 July 1766: PRO Adm 3/74).

The pay of a rear admiral was £1 os. od. per day ('An Establishment of Sea-Wages, and of the Number of Officers allowed to His Majesty's Ships', *Regulations and Instructions*, 142, 153).

[2] John Green, *Charts of North and South America . . . 1753* [(London), 1753; B.M. Maps 16.e.6], Chart VI, 'Land seen by Capt. Davis in 1686'.

Davis's Land is also shown on 'Carte Reduite des Mers Comprises entre l'Asie et l'Amerique . . . 1742 [corrected in 1756]', *L'Hydrographie Françoise* . . . [(Paris), 1756], 6.

The position of Davis's Land was thought to be 12° due east of Easter Island.

Saturday May 4th. Wind from SSE to NE moderate & cloudy weather. Course N° 89° W^t. Dist 95 M^s. Lat in 27°14′ S^o Long^{de} made 5°9′ W^t. M Dist 275 M^s W^t. Long^{de} in / from London 90°8′ *p. 135* W^t. Masa fuera S^o 33°54′ E^t. Dist 159 Leag^s.

Sunday May 5th. The first part little wind variable, the latter a moderate breeze NNW. Course W^t. Dist 66 M^s. Lat in 27°14′ S^o. Long^{de} made 6°21′ W^t. M Dist 341 M^s W^t. Long^{de} in 91°20′ W^t. Variation by Medium 3 Az^{ths} & Amplitude 7°50′ E^t. Masa fuera S^o 39°38′ E^t Dist 171 Leag^s.

Monday May 6th. PM wind NbW moderate & fair weather AM NNW. Fresh Gales & Cloudy with a great Swell from the SW. Course S^o 80 W^t. Dist 125 M^s. Lat in 27°36′ S^o. Long^{de} made 8°39′ W^t. M Dist 464 M^s. Variation by Amp^d 6°44′ E^t. Long^{de} in 93 38 W^t. Masafuera S^o 50°2′ E^t. Dist 194 Leag^s.

Tuesday May 7th. PM Strong Gales at NW & squally with rain AM strong Gales WNW & WbN with a prodigious great Western Swell. Course S^o 70° W^t. dist 49 M^s. Latt in 27°53′ S^o. Long^{de} made 9°31′ W^t. M Dist 510 M^s W^t. Long^{de} in 94°30′ W^t. Masafuera S^o 53°55′ E^t. 202 Leag^s.—Copiapo by the Draught E½S 364 Leag^s.

Wednesday May 8th. Little wind & variable with a vast Swell from the SW. Course N° 12° W^t. Dist 69 M^s. Latt in 26°46′ S^o. Long^{de} made 9°46′ W^t. M Dist 524 M^s W^t. Long^{de} in 94°45′ W^t. Variation p^r Amp^d 5°30′ E^t Masafuera S^o 50°2′ E^t. Dist 220 Leag^s.

Thursday May 9th. PM light airs of wind SW & cloudy. AM calm with a most uncommon great Swell from the SW. Finding there was little prospect of getting to the Westward in the Latitude I first / proposed as the winds then seem to hang from that quarter *p. 136* & we have an immense run to make, I intend if possible to make a NW Course til we get the true Trade wind,[1] and then to shape a Course to the W^tward in hopes of falling in with Solomons Islands if there are such, or else to make some new Discovery. Course N° 22° W^t. Dist 21 M^s. Lat in 26°27′ S^o. Long^{de} made 9°55′ W^t. M Dist 532 M^s W^t. Long^{de} in 94°54′ W^t. Masa fuera S^o 49°17′ E^t. Dist 226 Leagues.

Friday May 10th. PM Calm & a great Swell from the SW. AM

---

[1] The trades should be north of 20° S [M.O. 518, *Monthly Meteorological Charts of the Eastern Pacific Ocean* (London, 1950), 45]. The charts have no information in regard to the swell in the area (pp. 46–7).

little wind ENE & fine weather. Many Dolphins & Bonetas about the Ship. Course N^o. Dist 17 M^s. Latt in 26°10' S^o. Long^{de} made 9°55' W^t. Variation by Amp^{de} 5°0' E^t. Masafuera S^o 48°15' E^t. Dist 231 Leag^s.

Saturday May 11th Moderate & fair weather, wind NNE. We now & then see a straggling Bird, the back & upper part of the wings brown, all the rest of it white with a short beak & a short pointed tail.[1] Course N° 54° W^t. dist 74 M^s. Lat in 25°27' S^o. Long^{de} made 11°0' W^t M Dist 591 M^s W^t. Long^{de} in 95°59' W^t. Variation by Amp^{de} 4°45' E^t. Masa fuera S^o 48°44' E^t. Dist 254 Leag^s.

Sunday May 12th. PM Wind N^o moderate & fair. AM Wind NNE fresh gales & cloudy. Course N° 59° W^t. Dist 112 M^s. Lat by two *p. 137* Altitudes 24°30' S^o. Long^{de} made 12°46' W / M Dist 687 M^s W^t. Long^{de} in 97°45' W^t. Variation 4°45' E^t Masa fuera S^o 50° E Dist 291 Leag^s.

Monday May 13th. PM wind NBE fresh gale & cloudy, at 4 AM NW at 8 NNE D^o W^t. Course N° 61° W^t. Dist 114 M^s. Lat in 23°36' S^o. Long^{de} made 14°34' W^t. M Dist 786 M^s. Long^{de} in 99°33' W^t. Variation 4°45' E^t. Masafuera S^o 51°16' E^t. Dist 327 Leag^s.

Tuesday May 14th. Wind N^{o}erly fresh gale & cloudy weather, a great Swell from the SW. Several Grampusses blowing, & some Birds of the same kind mentioned before. Imagined by this we might be near some Land, kept a good look out, but saw nothing. Course N° 72 W^t. Dist 111 M^s. Latt in 23°2' S^o. Long^{de} made 16°29' W^t. M Dist 892 M^s W^t. Long^{de} in 101°28' W^t. Variation by Azimuth 3°20' E^t. Masafuera S^o 53°16' E^t Dist 361 Leag^s.

Wednesday May 15th. Wind N^{o}erly moderate & cloudy weather. A fine large Turtle passed the Ship this morning; brought the Ship too & hoisted the Boat out, as it would have been very acceptable to us, but the boat could not find him. Course N° 78° W^t. Dist 76 M^s. Lat in 22°46' S^o. Long^{de} made 17°49' W^t. M Dist 966 M^s W^t. Long^{de} in 102°48' W^t. Variation by Azimuth 4°0' E^t. Masa fuera S^o 54°25' E^t. Dist 381 Leagues. /

p. 138 Thursday May 16th. Wind from N^o to NNE. moderate & fair weather. This morning saw two very remarkable Birds, they flew

[1] A brown booby [Ernst Mayr, *Birds of the Southwest Pacific* (New York, 1945), 17].

high, were as large as Geeze, all over white, excepting their legs which were black.[1] *I imagine we have passed some Land or Islands to the S⁰ward of us,[2] for we generally had a prodigious Swell from that quarter, but last night we observed that the water became all at once quite smooth, & a few hours after we had as much Swell as ever.* Course N⁰ 78° Wᵗ. Dist 141 Mˢ. Latt in 22°17′ S⁰. Long^de made 20°17′ Wᵗ. M Dist 1104 Mˢ Wᵗ. Long^de in 105°16′ Wᵗ. Variation 4°0′ Eᵗ. Masa fuera S⁰ 57°7′ Eᵗ. Dist 425 Leagˢ.

Friday May 17th. Wind from NNE to ENE moderate & fair weather; a great S⁰ern Swell. Course N⁰ 75° Wᵗ. Dist 95 Mˢ. Latt in 21°52′ S⁰. Long^de made 21°56′ Wᵗ. M Dist 1196 Mˢ. Long^de in 106°55′ Wᵗ. Variation by Amp^d 4°0′ Eᵗ. Masa fuera S⁰ 58°16′ Eᵗ Dist 455 Leagˢ.

Saturday May 18th. Wind from Eᵗ to ESE moderate & fair. Course N⁰ 74° Wᵗ. Dist 130 Mˢ. Latt in 21°17′ S⁰. Long^de made 24°10′ Wᵗ M Dist 1321 Mˢ Wᵗ. Long^de in 109°9′ Wᵗ. Masafuera S⁰ 59°33′ Eᵗ. Dist 495 Leagˢ.

Sunday May 19th. Wind from ESE to ENE fresh breezes & cloudy weather with some Squalls & rain. Course N⁰ 85 Wᵗ. Dist 154 Mˢ. Latt in 21°4′ S⁰. Long^de made 26°54′ Wᵗ. M Dist 1474 Mˢ Wᵗ. Long^de in 111°53′ Wᵗ. Masafuera S⁰ 61°47′ Eᵗ Dist 540 Leagˢ.

Monday May 20th. Wind from EbN to / EbS moderate & fair p. 139 weather some Tropic Birds & a number of flying Fish about the Ship. Course N⁰ 88° Wᵗ. Dist 118 Mˢ. Lat in 21°0′ S⁰. Long^de made 29°0′ Wᵗ. M Dist 1592 Mˢ Wᵗ. Long^de in 113°59′ Wᵗ. Variation by Az^th 0°52′ Eᵗ. Masa fuera S⁰ 63°26′ Eᵗ. Dist 574 Leagues.

Tuesday May 21st. Wind from Eᵗ to SEbE Course N⁰ 85° Wᵗ. dist 93 Mˢ. Latt in 20°52′ S⁰. Long^de made 30°39′ Wᵗ. M Dist 1684 Mˢ Wᵗ. Long^de in 115°38′ Wᵗ. Variation by Amp^d 0°24′ Wᵗ Masa fuera S⁰ 64°29′ Eᵗ. dist 602 Leagues.

Wednesday 22^d May Wind from ESE to EbN a faint breeze & cloudy with so great a Swell from the S⁰ward that we were in danger of rowling our Masts over the side, so that I was obliged to haul more to the N⁰ward to ease the Ship, & at the same time by

---

[1] Probably terns.
[2] If Byron was where he thought he was, his position was 3°50′ due north of Sola-y-Gomez.

so doing was in hopes of getting the true Trade, which we certainly have not had as yet.[1] *Some of my best Men (to my great sorrow) begin to complain of the Scurvy.* We caught two Bonetas to day, being the first we got for the Voyage. Several Tropic Birds about the Ship, they are much larger than any of the kind I ever saw before, are all white, with two long feathers in their tail.[2] Course N° 75° W^t. Dist 84 M^s. Latt in 20°31′ S^o. Long^{de} made 32°5′ W^t.
M^n Dist 1765 M^s W^t. Long^{de} in 117°4′ W^t. Variation by Amp^d
p. 140 0°19′ W^t. Masa fuera S^o 64°55′ E^t. Dist / 628 Leagues.

Thursday May 23^d Wind NE moderate and cloudy weather. Course N° 55° W^t. Dist 130 M^s. Latt in 19°16′ S^o. Long^{de} made 33°58′ W^t. M Dist 1871 M^s W^t. Long^{de} in 118°57′ W^t. Variation 0°30′ W^t. Masa fuera S^o 64°18′ E^t. Dist 671 Leag^s.

Friday May 24th. Wind ENE Moderate & fair weather. Course N° 66° W^t. Dist 131 M^s. Latt in 18°23′ S^o. Long^{de} made 36°4′ W^t. M Dist 1991 M^s W^t. Long^{de} in 121°3′ W^t. Variation 0°36′ W^t. Masa fuera S^o 64°24′ E^t. dist 715 Leagues.

Saturday May 25th. PM Wind ENE. moderate & fair AM EbS fresh breeze & cloudy. Course N° 76° W^t. Dist 140 M^s. Latt in 17°48′ S^o. Long^{de} made 38°27′ W^t. M Dist 2127 M^s W^t. Long^{de} in 123°26′ W^t. Variation 0°30′ W^t. Masa fuera S^o 64°59′ E^t. Dist 761 Leagues.

Sunday May 26th. Wind from E^t to NE fresh gales & squally with rain. Two large Birds about the Ship, all black but the Neck & beak, which were white, very long wings & long feathers in their tails & flew very heavy, wch makes me imagine they are Birds that dont fly far from the Shore.[3] Course N° 78$\frac{1}{4}$° W^t. Dist 164 M^s. Latt in 17°14′ S^o. Long^{de} made 41°14′ W^t. M Dist 2287 M^s. Long^{de} in 126°13′ W^t. Variation by Azimuth 0°20′ E^t. Masafuera S^o 65°57′ E^t. Dist 812 Leagues. /

p. 141 Monday May 27th. PM Wind NbE fresh gale & cloudy. In the night wind variable from N^o to NEbE. AM little wind NbW & cloudy weather. I had flatter'd myself that before we had run 6

---

[1] This course change was disastrous. Byron's previous course would have taken him through the centre of the Tuamotu Archipelago (see Introduction, pp. lvii–lx and Fig. A).

[2] Obviously terns. 'Terns are easily recognized by their slender, graceful shape, by their long tapering wings and long tails (usually forked), and by their jerky non-soaring flight' (Mayr, 21).

[3] Possibly frigate-birds or man-o'-war birds (Ibid., 19–20).

Degrees to the N⁰ward of Masa fuera we should have found a settled Trade at SE. but we have generally had the winds from the N⁰ern Quarter,[1] tho' at the same time we have always had a mountainous Swell from the SW. Course N⁰ 79° Wᵗ. Dist 99 Mˢ. Latt in 16°55′ S⁰. Long⁽ᵈᵉ⁾ made 42°56′ Wᵗ. M Distance 2385 Mˢ Wᵗ. Long⁽ᵈᵉ⁾ in 127°55′ Wᵗ. Variation 0°00′. Masa fuera S⁰ 66°20′ Eᵗ. Dist 843 Leagues.

Tuesday May 28th. PM light airs of wind variable & cloudy weather with a great Swell from the S⁰ward. In the night calm. AM Little wind at Eᵗ & EbS. Two fine large Birds about the Ship, one of them brown & white, the other black & white, they wanted much to settle upon the Yards. Course N⁰ 71 Wᵗ. Dist 43 Mˢ. Latt in 16°41′ S⁰. Long⁽ᵈᵉ⁾ made 43°38′ Wᵗ. M Dist 2425 Mˢ Wᵗ. Long⁽ᵈᵉ⁾ in 128°37′ Wᵗ. Variation 0 30′ Wᵗ. Masa fuera S⁰ 66°24′ Eᵗ. Dist 857 Leagues.

Wednesday May 29ᵗʰ. Wind from Eᵗ to ENE moderate & fair weather. Course N⁰ 74° Wᵗ. Dist 110 Mˢ. Latt in 16°11′ S⁰. Long⁽ᵈᵉ⁾ made 45°28′ Wᵗ. M Dist 2530 Mˢ Wᵗ. Long⁽ᵈᵉ⁾ in 130°27′ Wᵗ. Variation 0 30′ Wᵗ. Masa fuera S⁰ 66°42′ Eᵗ Dist 892 Leagues. /

Thursday May 30ᵗʰ. Wind ENE a fresh breeze & cloudy weather. *p. 142* Course N⁰ 76° Wᵗ. Dist 135 Mˢ. Latt in 15°38′ S⁰. Long⁽ᵈᵉ⁾ made 47°44′ Wᵗ. M Dist 2661 Mˢ Wᵗ. Long⁽ᵈᵉ⁾ in 132°43′ Wᵗ. Variation 0°00′. Masa fuera S⁰ 67°7′ Eᵗ. Dist 936 Leagues.

Friday May 31ˢᵗ. Wind from NbW to NWbW for the most part fresh Gales. A great number of Birds about the Ship, by seeing of which, & the wind shifting to the Wᵗward & having lost the great SW Swell, I imagine we must be near some Land; we keep hands constantly looking out for it, and it would be a most agreable sight to us now, *as my People fall down daily in the Scurvy. The heat is excessive.* Course N⁰ 88° Wᵗ. Dist 73 Mˢ. Latt in 15°33′ S⁰. Long⁽ᵈᵉ⁾ made 49°0′ Wᵗ. M Dist 2734 Mˢ Wᵗ. Long⁽ᵈᵉ⁾ in 133°59′ Wᵗ. Masa fuera S⁰ 67°34′ Eᵗ. Dist⁽ᶜᵉ⁾ 958 Leag⁽ˢ⁾.

Saturday June 1ˢᵗ. PM Wind NW & WNW moderate & cloudy weather. In the night Wᵗ fresh gales & squally with rain. AM WSW & WbS moderate & cloudy. In the first watch last night I tacked & stood to the N⁰ward. Course N⁰ 62°Wᵗ. Dist 45 Mˢ. Latt in 15°12′ S⁰. Long⁽ᵈᵉ⁾ made 49°42′ Wᵗ. M Dist 2774 Mˢ Wᵗ. Long⁽ᵈᵉ⁾ in

[1] Byron's assumption was correct (*Monthly Meteorological Charts*, 45).

134°41′ W^t. Variation 0 40′ E^t. Masa fuera S^o 67°29′ E^t. Dist 973 Leagues.

Sunday June 2^d. Wind from WSW to SWbS moderate & cloudy
p. 143 weather AM a Swell from the S^{o}ward. Course / N° 47° W^t. Dist 82 M^s. Latt in 14°15′ S^o. Long^{de} made 50°43′ W^t. M Dist 2833 M^s W^t. Long^{de} in 135°42′ W^t. Variation 1°0′ E^t. Masa fuera S^o 66°57′ E^t. Dist 1000 Leagues.

Monday June 3^d. Wind variable from SWbW to E^t with a great Swell from the S^{o}ward. Course N° 78° W^t. Dist 94 M^s. Latt in 13°56′ S^o. Long^{de} made 52°19′ W^t. M Dist 2926 M^s W^t. Long^{de} in 137°18′ W^t. Variation 1°0′ E^t. Masa fuera S^o 67°16′ E^t. Dist 1030 Leag^s.

Tuesday June 4th. Wind from ESE to EbN Little wind & cloudy weather. Course N° 85 W^t. Dis 96 M^s. Latt in 13°48′ S^o. Long^{de} made 53°57′ W^t. M Dist 3017 M^s W^t. Long^{de} in 138°56′ W^t. Variation 2°0′ E^t Masa fuera S^o 67°46′ E^t. Dist 1059 Leag^s.

Wednesday June 5th. Wind E^t & EbS fresh gales & cloudy weather. A great number of Birds about the Ship, & no Swell, makes us imagine we are near some Land. *The weather extreamly hot. The Thermometer having stood for some time past at 80° & 81°. My People fall down daily in the Scurvy, & several of my best Men already so bad in it, that they are confined to their Hammocks.*[1] Course S^o 89 W^t. Dist 161 M^s. Latt in 13°50′ S^o. Long^{de} made 56°43′ W^t. M Dist 3178 M^s W^t. Long^{de} in 141°42′ W^t. Variation 4°0′ E^t Masa fuera S^o 68°47′ E^t. Distance 1106 Leagues. /

p. 144 Thursday June 6th. Wind EbN moderate & Cloudy. A great number of Birds about the Ship. Course S^o 83° W^t. Dist 129 M^s. Latt in 14°5′ S^o. Long^{de} made 58°55′ W^t. M Dist 3306 M^s W^t. Long^{de} in 143°54′ W^t. Variation 4°0′ E^t. Masa Fuera S^o 69°44′ E^t. Dist 1141 Leagues.

Friday June 7th. Course made (to the time *we made the Land* which was at 1 AM) W^t. dist 62 M^s. Latt in 14°5′ S^o. Long^{de} made 59°59′ W^t. M Dist 3368 M^s W^t. Long^{de} in from London 144°58′ W^t. Variation 4°30′ E^t. Masa fuera S^o 70°4′ E^t. Distance 1159 Leagues.

---

[1] The sick on board numbered about 30 men according to the 1767 Officer *Account*, 126. '. . . our people a few of which were down with the Scurvy' (Mouat, 133).

After making the Land I hauld upon a wind under an easy Sail til morning, & then saw it was a low small Island bearing WSW about 2 Leag^s from us; presently after we saw another Island to Windward of us bearing ESE distance 3 or 4 Leag^s.[1] This appeared to be much larger than the first we saw, and we must have passed very near it in the night. I stood for the small Island which appeared very beautiful as we drew near it, having a fine white Sandy Beach all round it, and the Inner part cover'd with tall shady Trees, which looked vastly green & pleasant & no underwood. This Island may be about 4 or 5 Miles round, off each end of it there runs a Spit on which the / Sea breakes with great fury, & all round it *p. 145* there runs a great Surf. We soon saw it was Inhabited, for the Savages shewed themselves upon the Beach with great long Spears of 15 or 16 feet in their hands. They made several large Fires which was immediately answer'd by those on the large Island to Windward. I sent a Boat with an Officer from each Ship to Sound all round the Island for an anchoring Place, but some time after they returned with an account that there was no Soundings within less than a Cable's length of the Shore, & that close to the Sandy Beach the whole Island was surrounded with a steep Coral Rock. This news was great grief to us, for had I found a place to anchor the Ships, I intended to have landed my Sick here, & have remained till they recover'd, as this little beautiful Spot seemed to promise all the Refreshments necessary for Scorbutick People. We saw abundance of Cocoa Trees, & I make no doubt but there are Limes, Bananas &c^a common to most places between the Tropics. Our People saw the Shells / of many Turtles upon the Beach. As to the *p. 146* Inhabitants they are of a deep Copper Colour, strong, stout

[1] The first island was Tepoto (Otooho); the second, Napuka (Wytoohee), about 12 miles to the south-east—the two atolls making up the Disappointment Group which was discovered and named by Byron. Tepoto and Napuka are the northernmost islands of the Tuamotu Archipelago, which consists of 78 islands, all atolls with the exception of Makatea and Tikea.

Tepoto is from 13 to 16 ft in height and of coral origin. It is still covered with coconut trees, which reach a height of about 60 ft above the sea; and there is still no anchorage around the island, although local craft can find poorly sheltered anchorage about 30 yd from the reef off the western side of the island by mooring stern to shore. Fish and turtle form the principal food of the some 50 natives now living on Tepoto, and they drink only the milk of the coconut since the two wells on the island give only brackish water. [*Sailing Directions for the Pacific Islands*, III, 'Eastern Groups', H.O. Pub. 80 (Washington, D.C., 1952, corr. to 1961), 87, 99–100.]

M

limbed Men, go quite naked,[1] & are very active & nimble, for I never saw fellows run faster. When I knew the Soundings I stood close round the Island with my Ship, & these Savages followed us hollowing and dancing, & every now & then brandishing their long Spears at us, & then of a sudden falling down upon their backs as if they were dead. I suppose to let us know what we had to expect if we offer'd to Land. They had fixed two Spears upright in the Sand & hung about them a number of trash, to which every moment they kneel'd down, praying them I suppose to deliver them from these Strangers. When our Boats went near in Shore to Sound, they set up a hideous Noise, pointed their Spears at them & some took up large Stones in their hands. Our Men made all the Signs of friendship to them they were able; they threw them Bread & other Things, but they would touch nothing they gave them. They *p. 147* wanted much to get / hold of the Boat & haul her on Shore that they might murder the Crew. Our People would have gladly saluted them with a few Balls, but as they had no Orders from me they desisted. However if it had been possible for us to have come to an Anchor, It would have been a most convenient place for us, for if we could not have made these Savages our friends, we should presently have drove them off, & as the Island was so small, I could easily have guarded every part of it, so that I should have been under no apprehension of being molested from the Savages of the Great Island. We saw 5 or 6 large Canoes, which they haul'd up to the side of the Wood upon our Peoples approaching the Shore. This Island is in the Latt^{de} of 14°5′ S^o & Long^{de} from the Meridian of London 145°4′ W^t; Finding it impossible to anchor here I intend to work up to the Easter-most Island, which as I mention'd before appears much larger than this./

p. 148 *Saturday June 8th.* PM Wind ESE moderate & hazey weather. At 4 the Westermost Island bore SbW½W 4. or 5 Leag^s. In the night fresh gales & squally with hard rain. At 6 AM brought too on the West Side of the E^{t}ermost Island about ¾ of a Mile from the Shore

---

[1] 'These Indians were of a very black complexion, with well proportioned limbs, and appeared to be extremely active and full of vigour. Their women, who were only to be distinguished by their bosoms, had something twisted round their waist, and hanging down from thence to hide what nature taught them to conceal; as had also the men, and this was their only cloathing' (1767 Officer *Account*, 125).

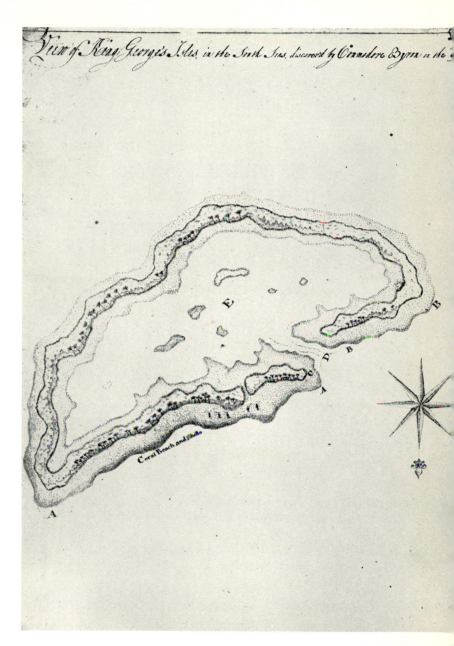

View of King George's Isles, in the South Seas, discovered by Commodore Byron in the

Coral Beach and Shoals

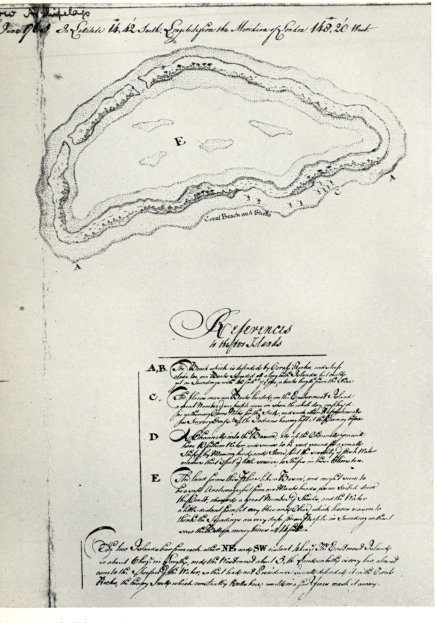

ing George's Isles

& had no Soundings with 140 f^m of Line.[1] These are several low Islands & full of Wood, appear vastly pleasant. Most of them are joined with a low neck of Land very narrow & almost level with the surface of the Water, which breaks high over it. The Coco Nut Trees are the first thing seen at making these Islands as they are by much the highest. I sent a Boat with an Officer from each Ship to sound along the Lee side of these Islands for an anchoring place. The Savages came down in great numbers, armed with long Spears, Clubs &c^a to oppose our Peoples Landing, and seemed to threaten much, following our Boats wherever they went. I sent a 9 Pound-Shot from the Ship over their heads which spoiled their diversion & made them scamper away into the Woods. / At 10 the *p. 149* Boats returned, could get no Soundings close in with the Surf, which broke very high upon the Shore. The middle of these Islands is in the Lat. of 14°10′ S^o & Long^{de} 144°52′ W^t from London and the Compass has 4°30′ Variation. At $\frac{1}{2}$ past 10. *Bore away & made Sail to the W^t ward greatly grieved I could procure no Refreshments for our Sick here, who are now most of them in a very desponding way.* At Noon the W^{t}ermost of these Islands (which I named the Islands of Disappointment) bore NEbE Dist 5 Leag^s. We had the wind at E^t a very fresh gale, squally & hard Rain.

Sunday June 9th. Wind E^t & EbS fresh Breezes & hazey weather. Course S^o 87° W^t. Dist 153 M^s. Latt in 14°12′ S^o Long^{de} made 2°37′ W^t. M^n Dist M^s 152 W^t from the Islands of Disappointment, Long^{de} in from London 147°42′ W^t. Variation 4°45′ E^t.—Islands of Disappointment N° 87°o′ E^t. Dist 51 Leagues.

Monday June 10th. PM Fresh Breezes & hazey weather; at $\frac{1}{2}$ past 5 *Saw / Land* bearing WSW Dist 6 or 7 Leag^s. At 7 bro^t too & lay by *p. 150* all night. Little wind E^t & ENE. At 6 AM the Extreams of the Land bore from SWS^o ward to SSE distance off Shore 3 M^s.— This is a long low Island with a white Beach & surrounded with a red Coral Rock, & appears extremely pleasant full of Coco Nut

---

[1] Napuka, the south-eastern atoll of the Disappointment Group, encloses a lagoon inaccessible from the sea. Today the eastern and western sides of the island are wooded but the southern is nearly bare. Landing is possible about one-half of a mile from the western point of the atoll, either on the north or the south side of the point. However, if there is any swell, only the native canoes can land. The huts of the 300 natives living on Napuka are completely hidden by the trees, although their canoes may be seen on the shore [H.O. Pub. 80 (1961), 99–100].

97

Trees &c. Much like the Islands of Disappointment.[1] We stood along the NE side of it, & within ½ a Mile of the Shore. The Savages no sooner saw us but they made great smokes to alarm their Neighbours & followed us in great Numbers armed as those mentioned before. This side of the Island is very narrow, over which we could see a great Salt water Lake which is between 2 & 3 Leag[s] wide to the opposite shore. *It has a small Inlet into it about a League from the SW Point*,[2] we bro[t] too off it's Entrance, & here the Savages have a little Town under the shade of a fine Grove of Coco Nut Trees. I sent the Boats away with an Officer in each to Sound, but they could find no ground. The Shore all along being

p. 151 quite steep to, *excepting the very mouth of the Inlet which | is hardly a Ship's length wide, & then they had 13 f[m] Coral Rock bottom.* We stood close in with the Ships & saw hundreds of the Savages draw up in pretty good order, standing up to their middles in the water all armed in their way, making a terrible noise. One of them carried a piece of Matt upon a Pole by the way of Colours. A great many large Canoes by this time came down the Lake to join them. Our Men in the Boats made all the signs of friendship to them that was possible, upon which some of the Canoes drew near them; but it was only with a design of hauling our boats ashore amongst them if they could. Many of them plung'd off the Rocks into the Water & swam to our Boats, & one of them got into the Tamar's boat, & in a moment's time a Seaman's Jacket & jumped overboard with it, & never appear'd above water again till he was close in Shore amongst his Companions. Another got hold of a Midshipman's hat, but not knowing how to take it off, he pull'd down, instead of lifting it off

p. 152 his head, or else it would have disappeared as / the Jacket did. Our Men bore all this wth a great deal of patience. At Noon finding there

---

[1] Takaroa, one of the two atolls of the King George's Group (14°30′ S, 143° 00′ W), the other being Takapoto, 4½ miles south-west of Takaroa. Like Tepoto and Napuka, Takaroa encompasses a lagoon; but the Takaroa lagoon has an entrance on the south-western side, the Tehavaroa Pass (Ibid, 108–9).

[2] Tehavaroa Pass, on the south-western side of the island, is the only entrance to the lagoon. It is about one mile long, runs east and west in a fairly straight fashion, and is about 80 yards wide at the seaward end. At the lagoon end it is much narrower, with a sharp bend to the northward limiting the size of vessels entering the lagoon to those of about 60 ft. in length. The *Dolphin's* keel was 93′ 4″. Submerged reefs fringe both sides of the pass, except for a short distance along the northern side where the southern shore of an island and a modern quay mark the northern edge (Ibid.).

was no anchoring here, I bore away & steered along shore to the W^{t}ermost Point. The Boats immediately followed us & kept Sounding close in Shore, but could get no Ground. From the W^{t}ermost Point we saw another Island, bearing SWbW about 4 Leag^s distance.[1] I was now above a League from the Inlet where we left the Savages, but it seems they were not satisfied with what they had done already, for I presently perceived two large Canoes coming after us with about 30 Men in each all Armed. Our Boats were now a good way to Leeward of us. The Canoes passed between our Ships & the Shore & appeared to be very eager in chacing our boats. Upon which I made the Signal for our Boats to speak with the Canoes. As soon as our people perceived the Signal they both gave chace to the Canoes. The Savages finding how the tables were turned, presently haul'd their Sails down, & paddled back again at a surprizing rate, however our Boats came up with them, & notwithstanding there run a prodigious Surf upon the Shore, the Canoes pushed thro' it, & the Savages presently haul'd them / up $p.$ 153 on the Beach. Our Boats followed them close in when the Savages began the attack with Clubs & Stones, & wounded two of our People; Upon which our Men fired & killed 5 or 6 of them.[2] One of them that had three Balls through him took up a large Stone to heave at one of our Men just before he died—Those that remained unhurt amongst them carried off all their dead (excepting this last who remained too close to our Boats for them to attempt it) & made the best of their way back again to their Companions at the Inlet. Our People bro^t off two of the Canoes which were very curious; and shews these people to be extremely Ingenious. One of them was 32 feet long, the other was something less, but they were made fast together at the distance of 6 or 8 feet by stout Spars, for separately they are of no use, as their bottoms is like a wedge; they have each a Mast but one Sail serves them both. The Sail I have kept & is as neat apiece of work as ever I saw, made of Matting. Several Men sit upon the Spars between both Canoes. Their

---

[1] Takapoto, the south-western of the King George's Group, is a well wooded atoll, with a lagoon inaccessible from the sea. Boats, however, can land today at Fakatopatere about $\frac{1}{4}$ mile northwestward of the southern point, and landing can also be effected about 2 or 3 miles farther northward. In fine weather, even schooners occasionally make fast to the reef at the latter place (Ibid.).

[2] Mouat, 133, said only two natives were killed.

p. 154 Paddles are very curious. There must be an / infinite deal of labour in making one of these Canoes; the Plank is extremely well worked & carved in many places. It is sewed together, & over every Seam is a strip of Tortoise Shell to keep the water out. Their Cordage is as good & well laid as any I ever saw tho' made of the rind of Coco Nutt. Finding it was impossible to procure any Re-freshments for the Sick at this part of the Island, as the Surf broke so high upon it, I resolved to work back again to the Inlet & try again what might be done there.

Tuesday June 11th. Hauled the wind & worked up to the Inlet again. In the Evening I saw a great Number of the Savages upon the Point near the Spot we had left them in the morning, they seemed to be very busy in loading a number of large Canoes that lay upon the Point, I fired a Shot over their heads & they all disappeared in a moment. I sent the Boats to sound again the mouth of the Inlet, but they found it impossible for a Ship to anchor there. Our People landed just before night & bro^t off a few Coco Nuts, but saw none of the Inhabitants. In the night I stood off & on with the

p. 155 Ships, & had dirty, squally, rainy weather. At 7 AM I / brought too off the Inlet, & sent the Boats ashore to look for Refreshments, & made all those that were not as yet very bad in the Scurvy, go with them. I went myself & staid ashore the whole day. We found the Savages Houses quite deserted, excepting by their Dogs which kept a dreadful howling all day long. They had left a great many fine large new Canoes behind them. Their Houses are but mean & low, thatchd with Coco Nut Branches, however they left a thousand marks of their Ingenuity behind them. The Spot they chose for their Habitations was delightfully situated under a fine Grove of stately Trees, many of them we were quite unacquainted with, but I have observed they always chuse to fix where there is the greatest plenty of Coco Trees, as that is food, sails, Cordage, Timber, & in short almost every thing to them. The women make themselves a bit of Cloth which hangs from the waist as low as the Knee from the same Tree. The Shore was cover'd with Coral & the Shells of large Pearl Oysters, & I make no doubt but there might be carried on here as fine a Pearl Fishery as any in the World. In rummaging

p. 156 the Hutts our People / found the carved Head of a Dutch Long boats Rudder, it is very old & worm eaten; we likewise found a piece of hammer'd Iron & a piece of Brass all which I brot away, together with some small Iron Tools used by the Savages, which I suppose their Ancestors got by cutting off one of those Dutch Ships,[1] who attempted to make Discoveries this way many Years ago, & who were never afterwards heard of; they make use of a Tool exactly like a Carpenters Adze made out of a Pearl Oyster Shell, which is I suppose in imitation of those they saw on board that Ship, & which in all probability are now worn out, for those I brought away I take to be the remains of a Carpenter's Adze, which by time they have worn away almost to nothing. They seem to have great veneration for their dead; their Burying Place being close to their Houses under large shady Trees, they are very decent, their Sides & Tops being made of Stone something like our Tombs in Country Church Yards. They have likewise many neat Boxes full of human Bones which they appear to preserve with great care. Over the Tombs upon the Boughs of Trees they / hang a number *p. 157* of Turtles Heads & Bones, & a great variety of Fish neatly platted rounds with Reeds; we took down some of them & found they had only left the Skin & teeth, the Bones & Entrails they had extracted without cutting the Skin. We sent off some Boat loads of Coco Nuts, & *the whole Island is cover'd with scurvy Grass* which has proved of infinite service both to the Sick & those that call themselves well, for I believe there is not a man amongst us but is touched with the Scurvy. *Fresh Water is scarce here but what I tasted of it was good.* The Wells the Nations make use of are very small, two or three Coco Nut Shells of water taken from them, drys them for a moment or two, but they are presently full again, *so that with some little pains to enlarge them I dare say a Ship might be supplied with water.* I saw no Venemous Creature here. The flies are very troublesome, they cover you all over & even the Boats, so that our Ships are now full of them. All this day the Savages kept very close, they did not even make a Smoke upon any Part of the Islands as far as we / could see, least we should find them out. In *p. 158* the Evening we all returned on board. This part of the Island is in the Latt of 14°29′ So & Longde 148°50′ Wt.—I haul'd a little way

---

[1] Takaroa was seen by Roggeveen in 1722. Although the two islands were named the King George's by Byron, they could possibly have been discovered in 1616 by Le Maire and Schouten.

off Shore & then brought too, intending to visit the W^termost Island in the morning. This Island is 69 Leag^s [1] W½S from the W^termost Island of Disappointment. The Birds we saw ashore were Parrots & Parokets, & a beautiful kind of Dove, which were so tame, that they came close to us, and often went into the Savages Hutts.

Wednesday June 12th. At 6 AM the SW^t Point of the E^termost Island bore EbN Dist 5 Leag^s & the Extreams of the W^termost Islands from SE S^oward to SW Dist off shore 2 miles. Made sail & steered SWBW close along the NE Side of this Island but could get no Soundings. This Side is about 6 or 7 Leag^s in length & in much the same form with a Great Salt water Lake between this & the opposite side as the other Island had; The Savages were very numerous here, they follow'd us armed in the same manner the others had, & run along shore some Leagues after us. As this Climate is most unsufferably hot, & they were pretty well warmed *p. 159* with this / exercise, they would every now & then plunge into the Sea or else would fall flat down for the Surf to beat over them, & then up again & run as fast as they could. Our Boats were Sounding along Shore as usual, & I had given strict Orders to the Officers who commanded them never to molest the Savages without they began first with them, but to try by all methods to procure their friendship; Accordingly our people put the Boats in as near as they durst for the Surf, and made Signs to them that we wanted water. The Savages pointed to run down farther along Shore which they did till they came opposite to such a Town as I mentioned we landed at on the last Island. Here a number of Savages joined those who first followed us. Our Boats haul'd close into the Surf, & we brought too in the Ships at a little distance from the Shore. A very stout venerable looking old Man, with a long white Beard, who seemed to be their King came down from the Hutts attended by a Young Man to the Waterside. The rest of the Savages he made *p. 160* keep off at some / little Distance, in one hand he held a Green Bough & with the other he held his Beard; he began a long Song which our People say was far from being disagreable, & tho' they threw him several trifling presents from the Boats, yet he would

---

[1] Actually, 196 miles. Byron's latitude is exact; his longitude should be 144°55′ W rather than 148°50′ W.

neither touch them himself nor suffer any one else to do so, til he had finished his Song which was very long one. He then waded into the water & threw our People the green bough & accepted the Presents they made him, after which our People & they seemed to be pretty familiar. Our men pointed to them to lay down their Arms, which most of them did, upon the strength of which one of our Midshipmen jumped out of the Boat with his Cloaths on, & swam thro' the Surf to them, they immediately gather'd about him & seemed to admire his Wastecoat much, which he immediately pulled off & gave to them, he had no sooner done that than one of them stole his Cravat off his Neck, finding how things was likely to go he made the best of his way off to the Boat again. Several of the Savages swam to our Boats, one would bring a little fresh water in a Coco Nutt Skell, / another would bring a Coco Nut; but all our *p. 161* People could do they could not make them understand that we would trade with them for Pearls by shewing them the Pearl Oyster Shells, which they carried with them for that purpose. The Misfortune here was that we could find no anchoring ground for our Ships, or I make no doubt but in a little time we should have made these People understood us, & in all probability have got a number of valuable Pearls from them in exchange for Hatchets, Nails & Bill-hooks of which they seemed prodigiously fond. We observed two or three large kind of Boats they had in the Lake, one one of them had two Masts & had some Rigging over head to support them. I honor'd these Two last Islands by the name of King George's Islands. This last lays in the Latt of 14°41′ S⁰ & Long^de in from London 149°15′ W^t. At Noon made sail to the Westward again.

Thursday June 13th. Wind East, moderate & hazey weather. Course West Dist 120 M^s. Latt in 14°42′ S⁰ Long^de made 2°24′ W^t. M Dist 120 M^s W^t from King George's Islands, / Long^de in from *p. 162* London 151°39′ W^t. Variation 5°0′ E^t, the W^t End of King George's Islands East Dist^ce 40 Leag^s.[1]

Friday June 14th. Wind East. The Weather most *excessively hot for some days past, the Thermometer has stood at 82 & 84 Degrees.* At

---

[1] This position puts Byron too far west, for he would be 16 miles north of and midway between Rangiroa and Tikahau Islands. Actually, he was east of Rangiroa, which he sighted the next day.

3 PM saw the Land bearing SSW Dist 6 Leag^s.[1]—Haul'd the Wind
& stood towards it. At 4 the Extreams bore from SSE to WbS. This
a low & very narrow Island & lies E^t & W^t & is near 20 Leag^s. in
Length, it looks very pleasant & we saw a great number of Savages
upon it. On the S^o side 2 or 3 Leag^s from it are several Rocks &
small Islands, then breaks a prodigious Surf on the Side we run
down along, & a great deal of foul ground lays at some distance
from it. I named it Prince of Wales's Island. It is in Lat 15°0′ S^o
& the W^{t}ermost End in Long^{de} 151°55′ W^t from London, & bears
S^o 80° W^t distance 48 Leagues from King George's Islands.
Course from the W^t End of Prince of Wales's Island N° 85° W^t.
Dist 112 M^s. Lat in 14°48′ S^o Long^{de} made 1°56′ W^t. M Dist 112
M^s from Prince of Wales's Island. Long^{de} in 153°51′ W^t. Variation
5°30′ E^t. Prince of Wales's Island S^o 85° E^t. Dist 37 Leag^s. /

p. 163 Saturday June 15th. Wind EbN Fresh Gales & hazey. Course N^o
82° W^t.Dist 149 M^s. Latt in 14°28′S^o. Long^{de} made 4°28′ W^t. M Dist
259 M^s. Long^{de} in 156°23′ W^t. Variation 7°40′ E^t.—Prince of
Wales Island S^o 83°23′ E^t. Dist 87 Leag^s.

Sunday June 16th. Wind East with a mountainous Swell from
the S^{o}ward. *For a day or two before we made the Islands of
Disappointment till this day we had entirely lost that great Swell &*

[1] Rangiroa (Rahinoa) Island (15°00′ S, 147°40′ W) the largest and now the
most populous island in the Tuamotu Archipelago, is about 44 miles long and
17 miles wide, and runs in an east-south-easterly and opposite direction. It is
wooded throughout, and its lagoon is infested with sharks. No dependence can be
placed on the accuracy of the charted topographical details of the north and south
coasts, and the north-western end of Rangiroa was reported to lie about three
miles farther westward than shown on H.O. Chart 5732.

Two passes, Avatoru Pass and Tiputa Pass, lead into the lagoon, while close to the
north-western point of the atoll, an inlet in the reef forms a tiny harbour called
'Avatika' by the natives. Avatoru Pass, which is about eight miles eastward of the
north-western point of the atoll, is about 400 yd wide, deep and clear of dangers,
and is navigable by large vessels as far as the turn into the lagoon. Then shoal
dangers make it dangerous for vessels drawing more than 10 feet to proceed
farther in. The *Dolphin* drew 15′ 6″ forward, 14′ 6″ aft. The second pass,
Tiputa Pass, near the middle of the northern side of the atoll, is available to large
vessels. However, it is subject to violent eddies. Also, in both passes, the tidal
currents attain the rates of 7 to 9 knots and cause rips and eddies, known as
'opape', which are dangerous for boats. During the flood these eddies are found
in the inner parts of the passes, and during the ebb near the outer parts. So
dangerous are the effects of the currents that even today local schooners with small
auxiliary motors will not attempt to pass against the current, and if the current is
unfavourable they wait until slack water which is indicated in calm weather by
the cessation of the 'opape'. (H.O. Pub. 80 (1961), 109–10.]

The island was discovered by the Dutch in 1616.

for some time before we first made the Land we saw vast Flocks of Birds which we observed towards Evening always flew away to the S^oward. This is a convincing proof to me that there is Land that way, & had not the Winds failed me in the higher Latitudes as mentioned before, I make no doubt but I should have fell in with it, & in all probability made the discovery of the S^o Continent;[1] Indeed if it had not been for the Sickness in both Ships, I would still have attempted it by hauling away to the S^oward immediately from those Islands. I remarked before that all the Islands we have seen are well peopled; Now if there are not a Chain of Islands reaching to the Continent how can we account for these / Peoples being here, *p. 164* situated we may say in the middle of this vast Southern Ocean. Course N° 84° W^t. Dist 110 M^s. Latt in 14°17′ S^o. Long^de made 6°20′ W^t. M Dist 368 M^s W^t. Long^de made from Masa fuero 73°15′ W^t. Long^de in 158°15′ W^t. Variation 7°50′ E^t. Prince of Wales Island S^o 83°40′ E^t. Dist 124 Leag^s.

Monday June 17th. Wind East with a great S^oern Swell. Many Birds of various Sorts about the Ship. Suppose we may be near some Island. This makes it a dangerous Navigation in the night, for those Islands we have seen already were so low, that a Ship is close to them before they are seen, even in a Moon light night. Course N° 82° W^t. Dist 137 M^s. Latt in 13°57′ S^o. Long^de made 8°40′ W^t. M Dist 504 M^s W^t. Long^de made from Masa fuera 75°35′ W^t. Variation 8°0′ E^t. Long^de in from London 160°35′ W^t. Prince of Wales Island S^o 83°6′ E^t. Dist 169 Leag^s.

Tuesday June 18th. Wind E^t. Fresh gales with some Squalls & rain. Course N° 82° W^t. Dist 136 M^s. Latt in 13°39′ S^o. Long^de made 10°59′ W^t. M Dist 639 M^s W^t. Long^de made from Masa fuero 77°54′ W^t. Variation 8°0′ E^t. Long^de in from London 162°54′ W^t. Prince of Wales Island S^o 82°57′ E^t. Dist 214 Leag^s.

Wednesday June 19th. Wind E^t. Fresh Gales with some Squalls of Rain. / A great number of Birds seen. Course N° 81° W^t. Dist 147 *p. 165* M^s. Latt in 13°14′ S^o Long^de made 13°27′ W^t. M Dist 784 M^s W^t. Long^de made from Masa fuero 80°22′ W^t. Variation ¾ P^t E^t. Long^de in from London 165°22′ W^t. Prince of Wales Island S^o 82°27′ E^t. Dist 263 Leag^s.

[1] See Introduction, p. lxvi, for a discussion of the influence which this opinion had upon subsequent voyages.

Thursday June 20ᵗʰ. Wind Eᵗ & ESE. Fresh Gales & Squally with rain. Course Nº. 74° Wᵗ. Dist 150 Mˢ. Latt in 12°33′ Sº. Longᵈᵉ made 15°52′ Wᵗ. M Dist 928 Mˢ Wᵗ. Longᵈᵉ made from Masa fuero 82°47′ Wᵗ. Variation 9°15′ Eᵗ. Longᵈᵉ in from London 167°47′ Wᵗ. Prince of Wales Island Sº 81°7′ Eᵗ Dist 313 Leagˢ.

Friday June 21ˢᵗ. PM Wind Eᵗ. Fresh Gales & Squally with rain AM NE Fresh Gales & Cloudy. Variation 10°20′ Eᵗ at 7 AM Saw a most dangerous Reef of Breakers bearing from us SSW dist about a League.[1] About half an hour afterwards saw the Land from the Mast head bearing WNW Dist 8 Leagues, which makes in 3 Islands with Rocks & broken Ground between them.[2] The SE side Lays NEbN & SWbS about 3 Leagˢ in length, & from both the extreme Points runs off a Reef of Rocks upon which the Sea breaks immensely high. We sailed round the Nº End & on the NW

---

[1] Tema Reef (see p. 107, n. 2).

[2] Isles of Danger; discovered by Byron.

'12–2 Danger Islands (10°55′. S., 165°50′ W. . . .) consist of three islands, Pukapuka, Motu Ko, and Motu Kavata with several smaller islets and sand cays, all lying on or within a barrier reef which surrounds a shallow lagoon. The islands are said to be diminishing in size, and tradition tells of a larger population at one time.

'The barrier reef is unbroken and there is no access to the lagoon for other than small boats and canoes. On its western side, the barrier reef is always awash. Its southern side is awash at low tide and its eastern side is partly awash and part dry sand.

'Tearai Reef, a sunken reef over which there are depths of 8 to 30 feet, extends in a westerly direction for about 3 miles from Motu Kavata Island. None of the patches on this sunken reef break in fine weather and some of them not continuously in bad weather. Toka Sand Cay marks the western extremity of Tearai Reef. Most of the sandbank was washed away by the tidal wave of 1914.

'12–3 Pukapuka, at the northern end of the atoll, is a horseshoe-shaped island with the two arms extending southward along the east and west sides of the barrier reef. It is densely wooded with coconut and other trees, some reaching a height of about 80 feet. The land part of the island is about 40 feet high at its highest point, but its surface is broken by uneven ridges and depressions, the latter filled with swampy ground and taro patches. The island is bordered on its north and west sides by wide, flat reefs and surf beats heavily on the narrower reef on the weather side. Three villages of which one has a large church and a school, are located on the south side of the island near the lagoon and inside the horseshoe.

'Motu Katava (Kotawa) (Kotava), about 3.5 miles south-southwestward of Pukapuka and connected with it by a flat reef always awash, is about 1 mile long east and west and one-half of a mile wide north and south, at its widest part. The western part of the island is densely wooded with buka trees, the tops of which are 80 feet above the sea. The land does not reach a height of more than 40 feet and is highest on the western half of the island. The taller buka trees, 40 to 50 feet high, grow in a lower central depression. The eastern half of the island is wooded with coconuts.

'12–4 Motu Ko (Koe) . . . , the southernmost island of the atoll, lies about

XV. View of the Isles of Danger

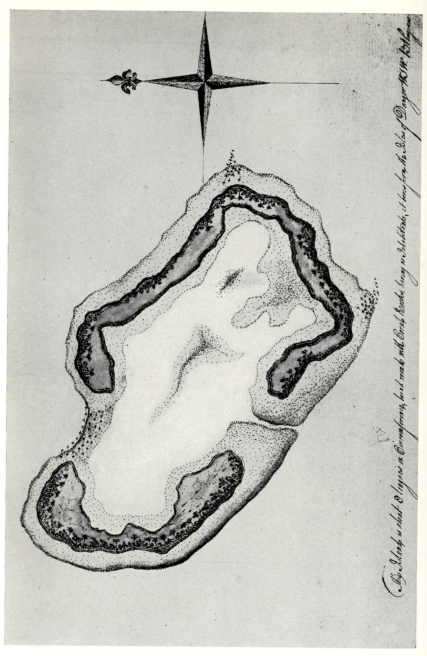

XVI. View of the Duke of York's Island

W^t Sides saw a great many dangerous Rocks & / Shoals which *p. 166* stretches off near two Leagues into the Sea. The Islands appear beautiful almost beyond description. We saw a great many Savages upon them & their Houses & a large Boat under Sail at some little distance from them. It grieved me much to leave these Islands without a further examination. But when ever we cast our Eyes round them, we saw nothing but Rocks & Breakers which made it too hazardous to attempt any thing more. I take these to be part of Solomon's Islands & am in hopes I shall fall in with some others of them that may possibly have harbours, tho' I take this to be as dangerous a navigation as any in the World. The Reef of Rocks first seen is in Latt 10°15′ S° & Long^{de} 169°28′ & bears from Prince of Wales Island N° 76°48′ W^t. Dist 352 Leag^s.—The Islands bears from the Reef WNW 9 Leag^s. I named them the Isles of Danger, Lattitude observed at Noon 10°43′ S°. Long^{de} in 170°0′ W^t. from these Islands I shape my Course NWbN allowing the Variation.

Saturday June 22^d. PM Wind E^t with some Squalls & hard rain. AM Wind NE & ENE Fresh Gales & hazey. After seeing that dangerous Reef of Rocks / Yesterday at a little after day break, I *p. 167* told some of my Officers that I supposed we should have frequent Alarms in the Night. Accordingly in a very hard Squall of Wind & Rain about 9 last night I heard a great noise upon Deck & was

1¼ miles east-southeastward of Motu Katava and is the flattest and least vegetated of the three islands. It is horseshoe shaped, larger than Pukapuka, but flat and sparsely wooded with coconut and other trees, the tops of which rise to a height of about 65 feet.

'The reefs on the south side of Ko and Katava are wide, flat, and awash, with a heavy surf breaking.

'The lagoon is blocked by reefs and coral heads at the north, southeast and southwest ends, but towards the middle it is clear and deep with depths up to 6 to 8 fathoms. The natives navigate the lagoon freely in canoes, paddling or sailing between the three islands.

'12–5 Tema Reef (11°05′ S., 165°35′ W.) lies about 4 miles east-southeastward of Danger Islands. It is about 600 yards in diameter and breaks heavily, but no rocks show above water. At 1,000 yards northeastward of Tema Reef no sounding could be obtained with 500 fathoms of line, and all around the reef, at a distance of 1 mile, 100 fathoms of line failed to find bottom. On a fine day, with the wind less than force 4, the reef has been sighted from a distance of 8 or 9 miles.' [H.O. Pub. 80 (1961), 334–5.]

'And the Islands [Isles of Danger] bear from the Prince of Whales Isl^d WbN 370 L^{gs} and agree in Lat^d with one laid down in the Neptune Francois by the Name of I Solitaire, wch Isl^d is laid down by them 160 L^{gs} to the Eastw^d of the Islands of Solomon' (Mouat, 134).

presently informed that the Tamar who was a head of us had fired a Gun & that our People saw Breakers to Leeward of us. I run upon Deck & saw the Moon going down which was what our People took for Breakers, & as for the Tamar I could see nothing of her, so we bore away again & about an hour after got sight of the Tamar. Course N⁰ 59° W^t. Dist 165 M^s. Latt in 9°24' S⁰. Long^{de} made 2°26' W^t. M Dist 144 M^s W^t from the Islands of Danger. Long^{de} made from Masa fuero 87°17' W^t. Variation 10°30' E^t. Long^{de} in from London 172°16' W^t. The Islands of Danger S⁰ 59° E^t. Dist 55 Leag^s.

Sunday June 23^d. Wind E^t fresh gales with frequent Squalls & rain Course N⁰ 61° W^t. Dist 140 M^s. Latt in 8°20' S⁰ Long^{de} made 4°30' W^t. M Dist 266 M^s W^t. Long^{de} in 174°21' W^t. Long^{de} made from p. 168 Masa fuero 89°20' W^t. the Islands of Danger S⁰ 61°4' E Dist / 101 Leagues.

Monday June 24th. AM Fresh Gales E^t & ESE & fair weather. PM Wind EbN, Squally with hard rain & thick weather. Fearing I might fall in with some Shoal or Island, I bro^t too & lay so all night. At Day break made sail & at 10 AM discover'd an Island[1] bearing SSW dist 7 or 8 Leag^s. Steered towards it & at noon the middle WNW 2 or 3 Miles. Course S⁰ 88 W^t. Dist 108 M^s. Latt^{de} in 8°32' S⁰. Long^{de} made 6°18' W^t. M Dist 373 M^s W^t. Long^{de} made from Masa fuero 91°9' W^t. Long^{de} in 176°8' W^t.— The Islands of Danger S⁰ 70°6' E^t. Dist 132 Leag^s. Variation by amplitude 10°30' E^t.

Tuesday June 25th. Little wind EbS & fair weather, The Island we saw yesterday is low, full of wood, amongst which are abundance of Coco Trees, & appears very pleasant. It has a large Lake in the middle like King George's Islands. It is near 30 M^s round, but upon the greatest part of it there breaks a most dreadful Sea, & a great deal of foul ground & Spits lay off it. It is not inhabited, &

[1] Atafu, which was discovered by Byron and named the Duke of York's Island and whose position is 8°32' S, 172°31' W, is an atoll consisting of a number of islets about 8 to 10 feet high, lying on a triangle-shaped reef which encloses the inevitable lagoon. There is no passage into the lagoon, and the sea breaks with violence on the reef enclosing the lagoon. However, at high water a boat may sometimes cross the reef. The reefs surrounding the atoll are mostly steep-to, and a long reef extends some 700 yards northwestward from Atafu. Today the islets are covered with coconut, pandanus, and low trees, and a conspicuous clump of casuarina trees is located on the southern islet of the atoll [H.O. Pub. 80 (1961), 331–2].

I believe we are the first People that ever saw it. I sailed quite round it & upon the Lee Side of it sent our Boats to sound in hopes of finding anchoring ground, but they could get no Soundings close in with the Shore. However I sent the Boats to try to Land & if possible to procure / some Refreshments for the Sick wch they *p. 169* did with great difficulty returning with about 200 Coco Nuts. They said there was no Signs of its ever having been inhabited, that there was Thousands of Sea Fowls setting upon their Nests which they made upon high Trees, & that they would not stir for our People, so that they knocked them down as they pleased, They may possibly take this method of building their Nests to secure them from the Land Crabs with which this Island Swarms. I was not willing to name this Island immediately as not being certain but it might be that called Maluita in the Neptune Francois, & laid down about a Degree to the E^tward of the Great Island of St Elizabeth one of Solomon's Islands, but since I am convinced that is no such thing, therefore named it Duke of York's Island after His Royal Highness.[1] I am much afraid there is no foundation for laying down Solomon's Islands in the Latitude & Longitude they are laid down in by the French; The only person that ever pretended to have seen them was Quiros, and I believe he left no Account behind him / to direct any other person to find them by.[2] Course S^o *p. 170* 85° W^t. Dist 82 M^s. Latt in 8°39′ S^o. Long^de made 7°40′ W^t. M Dist 455 W^t. Long^de made from Masa fuero 92°31′ W^t. Variation 11°10′ E^t. Long^de in from London 177°30′ W^t. The Islands of Danger S^o 74°17′ E^t. Dist 178 Leag^s.—The Middle of the Duke of York's Island is in Latt 8°30′ S^o. and Long^de from the Meridian

[1] The *Neptune François* . . . (Amsterdam, 1700), has no chart of the area. However, Chart 6, *L'Hydrographie Françoise*, does contain the information Byron mentions. Since Carteret carried *L'Hydrographie Françoise* (my source is Helen Wallis), Byron undoubtedly did too. Also, both Byron and Carteret had aboard *Le Neptune Oriental* . . . (Paris, 1745; B.M. Maps 14.e.18). Byron could have combined the titles of the latter two works into 'Neptune Francois'.
  Maluita's position is given on the chart as being 8°25′ S, 172°10′ W.
  Also puzzling is the fact that, although Quiros is mentioned on the chart, 'Teere et Isles veus par Quiros en 1605' refers to land 1700 miles to the south-east of Maluita.
[2] Why did Byron not have John Campbell's edition of Harris's *Voyages* (see Introduction, pp. xxxii–xxxvi), of which ch. I, sect. x is an account of 'The Voyages of Don Pedro Fernandez De Quiros, for the Discovery of the Southern Continent and Islands', I, 63–5, and which correctly ascribes the discovery of the Solomon Islands to Mendaña?

of London 176°10′ W^t. & bears from the Islands of Danger N° 70°4′ W^t. Dist 133 Leag^s.

Wednesday June 26th. Little wind, variable, with unsettled weather & some Showers of Rain. Course N° 88° W^t. Dist 59 M^s. Latt in 8°37′ S^o. Long^{de} made 8°40′ W^t. M Dist 514 M^s W^t from the Islands of Danger. Variation 10°50′ E^t. Long^{de} made from Masa fuero 93°31′ W^t. Long^{de} in 178°30′ W^t. The Islands of Danger S^o 75°49′ E^t. Dist 177 Leag^s.[1]

Thursday June 27th. Little Wind from ENE to S^o & back to SEbS. the Weather Sultry hot; the Thermometer for many days past not falling below 82 Degrees. Many Fish about the Ship, but we get only Sharks, which our People eat with a good appetite. The little Refreshments we have got from the Islands has been of great service to our Scorbutick Men. Course W^t. Dist 56 M^s. Latt in
p. 171 8°38′ S^o. Long^{de} made / 9°37′ W^t. M Dist 570 M^s. W^t Long^{de} made from Masa fuero 94°28′ W^t. Variation 10° E^t. Long^{de} in from London 179°27′ W^t. The Islands of Danger S^o 77°15′ E^t. Dist 195 Leag^s.

Friday June 28th. Wind SE moderate & fair weather Course N° 86° W^t. Dist 127 M^s. Latt in 8°29′ S^o. Long^{de} made 5°29′ W^t. M Dist 327 M^s W^t from Duke of York's Island, Long^{de} made from Masa fuero 96°37′ W^t. Variation 1 P^t E^t. Duke of York's Island E^t. Dist 109 Leagues.

Saturday June 29th. Wind ESE moderate & fair weather, but most excessively hot. The Thermometer at 83 Degrees. Finding there is no such Land as laid down in the Neptune Francois for Solomon's Islands, tho' I have run down in that track, & am now by my Reckoning near 10 Degrees to the W^{t}ward of them as laid down in that Chart, I intend to haul to the N^{o}ward to cross the Equinoctial, & afterwards shape my Course for the Ladrone Islands which tho' still a long run I am in hopes of reaching before we are distressed for

---

[1] 'We now look'd upon our selves not to be more than 30 or 40 L^{gs} dist. from the Isl^d of *Solomon*, and that this Island [Duke of York's] is what is called in the Draughts and Acc^{ts} the Isl^d Melita it agreeing in Lat^d to the East of the Largest Isl^d of *Solomon* & we therefore expected to make it the next Day.

[The next day] 'By our Acc^t and likewise by our Corrected Long^d we ran thro the Middle of the Isl^d in the Position it is laid down, wch I am very confident is erroneous, & whoever finds it must seek it to the East^d of 170°0′ W^t of London.

'We gave over our Search for Solomons Islands being certain if there are any such we were to the Westw^d of them; We therefore hauled to the N^{o}w^d in order to cross the Equinoctial Line' (Mouat, 135–6).

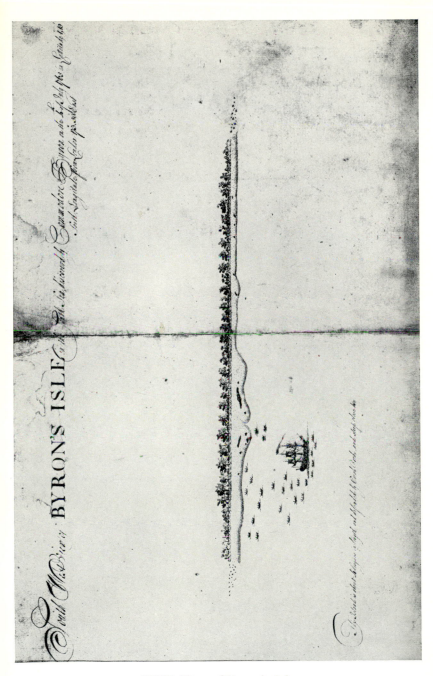

XVII. View of Byron's Isle

Water, which now begins to fall short. Course N⁰ 82° W^t. Dist 124
M^s. Latt in 8°13′ S⁰. Long^de made 7°33′ W^t. M Dist 449 M^s W^t.
Long^de made from Masa fuero 98°41′ W^t. Long^de in 176°20′ E^t.
Variation by Azimuth 10°10′ E^t. Duke of York's Island / S⁰ 87°50′ *p. 172*
E^t. Distance 150 Leagues.

Sunday June 30th. PM Wind ESE Moderate & Cloudy. AM NE
Squally with hard Rain. Course N⁰ 34° W^t. Dist 148 M^s. Latt^de.
in 6°10′ S⁰. Long^de made 8°56′ W^t. M Dist 531 M^s W^t. Long^de
made from Masa fuero 101°3′ W^t. Long^de in 174°58′ E^t. Variation
10° E^t. Duke of York's Island S⁰ 75°14′ E^t. Dist 183 Leag^s.

Monday July 1st. PM Wind E^t & SE Light Airs & Cloudy. AM
NE & ENE fresh gales & hazey. By Observation find the Ship 26
M^s to the S⁰ward of Account which I impute to a Current. Course
N⁰ 16° W^t. Dist 117 M^s. Latt in 4°18′ S⁰. Long^de made 9°29′ W^t.
M Dist 564 M^s W^t. Long^de made from Masa fuero 100°36′ W^t.
Long^de in 174°25′ E^t. Variation 10°4′ E^t. Duke of York's Island
S⁰ 65°55′ E^t. Dist 207 Leag^s.

Tuesday July 2^d. PM Wind variable, squally with hard Rain, &
much Lightning in the Night. AM Light Airs & the weather so
Sultry it is difficult breathing. Find the Ship 17 M^s to the S⁰ward
of Account. Course N⁰ 13° W^t. Dist 98 M^s. Latt in 2°44′ S⁰.
Long^de made 9°54′ W^t. M Dist 589 M^s W^t. Long^de made from
Masa fuero 101°1′ W^t. Long^de in 174°0′ E^t. Duke of York's Island
S⁰ 59°34′ E^t. Dist^ce 228 Leagues.

Wednesday July 3^d. Little wind from NE to SE & sultry weather.
Many Birds about the Ship. Course N⁰ 13° W^t. Dist 50 M^s. Latt in
1°55′ S⁰. Long^de made 10°15′ W^t. M Dist 600 M^s W^t. Long^de from
Masa fuero made / 101°12′ W^t. Long^de in 173°49′ E^t. Duke of *p. 173*
York's Island S⁰ 56°48′ E^t. Dist 239 Leag^s.

Thursday July 4th. Little wind from SSE to ESE & hazey weather.
At ½ past 4 PM discovered an Island bearing N⁰. Dist 5 or 6
Leag^s. Stood towards it, and at Sun set the Extreams of it bore
from NNE to NNW Dist 4 Leag^s. We haul'd the wind & stood off
& on in the night. In the morning made Sail & steere'd for it. It is
a low Island, appears delightfully pleasant, full of Wood amongst
which are a prodigious number of Coco Trees.[1] But there is a

---

[1] Byron Island is Nukunau, of the Gilbert Islands [William T. Brigham, 'An
Index to the Islands of the Pacific Ocean' (Honolulu, 1900), in *Memoirs of the*

great deal of foul ground lays off it, upon which the Sea breaks immensely high. We steered along the SW side of it which may be about 4 Leag^s in Length. We soon saw it was inhabited, & that they were very numerous, for there was at least a Thousand of them got together in an Istant [instant] upon the Beach, & presently after we counted above 60 Canoes (or rather Proas) coming off to us. I brought to for them, & they surrounded us with very little ceremony. Their Proas were extremely neat & kept in such order that they all appeared as if quite new. Each of them had

p. 174 from 3 to 6 Savages in them. They were very / clean Limbed, tall well proportioned Men, of a bright copper colour, extream good features & chearful Countenances, & very bold; they had long black hair which some wore tied behind in a great bunch, others in three Knots, some had long beards & some only Whiskers, & others only a little tuft at the end of their Chin; But they were all stark naked, not having the least covering, excepting ornaments of Shells about their Necks, wrists & waist, very prettily disposed. One of them jumped out of his Proa & swam to the Ship & ran up the Side like a Cat, & as soon as he was up, sat down upon the Gunnel & burst out into a violent fit of Laughter. He then run all about the Ship attempting to steal every thing he could lay his hands on. Our Seamen put him on a Jacket & Trowzers, & he appeared with all the gestures of a Monkey newly drest. We gave him & all the rest that were about the Ship Bread, which they were vastly fond of; After this fellow that was aboard had playe'd a thousand Asses tricks, he jump'd over board Jacket & Trowzers & all, & swam to his Proa. Others got into the Gun room Ports & stole every thing that was in their reach, & then jumped over

p. 175 board & swam away / at a prodigious rate with both hands full, holding their Arms up quite out of the water least the things they had got should be spoiled. I believe there was never a Set of more dexterous Thieves in the World. I observed one of them that I suppose was a person of some consequence amongst them, with a String of human Jaw teeth about his waist, he set a great value

Bernice Pauahi Bishop Museum, I (Honolulu, 1899–1903), 49].
The island is of coral formation and is surrounded by a reef. It is from 6 to 8 feet high and thickly covered with coconut and pandanus trees. In 1926, it was reported to lie 3 miles northeastward of its charted position, 1°19′ S, 176°23′ E [H.O. Pub. 80 (1961), 298–9].

upon them for we offered him several things in exchange for them, but he would not part with them. Their Ears are bored & hang down almost to their Shoulders & many had their Ears quite split thro' with the weight of the Ornaments they carry in them. We shewed them some Coco Nuts & made Signs that we wanted some from the Shore, but instead of offering to go for any, they wanted to have those we shewed them. I remarked a very dangerous weapon some of them had, it was a kind of Spear, very broad at the end, which for about three feet in length was of each side stuck full of Sharks teeth, which are as sharp as any Lancet. I sent the Boats in / Shore to Sound, & they had ground at 30 f^m within two Cables *p. 176* length of the Shore, but the bottom was Coral Rock, & other wise the Soundings much too near the Breakers for a Ship to lie in safety, so I was obliged to make sail again. This Island which my Officers chose to give my Name to, is in the Latitude 1°18' S° & Long^de 173°46' E^t from the Meridian of London.[1] At Noon it bore SEbE 3 or 4 M^s. Course N° Dist 40 M^s. Lat in 1°15' S°. Long^de made 10°5' W^t. M Dist 600 M^s W^t. Long^de made from Masa fuero 101°12' W^t. Duke of York's Island S° 54°3' E^t. Dist 247 Leag^s.

Friday July 5th. Wind from EbN to SE cloudy weather with some Squalls & hard rain. Course N° 14° W^t. Dist 72 M^s. Lat in 0°5' S°. Long^de made 0°17' W^t. M. Dist 17 M^s W^t from Byron's Island, Long^de made from Masa fuero 101°28' W^t. Long^de in from London 173°33' E^t. Variation 1 Point E^t, Byron's Island S° 14°0' E^t. Dist 24 Leagues.

Saturday July 6th. Wind from SSE to ENE with frequent Squalls & hard rain. Abundance of Fish seen for some days past, but we get nothing but Sharks, which however is now reckoned a good Dish at my Table. / *Many of our People are seized with the flux,* p. 177 *which our Doctor*[2] *Attributes to the violent heat & perpetual Rains.* Course N° 12 W^t. Dist 99 M^s. Latt in 1°33' N°. Long^de made 0 37' W^t. M Dist 37 M^s W^t. long^de made from Masa fuero 101°48' W^t. Long^de in 173°13' E^t. Variation by Azimuth 10°30' E^t. Byron's Island S° 12°17' E^t. Dist 57 Leag^s. Tinian N° 67°4' W^t. Dist 645 Leag^s.

[1] Latitude exact; longitude should be 176°25' E or 176°23' E.
[2] John Crozier. See Introduction, pp. lxiii–lxiv, for his troubles after the *Dolphin* returned to England.

Sunday July 7th. Variable winds and rain with Squalls & very unsetled weather Course N° 14° W^t. Dist 70 M^s. Lat in 2°40′ N^o. Long^{de} made 0°54′ W^t. M Dist 54 M^s W^t. Long^{de} made from Masafuero 102°5′ W^t. Long^{de} in 172°56′ E^t. Variation 10°30′ E^t. Byron's Island S^o 12°47′ E^t. Dist 80 Leag^s.

Monday July 8th. Wind very variable, with Squalls & hard rain. Course N° 23° W^t. Dist 70 M^s. Lat in 3°44′ N^o. Long^{de} made 1°21′ W^t. M Dist 81 M^s W^t. Long^{de} made from Masa fuero 102°32′ W^t. Long^{de} in 172°29′ E^t Variation by Azith 10°50′ E^t. Byron's Island S^o 15°1′ E^t. Dist 104 Leag^s.

Tuesday July 9th. Light airs of wind variable with Calms, & continual Rains with a great swell from the N^{o}ward. We saved a great deal of Rain water. Course N° 21° W^t. Dist 18 M^s. Latt in
p. 178 4°0′ N^o. Long^{de} made 1°27′ / W^t. M Dist 87 M^s W^t. Long^{de} made from Masa fuero 102°38′ W^t. Long^{de} in 172°23′ E^t. Variation 10°50′ E^t. Byron's Island S^o 15°18′ E^t. Dist 110 Leag^s.

Wednesday July 10th. PM Little wind W^t & Cloudy weather, In the night calm with hard rain. AM fresh gales SE very thick weather & much rain. Course N° 10° W^t. Dist 57 M^s. Lat in 4°56′ N^o. Long^{de} made 1°37′ W^t. M Dist 97 M^s W^t. Long^{de} made from Masa fuero 102°48′ W^t. Long^{de} in 172°13′ E^t. Variation 1 point E^t. Byron's Island S^o 14°32′ E^t. Dist 129 Leag^s.

Thursday July 11th. PM Fresh gales SSE & hazey weather. AM moderate Breezes E^t & EbN & Cloudy. Course N° 13° W^t. Dist 112 M^s. Lat in 6°45′ N^o. Long^{de} made 2°1′ W^t. M Dist 121 M^s W^t. Long^{de} made from Masa fuero 103°12′ W^t. Long^{de} in 171°49′ E^t. Variation 1 Point E^t. Byrons Island S^o 14°4′ E^t Dist 166 Leag^s.

Friday July 12th. A fresh Gale NEbE & Cloudy weather. Course N° 17 W^t. Dist. 147 M^s. Lat in 9°5′ N^o. Long^{de} made 2°44′ W^t. M Dist 164 M^s W^t. Long^{de} made from Masa fuero 103°55′ W^t. Long^{de} in 171°6′ E^t. Variation by Azth 8°24′ E^t. Byron's Island S^o
p. 179 14°46′ / E^t. Distance 215 Leagues.

Saturday July 13th. Fresh Gales NEbE by Observation find the Ship 5 M^s to the N^{o}ward of Account. Course N° 14° W^t. Dist 146 M^s. Lat in 11°27′ N^o. Long^{de} made 3°20′ W^t. M Dist 199 M^s W^t. Long^{de} made from Masa fuero 104°31′ W^t. Long^{de} in 170°30′ E^t. Variation 8°30′ E^t. Byron's Island S^o 14°34′ E^t. Dist 263 Leagues, Tinian N° 82°41′ W^t. Distance 578 Leagues.

Sunday July 14. A Fresh Gale NE & hazey weather. Course N° 58° W^t. Dist 203 M^s. Lat in 13°14′ N^o. Long^{de} made 6°17′ W^t. M Dist 372 M^s W^t. Long^{de} made from Masa fuero 107°24′ W^t. Long^{de} in 167°33′ E^t. Variation 9°0′ E^t. Byron's Island S^o 23°12′ E^t. Dist 316 Leagues.

Monday July 15th. Fresh Gales ENE. By Observation the Ship is 10 M^s to the N^{o}ward of Account. Course N° 89° W^t. Dist 176 M^s. Latt in 13°18′ N^o Long^{de} made 9°18′ W^t. M Dist 548 M^s W^t. Long^{de} made from Masafuero 110°29′ W^t. Long^{de} in 164°32′ E^t. Variation by Azth 9°12′ E^t. Byron's Island S^o 32°17′ E^t. Dist 345 Leag^s. Tinian N° 85°19′ W^t. Dist^{ce} 450 Leagues. /

Tuesday July 16th. Wind EbN moderate & fair weather Course S^o *p. 180* 85° W^t. Dist 133 M^s. Latt in 13°7′ N^o. Long^{de} made 11°33′ W^t. M Dist 680 M^s W^t. Long^{de} made from Masa fuero 112°44′ W^t. Long^{de} in 162°17′ E^t. Variation by Azth 10°3′ E^t. Byron's Island S^o 38°28′ E^t Dist 368 Leag^s. Tinian N° 84°17′ W^t. Dist 405 Leag^s.

Wednesday July 17th Wind EbN moderate & fair. Course W^t. Dist 111 M^s. Latt in 13°8′ N^o. Long^{de} made 13°27′ W^t. M Dist 791 M^s W^t. Long^{de} made from Masa fuero 114°38′ W^t. Long^{de} in 160°23′ E^t. Variation 10°30′ E^t. Byrons Island S° 42°25′ E^t. Dist 391 Leag^s. Tinian N° 84°0′ W^t. Dist 368 Leag^s.

Thursday July 18th. Wind ENE Light Airs & fair weather, but the heat excessive, the Thermometer never below 81 Deg^s. Course N° 89° W^t. Dist 91 M^s. Lat in 13°9′ N^o. Long^{de} made 15°0′ W^t. M Dist 882 M^s W^t. Long^{de} in 158°50′ E^t. Variation 10° E^t. Long^{de} made from Masa fuero 116°11′ W^t. Byron's Island S^o 45°29′ E^t. Dist 412 Leag^s. Tinian N° 83°16′ W^t. Dist 338 Leag^s.

Friday July 19th. Little wind NE & Cloudy Weather. Course N° 87 W^t. Dist 67 M^s. lat in 13°12′ N^o. Long^{de} made 16°9′ W^t. M Dist 949 M^s W^t. Long^{de} made from Masafuero 117°20′ W^t. Long^{de} in from London 157°41′ E^t. Variation 10° E^t. Byron's Island S^o 47°29′ E^t. Dist 429 Leag^s. Tinian N° 82°58′ W^t. Dist 316 Leagues. /

Saturday July 20th. Little wind ENE & Sultry weather. Course N^o *p. 181* 83° W^t. Dist 71 M^s. Latt in 13°21′ N^o. Long^{de} made 17°22′ W^t. M Dist 1020 M^s W^t. Long^{de} made from Masafuero 118°33′ W^t. Long^{de} in 156°28′ E^t. Variation 9°24′ E^t. Byron's Island S^o 49°30′ E^t. Dist 451 Leag^s. Tinian N° 83°0′ W^t. Dist 2992 Leagues.

Sunday July 21ˢᵗ. Little Wind EbN with very smooth water. The Heat most excessive. We have made little progress for many days past, having had nothing but light faint Breezes. *Our Coco Nuts failing, my People begin to fall down again in the Scurvy. It is astonishing the effect these Nuts alone had on those afflicted with that dreadful disease. Many that could not stir without the help of two Men, & who were in the most violent pain imaginable, their Limbs as black as Ink, & thought to be in the last stage of that Disorder were in a few days by eating those Nuts (tho' at Sea) sofar relieved as to do their duty, & even to go aloft as well as they had done before.* We are now heartily wishing for a fresh gale imagining that we cant be at a great distance from the Ladrone Islands, where we hope to get some Refreshments, which we all stand in great need of at present, /

p. 182 For certainly this is the longest, the hotest, & most dangerous Run that was ever made by Ships before. Course Nº 79° Wᵗ. Dist 87 Mˢ. Latt in 13°38′ Nº. Longᵈᵉ made 18°51′ Wᵗ. M Dist 1109 Mˢ Wᵗ. Longᵈᵉ made from Masa fuero 120°2′ Wᵗ. Longᵈᵉ in 154°59′ Eᵗ. Variation 9°11′ Eᵗ. Byron's Island Sº 51 4 Eᵗ. Dist 476 Leagˢ. Tinian Nº 83°26′ Wᵗ. Dist 263 Leagˢ. By the Observation find the Ship 12 Miles to the Nºward of Account.

Monday July 22ᵈ. Little wind ESE & hazey with some passing Squalls & rain. Course Nº 66° Wᵗ. Dist 114 Mˢ. Latt in 14°25′ Nº. Longᵈᵉ made 20°39′ Wᵗ. M Dist 1214 Mˢ Wᵗ. Longᵈᵉ made from Masa fuero 121°50′ Wᵗ. Longᵈᵉ in 153°11′ Eᵗ. Variation 8°50′ Eᵗ. Byrons Island Sº 52°10′ Eᵗ. Dist 513 Leagˢ. Tinian Nº 86°22′ Wᵗ. Dist 225 Leagˢ.

Tuesday July 23ᵈ. PM Little wind ESE. AM Fresh Gales SE & hazey. For these four days past have had a Nºerly Current. At Six this Morning imagining I was near the Latitude of Tinian, I shaped my Course for that Island. Course Nº 71° Wᵗ. Dist 126 Mˢ Lat in 15°6′ Nº Longᵈᵉ made 22°43′ Wᵗ. M Dist 1334 Mˢ. Longᵈᵉ made from Masa fuero 123°54′ Wᵗ. Longᵈᵉ in 151°7′ Eᵗ. Variation 8°0′ Eᵗ. Byrons Island Sº 53°31′ Eᵗ. Dist 553 Leagˢ. Tinian West Distᶜᵉ 183 Leagˢ.

p. 183 Wednesday July 24ᵗʰ. PM Wind from SbE / to Sº fresh gales & cloudy weather. AM Wind SbW & SSW with a Swell from the Westward, from which I am much afraid we shall have the wind from that Quarter. Course Nº 85° Wᵗ Dist 130 Mˢ. Latt in 15°18′

N^o. Long^{de} made 24°57′ W^t. M Dist 1463 M^s W^t. Long^{de} made from Masa fuero 126°8′ W^t. Long^{de} in 148 53 E^t. Variation 8°0′ E^t. Byron's Island S^o 56°4′ E^t. Dist 592 Leagues. Tinian S^o 88°40′ W^t. Distance 143 Leagues.

Thursday July 25th. PM fresh gales SbW & Cloudy weather with much Lightning in the night. AM wind SSW & SW. Squally dark weather. A great Swell from the NW. *The Thermometer for some days past at 83 & 84 Deg^s.* Course N° 78° W^t. Dist 74 M^s. Lat in 15°33′ N^o.—Long^{de} made 26°12′ W^t. M Dist 1535 M^s W^t. Long^{de} made from Masa fuero 127°33′ W^t. Long^{de} in 147°38′ E^t. Variation 7°30′ E^t. Byron's S^o 56°58′ E^t. Dist 616 Leag^s. Tinian S^o 86°1′ W^t. Dist 120 Leag^s.

Friday July 26th. Little wind variable between the S^o & W^t with Thunder, Lightning & rain, & very unsettled weather Course S^o 67° W^t. Dist 15 M^s. Latt in 15°27′ N^o. Long^{de} made 26°26′ W^t. M Dist 1544 M^s W^t. Long^{de} made from Masa fuero 127°37′ W^t. Long^{de} in 147°24′ E^t. Variation 6°50′ E^t. Byrons Island S^o 57 0 E^t Dist 621 Leag^s. Tinian S^o 86°52′ W^t. Dist 116 Leag^s. /

Saturday July 27th Little wind from S^o to SW^t & dark cloudy, *p. 184* sultry weather. Course N° 86° W^t. Dist 39 M^s. Latt in 15°30′ N^o. Long^{de} made 27°6′ W^t. M Dist 1583 M^s W^t. Long^{de} made from Masa fuero 128°17′ W^t. Long^{de} in 146°40′ E^t. Variation 6°30′ E^t. Byron's Island S^o 57°55′ E^t. Dist 633 Leag^s. Tinian S^o 85°53′ W^t. Dist 103 Leagues.

Sunday July 28th. PM Calm AM Little wind E^t & Cloudy weather. A great Number of Birds about the Ship. *The Thermometer at 83 & 84.* Course S^o 75° W^t. Dist 73 M^s. Lat in 15°11′ N^o. Long^{de} made 28°20′ W^t. M Dist 1654 M^s W^t. Long^{de} made from Masa fuero 129°30′ W^t. Long^{de} in 145°27′ E^t. Variation 7°0′ E^t Byron's Island S^o 59°32′ E^t. Dist 650 Leag^s. Tinian W^t. Dist 79 Leag^s.

Monday July 29th. PM Little wind variable with hard rain. In the Night a moderate Breeze NE & much Lightning to the W^{t}ward. AM Wind ENE a fine Breeze & fair weather. A great many Birds & Fish about the Ship. Course S^o 85 W^t. Dist 119 M^s. Lat in 15°1′ N^o. Long^{de} made 30°23′ W^t. M Dist 1772 M^s W^t. Long^{de} made from Masa fuero 131°34′ W^t. Long^{de} in 143°23′ E^t. Variation 7°30′ E^t. Byrons Island S^o 61°31′ E^t Dist 684 Leag^s.—Tinian West Dist 39. Leagues.

p. 185 *Tuesday July 30ᵗʰ* PM Fresh Gales at / East & fair weather. At 2 *Saw the Land bearing W½N which proved to be the Islands of Saypan, Tinian, & Aquigan.*[1] At Sun Set the Extremes of them bore from NW½N, Wᵗward to SW & makes all like one Island—& the high Hill of Saypan WNW 5 or 6 Leagˢ.—At 7 haul'd the Wind & stood off & on all night. In the morning had Squally weather. Wind Eᵗerly & hard Rain. At 6 the Extremes of the Islands (which still makes in one) from NWbN to SWbS Dis 5 Leagˢ.—The East Side of these Islands lies NEbN & SWbS & from the NE Point of Saypan (wᶜʰ is the Nᵒermost Island) to to SW point of Aguigan is 16 or 17 Leagˢ. The Islands are between 2 & 3 Leagˢ Distance from each other. Saypan is the largest & Aguigan is a small, high, round Island. We steered along the East side, & at Noon haul'd round the Sᵒ Point of Tinian, between it & Aguigan, & anchored at the SW End of the Island in 16 fᵐ hard Sand & Coral Rocks (for the water is so clear here that we can see the bottom very plain in 24 fᵐ) and opposite to a white Sandy Bay. The Extreme Points of

p. 186 the SW / Side of the Island from SEbS to NW, & the body of the Island of Aguigan SSW Dist 2 Leagˢ. And about a Mile & a quarter from the Shore & ¾ of a Mile from a Reef of Rocks which lies a good distance from the Shore, being the same place where the Centurion lay.[2]

Tinian is in Latt 15°8′ Nᵒ & Longᵈᵉ from London 142°16′ Eᵗ & our Longitude made from Masa fuero is 132°45′ Wᵗ.

I went immediately on Shore to look out for a spot to erect Tents for the Sick which were very numerous; *There is not I believe clear of the Scurvy one single Man in the Ship & many very near the last Stage of that dreadful Disorder.* We found on Shore several Hatts which the Spaniards and Indians had left last Year, for none have been here this, nor I suppose will not come till the bad Season is over, for the Sun is now almost vertical & the Rainy Season set in. We soon got Tents up and the Sick on Shore from both Ships. *As Mʳ Walter in Lord Anson's Voyage has particularly described this*

---

[1] Aguigan is Rota, not Guam which is a full day's run from Saipan. One name for Guam is Agana. The Mariana or Ladrone Group, which were named after Maria Anna of Austria, widow of Philip IV of Spain, in 1668, extends from 13°26′ N, 144°44′ E (Guam) to 20° 33′ N, 144° 48′ E (Pajoros). Guam was visited by Drake in the *Golden Hind* in 1579 and by Cavendish in 1586.

[2] Sunharon Roads.

Island, it might be thought unnecessary in me to | mention any thing p. 187
more than our own Transactions during the time we remained here.
But as it is now three & twenty Years since the Centurion was here,
we suppose it must be owing to that length of time, that we found the
Place so very different from what it was described to be by the above
mentioned Gentleman. After I had pitched upon a Spot for the
Tents, six or seven of us attempted to strike through the Woods in
order to get into those beautiful Meadows & Lawns & kill some
Cattle if possible. It was with the utmost difficulty imaginable that
we got thro' the Wood hollowing & calling to one another every
minute for it was impossible almost to see three Yards before you
for the Underwood, which tore our Shirts & Trowzers to pieced,
which was all we had on or in deed could bear for I believe it is the
hotest place in the World. When we came to the Lawns we found
it in many Places over grown with stubborn kind of Reed or Brush,
higher than / our heads, & all other Parts of it higher than our p. 188
middle.[1] This continually got about our Legs & cut us like so much
whip cord. We saved our Stockings, for we never wore any. I
should have mentioned that we were all this time cover'd with
large Flies and whenever we offer'd to speak we were sure of
having them in our Mouths, or what was worse down our throats.
After walking 3 or 4 Ms we saw a Bull & killed him & returned to
the Beach just before night as wet as if we had been dipped
overboard & as well tired as ever we was in our Lives. The next day
we were employed in Erecting more Tents, getting our Cask on
Shore & clearing the Well, which I imagine to be the same where
Lord Anson water'd, & is by much the worst we have met with for
the Voyage, as it is very brackish & full of Worms. The Road our
Ships lay in is a very dangerous one at this Season for the bottom
is a hard Sand with large Coral Rocks, so that your Anchor has no
hold in the Sand, & it is ten to one but your Cables are cut to
pieces, tho I took all the precaution I was able to prevent it, by
rounding / the Cables well, & buoying them up with Cask. I at first p. 189
moor'd & presently found the Cables much damaged, so that I
resolved to lay single for the future, that by veering away or
heaving in according to more or less wind we should always keep
the Cable from being slack & of course Rubbing, & we found it

---

[1] The grass was 6 to 9 ft. high (Mouat, 136).

119

answer very well. Upon the full & change of the Moon there tumbles in a prodigious swell here, & in my Life I never saw Ships rowl at an Anchor as our's did here. I was once obliged to put to Sea for a week such a Swell drove in from the W^{t}ward & broke so high upon the Ruff, that if our Cable had parted in the Night & the wind had been on the Shore (which sometimes happens for two or three days together) the Ship must innevitably have gone upon the Rocks.—As I had not escaped without a large share of the Scurvy I had my Tent fixed on Shore & remained there a Month. This Island abounds with Limes, Sower Oranges, Coco Nuts, Bread fruit, some Guavoss & Paw-pas, but no Water Melons, p. 190 Scurvy Grass, or Sorrel did we / find. *Our People recovered fast of their Scorbutick Complaints, but were daily falling down in Fevers. I buried two Men here,[1] the first I had lost during this long Voyage, thro' so many different Climates.* I take this to be one of the most unhealthy Places in the World, at least at this Season. The Rains are extremely violent & the Sun so scorching that it is difficult breathing. The *Thermometer was generally near 86 Degrees, this was kept on board, but had it been on Shore it would have rose much higher.* I have been upon the Coast of Guinea & West Indies, & even the Island of St Thomas's under the Line, I dont remember to have felt it any thing near as hot as it is here. The Flies by day & the Muscatos by Night give you not a moments respite, besides it swarms with Antipedes & Scorpions, & a large black Ant, whose bite is almost as painful as that of the two former, & there are a hundred other different venemous Insects so that we were afraid to lie down on our Beds, for several of our People had been bit by them, & we have numbers now in the Ship, brought aboard with p. 191 the / Wood. I sent our People to discover the haunts of the Cattle,[2] they found some at last, but at a great distance from our Tents & those very Shy. Parties were sent out to kill some, but they would be out sometimes two or three days & nights before they killed any, & then the bringing them perhaps 7 or 8 Miles thro' the woods, & such Lawns as I mentioned before, in such dreadful heat, us'd to fatigue the Men so much that few escaped violent fevers, & the

---

[1] Peter Evans, second gunner, and Thomas Watson, quarter master's mate.
[2] Mouat, 136, complained that there were only 1,500 or 2,000 head on the whole island, not the droves of a thousand as Walter claimed.

Meat generally stunk, & was full of flie blows before it reached the Tents. At last one of our Mates found *a pleasant Spot upon the N°west part of the Island where the Cattle were in great Plenty*. It was about 8 Miles from our Tents. I sent our Boat every day there for Beef when the weather permitted, for some times there broke such a Sea upon the Rocks that it was impossible for a Boat to approach them, and the Tamar by an accident of that sort lost three of her best Men. Poultry is in great abundance here & are easily killed, but the / Climate is so excessively hot that in an hour or two after *p. 192* they are killed, the flesh of them is as green as Grass, & swarm with Maggots, but the best of them are very bad tasted. Wild Hogs are likewise in plenty & some of them so large that they weigh near 200 weight. A Black belonging to the Tamar got several of them by laying Snares some of them we have aboard now by way of Sea Stock, they are a very dangerous fierce Animal. Whilst we lay here I sent the Tamar to examine the Island of Saypan. They anchored to Leeward of the Island in 10 f^m about a Mile from the Shore, much the same sort of Ground as the Road of Tinian.[1] They landed upon a Sandy Beach that was 6 or 7 Miles in length; *they found many Trees among the Woods fit for Topmasts*. They saw no signs of Cattle, nor fowls; Hogs there are & guanoes in plenty; they saw a large Pond some distance in Land, but found no fresh water near the Beach. Saypan is a larger Island than Tinian[2] & the Land much higher, & in my opinion appears much pleasanter; they / observed large heaps of Pearl Oyster Shells thrown up together, & *p. 193* signs of People having been there not long before. Possibly the Spaniards come here at a certain time of the Year & carry on a Pearl Fishery. Our People saw many of those Ruins of Rows, consisting of square Pyramidal Pillars that there are at Tinian. Mr Walter says that they thought it prudent to abstain from fish, as the few they caught at their first arrival, surfeited those who eat of them. We wish he had said poisoned, for the word Surfeit I believe implies having eat too much of any particular food, and we imagining that to be the case, *several of us eat sparingly of some very fine looking Fish we caught & got violently poisoned by it*, insomuch that the recovery of some was doubtful for a long time. Before I

[1] Probably off Irai Fahan.
[2] Next to Guam, the largest of the Marianas.

leave this Island it will be necessary to say it produces Cotton & Indigo in great plenty, & would certainly be a valuable Island if it was situated in the West Indies. The Surgeon of the Tamar *p. 194* inclosed / a large spot of Ground & made a very pretty Garden, which however we did not stay long enough to reap any great benefit from. Having been here now *nine weeks & our Sick pretty well recovered*, I got off our Tents, Forge & Oven (for we baked fresh Bread every day for the Sick) & prepared to leave this Island, hoping the NE Monsoon would be set in before we are the length of the Bashe Islands. I laid in about *Two Thousand Coco Nutts for the Ship's Company which I take to be an excellent Antiscorbutick* And the 1st of October weighed & stood along shore in order to take off our Beef Hunters. We had very little wind that day & the next. In the Evening it came to the W^{t}ward, & began to blow fresh. I stood to the N^{o}ward & the next morning made the Island of Anatacan, it is remarkable high Land & was one of those Islands Lord Anson fell in with first.[1]

Friday October 4th Wind from NW to WNW. fresh gales, cloudy with a great Western Swell Course N° 5° W^t. Dist 72 M^s. Latt in *p. 195* 16°15′ N^o. Long^{de} / made 0°6′ W^t. M Dist 6 M^s W^t from Tinian Long^{de} in 142°22′ E^t from London Variation 7°0′ E^t. Tinian S^o 5° E^t. Dist 24 Leagues.

Saturday Octo^r 5th. Wind from NW to WSW hard gales & much rain with a very great Sea. Course N° 64° W^t. Dist 19 M^s. Latt in 16°23′ N^o Long^{de} made 0°24′ W^t. M Dist 23 M^s W^t. Long^{de} in from London 142°40′ E^t. Tinian S^o 16°0′ E^t Dist 28 Leagues.

Sunday Octo^r 6th. Wind from WSW to S^o hard gales & Squalls with much rain, Thunder & Lightning & a very great Sea. Course N° 55° W^t. Dist 78 M^s. Latt in 17°7′ N^o. Long^{de} made 1°31′ W^t Dist 87 M^s W^t. Long^{de} in 140°47′ E^t. Tinian S^o 35°30′ E^t. Dist 50 Leagues.

Monday Octo^r 7th. Strong Gales at South & SbW, Lightning, Rain, & a great Sea. Course N° 63 W^t. Dist 89 M^s. Latt in 17°47′ N^o. Long^{de} made 2°54′ W^t. M Dist 166 M^s W^t. Long^{de} in 139°22′ E^t Variation 7°0′ E^t. Tinian S^o 45°31′ E^t. Dist 77 Leagues.

Tuesday Octr 8th. Wind S^o & SSW Fresh Gales & a great Sea. Course N° 77° W^t. Dist 69 M^s. Latt in 18°2′ N^o. Long^{de} made

[1] Anatahan or Anataxan, about 1,200 ft high (Brigham, 37).

4°4′ W^t. M Dist 233 M^s W^t. Variation 6°0′ E^t. Tinian S^o 52°19′ E^t. Distance 98 Leagues. /

Wednesday Octo^r 9th. Wind S^o & SbE dark weather with a great *p. 196* Western Swell. Course N° 70° W^t. Dist 64 M^s. Latt in 18°24′ N^o. Long^{de} made 5°7′ W^t M Dist 293 M^s W^t. Long^{de} in 137°9′ E^t. Tinian S^o 55°33′ E^t. Dist 118 Leagues.

Thursday Octo^r 10th. Wind PM S & SSW Fresh Gales & Squally. AM WbN & WNW moderate & clear. By Observation find the Ship 22 Miles to the S^{o}ward of Account, owing to a strong Current. Course N° 63 W^t. Dist 20 M^s. Latt in 18°33′ N^o. Long^{de} made 5°26′ W^t. M Dist 311 M^s W^t. Long^{de} in 136°50′ E^t. Variation 5 10 E^t. Tinian S^o 56°6′ E^t Dist 125 Leagues.

Friday Octo^r 11th. Wind from WNW to NbE. fair weather with a great Swell from NW^t. By Observation 9 M^s to the S^{o}ward of Account. Course S^o 67° W^t. Dist 37 M^s. Latt in 18°19′ N^o. Long^{de} made 6°1′ W^t. M Dist 344 M^s W^t. Long^{de} in 136°15′ E^t. Variation by Amp^{de} 3°10′ E^t. Tinian S^o 60°20′ E^t. Dist 132 Leagues.

Saturday Octo^r 12th. Fresh Gales at North & NbE & cloudy weather. Course N° 80° W^t. Dist 105 M^s. Lat in 18°38′ N^o. Long^{de} made 7°51′ W^t. M Dist 449 M^s W^t. Long^{de} in 134°25′ E^t. Variation 3°0′ E^t. Tinian S^o 64°34′ E^t. Dist 167 Leag^s. /

Sunday Octo^r 13th. PM Wind NbW & NNW. AM WNW & W^t. *p. 197* Fresh gales & Squally & a great Swell from the N^{o}ward. Course S^o 84° W^t. Dist 84 M^s. Latt in 18°30′ N^o. Long^{de} made 9°19′ W^t. M Dist 553 M^s W^t. Long^{de} in 132°57′ E^t. Variation 2°30′ E^t. Tinian S^o 68°52′ E^t. Dist 191 Leag^s.

Monday Octo^r 14th. PM Fresh gales at W^t & hazey weather. AM Light Airs of Wind W^{t}ly & calm, with a very great Swell from the N^{o}ward. Course N° 23° E^t. Dist 40 M^s. Latt in 19°7′ N^o. Long^{de} made 9°3′ W^t. M Dist 538 M^s W^t. Long^{de} in 133°12′ E^t. Variation by Amp^{de} 2°20′ E^t. Tinian S^o 64°50′ E^t. Dist 191 Leag^s.

Tuesday Octo^r 15th. Wind from NNE to NE with a great NW Swell. Course N° 77° W^t. Dist 107 M^s. Latt in 19°31′ N^o. Long^{de} made 10°53′ W^t. M Dist 642 M^s W^t. Long^{de} in 131°22′ E^t. Variation 2°0′ E^t. Tinian S^o 66°30′ E^t. Dist 226 Leag^s.

Wednesday Octo^r 16th. Wind NE & NEbE fresh gales & cloudy. Course N° 79° W^t. Dist 175 M^s. Latt in 20°3′ N^o. Long^{de} made 13°55′ W^t. M Dist 773 M^s W^t. Long^{de} in 128°20′ E^t.

Variation by Amp^de 1°20′ E^t. Tinian S^o 69°23′ E^t. Dist 284 Leagues.

p. 198 Thursday Octo^r 17th. Wind from NE / to ENE & E^t. Fresh Gales & Cloudy. Course N° 78° W^t. Dist 145 M^s. Lat in 20°33′ N^o. Long^de made 16°26′ W^t. M Dist 885 M^s W^t. Long^de in 125°49′ E^t. Variation 1°10′ E^t. Tinian S^o 70°40′ E^t. Dist 333 Leagues. The middle of the Bashu Islands N° 85°13′ W^t. Dist 124 Leag^s.[1]

Friday Octo^r 18th. PM Wind variable between SSE & E^t & Squally with Rain. AM Little wind WNW & cloudy weather. By Observation find the Ship 18 M^s N^oward of Account. Several Land Birds about the Ship very tired. We caught one which was resting upon the Booms, a very remarkable Bird, he is as big as a goose, is all white excepting his Legs & beak, which are black, the Bill is carved & of such a prodigious length & thickness that one would imagine it must be a pain to him to hold his head up. I suppose these Birds to be blown off of some Island to the N^oward of us not laid down in the Charts.[2] Course N° 71° W^t. Dist 60 M^s. Latt in 20°53′ N^o. Long^de made 17°27′ W^t. M Dist 942 M^s W^t. Long^de

p. 199 in 124°48′ E^t. Variation 0°50′ E^t. Tinian / South 70°38′ E^t. Dist 352 Leagues. The middle of the Bashu Islands N° 88°4′ W^t. Dist 104 Leagues.

Saturday Octo^r 19th. Little wind Variable & calm for the first part with showers of Rain. AM Little wind NE. & fair weather. Course N° 60° W^t. Dist 36 M^s. Latt in 21°10′ N^o. M Dist 972 M^s W^t. Long^de in 124°17′ E^t. Variation 0°0′ Tinian S^o 70°29′ E^t. Dist 365 Leag^s. The middle of the Bashu Islands S^o 88° W^t. Dist 92 Leagues.

Sunday Octo^r 20th. Fresh Gales at NE & ENE & Squally with hard Rain, & a great following Sea. Course W^t. Dist 162 M^s. Latt in 21°11′ N^o. Long^de made 21°3′ W^t. M Dist 1134 M^s W^t. Long^de in 121°23′ E^t. Variation 0°0′ Tinian S^o 73°18′ E^t. Dis 419 Leag^s.— The middle of the Bashu Islands W½S Dist 38 Leagues.

Monday Octo^r 21st. Fresh Gales ENE & hazey weather. By Observation find the Ship 17 M^s to the S^oward of Account. Course

---

[1] See 'Carte Réduite de l'Ocean Oriental depuis le Cap de Bonne Esperance, jusqu'ai Japan', in Apres de Mannevillette, *Le Neptune Oriental* (Paris, 1745; B.M. Maps 14.e.18): Bashi Islands, a small group of islands, the largest of which are Orange and Grafton, about midway between Formosa and Luzon on the chart. The true position is in the centre of the Luzon Strait but eastward of the *Neptune Oriental* position.

[2] There are no nearby islands to the north. Formosa, to the west-north-west, is the nearest large island.

S^o 81 W^t. Dist 108 M^s. Latt in 20°53′ N^o. Long^{de} made 22°55′ W^t. M D 1240 M^s W^t. Variation 0°0′ Long^{de} in 119°31′ E^t. Tinian S^o 75°1′ E^t. Dist 452 Leagues.

Tuesday Octo^r 22^d. Fresh Gales NE & hazey weather. At 11 PM Saw the Bashu Islands bearing WNW Dist 4 Leag^s.—Haul'd the Wind & stood to the N^{o}ward till day light. At 6 AM the N^o E^t most or / Grafton's Island bore S^o. Dist 6 Leag^s. Bore away & _p. 200_ stood towards it as I did design touching at these Islands. But as it is a very dangerous Navigation from hence to the Streights of Banca,[1] & we have now a fine morn, as well as a fine Gale in our favor, I thought it would be best to proceed on our way, so steered W^t W^d again. At Noon the S^o W^{t}most called Orange Island bore SE & Grafton Island E$\frac{1}{2}$N Dist 12 or 13 Leagues. These Islands which are 5 in number, beside some small ones, lie NE & SW^t & by a good Observation Grafton's Island is in Lat 21°8′ N^o & by our Reckonings with the first Bearing & Distance included, made 24°12′ W^t. Longitude from Tinian. It's Longitude in from London 118°14′ E^t & the Compass hath 1°20′ W^t. Variation.

Wednesday Octo^r 23^d. Fresh Gales ENE & Cloudy weather. Course S^o 69° W^t. Dist 228 M^s. Latt in 19°48′ N^o. Long^{de} made 3°48′ W^t. M Dist 215 M^s W^t from Grafton Island. Long^{de} in 114°26′ E^t. Variation 1°20′ W^t. Grafton Island N° 69° E^t. Dist 76 Leagues.

Thursday Octo^r 24th. Wind ENE & NE Strong Gales & Squally; Kept a good look out for the Triangles, which / lays without the _p. 201_ N^o End of the Pracel, & is a most dangerous Shoal.[2] Course S^o 26° W^t. Dist 187 M^s. Latt in 16°59′ N^o. Long^{de} made 5°13′ W^t. M Dist 296 M^s W^t. Long^{de} in 113°1′ E^t. Variation 2°0′ W^t. Grafton Island N° 50°2′ E^t. Dist 129 Leagues.

Friday Octo^r 25th. Fresh Gales NNE & Cloudy weather. Course S^o 15° W^t. Dist 172 M^s. Latt p Ac^t. 14°12′ N^o. Mr Dist 340 M^s W^t. Long^{de} made 5°59′ W^t. Long^{de} in 112°15′ E^t. Grafton Island N^o.

Saturday Octo^r 26th. PM Wind shifting between NNE & ENE &

---

[1] See William Herbert, *A New Directory for the East-Indies* . . . , 4th ed. (London, 1775), 114–17. The 1st ed. was 1758.

[2] Byron now using 'Carte Plate Qui comprend les Costes de Isiompa de la Cochinchine le Golfe de Tunquin une partie des Costes de la Chine avec une partie de l'Archipel des Isles Philippines', *Le Neptune Oriental*.

Squally with rain. In the Night had variable winds from NE to WNW with Lightning & hard Rain. AM Wind NNE & NE dark weather. Course S^o 24°W^t. Dist 145 M^s. Latt p Ac^t 11°59' N^o. M Dist 399 M^s W^t. Long^{de} made 6°59' W^t. Long^{de} in 111°15' E^t. The S^o End of the Shoals of Pracel SWbW $\frac{1}{2}$W^t as laid down in the English Pilot Dist 60 Leag^s.[1] The Rocks laid down in Latt 10°50' N^o bears SWbS Dist 25 Leagues.

Sunday Octo^r 27th. Wind between the NNE & ENE Squally with Rain. Course S^o 45° W^t. Dist 150 M^s. Latt p Ac^t 10°18' N^o. M Dist 505 M^s W^t. Long^{de} made 8°47' W^t. Long^{de} in 109°27' E^t.

p. 202 Variation by Azth 0°30' W^t. Pulo Condore / S^o 66°26' W^t. Dist 84 Leagues.

Monday Octo^r 28th. PM Wind NE & NEbN Fresh Gales & Cloudy. AM variable between NE & ESE & Squally with Thunder Lightning, & hard Rain. Course S^o 61 W^t. Dist 134 M^s. Latt p Account 9°16' N^o. M D 623 M^s W^t. Long^{de} made 10°47' W^t. Long^{de} in 107°27' E^t. Variation 0°0' Pulo Condore S^o 72° W^t. Dist 42 Leagues.

Tuesday Octo^r 29th. PM Little Wind variable between the NE & SE with hard Rain. AM Wind ENE dark weather & squally with rain. Course S^o 66° W^t. Dist 113 M^s. Latt in 8°29' N^o. M Dist 726 M^s W^t. Long^{de} made 12°31' W^t. Long^{de} in 105°43' E^t. Variation 0°30' W^t. Pulo Condore N° 71° W^t. Dist 32 Miles.

Wednesday Octo^r 30th. Little wind variable between the S^o & E^t & hazey with rain. Several Trees & large Bamboo Canes floating about. Soundings since Yesterday at Noon 23 f^m dark brown Sand & small pieces of Shells. Course S^o 49° W^t. Dist 108 M^s. Latt in 7°17' N^o. Long^{de} made 13°53' W^t. M Dist 807 M^s W^t. Long^{de} in 104°21' E^t. Variation 0°30' W^t. Pulo Timoan SbW$\frac{1}{2}$W. Dist 96 Leagues.

Thursday Octo^r 31st. PM Little wind SE & E^t & fair. Soundings 24 f^m dark brown Sand. AM Wind NE & NNE. Soundings 30 f^m mud. By Observation find the Ship 13 M^s to the N^{o}ward of Account. Course S^o 18° W^t. Dist 59 M^s. Lat Obs^d 6°21' N^o. /

p. 203 Long^{de} made 14°11' W^t. M Dist 825 M^s W^t. Long^{de} in 104°3' E^t. No Variation. Pulo Timoan S^o 19 4 W^t. Dist 76 Leag^s.

[1] Now using *The English Pilot. The Third Book. Oriental Navigation* (London, 1734).

Friday Novem^{r} 1st. Little wind variable, Thunder & Lightning & very unsettled weather. PM Soundings 32 f^{m} AM 36 f^{m} soft Ground. Two Water Snakes passed close along side the Ship, they are said to be so venemous that there is no cure for their bite. But at Tinian two or three of our People were bit by them with without any bad consequences attending it. Course S^{o} 26° W^{t}. Dist 60 M^{s}. Latt in 5°27' N^{o}. Long^{de} made 14°37' W^{t}. Long^{de} in 103°37' E^{t}. M Dist 845 M^{s} W^{t}. Pulo Timoan S^{o} 19° W^{t}. Dist 56 Leagues.

Saturday Novr 2^{d}. Little wind W^{t}erly & Calm with Thunder, Lightning & rain. Since the last Observation to this day at Noon find the Ship 38 Miles to the S^{o}ward of Account. Soundings 42 & 43 f^{m} Mud. Course S^{o} 12° W^{t}. Dist 95 M^{s}. Lat Obs^{d} 3°54' N^{o}. Long^{de} in 103°20' E^{t}. Variation 0°52' W^{t}. Pulo Timoan S^{o} 44° W^{t}. Distance 25 Leagues.

Sunday Novr 3^{d}. Little wind variable from the NW^{t} W^{t}ward to SW^{t} with much Thunder, Lightning & Rain. By Observation find the Ship 18 / Miles to the S^{o}ward of Account. At 7 AM Saw the $_{p.\ 204}$ Island of Timoan bearing SWbW^{t} 12 Leagues. At Noon D^{o} WSW 10 Leag^{s}. Pulo Pisang SW½W 13 Leag^{s}. Pulo Auror SbW½W 14 or 15 Leagues. Course made to Pulo Timoan with the Bearings & Distance included S^{o} 40 W^{t}. Dist 75 M^{s}. Lat of Timoan 2°56' N^{o}. Lat Obs^{d} 3°7' N^{o}. Long^{de} made from Grafton's Island 15°45' W^{t}. M Dis 918 M^{s} W^{t}. Long^{de} in 103°1' E^{t}. Variation 0°52' W^{t}.— Dampier in his Voyages having mentioned Pulo Timoan as a Place where some kind of Refreshments were to be had,[1] I endeavoured to touch there, having lived upon nothing but bad Salt Provisions since we left Tinian; But light Airs, Calms, & S^{o}erly Current prevented our coming to an anchor till the 6th late in the Evening, in a Bay on the East side of the Island in 16 f^{m} about a Mile from the Shore.[2] The next day I landed in order to

---

[1] William Dampier, 'A Supplement to the Voyage round the World', *A Collection of Voyages* (London, 1729), II, 109, listed Pulo Tumaon as a port of call for larger ships sailing northward from Batavia. The run was too long for smaller vessels.

[2] 'Carte des Mers Comprises entre le Detroit de Banca et P^{o}. Timon avec la partie orientale du Détroit de Malacca,' *Le Neptune Oriental*, is excellent for this area. It lists a bay on the west side of the island as an anchorage. However, Byron used the east side.
'On the South end is a Bay, with a Town being inhabited; in which Bay is good Anchor-ground, where is good Water and necessaries to be had' (*The English Pilot*, 73).

see what was to be got; the Inhabitants are Malagans, a Surly, insolent set of People, they came down Armed every one of them having a long drawn knife in one hand, a Spear in the other, headed p. 205 with Steel or Iron, & a Cresset or Dagger by their Sides; / they seemed not at all pleased with our Company, which however we did not much trouble our heads about; All we could procure from them was about a dozen of Fowls, & a Goat & Kid & those very dear. They turned their Noses up at our Truck which consisted of Knives & Hatchets &c^a & chose nothing but Rupees wch we had none of, or Pocket Handkerchiefs which were not very plenty with us neither, & they would not take them if they was not very good. These People are but small in Stature, but very well made. They hid all their Women so that we saw not one of them. Their Houses are neat enough of Slit Bamboo, built upon Posts about 8 feet from the ground. The Men we saw are of a dark copper Colour, they wear a Handkerchief about their heads by way of Turbant, two or three Cloths about their Middle made fast by a large Silver plate, & all the rest of their bodies naked, excepting one old Man who had a kind of Dress something like the Persians. They have neat large p. 206 Boats in which I suppose they trade to / Mallaca. This Island is mountainous & woody, but pleasant enough ashore. They have Rice & the Cabbage Tree & Coco Nut Tree in great plenty, but they did not chuse we should have any of these. There is excellent Fishing in this Bay tho' the Surf runs high. We haul'd our Seynes here & got abundance of fine Fish tho' it did not seem to please the Inhabitants, who look upon all the Fish about these Islands as their own. Two fine Rivers run into this Bay & the Water is extremely good. I filled two Boat loads, as it was so much better than what we had on board. The two Nights we lay here we had violent Thunder, Lightning & Rain. One of our Officers bought a small Animal here which one of the Inhabitants brought down. It had the body of a Hare & the Legs of a Deer, & was very good Eating. Finding there was nothing more to be got here, I sailed again a Thursday Morning with a fine breeze off the Land.

Friday Novr 8th. Little wind S^oerly & calm. Tried the Current & found it set SE a Mile an hour. Soundings 26 & 28 f^m coarse Sand p. 207 & Shells. Course / S^o 48° E^t. Dist 75 M^s. Latt Obs^d 1°40′ N^o. Long^de made from Pulo Auror 0°35′ E^t. Long^de in 105°30′ E^t.

Variation 0°38′ W^t. Pulo Auror N° 48° W^t. Dist 25 Leag^s. Daynon's Shoal SbW$\frac{1}{2}$W Dist 25 Leag^s.

Saturday Novr 9th. Light Airs of Wind at NE & Calms. Soundings 26 & 25 f^m coarse Sand. By Observation find the Ship 12 M^s to the S^{o}ward of Account. The weather most excessively hot, tho the Thermometer is not so high by two Degrees as it was at Tinian. Many Fish about the Ship & several of those water Snakes mentioned before. This must be a wrong time for making this Passage, for since we were in the Latt^{de} of Pulo Condore, we have had nothing but light Airs of wind (excepting now & then Tornados) Calms, violent hard Rains & Thunder & Lightning. Course 4° E^t. Dist 49 M^s. Latt^{de} Obser^d 0°51′ N^o. Long^{de} made 0°58′ E^t. M Dist 58 M^s E^t from Pulo Auror. Long^{de} in 105°42′ E^t. Variation 0°58′ W^t. Pulo Auror N° 31°0′ W^t. Dist 38 Leag^s. Daynon's Shoals SWbW 11 Leagues.[1]

Sunday Novr 10th. PM Little wind Variable from the NW to SW^t with Rain. In the night Calm. AM Little / Wind W^{t}erly & *p. 208* fair. At 7 AM Saw the East End of the Island Lingen[2] bearing SWbW dist^{ce} 11 or 12 Leag^s. Variation by an Azimth 0°24′ W^t. At Noon Calm, Anchored with the Kedge in 20 f^m. The E^t End of Lingen SWbW$\frac{1}{2}$W 12 or 13 Leag^s. Found the Current set ESE$\frac{1}{2}$E a Mile an hour. Soundings from 23 to 20 f^m Oazy with small Shells

Monday Novr 11th. PM Calm & clear weather—at 1 Saw a Small Island bearing SW$\frac{1}{2}$S. Dist 10 or 11 Leag^s AM Little wind & fair. At 1 AM weighed & made sail Wind WbS & SW. at 6 a very remarkable double peak on Lingin bore WbS 10 or 12 Leagues.[3] The Small Island[4] WSW 6 or 7 Leagues; and some very small Islands, which we take to be the Dominis Island[5] W$\frac{1}{2}$N 7 or 8 Leagues. At Noon the High Peak on Lingin bore WbN 10 or 12 Leag^s. Latt Obs^d 0°18′ S^o. The East End of Lingin is in Latt 0°10′ S^o & Long^{de} 105°15′ E^t from London. Soundings from 20 to 17 f^m Oazy Ground.

Tuesday Novr 12th. PM Wind SW Squally & hard Rain. At 6 AM

---

[1] 'A Large Chart Describing ye Streights of Malacca and Sincapore;' *The English Pilot*: shoals 0°30′ N, listed as 'Loos Duynens Droogte'.
[2] Large island on the equator, 0°20′ N—0°40′ S.
[3] Height, 3,957 ft, on the southern part of the island.
[4] Sebangka Island, 17 miles long, only 5 wide.
[5] The old charts show them as a group of small islands ten miles north of the east end of Lingen.

p. 209 anchored in 19 f^m. The double Peak on Lingin / WNW½W 11 Leagues. Found the Current Set NE 1 Knot. AM fresh Gales SW & squally with hard rain. At 1 made the Signal & weighed. At 6 the high Land of Lingin bore WNW½W^t. 12 or 13 Leagues, & Pulo Taga from the Mast head SW 13 or 14 Leagues.[1] Pulo Taga is in the Latt 0°44′ S^o & bears about SbW from the E^t End of Lingin dist^ce 12 Leagues. At 10 Saw a small Chinese Junk to the NE^t. Soundings 16 & 17 f^m Oazy ground

Wednesday Novr 13th. PM moderate breezes W^terly & cloudy. At 6 Pulo Taga bore SWbW 10 or 11 Leag^s, & the E^t End of Lingin WNW 8 or 9 Leag^s.—AM Little wind from SW to W^t & hard rain. At 6 the High land of Lingin NWbW & Pulo Taga WSW½W 8 or 9 Leag^s.—The Seven Islands S^o 10 or 11 Leag^s.[2]—At 7 saw a small Island called Pulo Toty bearing SEbE 11 or 12 Leag^s.—At Noon the wind shifted to NE & NNE with hard rain, thunder & Lightning. The Extreams of the 7 Islands from SSE to S. Dist 5 or 6 Leag^s.—Two small Vessels in sight. Soundings 14 f^m oazy ground.—The Middle of the 7 Islands is in Latt 1°10′ S^o & about 10 Leag^s SE from Pulo Taya. A Little to the N^oward of Pulo Taya *p. 210* is a very / small Island called Pulo Toupoa.

Thursday Novr 14th. PM Wind NE moderate & hazey weather. At 4 Calm. Anchored with the Stream in 14 f^m soft ground. Pulo Taya bearing NW 7 Leag^s. Found the Current set EbS 2 Knots 2 F^m an hour. A Sloop at an Anchor about 4 Miles from us hoisted Dutch Colours. In the night Squally with very hard Rain, Thunder & dreadful Lightning. Wind SW. At 1 parted the Stream Cable & let go the small Bower Anchor. At 8 Wind variable from WNW^t to WSW moderate & cloudy. Got the Longboat out & weighed the Stream Anchor. At 9 made the Signal, weighed & came to Sail. At Noon Pulo Taya bore NW½N 7 Leag^s, and the largest of the 7 Islands SEbE 3 or 4 Leagues. Soundings 15 f^m. Latt Obs^d 1°5′ S^o. Find the Current still set very strong to the Eastward.

Friday Novr 15th. Wind W^t & WbN moderate & cloudy. At 2 Anchor'd with the small Bower in 14 f^m. Pulo Taya NW½N 7 or 8 Leag^s.—Found the Current set SE 1 Knot. I sent a Boat with an

[1] '. . . Malacca and Sincapore', *The English Pilot*: a small island 13 leagues south of the eastern end of Lingen. Modern name and position: Saya Island, 0°47′ S, 104°55′ E.
[2] Tudju Eilanden is the modern name.

Officer on board the Sloop that still lay at an Anchor where she did yesterday & had Dutch Colours flying; But when they got on board they could not make / themselves understood for they were *p. 211* all Malays without one white Man amongst them. They were civil to our People & made tea for them the moment they came on board. The Vessel was of an old construction, her Deck was of Split Bamboo, & instead of a Rudder they have two large pieces of Timber to steer with upon each Quarter. In the night wind SSW & SW. Fresh gales & squally with Thunder, Lightning & hard rain. AM Fresh Gales WSW & cloudy weather. At 6 weighed & made sail At 9 Pulo Taya NWbN 5 or 6 Leag^s & Pulo Toapoa NNW$\frac{1}{2}$W & the largest of the 7 Islands SEbE 5 Leag^s.—Soundings 14 f^m. The Current setting SE 1 Knot Latt Obs^d 1°14′ S^o.

Saturday Novr 16th.[1] Moderate & cloudy weather. Wind variable from NNW to WSW. At 2 PM Monopin Hill bore SbE 10 or 11 Leag^s, & makes like a small Island. It bears SbW 10 or 12 Leag^s from the 7 Islands, & is in the Latt of 2°0′ S^o.—From the 7 Islands steered SWbS & had regular Soundings from 12 to 7 f^m, then saw the Sumatra Shore bearing from WSW to WbN Dist 7 Leagues. At 6 Monopin Hill bore SEbS 9 Leag^s.—Anchored in / 7 f^m. At 4 AM *p. 212* weighed. At 8 Monopin Hill SEbE 6 or 7 Leag^s, and Batacarang Point on the Sumatra Shore SSW Dist 5 Leag^s. Soundings all along 7 f^m.—Course Steered SbE. At Noon when Monopin Hill bore E^t & Batacarang Point SWbS then depen'd the water from 7 to 13 & 14 f^m.

Sunday Novr 17th. PM Wind N^{o}erly moderate & cloudy. Continued the Course SbE till the Peak of Monopin Hill bore E^t & Batacarang Point on the Sumatra Shore SW to avoid a Shoal called Frederick Hendrick, which is about midway between the Banca &

[1] 'Of Sailing through the Streights of Diron from Mallaca.' 'From hence steer away South East by East, and East South East, and you will discover the high Land of *Monopin*, appearing in the Form following. [A profile view is given.] Continue the aforesaid Course more Southerly, in 7, 8, and 9 fathom, till *Monopin* bears South East, and Batacarang South West; from whence stands in for *Sumatra* shore, till you deepen your water to 14 and 15 fathom (to avoid a sunken Rock which is called *Frederick Hendrick*, which lies much about mid-way, between the Head *Banca* and *Sumatra*, as by the Draught doth plainly appear. This Rock bears West South West, from the Westermost Point of *Banca*, about 8 or 10 miles distance.) From hence, with the Tide under foot, continue your Course Southerly, till the high-Land of *Monopin* bear North, and the fourth Point of *Sumatra* South East; here, if necessity require, you may anchor in 13 fathom' (*The English Pilot*, 69–70).

Sumatra Shore. The Soundings 13 & 14 f^m then steered ESE & kept mid-channel to avoid the Banks of Palambam River[1] & the Bank off the W^{t}most Point of Banca; and when abreast of Palambam River had shoal'd the water regularly from 14 to 7 f^m & when past it, deepen'd it again to 15 & 16 f^m.—Continued the Course ESE between the 3^d & 4th Points of Sumatra which are distant 9 or 10 Leag^s—the Soundings all along from 11 to 13 f^m nearest the Sumatra Shore & will see the high Land of Queda Banca[2] over the

p. 213 3^d Point of Sumatra bearing ESE. From the 3^d Point to / the Second the Course is SEbS Dist^{ce} 11 or 12 Leag^s and many borrow the Soundings in 7. 8. & 9 f^m on the Sumatra Shore, about 3 or 4 M^s off. The high Land of Queda Banca & Second Point of Sumatra bear ENE & WSW of each other. The Streights about 5 Leag^s over, & in midchannel had 24 f^m.—At 6 PM anchored in 13 f^m. Monopin Hill bearing N$\frac{1}{2}$W & 3^d Point of Sumatra SEbE between 2 & 3 Leag^s. Saw many small Vessels this day most of them with Dutch Colours.—In the Night SW fresh gales & squally with hard rain, Thunder & Lightning; But there is no danger if your Cables are good, for your Anchor will never come home, as it is buried all over in a stiff Clay. AM the Current or Tide set to the SE 3 Knots. At 5 weighed Wind W^{t}erly, moderate & hazey weather. At 8 the 3^d Point of Sumatra SEbE$\frac{1}{2}$E 3 Leag^s. At 10 Pulo Nanca Islands[3] E^t & 3^d Point of Sumatra WNW$\frac{1}{2}$W^t.—At Noon the high Land of Queda Banca ESE & 2^d Point of Sumatra SSE 3 Leag^s.

Monday Novr 18th. PM Little wind N^{o}ly & fair weather. At *p. 214* $\frac{1}{2}$ past 4 Anchored in 12 f^m. The 2^d Point of / Sumatra bearing NWbN 3 or 4 M^s. A Tide running to the SE 3 Knots. In the Night Wind S & SSW squally weather with Thunder, Lightning & Rain. At 2 AM the Tide shifted & ran as strong to the NW^t so that it flows & ebbs here 12 hours. At 4 little wind W^{t}erly. At 7 weighed. At Noon the high Land of Queda Banca NEbN & the 2^d Point of Sumatra NWbN 3 Leag^s.—The Soundings 11, 12, 13, & 14 f^m 4 Miles from the Sumatra Shore.

Tuesday Novr 19th. PM Wind ENE moderate & hazey. At 3 Anchor'd with the small Bower in 9 f^m the Land of Queda Banca

---

[1] On Sumatra coast.

[2] Permisan Geb, on Adm. Chart 3471; el. 1,539′. The high land consists of three peaks close together.

[3] Group of three islands called Nanga Eil on Adm. Chart 3471.

bearing NbE & the first point of Sumatra SEbE 5 Leag^s. The Course from the 2^d to the 1st point is SEbS 9 or 10 Leag^s.—The Soundings from the Sumatra Shore about 4 Miles off 10, 11, 12 f^m. —In the night little wind & calm. At 5 AM weighed Wind WSW. At 8 the high Land of Queda Banca N^o & the 1st Point of Sumatra SEbE 2 Leag^s. Soundings 13 f^m.—Spoke with an English Snow belonging to the India Company from Bencola, bound to Mallaca & Bengal. The Master of her, hearing that I had nothing to Eat but the Ship's Provisions (which is very bad for *all | our Beef & Pork* p. 215 *stinks abominably & our bread is quite rotten & full of Maggots & Worms*) sent me I believe near half his Stock, consisting of a Sheep, a Dozin of Fowls, & a Turtle, besides 2 Gallons of Arrack, which he would take nothing for, so that I was afraid this good man by his generosity must have distressed himself.

Wednesday Novr 20th. PM Wind SSE fresh Gales & hazey, working round the first of Sumatra. Soundings on the N^{o}Side 14 f^m a Mile & a half from the Shore. At $\frac{1}{2}$ past 3 Anchored in 5 f^m. The first point of Sumatra WNW$\frac{1}{2}$W^t 3 M^s & the Island Lasipara^1 SEbS 6 Leag^s. Sent a Boat to sound for the Shoals to the N^{o}ward of Lasipara. At 6 AM weighed little wind WNW & hazey; the weather excessively hot. Steered SSE about 3 M^s. Soundings 4 & 5 f^m 2 or 3 Miles from the Shore. At 8 Little wind & a strong tide of Flood setting to the N^{o}ward, we lost ground so was obliged to anchor again. At Noon Latt Obs^d 3°2' S^o.

Thursday Novr 21st. Fresh Gales SbE & SSE & hazy. At 3 weighed & worked between the Shoals to the N^{o}ward / of Lasipara & the p. 216 Sumatra Shore, the Channel 1$\frac{1}{2}$ Mile over. The Soundings very regular. In standing over to the Island side, found 9 & 10 f^m & over to the Sumatra Shore 5 & 6 f^m when Lasipara bore SE & the 1st Point NNW had 9 f^m & in standing over to the Shoal on the Island side, shoal'd at once to $\frac{1}{2}$ 6 f^m then K^d imagining we were near it. At 6 anchor'd in 5 f^m. Lasipara SEbE$\frac{1}{2}$E^t. 3 Leag^s & dist from the Sumatra Shore 3 M^s. A Strong flood tide setting to the N^{o}ward & continued at Noon.

Friday Novr 22^d. Little wind variable & Calms. At 2 PM the Tide shifted to the S^{o}ward, weighed, Wind SbE, and worked between

---

^{1} 10 miles east of Lucipara Point, the final point before Byron leaves the Strait. He is now in Stanton Passage.

the Island & Sumatra Shore. In standing to the Sumatra Side had a $\frac{1}{2}$ 4 f^m at 3 Miles distance, & to the Island no Less than 6 f^m when you have brought Lasipara ESE you have no danger to fear from that side, And the best of the Channel is nearest the Island in 5 & 6 f^m. At 7 Anchored in $\frac{1}{2}$ 5 f^m. Lasipara ENE$\frac{1}{2}$E 2 Leag^s.—Sent the Boat ashore to try for Turtle. In the Morning she returned with only one, it weighed 270^{lb} & was full of Eggs. The Island was full of the Trees they call Rosewood, & smelt sweeter than a bed of Flowers. This / Passage has been very tedious having for three weeks past had nothing but calms or light airs of wind & strong Currents. Our People wish much to get to Batavia that they may have something better than bad water to drink, for our Brandy has been out for some time on board of both Ships. At 6 AM weighed Wind WSW^t. At 8 Lasipara NEbE 3 M^s. Depth 6 f^m. By Observation Lasipara is in Latt 3°16′ S^o.

p. 217

Saturday Novr 23^d. PM Calm at 1 anchored in 5 f^m. Lasipara bearing NbE 8 or 9 M^s. At 3 weighed Little wind SE. At 6 Anchored again in 5 f^m. Lasipara NbE 6 or 7 Leag^s. In the Night little wind variable & hard rain. At 8 weighed, a light Air at WbS & cloudy weather. At 9 Lasipara N^o. Dist 8 Leag^s. Steered SbE 4 Leag^s & deepen'd the water from 5 to 8 f^m. Latt in 3°51′ S^o. Lasipara N$\frac{1}{4}$W 11 Leagues.

Sunday Novr 24th. Light Airs of wind variable & calms. PM tried the Current & found it EbS a 1$\frac{1}{2}$ Knot. At 7 Anchored in 13 f^m. At 6 AM weighed Little wind SW & fair Weather. At 8 saw Tree Island from the Masthead bearing W$\frac{1}{2}$S dist^{ce} 8 or 9 Leagues. / Soundings 12 & 13 f^m. Course E^t. Dist 10 M^s. Latt Obs^d 3°50′ S^o. M Dist 10 M^s E^t. Long^{de} made 10 E^t from Lasipara Variation 0°0′. Lasipara N° 16° W^t. Dist 12 Leagues.

p. 218

Monday Novr 25th. PM Little wind from S^o to SE & cloudy weather. At 9 Anchor'd with the Stream in 13 f^m. At 11 weighed fresh gales W^{t}erly & squally with rain. At 9 AM saw the N^o Watcher bearing SbE$\frac{1}{2}$E 7 Leag^s.—The two Sisters[1] WSW & high Land of Bantam SW^t. Soundings 10 to 12 f^m. At Noon the high Land of Bantam[2] SW$\frac{1}{2}$W^t.—The N^{o}ermost of the Thousand

[1] Tree Island, the Two Sisters, and the Thousand Islands are all islands down the east coast of Sumatra.

[2] The high Land of Bantam is the south-west section of Sumatra, a mountain range with an elevation of from 5,000 to 7,000 feet. Byron was probably using a

Islands[1] SSE 7 or 8 Leag^s & the North Watcher ESE$\frac{1}{2}$E^t 4 Miles. Latt Obs^d 5°12′ S^o.—The North Watcher is in the Latt 5°10′ S^o & bears from Lasipara SbE 40 Leagues.

Tuesday Novr 26th. PM fresh gales SW & hazy. At 5 the N^o Watcher bore NWbN 7 or 8 Leag^s & the S^o Watcher SEbS 6 or 7 Leag^s, and the Body of the Thousand Islands SSW Dist from the nearest 1 Mile. Soundings 18 f^m. In the Night light airs variable & calm. At 6 AM Little wind S^o & fair weather. At 7 the S^o Watcher SEbE 2 or 3 Miles. 20 f^m. At 8 Pulo Pari[2] SbW$\frac{1}{2}$W 4 Leag^s. At Noon the S^o Watcher[2] NEbN 1 Mile 27 f^m. Latt obs^d 5°42′ S^o. /

Wednesday Novr 27th. Land & Sea Breezes & fair weather. At 3 PM *p. 219* the S^o Watcher bore NbW 7 or 8 Leag^s Edam E$\frac{1}{2}$S 3 or 4 Miles, & the Island of Onrust[3] SWbS 6 or 7 Miles. Island Edam bears from the S^o Watcher SSE a little E^{t}erly Dist 8 Leag^s.—Soundings 18 or 19 f^m. The true Course from the S^o Watcher into Batavia Road is SSE 9 Leag^s. The Ships at Onrust appear first, but soon after you see the Ships in the Road & the Cupola of the Great Church in the City of Batavia. At 6 PM Steered between the Islands of Edam & Horn[4] into Batavia Road. At 8 Anchored in 8 f^m about 1$\frac{1}{2}$ Mile without the Ships—Onrust bearing WNW 5 or 6 Miles. Edam NNE 5 or 6 M^s & the Cupola S^o 6 Miles.

Thursday (the 28th by our Account but the 29th by the Dutch) weighed & soon after anchor'd amongst the Ships in Batavia Road in 5 f^m soft mud, where you may always lay single without any danger of fouling your Anchor, as it is buried in the mud. The Island of Edam NbE$\frac{1}{2}$E. Horn Island NbW$\frac{1}{2}$W^t.—Onrust NW$\frac{1}{2}$W & the Cupola of Batavia S^o 1$\frac{1}{2}$ Mile from the Shore / Saluted the *p. 220* Water Fort with 11 Guns which was returned. Found above a hundred Sail great & small here, amongst them was a large English Ship belonging to Bombay, who Saluted the Dolphin with 13 Guns.[5] They have always a Dutch Commodore belonging to the

large-scale, untitled chart of Java in *Le Neptune Oriental,* and an excellent chart in *The English Pilot,* 'A Large Draught of the Coast of Iava from Bantam Point Batavia'.

[1] See p. 134, n. 1.
[2] Pilo Pari (North Watcher or Noord Wachter on modern charts) and South Watcher: islands on the approaches to Batavia.
[3] North-west corner of Batavia Bay.
[4] Just off shore.
[5] AB John Robinson, who was probably from this English ship, joined the *Dolphin* 'for single pay'.

Company, who is a Man of great consequence amongst them; He sent his boat on board of me with only the Coxswain in her, who was a very dirty ragg'd fellow, to demand where I ame from, where bound & &cᵃ & pulled out a Book, Pen & Ink to set down the Answers; But to save him all that trouble, he was desired immediately to walk over the Side again & to put off. *I came in here without a Man Sick in either Ship*, but as this is one of the most unhealthy Places in all the East Indies, the rainy Season at hand, & arrack in great plenty, I dreaded the consequences that might attend it, and was resolved to make my stay as short as possble. I went on Shore to wait upon the Dutch General, but was told he was at his Country House about 4 Miles out of Town, and that if

p. 221 I / chose to wait upon him there the Shabander (who is properly the Master of the Ceremonies) would accompany me; accordingly I went with him in his Chariot. The General told me I was welcome to every thing the Place afforded, & that I might take a House in any part of the City I chose for myself, or lodge at the Hotel as should be most agreable to me. The Hotel is kept by a Frenchman, an artful sly fellow & put in by the General himself. It seems there is a Penalty of 500 Dollars to any Person in the City of Batavia who suffers a Stranger to sleep one Night in his House, so that they are obliged to repair to the Hotel the only licensed Lodging House in the Place; Indeed it has more the appearance of a Palace than a Tavern, as it is the finest House in all Batavia, & as several Strangers told me in all the East Indies. Almost all their Houses here are not only finely built in the Inside but a great many of the Out. This is all done by the Chinese who are innumerable here.

p. 222 Carriages / are in such plenty that it is looked upon as a disgrace to be seen walking in the Streets, & if you send for a Taylor he comes in his Chariot with a Slave or two behind. Batavia is a large City, the Streets well laid out, & a Canal runs through most of them, with Rows of Trees planted of each side; this makes it very convenient for the Merchants who have every thing brought up to their own Doors by Water. This City swarms with People, Chinese, Persians, Moors, Malagans, Javans &cᵃ &cᵃ. The Chinese have a large Town to themselves without the Walls. They have 10 or 12 large Junks every Year from China, & indeed the Dutch are indebted to the Chinese chiefly for the considerable figure they make here. The Roads for many Miles about Batavia are as good as the best of the Turnpikes about London, they are very broad, a Canal navigable for large boats, with Rows of fine tall shady Trees runs of each side of them, & of the Side of these again are beautiful Gardens with fine Houses.—As the City is very unhealthy most people chuse to pass as much of their time at their Country Houses as possible, / for the Europeans die here like rotten Sheep. The *p. 223* Heat is excessive & there is no getting a moments rest for Muscatos; for the Trees, the Canals, & a Swampy Ground the City is built on, breed these poisonous troublesome Insects in such numbers that every House is full of them, Antipedes & Scorpions abound here likewise. They have the greatest plenty, as well as the greatest variety of fine Fruits I ever saw in any hot Climate. There Beef is bad, Mutton very scarce, but Poultry good & in great abundance, & have every day a Fish Market well supplied with choice of excellent Fish. Having procur'd what Refreshments I could for my People, & taken on board Rice & Arrack for the rest of the Voyage, *We weighed from Batavia the 10ᵗʰ of December*, The Fort saluted me with 11 Guns & the Dutch Commodore with 13, which I returned. The English Ship likewise saluted us. We worked down to Princes Island in the Streights of Sunda, & came to an Anchor there the 14ᵗʰ.[1] In this Passage Boats came off to us from the Java Shore, & supplied / us with such Quantities of Turtle that our *p. 224* Ships Companies lived upon nothing else; In the same manner they lived all the time they were at Princes, for Turtle is there in great plenty. By the 19ᵗʰ having taken on board as much wood & water as we could stow, we weighed from Princes & got without Java Head[2] before night. *Two or three days after we left Batavia a dangerous putrid Fever broke out amongst our People*, indeed it was only what I expected, for I was told by a Gentleman there, that if we left the Place without burying a Man, he believed we were the first Ship that ever did not withstanding we remaned there so short a time. I lost three of my People[3] in it in a very few days & had many others seized with it, who lay in a wretched condition for

[1] Princes Island: a large island off the western tip of Java. Kassauris Bay is the anchorage.
[2] Java Head: name of the first point of Java and used by Herbert, 129, n.t.
[3] The dead were Cooper Jonathan Godfrey, d. 15 Dec., Carpt. John Dancey, d. 31 Dec., and AB Alexander Fullerton, d. 30 Dec.

along time. The 25th one of my best Men fell overboard & was drowned.[1]

Monday Feby 10th 1766. At 7 in the afternoon thinking ourselves in Soundings brought to, but had no Ground with 120 f^m of Line. At 6 in the Morning saw the Land bearing / from NNW to NE dist^{ce} about 7 Leagues. It makes in several high Hills, & some white Sandy Cliffs, & is in Latt 34°15′ S° & Long^{de} 21°45′ E^t from the Meridian of London. Variation 22° W^t. Depth of Water 53 f^m. Coarse brown Sand. I stood in for the Land & when about 2 Leagues from it saw a great smoke made upon a Sandy Beech, tho' I imagined it might have been made by Hotentots, yet I was astonished at their chusing such a part of the Coast to reside on, for all the Land as far as we could see was nothing but Sand Banks without the least Bush or Verdure, & there breaks a heavy Sea upon the Coast, so that it is impossible for them to get any Fish. Upon my arrival at the Cape I was mentioning this Circumstance to the Governor, & some Gentlemen that dined with him, they told me that some time since a Ship fell in with that part of the Coast & had seen large Smokes made as we had done, that there was no Inhabitants that way, and it was imagined to be an Island. That about two Years ago / two Dutch India Men sailed from Batavia for the Cape & had never since been heard of, & that it is now supposed that either one or both of them might have been lost there, & that the Smokes we saw were made by some of the unfortunate Crew. That they had once or twice sent out Vessels to look for them but there broke so great a Sea upon the Coast they were obliged to return without doing anything. I wished much to have known this melancholly Account before, as I would have tried all in my power to have relieved those poor people who I think have now but a small chance of ever getting from thence.

Thursday Feby 13th.[2] At 3 PM was abreast of Cape Lagullas, from this Cape the Coast lies WNW 30 Leag^s to Cape Bona Esperance.

p. 225

p. 226

---

[1] Qtr. gunner William Walker.
[2] Byron probably used *The English Pilot* chart 'A Draught of the South Part of Africa from Cape Bona Esperance to Delagoa' facing p. 25.

Friday Feby 14th. Passed between Penguin Island & Green Point & worked into Table Bay[1] with close Reeft Topsails, wind SSE Strong Gales with excessive hard Squalls. At 3 Anchored with the small Bower in 7 f^m & moored; Got down / Top Gallant Yards & *p. 227* struck Yards & Top Masts. The Dutch told me none of their Ships could have worked in, in such a Gale of Wind, & that we seemed to come in faster that way than they generally do with a fair wind. Saluted the Fort which was returned.—The next morning I waited on the Governor who had sent his Coach & Six to the Water side for me. He is a Man of an exceeding good Character, much liked by all the Inhabitants of the Cape. He was extremely polite & civil to me, not only at this visit but all the time I was here; & was so obliging to offer me the Company; House in the Garden to live in, & the use of his Coach while I remained here. This is certainly a most excellent place for Ships to touch at, a healthy Climate, a fine Country, & refreshments of all kinds in the greatest abundance. I allowed all all People to come on Shore by turns, & they always contrived to get very drunk with the Cape Wine before they returned. The Company's Garden is a delightful / Spot, at the end of it the Governor has a Paddock with a number of *p. 228* curious Animals in it, & three fine Ostriches, which kind of Bird are in great plenty in the Plains about the Cape. The Governor shewed me four very large Zebras, which he intends sending to Holland as soon as he gets two more. Whilst we lay here, there came in many Ships, Dutch, French & Danes all outward bound. Having been here three weeks, our Water compleat & our People well refreshed, I took my leave of the good old Governor and prepared to Sail.[2]

Thursday March 6th. Weighed in the Evening with a fine breeze at SE. Sailed out to the E^tward of Penguin Island which is the best channel for Ships bound to the N^oward. There is no danger in going out, only observe to come no nearer Penguin Island than 7 or 8 f^m.

Sunday March 16th. At 6 in the Morning saw the Island of S^t

[1] Penguin Island is 4½ miles north of Green Point. The channel into Table Bay, the anchorage, lies between Penguin Island and Green Point (see *The English Pilot*, chart 'monomatapa', facing p. 21).
[2] The Muster Sheet lists marine Pte Samuel Holding as having run from the ship on March 17 at the Cape of Good Hope. The date must be inaccurate.

Helena bearing WbN 15 or 16 Leag^s.—Soon after saw a large Ship off the S^o End of the Island who shewed French Colours.

Tuesday March 25th. At 4 in the Afternoon crossed the Equator in Long^{de} 17°10′ W^t from London. Early next morning Capt *p. 229* Cumming came on board & / informed me *that the Tamar's three Lower Rudder Braces on the Stern were quite broke off, which render'd the Rudder unserviceable.* I immediately sent our Carpenter on board, who found it even worse than reported, & accordingly went to work directly in order to fix a Machine to steer by, after the manner of that the Ipswich came home with, & in five days time compleated & hung it, & with some little Alterations of his own made an excellent piece of work of it. The Tamar steered well with it, but as this Machine at best is only a make Shift, & not calculated for bad weather, or a Lee Shore, & we now imagined we had got the NE Trade, I gave Capt Cumming Orders to run down to Antigua, *there to heave down & get his Rudder hung again, having with him a new Set of Braces for that purpose, as it was not imagined when we left England that Iron Braces would hold out with a Copper* *p. 230* Sheathed Bottom. *All our lower ones being of Copper, dont / complain in the least, but the two upper ones, which are Iron, are prodigously worn.*

April 1st. The Tamar parted company & steered for the Carribee Islands. In our Run between St Helena & the Equator with a fresh Trade, *our Ship one morning received a very rude Shock as if she had touched the Ground, & presently after we saw the Water for a large space covered with Blood, so that we struck either a Whale or Grampuss, but we have not perceived the Ship has got any damage by it.*

In this passage we buried our Carpenter's Mate a very clever Young fellow, he had never been well since we left Batavia.[1]

In the Latt^{de} of 34° N^o & Long^{de} 35° W^t from London, we had strong Gales from WSW to NNW with a prodigious great Sea which broke over us continually for six days together, at the end of which time it run us into the Latt^{de} of 48° & Long^{de} 14° by our Reckoning.

p. 231 Wednesday May 7th. At 8 this / morning made the Islands of Scilly, having been just nine weeks from the Cape of Good Hope, & a little more than Twenty two months upon the Voyage.

[1] Thomas Madison. The Muster Sheet shows him as having died on 13 Sept. 1765, 'At Sea'. Again the date is wrong.

Appendix I

THE DOLPHIN'S CREW

The Dolphin's Crew

This list was compiled from the *Dolphin*'s Pay Book (PRO Adm 33/441) and from the alphabetical Muster Roll contained in the Pay Book. It includes only those men who actually sailed on the *Dolphin*. It omits members of the ship's company who either 'ran' or were discharged before the ship sailed from Plymouth.

Name	Rank	Reported aboard
Adams, Thomas	AB	10 May 1764
Attwell, Samuel	AB	12 May 1764
Baker, Henry	AB	1 July 1764
Baxter, William	Boatswain	18 April 1764
Discharged 23 February 1765		
Benson, William	Yeoman of the Sheets	5 May 1764
Bevan, Thomas	Boatswain's Mate	30 June 1764
Blackford, John	AB	7 May 1764
Blythe, Henry	AB	24 May 1764
Discharged 23 February 1765, 'unsble' [unsuitable]		
Bolton, John	AB	26 May 1764
Bowers, Nathanial	AB	19 May 1764
Bowles, Robert	AB	1 June 1764
Brine, James	Master's Mate	7 May 1764
Brodie, Robert	AB	21 April 1764
Broom, Joseph	AB	12 May 1764
Ran 31 October 1764, Rio de Janeiro		
Bulson, William	AB	10 May 1764
Byron, Hon. John	Captain and Commander-in-Chief	28 March 1764
Discharged 27 April 1765		
Byron, Michael	Quartermaster	8 May 1764
Canty, Dennis	AB	29 May 1764
Carteret, Philip	Lieutenant	28 April 1765
From *Tamar*		
Castle, Robert		15 May 1764
AB to 3 July 1764, then Mid. to 11 January 1765, then AB to 7 February 1765, then Mid.		

Chalmer, William	AB	29 May 1764

Ran 30 November 1764, Rio de Janeiro

Clarke, Charles	AB	17 May 1764
Clear, James	Armourer (Warranted)	3 July 1764
Clover, Jacob	AB	1 June 1764
Cole, John	AB	29 May 1764
Conolly, William	Master at Arms	12 May 1764
Cragg, William	Gunner	5 May 1764
Crews, Walter	Gunner's Mate	15 June 1764
Crosby, Wilson	Carpenter's Mate	23 April 1764
Crosier, John	Surgeon	28 March 1764
Cumming, James	Lieutenant	28 March 1764

Discharged 27 April 1765 to *Tamar*

Dancey, John	Carpenter	28 April 1764

Died 31 December 1765, Indian Sea

Darvell, Thomas	AB	20 April 1764

Ran 31 October 1764, Rio de Janeiro

Dawson, William	AB	30 June 1764
Dennis, William	Carpenter's Crew	30 June 1764
Dobson, Barney	AB	8 May 1764
Eastley, Charles	AB	30 June 1764

AB to 3 July 1764, then Mid. to 2 April 1765,
then AB to April 29 (fol.), then Mid.

Elvey, Joseph	Boatswain's Mate	29 May 1764
Evans, Peter	Second Gunner	15 June 1764

Died 13 September 1765, Tinian Hospital

Fallow, Joseph	AB	1 May 1764
Forster, John	Coxswain	21 May 1764
Francis, John	AB	1 May 1764

AB to 26 March 1766, then Carpenter's Crew

Fraser, James	AB	5 May 1764
Fullerton, Alexander	AB	1 June 1764

Died 30 December 1765, at Sea

Gardner, Joseph	AB	12 Sept. 1764
Gill, Peter	AB	19 May 1764

AB to 3 July 1764, then Quartermaster

Godfrey, Jonathon	Cooper	7 June 1764

Died 15 December 1765, Strait of Sundra

Goodman, Peter	Quartermaster	28 June 1764
Gore, John	Midshipman	23 May 1764

Mid. to 25 May 1764, then Master's Mate

Gosling, Thomas	Sailmaker (Warranted)	1 July 1764
Gower, Erasmus	AB	29 June 1764

AB to 9 July 1764, then Master's Mate

Graves, Frederick	Master's Mate	8 May 1764
Gray, James	AB	3 July 1764

Discharged 12 May 1766, 'for single pay'

Greenstade, Stephen	Quarter Gunner	16 April 1764
Grigg, John	AB	7 June 1764
Grosvenor, William	AB	7 May 1764

AB to 3 July 1764, then Mid. to October 20 (fol.),
then AB to November 18 (fol.), then Mid.

Hait, Francis	Carpenter's Crew	23 April 1764
Hardyman, Samuel	Yeoman of the Powder Room	5 May 1764
Harris, Joseph	Midshipman	28 March 1764

Mid. to 3 July 1764, then AB to July 31 (fol.), then Mid.

Holland, John	AB	23 May 1764
Hughes, Joseph	AB	21 April 1764
Hunter, Thomas	AB	11 May 1764
Jarrett, Joseph	Quarter Gunner	7 April 1764
Jeggar, Francis	Quarter Gunner	30 June 1764
Jenkins, Arthur	Coxswain	24 May 1764

Cox. to 23 February 1765, then Boatswain

Johnson, Archibald	AB	19 May 1764
Johnson, Stephen	AB	15 June 1764
Kelson, Peter	AB	1 May 1764
Kempe, Arthur	Midshipman	27 April 1764

Mid. to 23 September 1764, then AB to October 20
(fol.), then Mid.

Kendall, John	Master's Mate	28 March 1764

Master's Mate to 3 July 1764, then Mid.;
discharged 27 April 1765 to the *Tamar*

Kennedy, Thomas	AB	30 June 1764

Ran 31 October 1764, Rio de Janeiro

Kerr, John   AB   7 May 1764
     AB to 3 July 1764, then Mid. to November 18 (fol.),
         then AB to December 13 (fol.), then Mid.

Kerton, William   AB   28 April 1765
               [from *Tamar*?]

Lake, Thomas   AB   16 April 1764
       'Straggling' in Rio de Janeiro

Langman, William   AB   1 July 1764
     AB to 3 July 1764, then Mid. to 20 April 1765,
         then AB to May 25 (fol.), then Mid.

Leonard, William   Quarter Gunner   30 April 1764
Lippingwell, James   AB   4 June 1764
Ludlow, William   Sailmaker's Crew   23 May 1764
Lugge, Henry   AB   14 April 1764
Madison, Thomas   Carpenter's Mate   15 June 1764
        Died 13 September 1765, at Sea

Manley, Joseph   AB   30 June 1764
     AB to 5 July 1764, then Mid. to 7 February 1765,
         then AB to March 6 (fol.), then Mid.

Marshall, John   Second Lieutenant   12 June 1764
Meuse, Dominick   AB   27 April 1764
Midwinter, Samuel   Quartermaster's Mate   7 April 1764
              and Smith

Miles, William   Quartermaster   27 April 1764
Morgan, Henry   AB   7 June 1764
     AB to 16 December 1765, then Cooper

Mouat, Patrick   Captain   28 April 1765
             from *Tamar*

Murray, James   Cook   28 March 1764
Nashe, John   AB   23 April 1764
Nicholas, Francis   AB   18 April 1764
      Ran 31 October 1764, Rio de Janeiro

Ogelvie, William   AB   7 June 1764
Painter, Charles   AB   19 May 1764
Parum, Charles   AB   19 May 1764
Peacock, James   AB   24 Feb. 1765
             [from *Tamar*?]

Peppon, William	AB	15 May 1764

AB to 3 July 1764, then Mid. to December 15 (fol.),
then AB to 11 January 1765, then Mid.

Phillips, George	Steward	5 June 1764
Price, Robert	AB	7 April 1764
Purton, Patrick	Quarter Gunner	5 May 1764
Ranter, William	AB	29 May 1764

Ran 30 November 1764, Rio de Janeiro

Reede, Edward	Sailmaker's Mate	4 May 1764
Richardson, Robert	AB	23 April 1764
Roberts, Robert	AB	14 May 1764
Robertson, George	Third Lieutenant	12 June 1764
Robinson, Daniel	AB	28 April 1764

Ran 31 October 1764, Rio de Janeiro

Robinson, John	AB	27 Nov. 1765

At Batavia, 'for single pay'

Robinson, William	Midshipman	21 April 1764

Mid. to 31 July 1764, then AB to August 27
(fol.), then Mid.

Royal, John	AB	30 June 1764
Russell, Antony	AB	11 May 1764

AB to 9 August 1765, then Quartermaster's Mate

Russell, Phillip	AB	26 May 1764
Sharkay, John	AB	19 May 1764
Shaw Robert	AB	26 May 1764

Discharged 23 February 1765, 'unsble'

Simpson, John	AB	30 June 1764

AB to 3 July 1764, then Mid. to 6 March 1765,
then AB to April 30 (fol.), then Mid.

Skelton, Hill	AB	15 June 1764
Skyrme, William	AB	29 May 1764

Discharged 23 February 1765, 'unsble'

Smith, Richard	AB	28 March 1764
Spicer, William	AB	15 May 1764
Stacey, Henry	Purser	23 April 1764
Stanley, John	Captain's Cook	30 June 1764
Stevens, Thomas	AB	7 May 1764
Stroke, Patrick	AB	10 May 1764

Symonds, John	AB	5 April 1764

Ran 31 October 1764, Rio de Janeiro

Taylor, James	AB	11 May 1764
Taylor, James	AB	19 May 1764
Thomas, George	Trumpeter	17 May 1764
Tichfield, Samuel	AB	7 May 1764
Tothill, William	Clerk	1 April 1764
Treadway, William	AB	23 May 1764
Vickous, James	AB	27 April 1764

'for single pay'

Walker, William	Quarter Gunner	11 May 1764

Died, 25 December 1765, at Sea

Walter, George	AB	2 May 1764

Discharged 31 December 1765

Warron, Nickolas	AB	30 June 1764
Watson, Thomas	Surgeon's Mate	6 April 1764
Watson, Thomas	Quartermaster's Mate	4 May 1764

Died 7 August 1765, at Tinian Hospital

Webster, James	AB	12 Sept. 1764

Discharged 23 February 1765, 'unsble'

Weston, John	Carpenter's Crew	30 June 1764
Widows, Man	AB	28 March 1764
Williams, John	AB	24 May 1764

AB to 14 September 1765, then Quarter Gunner

Wisondon, Robert	AB	8 May 1764
Yates, Robert	Carpenter's Crew	17 April 1764

Carpenter's Crew to 26 March 1766, then
Carpenter's Mate

MARINES

Name	Rank	Reported Aboard[1]
Adams, Joseph	Drummer	
Bowdon, John	Private	
Douglas, Matthew	Sergeant	
Fenny, Daniel	Private	
Grimes, Richard	Private	

[1] All marines reported aboard on 28 June 1764.

Holding, Samuel	Private
Ran 17 March 1766, Cape of Good Hope	
Meadass, William	Private
McGeary, John	Private
McGinnis, Christopher	Private
Parslow, Thomas	Captain
Pasco, James	Private
Quinn, John	Private
Stoneman, Henry	Private
Discharged, 23 February 1765, because of sickness	
Taylor, John	Private

Appendix II

DOCUMENTS

Document 1

Letter from Byron to the Earl of Egmont sent via Florida *Storeship, 24 February* 1765[1]

24 Feb. 1765.
Capt. Byron.
Communicated in Circulation
to
    M^q Conway
    Duke of Grafton
    Mar^q of Rockingham—1^t Comm. Treas.
    Earl of Winchelsea—Pr. Coucl.

    SECRET

Rec^d by Lord Egmont Saturday
22^d June 1765 in the Evening.

My Lord
    When I had the Honor of writing last to Your Ldship from Rio
Janiero, I informed You that Our Ships were then ready for the
Sea, but after dropping down to the Harbours Mouth We were
detained a Week for a Wind to carry Us out. It was the 21st of
Octo^r. We sail'd from hence & arrived at Port Desire the 21st
Novem^r after a Passage of continued Hard Gales, in One of which
(the hardest I ever remember to have been in) the Dolphin was
near overset. I remain'd at Port Desire about a Fortnight, & then
put to Sea again to look for Pepys Island but after cruizing for It
for some time We are well assured there is no such Island, at least
any where near to the Latitude & Longitude it is laid down in, in
Lord Anson's Voyage. We met with much bad Weather in this
Cruize I then intended to look for Falklands Islands but as We
were both Ships in great Want of Wood & Water, neither of which
are to be had at Port Desire, I thought it would be most prudent to
put into the Streights of Magellen, the only certain place We knew

[1] PRO Adm 1/162 and PRO SP 94/253.

of for finding either, & supposing We had not / been able to find
Falklands Islands, the Westerly Winds blowing with such Violence
in these High Latitudes, it would have been ten to one if We had
recover'd the Main afterwards. For these Reasons I stood for the
Streights & had no sooner enter'd them than We saw a great
Smoke a little to the Northward of Cape Virgin Mary, and near to
the Spot where Bulkeley mentions his having seen those Horsemen,
who rode in great Order & waved white Handkerchiefs to him to
come on Shore, which Your Ldship will please to remember I told
You always stagger'd me much, no Horsemen having ever been
seen before by any of the Voyage Writers near the Streights of
Magellan, nor for many degrees to the Northward of It, & for that
Reason I said to Your Ldship that if it were possible I would
discover what those People were: accordingly the next day I stood
in with my Ship as near as I could to the Shore (which was still
kept up) and came to an Anchor. I could then easily perceive with
my Glass a Number of Horsemen riding along the Strand just in
the Order Bulkeley mentions to have seen / them & waving to Us
to come on Shore. I hoisted my Boat out & rode towards them &
Mr Cumming the first Lieutenant followed me in another: When I
came near the Shore I saw near 500 People, some on Foot, but most
on Horseback. They drew up upon a strong Spot that ran some
way into the Sea, where it was very bad landing. These People kept
waveing & hollowing to Us to come on Shore as We understood
them. I made Signs to them to retire to some distance which they
did. We could not perceive they were armed, but they made a
prodigious Noise. after some time We landed with a great deal of
difficulty, being up to the Middle in Water—I drew up my people
on the Beach with two Officers at their head, being all well arm'd, &
gave Orders that none should move a Step till I either call'd or
beckon'd to them.—I then went up alone to these People, but they
retired as I advanced. I made Signs for One of them to come near
which they understood, & seeing I was followed by nobody
accordingly One of them came . . . This Person was / a Chief
amongst them & was One of the most extaordinary Men for
Size I had ever seen till then; We mutter'd something to One
another by way of Salutation, & I walk'd a little farther with him
to the rest. I observ'd he constantly kept his Eye upon my People

who I had left drawn up as mention'd before. As soon as I had got among such Numbers, I made Signs to them to sit down, which after some little time they complied with, but I never was more astonish'd than to see such a set of People, the stoutest of Our Grenadiers would appear nothing to them. They were painted in the most frightful Manner imaginable, some of them had a large Circle of White Paint round One Eye & about the other a Circle of Black or red; others had their Faces streaked all over with different Colour'd Paint.—Nothing in Nature could appear more terribly frightful than these People did both Men & Women. Our People before We landed swore they were all mounted on Guanicoes, their Horses appear'd so small in Comparison to their Riders, tho' when I was near them I observ'd their Horses were of / the Common Size, and Our People on Board, who were looking at Us thro' their Glasses, said We look'd like meer Dwarfs to the People We were gone amongst. Many of the oldest amongst them kept singing a most doleful Tune & seemed extremely earnest all the time—They were all Cloath'd in Skins of Wild Beasts of different kinds which they wore as a Highlander does his Plaid—Many of these Skins were very curious & very large, as indeed they ought to be to cover these People, who in Size come the nearest to Giants of any People I believe in the World—Excepting the Skins which they wore loose about them with the Hair inwards, they were most of them naked. I made them some trifling Presents which pleased them greatly. I observed One Woman amongst them with Bracelets on her Arms which were either of Brass or Pale Gold—I wanted much to know where they got them, but could never make them understand Me—however after being with them some time they made me understand that they wanted me to get upon One / of their Horses & Go some where with them, but I made Signs to them in return that I must go on Board upon which they seem'd to express great concern.—When I left them not One offer'd to follow me, but as long as I could see them after they all continued seated on the same Spot I left them.—These People are not Inhabitants of the place I saw them in, for I intended paying them another Visit as I came down again but they were all gone. From thence I proceeded up as high as this place which is an exceeding good Port with Plenty of Wood & Water—I went from hence to Port Froward in my Boat, which I take to be half thro' the Straits & had I been bound at that time into the South Sea, I make no doubt but We should have got thro' in a Fortnight from the time of Our first entering the Streights. After We had finished Our Business here I return'd the same way in Order to look for Falklands Islands which We found & in them One of the finest Harbours in the World. I named it after Your Ldship & of what / Import such a Discovery of such a place may be One time or other to Our Nation Your Ldship will be the best Judge of It has the greatest plenty of good Water & Nothing wanting but Wood.—The Soil is extremely good Wild Fowl of different kinds in such Abundance that Our People lived upon nothing else whilst We were there—It was seldom that We took less than an hundred Wild Geese in a day for each Ship & that by only knocking them down with Stones The Land is all cover'd with Wood Sorrel & Wild Sellary, which are the best Anti-scorbuticks in the world. I had always a large Quantity of them boild every Morning for the Ships Company mix'd with Oatmeal & portable Soup, which last Article is One of the best things that ever was thought of for such a Voyage—Mr Stephens informs me the French have been lately at the Isles Malouins So Falklands Islands are call'd in some Charts: if Your Ldship will please to look over Freziers Voyage You will see that the French themselves acknowledge Our Countryman Sir Richd Hawkins to / have been the first Discoverer of Falklands Islands—As for Port Egmont I am almost certain that We are the first Ships that ever have been there since the Creation, & I coasted the Island above 70 Leagues afterwards but saw no Smokes nor Signs of any Body's being there —This Island is very large—I dare say at least 6, or 700 Miles round, but part of the Coast is extremely dangerous; I went as far as any Ship would dare to venture & quite to the South End of It, after that it becomes a Lee Shore a prodigious Sea tumbles in upon It & sunken Rocks lay off 3 or 4 Leagues from It, & besides after that the Country appears just like Staten Land, nothing but high barren rugged Rocks—I fancy there may be many Mines in it, for the Country seems to promise It.—I dug in several places & found Iron Ore in Abundance, but if proper Persons were sent who understand It, possibly something more valuable might be found. —I took Possession of this Country in form for His Majesty &

Heirs— / I have kept a Journal of this Voyage which, in Case any thing happens to me and the Ships ever return home I shall desire may be deliver'd to Your Ldship.—No Soul has ever seen it besides myself and in it I have been as particular as possible.—I wish'd much to have sent it now but I was afraid to trust it to the Storeship and I have no time to copy it, & I don't chuse any body else should.—After I had done with Falklands Isles, I return'd to Port Desire & found the Storeship there a perfect Wreck Our Carpenters & Blacksmiths work'd very hard to get her into some Condition to proceed with Us to this place for it is impossible to get any thing out of her at Port Desire from the rapid Tides that run there which makes it One of the most dangerous Harbours in the World—The Storeship had been twice ashore there, & otherwise I must have come up here as soon as possible for the Tamer's Rother is Sprung or rather split all to pieces and there is no finding Timber for a new One at any other place than This— The Dolphin's Main Mast is Sprung & She has been twice ashore / and both times in great Danger of being lost.—Now in coming from Port Desire to this place between Cape Fair Weather & Cape Virgin Mary early in the Morning We saw a strange Ship who kept at a great distance from Us, but always Shaped the same Course I did—The next Morning We were off Cape Virgin Mary & then made all the Sail We could to get into the Straits imagining the strange Sail might be a South Sea Man bound round Cape Horn, tho' very late in the Season for that;—but We were much mistaken for We soon after saw her steering directly after Us—It blew hard & I was in great hopes She would have run ashore for the Navigation is extremely difficult to those who are not well acquainted—The Misfortune was that the Store Ship was a great way aStern of Us, therefore serv'd as a Pilot to the other—After We had pass'd the first narrow, which is 17 Leagues from Cape Virgin Mary, I brought to for the Florida & after putting my Ship in the best Order I could for It, I was resolved to speak with the / Stranger & ask him the Reason he followed Us in the Manner he had done for two days past, but after he had got thro' the narrow & saw me laying to, he did the same about 4 Miles to Windward of me—Night came on & the Tide setting me over to the South Shore We came to an Anchor. At night the Wind shifted to the Westward

& at day break I saw the same Ship about 2 or 3 Leagues to Leeward of me at an Anchor—The Tide of Flood making, I thought of working thro' the Second narrow, but seeing the Stranger getting under Way & working up towards Us, I ran directly over into Gregory's Bay & brought my Ship to an Anchor with a Spring upon Our Cable, & got all Our Guns over of One Side which was Right & those I got out of the Hold on the Occasion & was all I could get at—I was obliged to throw Six overboard in a hard Gale of Wind—In the mean time this Ship work'd up to Us & various were Our Conjectures upon the Appearance She made—She shew'd no Colours, nor did We—The Florida in attempting to come to an Anchor near us ran aground—The Stranger / who came to an Anchor some little way a stern of her, hoisted French Colours & very officious in sending his Launch with an Anchor & another Boat to assist her I shew'd him no Colours but sent the Tamer's & our Boats to assist the Storeship & with Orders to the Officers who commanded them not to let the French Boats come on Board of her, but to thank them for their intended Assistance which was accordingly done & the Storeship got off presently after. —This French Ship is full of Men & seems to have a great many Officers . . . She followed Us up as high as this & is gone on toward Point Froward—I imagine She is either from the Islands to get Wood here, or else upon a Survey of these Straits;—I shou'd rather think the latter, for if the first had been his Intention, it certainly was not necessary for him to come up as high as this to procure It.—In all probability I shall soon know, for I intend if possible, to push thro' the Straits before the Season is too far advanced, for it would be impossible to follow the first / Scheme of wintering in these parts as it would be full Eight Months from this time before I could put to Sea again, for We came upon this Coast much too soon & paid for it accordingly besides that I should not have Provisions (but especially Brandy) to proceed any where afterwards, for I have been obliged to keep the People all along upon whole Allowance or they would never have been able to have gone thro' half the fatigues they have already and I must say here that I never saw better Provisions put on board a Ship than We brought out with Us—owing in a great Measure to that, I have but very few sick, & they have been so for a long time—Amongst them is my Boatswain, as good a Man as ever came into a Ship—I intend to send them home, I question much whether the Boatswain will live to return, & if he does & should recover, I humbly hope Your Ldship will give him a large Ship, as he left the Fame to come with me—As for the Rest of the People they are all healthy strong & stout & willing to go thro' any thing from the / Encouragement that has been promised them if they behave well. There was not One person in either Ship that had the least Suspicion where they were coming to, till I made them acquainted with It after leaving Rio Janiero.—I hope I have done everything here Your Ldship could expect, as to running 2 or 300 Leagues to the Eastward from Falklands Islands, it is an utter impossibility to do it without One was to proceed on to the Coast of Africa afterwards, for there is no getting back to the Westward, as the Easterly Winds blowing with the utmost Fury constantly prevail here & there runs such a Mountanous Sea that there is not the least Chance of gaining any thing to Windward—I intend now to run over for India by a new Track which if I succeed in I hope Your Ldship will approve of— Our Ships are too much disabled for the California Voyage—If Your Ldship should ever get my Journal You will see that We have gone thro' already an infinite deal of Fatigue & many dangers the / natural Consequence of such an Undertaking but I protest for my self that I have gone thro' them with the greatest Chearfulness and I can safely say that in either Ship no man has had so large a Share of them as I have—I now know of several convenient places where Ships may get every thing they could expect.—I hope I shall one day have the Honor of informing Your Lordship of all particulars myself—I intended at first to have given the Storeship orders to have remained here Six Weeks in Case I should not be able to get through the Straits We might have taken the rest of the Provisions out of her, for We have now as much as We can hold allowing for a great Quantity of Water We are obliged to take with Us for so long a Run—but as that French Ship may possibly turn back or others come into the Straits, I think it by no means safe for her to lay here with my letters on board, as I make no doubt those Gentlemen would make very free with her (probably under Spanish Colours) when I was not here to protect her.—I am &c^a.

J. B.

I send Your Ldship some Drafts,
& Charts that I hope will come safe
to Your Hands—My Opinion of
Copper Bottoms is that it is the
finest Invention in the World

Dolphin Port Famine Feb. 24. 1765.

[*Endorsement on Byron's Letter to Egmont*]

Copy of a Letter from Comm^re Byron to Lord Egmont dated
Port Famine 24 Febr 1765.
Giving Acc^t of his proceedings to Port Famine in the Streights of
Magellan
&
Description of Falklands Islands.

Document 2

Copy of a Letter from the Earl of Egmont to the Duke of Grafton. July 20. 1765[1]

Duke of Grafton [*at bottom of first page*]
                            20. July 1765. 9 oClock PM
My Lord,
    I have the honor to enclose the Charts & Surveys which were
transmitted with the Letter your Grace has lately read from Com^re
Byron.
    With these I have likewise sent full Extracts of all such accounts
as have hitherto come to our Knowledge concerning Falkland's
Island from its first Discovery to this day—Your Grace will please
to lay them before his Mty^s & those of his principal Servants whose
opinion can alone be taken on a Subject of this very great Moment
& of the most secret nature.
    The Perusal of these Papers will, I believe compleatly prove his
Mtys. Title. It will also shew the great Importance of this Station,

[1] PRO SP 94/253.

which is undoubtedly *the Key to the whole Pacifick Ocean*. This Island must command the Ports & Trade of Chili Peru, Panama, Acapulco, & in one word all the Spanish Territory upon that Sea It will render all our Expeditions to those parts most lucrative to ourselves, most fatal to Spain, & no longer formidable tedious, or uncertain in a future War and the Coast of Chili from the Streights of Magellan to the Isle of Chiloe being wholly Savage— uninhabited by the Spaniards, & possess'd by the most warlike of all the Native Indians in perpetual Hostility with Spain. The Country also abounding above all the rest in mines of Gold & Silver, & the Navigation through those Streights from this Island to Chiloe being now well known & such as will seldom exceed a Month. Your Grace will presently perceive the prodigious Use hereafter to be made of an Establishment in this Place by that / Nation who shall first fix a firm Footing there.

What farther advantages may be derived from Discoverys in all that Southern Tract of Ocean both to the East & West of the magellanick Streights, it is not possible at present to foresee, but those Parts (now almost entirely unknown) will from such a Settlement be soon & easily explor'd—and a Trade may be probably carried on with Paraguay, the Brazils &c hereafter with great Facility, & great Profit from this Island as well in time of Peace as War

Your Grace & the rest of the King's Servants will no doubt particularly consider how far & in what Manner this Project may commit G. Britain either with the Spaniards or the French

First, as to Spain, it is impossible that even their pretended Title from the Pope's Grant, or any Treaty (so far as I can recollect) can give them the least Claim to an Island lying 80 or 100 Leagues in the Atlantick Ocean Eastward of $\frac{c}{y}$ Continent of South America, to which it cannot be deem'd appurtenant. and the attempt of France to settle there seems to confirm this argument against all that can be urg'd hereafter by either of those Powers to that Effect.

With respect to France . . . the 1st & 2nd Discoverys of this Island were both made by the Subjects, & under the authority of the Crown of G. Britain in the reigns of Q. Elizabeth & Charles the Second, & the French never saw them till in the reign of Q. Anne.

Their present Projector Frezier owns that they were first discover'd by the English. It was many Months after Capt Byron's Expedition was plann'd & 6 or 7 Weeks after he had sail'd that the first suspicion was entertain'd in England of any Design on the Part of France to attempt this Island. In Sept. 1764 a Paragraph in the foreign gazettes first mention'd that some frigates were returned to St Maloes from visiting & exploring the Coast there ... and in the ... Month of March last the famous old Voyager Frezier himself told a Person employ'd to view the Ports of France (whose important Intelligence your grace has lately seen) that he had been consulted by the French ministers upon this undertaking & that 3 or 4 French Frigates were to be employ'd this Summer to make the Settlement. This being all that We have yet learn'd of the french Intentions & coming to Us from no avowed authority, & Capt Byron so late as Febry' last having rang'd the Coast for 200 Miles in Length & remain'd long upon it witho^t finding the least Trace of any Possession taken by the French We may either suppose the Intelligence above ment^d to have been such as deserv'd our Notice, or pretend a total Ignorance upon the Subject as it shall best suit the Conduct which his Mty. may think proper to hold upon this delicate affair—I have only to add that as things now stand, the King's Ministers sho^d immediately take this matter under Consideration & come to a very speedy Resolution upon it that the Admiralty may receive his Mty's orders if any thing is to be done witho^t delay. It will not be possible to fit out an Equipment proper to take possession of this Island later than the Middle of Sept^r—This Interval is very short to prepare for such an undertaking—and if We sho^d let this Season pass another will not return till the same month in the ensuing year. By that time the French will have certainly fix'd a Colony which will have taken root full 19 months before any that in that Case can be made by Us & may be then probably out of our Power to expell, at least witho^t direct & avow'd Hostilities which may bring on an immediate Rupture both with France & Spain Whereas (for many reasons too tedious to be inserted here) this will be less likely to ensue, if as things are now circumstanc'd We take our measures sooner or at least as soon as France.

I beg Your Grace's Pardon for troubling You with this very long

Letter, but I thought it might be necessary to submit the whole Matter thus at large & in this mannor for Your Information previous to the Consultation which his Mty. I presume will think proper to be had upon it.

I have the honor to be &c

Egmont

Document 3

Voyages & Journals, from whence the Extracts relative to Falkland's Islands, referred to in the Earl of Egmont's Letter to the Duke of Grafton, were taken[1]

159¾ Febry 2ᵈ	Sir Richard Hawkins first - discovered them, & named them Hawkins's Maiden Land - -	Hawkins's Voyage p. 69 & 70.
1600. Janʸ 21.	Sebald de Wert saw three small Islands that lye off Falklands' Islands & named them Sebaldine Islands	Harris's Coll. Voyages vol. 1. p. 44. & Purchas's Pilgrim vol. 1. B. 2. C. 5. p. 79.
1684. Janʸ 28.	Capᵗ Jnᵒ Cook & Capᵗ Dampier saw the Sebaldine Islands & anchored at one of them - - - - -	Harris's Coll. Voyages vol. 1. p. 79. 87. Dampiers Voyage vol. 1. p. 80.
1703. Decʳ 23ᵈ	Wᵐ Funnel Mate with Capt Dampier sailed past the Sebaldine Islands -	Harris's Coll. vol. 1. p. 132. Dampiers Voyage vol. 4. p. 9.
1708. Decʳ 23ᵈ	Capt Edwᵈ Cooke saw Land, which he supposed to be Falkland's Island, & the next Day sailed along the Shore	Capᵗ Edw. Cooke's Voyage. p. 29. & 30.
1708. Decʳ 23ᵈ	Woods Rogers saw Falkland's Land, as he calls it, & gives a very good Description of the great Island —	Woods Rogers Voyage p. 103.
1706. 1708. 1711. & 1713. —	Frezier mentions these Islands, but calls them Isles Nouvelles, or New Islands, tho' he expressly says they are certainly the same which Sir Richᵈ Hawkins discovered in 159¾ —	Translation of Frezier's Voyage p. 289.

[1] PRO SP 94/253.

1689 Jan^{ry} 27. 90	Capt John Strong of the Welfare or Farewel of Bristol, in his voyage to the Streights of Magellan, saw these Islands, sailed between them, & gave the Passage the name of Falkland's Sound, & from whence probably the Islands acquired that name, for I do not find them called so before that time———	Capt Strong's Journal in the British Museum in Manuscript.

1689 Jan^{ry} 27.
90

Capt John Strong of the Welfare or
Farewel of Bristol, in his voyage to
the Streights of Magellan, saw these
Islands, sailed between them, & gave
the Passage the name of Falkland's
Sound, & from whence probably
the Islands acquired that name,
for I do not find them called so
before that time———⎫ Capt Strong's
⎬ Journal in the
⎭ British Museum
in
Manuscript.

Dr Halley, in a Paper concerning
the Longitude of the Magellan
Streights, published in the Philoso-
-phical Transactions, makes very
honorable mention of this Journal
of Capt Strong. And in the Chart,
which he published in 1701, lays
down Falkland's Islands ——— ⎫ Philos: Trans:
⎬ N° 341.
⎭ p. 168.

For the Importance of these Islands see Ld Anson's
voyage p. 91. etc

Mem^d

Vol. 3^d p. 846.

Since Extracts were made from the foregoing —
voyages &c I find in Hakluyt's Collection, that —
Capt John Davis of the Desire, one of the Ships that —
sailed with Sir Th^{os} Cavidish in his last Voyage

*1592 Augt 14.

to the South Sea, saw these* Islands before Sr Rich^d
Hawkins — But as Davis did not return from that —
Voyage till 11. June 1593. Sir Richd Hawkins could
not have had any Account of that Voyage, as he —
sailed from England in April 1593.

1615 Decr 18.

I also find, upon searching into
Purchas's Collection of Voyages &c,
that LeMaire & Schouten saw the
Sebaldine Islands ——— ⎫ Purchas.
⎬ vol. 1. B. 2.
⎭ C. 7. p. 91.

1721. Dec^r

Commodore Roggewit also
saw these Islands, & gives them
another Name ——— ⎫ Harris's Coll.
⎬ Vol. 1. p. 262.

Extracts from Journals & Accounts of Voyages so far as they relate to Falklands Islands & Pepys's Island

Sir Richard Hawkins's Voyage to the South Sea page 69. & 70. Printed in the year 1622.

The 2nd of February 159$\frac{3}{4}$ about 9 of the Clock in the Morning, We descried Land, which bore SW. of Us, which We look'd not for so timely & coming nearer & nearer unto it, by the Lying, We could not conjecture what Land it should be, for We were next of any thing in 48. Degrees, & no Platt or Sea Chart which We had made mention of any Land which lay in that Manner near about that height. In fine We brought our Larboard Tack on board & stood to the North Eastward all that Day & Night, & the Wind continuing Westerly & a fair Gale We continued our Course along the Coast the Day & Night following, in which Time We made account We discovered well, near Three score Leagues off the Coast. It is bold & made small Shew of Dangers. The Land is a goodly champain Country & peopled We saw many Fires, but co^d not come to speak with the People, for the time of the Year was far spent to shoot the Streights, & the Want of our Pinnace disabled Us for finding a Port or Road, not being Discretion with a Ship of Charge, & in an unknown Coast, to come near the Shore before it was sounded, which were causes, together with the Change of the Wind (good for Us to pass the Streights) that hindered the farther Discovery of this Land with its Secrets—This I have sorrowed for many times since, for that it had Likelyhood to be an excellent Country. It hath great Rivers of fresh Waters, for the out Shoot of them colours the Sea in many Places as We ran along it—It is not mountainous, but much of the Disposition of England & as temperate. The Things We noted principally on the Coast are these following—The Westermost Point of the Land, with which We first fell, is the End of the Land to the Westward as We found afterwards. If a Man bring this Point S. W. it riseth in 3. Mounts, or round Hillocks, bringing it more Westerly, they shoot themselves all into one & bringing it Easterly, it riseth in two Hillocks. This We call'd Point Trem cuntaine [? coutaine], some 12 or 14. Leagues from this Point to the Eastward, fair by the Shore lieth a low flat Island of some 2 Leagues long, We named it Fayre Island, for it was all over as green & smooth as any Meadow in the Spring of the Year

Some 3 or 4 Leagues Easterly from this Island is a good opening as of a great River or an arm of the Sea with a goodly low Country adjacent. and 8. or 10. Leagues from this opening some 3. Leagues from the Shore lieth a big Rock which at first we had thought to be a Ship under all her Sails, but after as We came near it discover'd itself to be a Rock which We call'd Condite head, for that howsoever a Man cometh with it, it is like to the Condite heads about the City of London.

All this Coast so far as We lyeth next of any thing East & by North & West & by South. The Land for that it was discover'd in the reign of queen Elizabeth my Sovereign Lady & Mistress & a Maiden queen, & at my cost & adventure, in a perpetual memory of her Chastity & remembrance of my Endeavours, I gave it the name of Hawkins Maiden-land.—Before a Man fall with this Land, some 20 or 30 Leagues he shall meet with Beds of Oreweed, driving to & fro in that Sea, with white Flowers growing upon them & sometimes farther off, which is a good Show & sign the Land is near, whereof the Westermost part lyeth some 60. Leagues from the nearest Land of America.

Harris's Collection of Voyages Vol. 1st Page 44.
Printed in the Year 1744.

Sebald de Weerts Voyage to the South Sea, & Streights of Magellan

The 21st of Jany 1600. he sail'd out of the Mouth of the Channel (Streights of Magellan) with a S. W. Wind chopping sometimes to the East North East after having spent 9. Months in those Seas in a dangerous & dismal Condition In the afternoon having got into the main, they left the Sloop to drive into the Sea because the Stormy Weather had made her unfit for Service. The 24. in the morning they found 3 small Islands to the Windward, which are not mark'd in the Map, they nam'd these the Sebaldine Islands: They are 60 Leagues off the Continent in 30° 40°. There was Plenty of Penguins in those Islands but they cod catch None, because they had neither Sloop nor Boat.

Harris's Collection of Voyages.—Vol. 1. P. 79.

Capt Cowley's Voyage round the World.

They continued their Course till they arrived on the Coast of Brazil, from whence they steer'd S.W. till they were in 4 Degrees South Latitude, where they observed the Sea to be as red as Blood. This was occasion'd by vast Shoals of Shrimps which are there of a red Colour in the Water. They likewise observed vast quantities of Seals, and so many Whales that Capt Cowley remarks there were an hundred for One found in the same Degree of

166

Northern Latitude, holding their Course still S.W. till they came into the Latitude of 47 degrees, where they met with an Island not known before on, which Captain Cowley bestowed the Name of Pepys's Island, in honor of that great Patron of Seamen Samuel Pepys Esqr Secretary to His Royal Highness—James Duke of York, when Lord High Admiral of England. This Island had a very good Harbour where One Thousand Ships might safely ride at Anchor; was a very commodious place for Wood & Water; abounded with Fowls; and as the Shore was either Rocks or Sands, promised fair with respect to Fish. In the Month of Janu^{ry} 1684 they bore away for the Streights of Magellan; and on the 28th of that Month, they fell in with the Sebaldine Islands in the Latitude of 51—25 then steering S.W.&bW they came into the Latitude of 53 where they made the Land of Terra del Fuego.

Harris's Collection of Voyages Vol 1. page 87.

Capt Wm Dampiers first Voyage round the World.

The 28 Janry 1684, We made three Isles of Sebald de Weert in 51,, 25. South Latitude & 57—28 Longitude West from the Lizard in England, the Variation 33. 10. I persuaded Capt Cooke to anchor near those Islands, being sensible of danger in Our Passage through the Streight of Magellan considering, especially that Men"aboard the Privateers are not so strictly at Command as in other Vessels. We came to an Anchor within two Cables length of the Shore of the furthermost of those three Islands where We found foul rocky Ground & the Island barren & destitute of Trees, but some Dildo Bushes growing near the Sea Side

Dampiers Voyage round the World Vol. 1. page 80. Printed in the Year 1729.

The 28 Janry 1684 We made the Sibbel de Wards, which are three Islands lying in Latitude of 51. 25. South and Longitude West from the Lizard in England by my Account, 57" 20 The Variation here We found to be 23. 10.—I had for a Month before We came hither, endeavour'd to persuade Capt Cook & his Company to anchor at these Islands, where I told them We might probably get Water as I then thought, & in Case We should miss of it here, yet by being good Husbands of what We had, We might reach John Fernandos in the South Seas before our Water was spent   This I urged to hinder their designs of going through the Streights of Magellan which I knew would prove very dangerous to Us; the rather, because Our Men being Privateers & so more willfull and less under Command, would not be so ready to give a watchfull Attendance in a Passage so little Known. For althô these Men were more under Command, than I had ever seen any Privateers, yet I could not expect to find them at a Minute's Call in coming to an Anchor, or weighing Anchor: Besides, if ever we should have Occasion to moor, or cast out Two Anchors, We had not a Boat to carry out or weigh an Anchor. These Islands of Sibbel de Wards were so named by the Dutch. They are all Three barren rocky Islands, without any Tree, only some Dildoe Bushes growing on them: And I do believe there is no Water on any One of them, for there was no Appearance of any Water. The Two Northermost We could not come near, but the Southermost We came close by, but could not strike Ground, 'till within Two Cables Length of the Shore, and there found it to be foul rocky Ground.

Harris's Collection of Voyages—Vol: 1: P. 132.

Mr Wm Funnell, Mate, with Capt. Dampier, his Acct of the Voyage round the World.

The 29th of December 1703. We sailed near the Islands of Sebalt de Weert; from which Island there came a very remarkable Bird, which because it pleased me very much then, I will now describe. It was about the Bigness of a Duck, and of a very fine white Colour; His Bill Yellow, & both above & below the Bill, were long grey Hairs, like Whiskers; & instead of Feathers at the bottom of his Eye Lids, he had short stiff Hairs, which were black.

Funnel's Voyage round The World, Pag. 13. Printed 1707.

The 29th of December 1703. betimes in the Morning, We saw the Islands of Sibil de Wards, which are Three in Number, lying in the Latitude of 51°:35' South, Longitude W: from London by my Account 51°: 37'. & had a good Observation by Azimuth Compass, & found Variation to be 24°: 0. Easterly.

168

Capt: Dampier in his Voyage round the World, computes the Longitude of these Islands West from the Lizard to be 57°: 28'. The Occasion of which Difference I suppose to be his having made longer Turns in that Voyage, & so more liable to Mistakes of this nature. Whether there be any Water upon these Lands I know not, but never did hear of any.

Capt: Edwd Cooke's Voyage. Vol. 1. P: 29 & 30.
Printed 1712.

The 23^d December 1708. had smooth Water in the Morning, saw several Fish & Fowles about the Ship, & at Ten made the Land, which I suppos'd to be Falkland's Island, bearing S.S.W., distant Nine Leagues, Latitude & Estimation & indifferent Observation 51°: 25'. Longitude from The Island Grande 13°: 0. Ran along the Shore, steering away E. by N. 'till Ten at Night, & then brought too with our Foresail and Mizen, not being satisfied that We were the Length of the Eastermost Land.

Friday the 24th at Five in the Morning, made sail again. As We ran along this Shore, the Land look'd like some part of England, having several good Bays, & Vallies, but believe it is not inhabited, no Signs of People appearing, nor can I give any better Account of it, The Weather not permitting us to come any nearer with our Ships, nor to send our Boats ashore. What We cou'd discern, look'd very pleasant, & We saw Abundance of Ducks & small Fowl, besides Shoals of Fish; Yesterday at Four in the Evening, The East End of it bore S.E. by E. distant Six Leagues, & the Northermost part S.E. by E. distant Five Leagues. The body of This Island lies in about 51°: 20': South, & Longitude from London 64°: 00. West. I Guess it to be about 90 Miles long, & 70. in Breadth.

Woods Rogers's Voyage: Pag 103. & 104. Printed 1718.

The 23^d of December 1708, at Ten this Morning We saw Land, bearing S.S.E. distant Nine Leagues. It appear'd first in Three, afterwards in several more Islands. At Twelve it bore S.½W. the West End distant Six Leagues, a long Tract of Land. We saw most of that which appear'd at first to be Islands, join with the low Lands. The Wind being Westerly, & blowing fresh, We cou'd not weather it, but was forced to bear away, & ran along Shore, from Three to Four Leagues Distance. It lay as near as We could guess E.N.E. & W.S.W. This is Falkland's Land described in few Draughts and now lay it down right, thô the Latitude agrees pretty well. The Middle of It lies in Latitude 51, 00′ S° and I make the Longitude of it to be 61.: 54′ West from London. The Two Islands extend about Two Degrees in Length, as near as I could judge by what I saw.

The 24th Last We reefed both Courses, it blowing strong, lay by from 8. 'till 3. in the Morn, with Our Heads to Northward, Wind at W. by S. because We could not tell how far Falkland's Isles ran to the Eastward. Between Two & Three o'Clock Yesterday in the Afternoon, We ran by a high, round large White remarkable Rock, which appeared by itself near Three Leagues without the Land; which is not unlike Portland; but not so high, & the Rock like that called the Fastness to the Westward of Cape Clear in Ireland. At Four Yesterday in the Afternoon the North East End bore S.E. by S. 7 Leagues the white Rock bore S° 3. Leagues. At Six the Eastermost Land in Sight bore S.E. 7. Leagues. All this Land appears with gentle Descents from Hill to Hill, and seemed to be good Ground, with Woods and Harbours. At Three o'Clock we made Sail, steering S.E. Latitude 52. South.

The 25th. Yesterday noon We saw the Land again, and find it to trim away Southerly from the White Rock.

Translation of Freziers Voyage page 287. 288 289 & 290—
Printed in the Year 1717.

If I have in this Chart suppressed immaginary Lands, I have also added some real in 51 Latitude which I have called New Islands because discovered since the Year 1700, most of them by Ships of St Malo. I have laid them down according to the Memoirs or Observations of the Maurepas & the S. Lewis Ships belonging to the India Company which saw them near at hand & even the latter was water'd there in a Pool which I have set down near Port S. Lewis. The Water was somewhat ruddy & unsavory, in other respects good for the Sea. Both of them ran along several parts of them but none coasted along so close as the S. John Baptist commanded by Doublet of Havre who endeavor'd to pass into an Opening he saw about the middle but having spy'd some low Islands as almost level with the Water, He thought fit to tack about. This Range of Islands is the same that Monsr Fouquet of St Malo discoverd, & to which he gave the Name of Anican the person that had set him out. The Tracts I have traced will shew the bearing of those Lands in regard to Streight le Modire which the S. John Baptist was come out of when he saw them & with respect to Staten Land, which the other two had seen before they found them.

The North part of those Lands which is here under the Name of the Coast of the Assumption was discover'd on the 16th July, 1708 by Porce of S. Malo, who gave it the Name of the Ship he commanded. It was looked upon as a new Land 100 Leagues East of the new Isles I speak of; but I have made no difficulty to join it to the others, having convincing Reasons for so doing.

The first is that the Latitudes observed to the Northward & to the Southward of those Islands & the bearing of the parts known, answer exactly to the same point of Reunion on the East Side, without leaving any Space between them.

The Second is that there is no Reason to judge that Coast of the Assumption to be East of the Isles of Annican; for Monsr Le Gobien de Saint Jean who has been pleased to shew me an Extract of his Journal, judges it to lie South from the Mouth of the River of Plate, which being taken strictly, could not remove it above 2 or 3 degrees to the Eastward, that is about 25 or 30 Leagues but the diversity of Judgements is always a Token of Uncertainty. The first time they saw that Coast, as they came from the Island of S. Katharine, they judged it to be in 329 Degrees; & the Second coming from the River of Plate, whither the contrary Winds had obliged him to go and Anchor, after having attempted to pass Cape Horn, they judged it to be in 322 Degrees, and according to some in 324 on Peter Goos his Charts, the Errors whereof We have taken notice of at Page 30 so that little regard is to be had to them. However they reposing Confidence in them thought themselves very far from the Continent & reckoning they were too much to the Eastward, ran also 300 Leagues too far West in the South Sea, so that they thought they had been running upon Guinea, when they made land at Hilo: but the third & most convincing is that We &

Our Comrades must have run over that New Land, according to the Longitude in which It was laid down in the Manuscript Chart, and it is morally impossible that a Ship should have had no Sight of it being abo^t 50. Leagues in Length ESE & W.N.W. Thus there is no Room to doubt, but that it was the North Part of the new Islands whose Western Part which is yet unknown time will discover.

These Islands are certainly the same which Sir R^d Hawkins discover'd in 1593. Being to the Eastward of the Desart Coast in abo^t 50. Degrees, he was drove by a Storm upon an un Known Land: He ran along that Island abo^t 60 Leagues & saw fires which made him conclude that it was inhabited.

Hitherto those Lands have been call'd Sibald's Islands because it was believ'd that the 3. which bear that Name on the Charts were so laid down at Will for Want of better Knowledge, but the Ship the Incarnation comanded by the Sieur Brignon of S. Malo, had a near View of them in fair Weather in 1711. coming out of Rio de Janeiro—They are in short 3. little Islands about half a League in Length lying in a Triangle as they are laid down in the Charts— They passed by at 3 or 4 Leagues distance & they had no Sight of Land tho' in very open Weather which proves that they are at least 7 or 8 Leagues from the new Islands.

In fine I have set down in Roman Numbers the Variation of the Needle observ'd in these Parts where its Declination is very considerable to the N. E. for We have observ'd it to 27. Degrees, being to the Eastward of the new Islands

Capt Strong's Journal in Manuscript in the British Museum— Never published

The 26. of Jany 1689/90 being Sunday from noon the 25. to noon the 26. our Course made good was W. & S. 6.. o.. S. distance 80 Miles, Wind from S.W. to N.W. fresh Gales & fair Weather, We see several Fowls that are call'd Penguins that dive, & at 4 o Clock at Night We sounded & had Ground 80 Fathoms Water, some small Sand & ozey, that washed from the Lead, & at 8. at Night, We had 82 Fathoms Water, & at 12. 80 fathoms Latitude & observation 50. 33. S. Difference of Longitude from St Jago 42:

00: Meridian distance from St Jago 689 1/3 Leagues Monday 27.
from Noon the 26. to right in the morn^g this day that We see the
Land, our Course was W.S.W. 3..0 S. distance 81. Miles, Wind at
NW. & W.N.W. fair Weather, at 4 in the morning We had 75
Fathoms Water & within 3 or 4 Leagues of the Shore We had 36.
Fathoms. This Land doeth show like a great many Islands. It is a
great Land & lyeth E. & W. nearest, there are several Keys that lie
along the Shore. We sent our Boat on Shore to one of them & they
brought on board abundance of Penguins & other Fowl & Seals, &
at 3. in the afternoon We stood down along Shore & steer'd E. &
N. & at 8. at Night We see the Land, run to the Eastward as far as
We co^d discern. Lat. 51: 03 S. Difference of Longitude from S^t
Jago 43: 55. West. meridian distance 713:⅔ Leagues. Difference of
Longitude from the Lizard to Hawkins Land 60..55. West.—
Tuesday 28th. This morn^g at 4 o Clock We see a Rock that lyeth off
the main Island, abo^t 4 or 5 Leagues it makes like a Sail We tack'd
& stood to the Westward, & at 6 o'Clock, We did stand into &
through a Sound that lies abo^t 20. Leagues from the Westermost
Land We saw, but what Length this Island is I do not know. The
Sound lieth N. & S. nearest, there is 24 Fathoms Water, 3. Leagues
wide & shoals gradually till you come close on board of the West
End, & then you have 8 & 9 fathoms good Ground. It is abo^t 4.
Leagues the mouth of it, but as you run in it is broader. at 8. at
Night We came to an anchor in 14. Fathoms Water abo^t 6 or 7
Leagues within, the Wind was N.S.W.

Wednesday 29. this morn^g We weigh'd & stood into an harbour
on the West Side, & there came to an anchor & sent our Boat on
shore for fresh Water, & We did kill abundance of Geese & Ducks
but as for Wood there is none

Thursday 30—We rid at anchor in this harbour filling of fresh
Water, there is a great many good harbours in this Sound, & at 8.
o Clock at night We made an End of filling of Water. This harbour
is abo^t 8. Leagues within the Cape on your Starboard Side.
Friday the 31. This morn^g at 5. o Clock We weigh'd from this
harbour, the Wind at W.S.W. We sent our Long Boat ahead of
the Ship to sound before Us, We kept the West Side on board all
the Way till you come about 12 Leagues up, & then You take one
small Island on the Starboard Side of You, at Eight o'Clock We

came to an anchor in 9. Fathoms Water by reason it was Night
Saturday the 1st February

This Morning at 4 [or 7] o'Clock, We weighd and sent our Long
Boat before the sound, and at 10 We got clear out of the Sound, and
at Noon We set the West Cape, which We gave the Name of Cape
Farewell, and it bore NNE—Distance about 4 Leagues, Wind at
WS.W; This Land lies nearest East and West, but as for the
Length of it I do not know. From the Westermost End that We see
to Falkland, Sound as I named it, is 24 Leagues. This Sound is
about 17 Leagues long, the first Entrance lies S b E 7 & 8 Fathoms,
three and four Leagues over, and afterwards S b W.

Extract from a Paper of Dr Halley's concerning the Longitude of the Magellan Streights,—published in Philos: Trans. NO. 341. page 168.

I have had in my Custody a very curious Journal of one Capt
Strong, who went into the South Seas in quest of a rich Plate
Wreck, and who discovered the two Islands *he called Falkland's
Isles*, lying about 120 Leagues to the Eastward of the Patagon
Coast, about the Latitude of 51½.

This Capt Strong had a quick Passage from the Island of
Trinidada (in 20½ South) to the Magellan Streights; and in this
Journal, which was very well kept, I found that Cape Virgin was,
by his Account, 45 Degrees of Longitude more Westerly than that
Island, whose Longitude I know to be just 30 Degrees from
London, that is, in all 75 Degrees.

NB. Dr Halley in the Chart published by him in 1701, wherein
he delineates the Variation of the Compass, has laid down
Falkland's Islands.

Lord Anson's Voyage round the World. Page 90, 91, & 92.

It appears that all future Expeditions to the South Seas must run a
considerable Risque of proving abortive, whilst We are under the
Necessity of touching at Brazil in our Passage thither, an Expedient
that might relieve us from this Difficulty, would surely be a
Subject worthy of the Attention of the Publick; and this seems
capable of being effected, by the Discovery of some Place more to

the Southward, where Ships might refresh and supply themselves with the necessary Sea Stock for their Voyage round Cape Horn. and We have in reality the imperfect Knowledge of two Places, which might perhaps, on examination, prove extremely convenient for this purpose. The first of them is Pepys's Island, in the Latitude of 47° South, and laid down by Dr Halley, about 80 Leagues to the Eastward of Cape Blanco, on the Coast of Patagonia; the Second is Falkland's Isles, in the Latitude of 51½ nearly South of Pepys's Island. The first of these was discovered by Capt Cowley, in his Voyage round the World in the Year 1686; who represents it as a commodious Place for Ships to wood and water at, and says, it is provided with a very good and capacious Harbour, where a Thousand Sail of Ships might ride at anchor in great Safety; that it abounds with Fowls, and as the Shore is either Rocks or Sands, it seems to promise great Plenty of Fish. The Second Place, or Falkland's Isles, have been seen by many Ships both French and English, being the Land laid down by Frezier, in his Chart of the Extremity of South America, under the Title of the New Islands. Woods Rogers, who run along the N. E. Coast of these Isles in the Year 1708, tells us, that they extended about two Degrees in length, and appeared with gentle Descents from Hill to Hill, and seemed to be good Ground, with Woods and Harbours. Either of these Places, as they are Islands at a considerable Distance from the Continent, may be supposed, from their Latitude, to lie in a Climate sufficiently temperate. It is true, they are too little known to be at present recommended for proper Places of Refreshment for Ships bound to the Southward: But if the Admiralty should think it adviseable to order them to be surveyed, which may be done at a very small Expence, by a Vessel fitted out on purpose, and if, on this examination, one or both of these Places should appear proper for the Purpose intended, it is scarcely to be conceived, of what prodigious Import a convenient Station might prove, situated so far to the Southward, and so near Cape Horn. The Duke and Dutchess of Bristol were but 35 Days from their losing Sight of Falkland's Isles to their Arrival at Juan Fernandes in the South Seas: And as the returning back is much facilitated by the Western Winds, I doubt not but a Voyage migh be made from Falkland's Isles to Juan Fernandes and back again, in little more than Two Months. This, even in time of Peace, might be of great Consequence to this Nation; and, in time of War, would make Us Masters of those Seas.

Capt Cowley's History of the Voyage he made to the South Seas in the Revenge, commanded by Capt Cook. Page 6.

Being in Latitude 47°. We saw Land, the same being an Island not before known lying to the Westward of Us. It was not inhabited, and I gave it the Name of *Pepys's Island*. We found it a very convenient Place for Ships to water at, and take in Wood, and it has a very good Harbour, where a Thousand Sail of Ships may safely ride. Here is great Plenty of Fowls, and, We judge, Abundance of Fish, by reason of the Ground's being Nothing but Rocks and Sands. The new Year being now come, when We had taken a View of this Island, and that the Wind was so extraordinary high that We could not get into it to water, We stood to the Southward &c^a. This was the last of December 1683 & first of January 1684.

NB. He does not mention the Sebaldine Islands or Falkland's Islands.

Document 4

Extracts from Voyages had Recourse to, since the Extracts which accompanied the Earl of Egmont's Letter to the Duke of Grafton were made[1]

Authorities

Captain Davis, of the Desire, one of the Ships that sailed with Mr Cavendish in his last Voyage to the South Sea.

Hakluyt, Vol. 3. Page 846. Printed in the Year 1600.

The 7th of August 1592, towards Night, we departed from Penguin Isle (near Port Desire, on the Coast of Patagonia) shaping our

[1] PRO SP 94/253.

Course for the Streights, where we had full Confidence to meet with our General. The 9th we had a sore Storm, so that we were constrained to hull, for our Sails were not to indure any Force. The 14th we were driven in among certain Isles, never before discovered by any known Relation, lying 50 Leagues, or better from the Shore, East and Northerly from the Streights. In which Place, unless it had pleased God of his wonderful Mercy to have ceased the Wind, we must of Necessity have perished.

Le Maire and Schouten's Voyage round the World. Purchas, Vol. 1. B. 2. C. 7. Page 91. Printed in the Year 1625.

The 13th of Dec[r] 1615, about Noon, we sailed out of Port Desire, but the Sea being calm, we anchored before the Haven, and when the Wind began to rise, hoisted Anchor, and put to Sea.

The 18th we saw Sebaldes Islands, SouthEast from us, about 3 Leagues. They lie, as Sebald de Wert writes, distant from the Streight, East North East, and West South West, about 50 Leagues. Then we were under 51. Degrees.

Harris's Collection of Voyages, Vol. 1. Page 262.

Comm[re] Roggewein's Expedition for the Discovery of Southern Lands, from an original Journal, in the Year 1721.

Commodore Roggewein, and his Consort, the African Galley, continued a S.S.W. Course, 'till, by the Assistance of the Lands Winds, they were in the height of the Streights of Magellan. There they discovered an Island, of near 200 Leagues in Circumference, and at the Distance of about four score Leagues from the main Land of America; and, as they saw no Smoke, nor any Boat, or other Embarkation, on the Coast, they concluded that it was uninhabited. A French Privateer discovered the West Coast of it, and called it the Island of S[t] Lewis; but the Dutch, observing its many Capes, fancied them to be so many different Islands, and therefore bestowed on them the Name of the new Islands. This Squadron first discovered the Island all round, & particularly the East Coast of it; the first visible Points of which they named the Points of Rosenthall, because they were first discovered by a Captain of that Name, who commanded the African Galley. The

* 1st Jan^{ry} 172½

uttermost Eastern Point they called New Year's Cape, because discovered upon *that Day. This Island lying in the Latitude of 52° South, and in the Longitude of 95°, they called it Belgia Australis; because, whenever it comes to be inhabited, such as dwell thereon will be strictly and properly Antipodes to the Inhabitants of the Low Countries. The Land appeared extremely beautiful, and very fertile. It was chequered with Mountains and Valleys, all of which were clothed with very fine strait Trees. The Verdure of the Meadows, and the Freshness of the Woods, afforded a most delightful Prospect, insomuch that all the Ships Companies agreed, that, if they had landed, they should have found excellent Fruits: But the Commodore would not allow them to land for Fear of losing Time; and, from an Apprehension, that any Delay might hinder his getting round Cape Horn, he therefore chose to defer a thoro' Examination of this new Country, 'till he should return from the Discovery of the Southern Continents and Islands; but that, alas! however reasonable, proved, as in the Sequel we shall see, a vain Expectation, because he was obliged to return home with his Squadron by the East Indies. This fine Island therefore is like to continue still, in a great Measure, unknown; and the Commodore regretted excessively his not laying hold of that Opportunity of spending a few Days there; which, perhaps, might have produced the fixing a Colony on that Island; from whence, without Doubt, many other considerable Discoveries might, in a short Time, have been conveniently made.

Document 5

Letter from the Lords of the Admiralty to the Commissioners for Victualling, 20 March 1765[1]

By &c^a——

Whereas you have represented to us, by your Letter of the 15th Instant. 'That the Honble Capt Byron has acquainted you, by his Letter dated at Rio de Janeiro the 16th of Octr last, that, as the Voyage on which His Majesty's Ship Dolphin & the Tamer

[1] PRO Adm 2/92.

Frigate are bound may run them short of Bread, he had, in order to prevent it as much as possible & to make the Bread, then on board, last them to India, ordered the Purser of the former to purchase a quantity of Yams, and to serve them in lieu of Bread; That the People had likewise been served with fresh Beef, from the time of their arrival at the said place, & as the quantity of Greens & Vegetables which he had thought necessary to have boiled with the Beef, must have greatly injured the two Pursers to pay for out of their pockets, he had also ordered Mr Stacey, Purser of the former, in addition to the quantity furnished by him to purchase Vegetables of different Kinds for the two Ships to the Amount of seven Shillings a Sixpence a day, which he had found of the greatest Efficacy in restoring the Sick people, and that Mr Stacey had drawn upon you for those Articles & for Watering the said Ships, in favour of Scott & Pringle, or Order, for One hundred & Twenty four pounds, Eleven shillings & Sixpence.' And Whereas you have desired to receive our directions touching the Acceptance of the said Bill; You are hereby required and directed to accept & pay the same Charging the amount as Imprest to the said Mr Stacey.
Given &c^a the 20th March 1765.

To the Commiss^rs for Victualling   Egmont
  His Majestys Navy—   Carysfort
                                           Howe
          By & PS

Document 6

Byron's Memorial to the Earl of Egmont, August 1766[1]

To The Right Honble the Earl of
Egmont, first Lord Commissioner of
the Admiralty &c^a &c^a
The Memorial of the Honble John Byron.

Sheweth,
   That your Lordships Memorialist on his being appointed Commodore and Commander in Chief in June 1764 bound on

[1] PRO Adm 1/162.

Discoverys, he was verbally authorized by your Lordship (for the better preservation of the Health of the Officers & Seamen of His Majestys Ship Dolphin and Tamer Frigate,) to purchase Vegetables at all such places as your Lordships Memorialist might touch at, during the said intended Voyage. And that he was likewise verbally authorized by your Lordship, to cause the Ships Companys to be served any quantity of Provisions, beyond the established Allowance as your Lordships Memorialist might judge necessary, the better to enable them to undergo the fatigues & Hardships of the Voyage.

That in consequence of such your Lordships Authority, your Lordships Memorialist, directed Mr Henry Stacy Purser of the Dolphin, to furnish that Ship and the Tamer with Onions at Madiera, at the rate of twenty pounds in weight to each Person on board them for a Sea Store, and at the Cape of Good Hope a quantity of Pumpkins for the same purpose. And that at Rio de Janeiro, Batavia and the Cape, he finding that the Pursers quotas of Vegetables, which they furnished the Ships with, (being as much as they could afford) were not near sufficient, your Lordships Memorialist also directed Mr Stacy to purchase Vegetables, to Boil with the fresh Beef every Day for Dinner, limitting him to the Prices, which he was not to exceed, and to draw Bills on the Victualling Board for the same.

And that your Lordships Memorialist observing that the established Allowance of Provisions was not sufficient for the Officers and People, (who had nothing else to Eat or Drink for a great part of the time,) he order'd Breakfasts to be given them, every Day in the Week in the Straits of Magellan and the Coast of Patagonia, also as much Pease above their Allowance as they could eat in the Voyage; the Beef and Pork being very small when Boiled he frequently gave them double Allowance, he also gave them as much Bread as they could eat, with double Allowance of Sugar, and Spirits as often as necessary. The Raisins being in a perishing Condition, they were Served out by my directions, to prevent their being all thrown overboard.

Your Lordships Memorialist therefore begs your Lordship will be pleased, (in consideration of the Circumstances) to cause the necessary Orders to be sent to the Victualling Board, to Dispence with the said Mr Stacys Charges in his Imprest Account for Onions, Pumpkins and other Vegetables. And also to allow him Credit for such Extra Expence of Provisions as appear by my Certificates and Orders, which are lodged in that Office. And your Lordships Memorialist further begs, that the Purser of the Tamer, may likewise be allowed Credit for such Extra Expence of Provisions as shall appear by my Certificates and Orders, when the same shall have been Vouched by me, and deliver'd into the Victualling Office.

And your Lordships Memorialist
shall ever Pray &c^a &c^a

August 1766

Appendix III

THE PATAGONIANS

1. *The Patagonian Giants*

by Helen Wallis

The legend of the Patagonian giants originated in June 1520 with the discovery of Patagonia by the Spaniards of Magellan's expedition and with their reports (notably that of the Italian chronicler Pigafetta) of gigantic men, whom they named *patagones* or 'big feet'. Successive voyages to the region of the Strait provided conflicting evidence for and against the existence of this race of giants.[1] Sir John Narborough's expedition which visited Patagonia in 1670 found the Patagonians to be ordinary men. His map published in 1694 with the account of his voyage[2] notes against the north coast of the Strait 'Many Savage people here of a common stature', and his large MS chart describes 'the Natives' as 'not taller than Generally Englishmen are'.[3] Captain John Wood, of Narborough's ship the *Sweepstakes*, wrote in his Journal that seven country people who intercepted him 'were Very Well sett men of noe such Exterordenary Stature as is reported by Magellanes & other Spaniards; to be 10 or 11 foot hie none of these being above 6 at ye Most but I soppose they did Inmaging none would come here to disprove them'.[4] In 1741 John Bulkeley and John Cummins made similar observations: 'The Indians we saw in the Streights of Magellan, are People of a middle Stature and well-shaped';[5] 'the Patagonian Indians, at least those in that Part of the Country where we resided, were tall and well-made, being in general, from five to six Feet high'.[6] Although the account showed that the Patagonians were no giants, it was notable as the earliest report of

[1] See R. T. Gould 'There were giants in those days', *Enigmas* (1946), 13-25; and P. G. Adams, *Travelers and Travel Liars* (1962), published too late for use.
[2] See Pl. VII.
[3] 'The Land of Patagona &c The Draught of Magellan Straits drawn by Captain Iohn Narborough ann⁰ 1670'. (British Museum. K.Top.CXXIV.84).
[4] British Museum, Sloane MS 3833, fol. 20.
[5] Bulkeley and Cummins, *A Voyage to the South Seas . . .* (1743), 143.
[6] Bulkeley and Cummins, *A Voyage* (2nd ed. 1757), 280.

them as horsemen,[1] a fact which Byron told Lord Egmont 'always stagger'd me much' when he spoke to him before his departure in 1764.[2]

It was with the promise to Lord Egmont 'that if it were possible I would discover what those people were' that Byron, armed with Bulkeley's account, arrived off the coast of Patagonia in December 1764. He approached the place a little north of Cape Virgin Mary where Bulkeley had seen the horsemen and there, as the reviewer of Hawkesworth's *Voyages* in *The Annual Register* enthusiastically relates (referring to the giants), he 'had the good fortune to re-establish the credit of the old navigators, by meeting with a large party of them'.[3]

The first report of the encounter reached England on 22 June 1765 in Byron's letter to Lord Egmont written at Port Famine.[4] This showed the Patagonians to be a race formidable indeed: 'The stoutest of our Grenadiers would appear nothing to them. . . . Our People on Board, who were looking at us thro' their Glasses, said we looked like meer Dwarfs to the People we were gone amongst', Byron wrote, summing them up as 'People, who in size come the nearest to Giants of any People I believe in the World'.[5] The Admiralty kept this remarkable information to itself. It was not until Byron's return in May 1766 that the sensational news of Byron's giants became the talk of Europe. The report that Byron had encountered men 'of extraordinary bigness', 'nine feet high',[6] when passed on through French intelligence drew from the French Minister of Foreign Affairs, Praslin, the dry comment that Byron must surely have seen them through a microscope.[7] The Royal Society Club discussed the news of the giants at one of its weekly dinners at the Mitre in July 1766, and Dr Maty hastened to report

[1] Bulkeley's first encounter with the horsemen was near Cape Virgin Mary on 12 December 1741. [See Bulkeley and Cummins (1743), 149.]

[2] See Byron's letter to Lord Egmont from Port Famine, 24 February 1765, Document No. 1 (above, p. 154).

[3] *Annual Register for the year 1773* (1774), 268. The reviewer filled seven columns (pp. 268-72) with a verbatim transcript of the meeting with the giants from Hawkesworth's *Voyages*, presuming that 'the reader will not be displeased with the account'.

[4] Document No. 1.

[5] See above, p. 155.

[6] Corney, I, 24.

[7] Coquelle, 461.

the facts in a letter to M. de La Lande, President of the French Académie de Sciences.[1] All Paris was amazed, as the Abbé Coyer sardonically reports, until on 1 August 1766 the French naturalist, M. de La Condamine answered in a letter to the *Journal encyclopédique* that the story of the Patagonian giants was a fable, and that the English government had put the story about to conceal the real objective of the fleet of four ships then being made ready for South America—Wallis's ships and the *Swift*—the exploitation of a mine which the English had discovered.[2]

The British Government had certainly played up the giants, for when questioned about Byron's activities by Masserano the Spanish ambassador, the Duke of Richmond had replied in a bantering tone, 'they had been out looking for giants.'[3] That the government was behind the story was also implied by Horace Walpole, who lost no time in seizing upon the new Brobdinag as a field for satire on the British administration. Writing, under the pseudonym 'S.T.', an account of the giants in the form of a 'letter to a friend in the country' dated 1 July 1766 and published in 1766, he called the affair 'a political mystery, and a very wonderful one too, for it is really kept a Secret.—The very Crew of the Ship, who saw Five Hundred of these lofty Personages, did not utter a word of the Matter for a whole Year;[4] and even now, that a general Idea

---

[1] These details are given in La Condamine's letter to the *Journal encyclopédique* (see below, note 2), and by the Abbé Gabriel François Coyer, *Lettre au Docteur Maty* (1767), 16, 22–5. English translation, *A Letter to Doctor Maty* (1767), 14–15, 21–4.

[2] Extracts from a letter written by La Condamine, *Journal encyclopédique*, tom. V, 1 août 1766, pp. 132–3. M. de B . . . of the Académie des Belles Lettres who provided La Condamine with details of the dinner of the Royal Society Club, was evidently Louis George de Bréquigny. See Sir Archibald Geikie, *Annals of the Royal Society Club* (1917), 94. La Condamine also reveals the fact that the French Minister had suppressed an article, based on Bougainville's experiences, with extracts from the letter of Dr Maty, which was to have been inserted in the *Gazette de France*.

[3] Report by the Spanish ambassador of 10 June 1766; see Corney, I, 27. It is significant that the following report (somewhat garbled, but evidently referring to the Patagonian giants) appeared in *The Scots Magazine* (1766) as news from London on Byron's expedition, dated June 1766:
'It was reported that they had found out a new country in the East [sic], the inhabitants of which were nine feet high; but the report concerning the stature of the inhabitants was afterwards said to be fictitious'—*The Scots Magazine*, XXVIII (1766), 329.

[4] This may be a reference to the fact that no news of the giants had circulated on the return of Byron's store-ship the *Florida*, 21 June 1765.

has taken wind, can scarce be brought to give any Particulars to their most intimate Friends'.[1]

The sudden outburst of news on Byron's return and the reticence of the crew do suggest that the British Government used the giants to divert attention from the more serious and controversial episode of Byron's voyage, the visit to the Falkland Islands. How far the Government actually believed the reports of the giants is not known, but the Royal Society under Maty's auspices apparently did, and (as we have seen) publicized the reports with uncritical zeal. It is significant perhaps that when the crew did break their silence, the pronouncement came in the form of a letter to the Royal Society. One of Byron's midshipmen, Charles Clerke, sent an account of the giants to Dr Maty on 3 November 1766. The letter was read to the Royal Society on 12 February 1767 and published in the *Philosophical Transactions* for 1767.[2] It appeared to confirm the previous reports, for writing with what he called (pointedly, perhaps) 'the embellishment of truth', Clerke asserted that 'there was hardly a man there less than eight feet, most of them considerably more'. The publisher of a new edition of Walpole's *Account* accordingly corrected the statement that no account of the giants had yet been transmitted to the Royal Society, and declared that Clerke's account 'bordered so nearly on the marvellous, that it was deemed by many an imposition on that respectable Society'.[3] If Clerke was taking a rise out of the Royal Society, as Beaglehole thinks he may have been,[4] he was not alone in the jest. A similar account was published as a footnote in the anonymous journal of Byron's voyage (1767), its striking descriptions enlivened by a picture of an English sailor whose head reached the waist of his

---

[1] S.T., *An Account of the Giants lately discovered; in a letter to a Friend in the Country* (1766). Horace Walpole is identified as the author in J. Kennedy, W. A. Smith and A. F. Johnson, *Dictionary of Anonymous and Pseudonymous English Literature* (*Samuel Halkett and John Laing*), I (1926), 15. Coyer mentions the satire in his *Letter*, p. 65. Printed below, pp. 200–9.

[2] *Philosophical Transactions . . . for . . . 1767*, LVII (1768), 75–9. Printed below, pp. 210–13.

[3] *An Account of the Giants . . . First printed in 1766* (1783), 116n.

[4] *Journals of Captain Cook*, I, lxxxviii, note 1. The wording of Clerke's letter does give some support for this view: he writes of the account: 'it will make me extremely happy if I can render it in the least amusing or agreeable to you' (p. 75).

Patagonian hosts.[1] Byron himself wrote in his memorandum to the naturalist Thomas Pennant (1771): 'They were certainly of a most amazing size ... to this instant I believe there is not a man that landed with me, though they were at some distance from them, but would swear they took them to be nine feet high. I do suppose many of them were between seven and eight, and strong in proportion'.[2] It will be noted that Byron's more sensational statements were derived from the observations of his men, and that while Byron did not contradict these, he did not go all the way with them. Thus the reports of the giants cannot be said to be just the result of either innocent or calculated exaggeration at second-hand, yet when carefully examined they reveal two levels of testimony, the evidence of the officers who actually met the giants at close quarters, and that of the men who watched from a distance or even from the ship. Byron's own account in his manuscript journal was not as exaggerated as the version of it which appeared in Hawkesworth's *Voyages*, and which gave final authority to Byron's giants.[3] Byron had described their chief as 'one of the most extraordinary men for size I had ever seen till then'.[4] In Hawkesworth the man attained 'a gigantic stature', and 'seemed to realize the tales of monsters in a human shape'.[5] Where Byron wrote that 'Mr. Cumming ... was as much astonished at the size & figure of these People as I was, for tho' he is very tall himself he appeared comparitively speaking a mere shrimp to them', Hawkesworth, ostensibly in Byron's own words, referred to Mr Cumming's astonishment 'upon perceiving himself, though six feet two inches high, become at once a pigmy among giants; for these people may indeed more properly be called giants than tall men'.[6] This was a material change from Byron's words, that these people

---

[1] *A Voyage round the world* (1767), 49–53 and frontispiece (see Pl. VII). An appendix to the volume outlined the whole history of the giants from Magellan's discovery onwards. (Printed below, pp. 197–9.) C. de Pauw in his *Recherches philosophiques*, I, (1770), 306, wrote of the anonymous account that 'Byron ... pour se prêter aux vues du Ministère Anglois, a bien voulu se déclarer auteur d'une relation que le moindre matelot de son escadre n'auroit osé publier'.

[2] Pennant, *Of the Patagonians* (1778), 16.

[3] See above, pp. lxxvi–lxxxii, for a discussion of Hawkesworth's faults of editing in dealing with this and other topics.

[4] Byron's MS Journal, 57–8, N.M.M., MS 57/053.

[5] Hawkesworth, I, 28.

[6] Hawkesworth, I, 31.

'come the nearest to Giants I believe of any People in the World'.[1]

As Byron and his men had been genuinely astonished at the size of the Patagonians, and the matter had rapidly become an issue of national and international interest, it was natural that Byron's successors, Wallis and Carteret, should plan to make further and more exact observations of the Patagonians on their voyage in 1766; indeed the belief that this was one of the Admiralty's objectives in dispatching their expedition—either genuine or pretended—was still current in 1767.[2] Dr Maty himself evidently commissioned Carteret—a personal friend—to make a report and to send it back without delay;[3] and he had good reason for this importunity; for (unknown to Walpole) he was already being criticized in France for allowing his good name and that of the Royal Society to be involved in the controversy. La Condamine, in his letter published in the *Journal encyclopédique* of 1 August 1766, was pained (he wrote) that his friend Dr Maty should have been taken in by the reports and rumours of the giants, and that the Royal Society should have treated the matter so lightly.[4] An urgent appeal for information from Maty would explain why Carteret sent home a letter on the Patagonians to him by the store-ship from Port Famine.[5] As Maty never received it, the first report of Wallis's and Carteret's encounter with the Patagonians appeared in a letter written at Port Famine by one of the carpenters in the *Dolphin*. This letter did reach home safely in the storeship, and was published in London in May 1767. It reported that the expedition 'had been at the land of Giants, of whom the biggest are eight feet in height, but that the ordinary stature obtaining among them is seven and a half feet'.[6] Wallis's barber Rogers Richardson,

---

[1] See above p. 46.

[2] Coyer writes in his *Lettre au Docteur Maty . . . sur les Géants Patagons* (1767), 71–2: 'S'il est vrai, comme je l'apprends, que votre Amirauté vient d'expédier le *Dauphin* pour suivre cette découverte, nous serons *instruits*.' In fact the Patagonians were not specifically mentioned in Wallis's instructions in 1766.

[3] Maty never received the first letter sent by Carteret, who forwarded a copy later (20 April 1769).

[4] *Journal encyclopédique*, V (1766), 133.

[5] See Helen Wallis (ed.), *Philip Carteret's Voyage round the World* (Hakluyt Society, ser. II, no. 124), Document No. 39.

[6] Quoted by the Spanish ambassador to the Spanish Minister of State, 1 June 1767 (Corney, I, 71–2). A report in the Spanish newspaper *Mercurio*

AB, under the inspiration of poetic licence, went further in the 'poetical essay' which he presented to Wallis:

> The well known Streights we enter then
> So famed for its Gigantic Men
> Whose Height from six feet, reach'd to ten.

To this Wallis carefully appended a note that 'ten' meant 'six feet ten inches'![1]

Wallis and Carteret in fact showed the Patagonian to be what Walpole's 'Mrs ——' called 'only a well-made Man'.[2] Carteret's statement that none of the Patagonians was above six feet seven inches high was borne out by Wallis's description of them as 'a very stout People, few of them if any under six feet; many six feet six inchess, and one six feet seven inchess—for I took a measure in shoar with me, and measured more than twenty'.[3] Wallis measured only the tallest, and estimated that 'the major part of them were from 5 feet 10 inches to six feet'.[4] These moderate statements did not deter Hawkesworth from drawing the following conclusion, at the end of his survey of the history of the Patagonian giants in his General Introduction: 'Upon the whole, it may reasonably be presumed, that the concurrent testimony of late navigators, particularly Commodore Byron, Captain Wallis, and Captain Carteret, Gentlemen of unquestionable veracity, who are still living, will put an end to all the doubts that have been hitherto entertained of their existence'.[5] Hawkesworth's engraved plate illustrating Byron's interview with the Patagonians bore out these remarks; and for many years after the publication of Hawkesworth popular collections of voyages included illustrations of still more substantial giants.[6] The reviewer in the *Annual Register* likewise

Histórico y Político for May 1767 reported that the *Prince Frederick* had brought back three men and a boy 'of gigantic stature'. (Corney, I, 153.) This statement presumably arose from a confused version of the report that three men and two women went on board the *Dolphin* in Patagonia. (See Corney, I, 139.)

[1] The poem is copied out by Wallis in his *Journal* (Willyams MS).
[2] S.T., *Account* (1766), 4.
[3] Wallis's log, Willyams MS, 17 December 1766.
[4] Wallis's log, P.R.O. Adm. 55/35, 17 December 1766. See also Hawkesworth's account (I, 374), which was based on this log.
[5] Hawkesworth, I, xvi.
[6] Bernard Smith, *European vision and the South Pacific 1768–1850* (1960), 21, 29; and pl. 27.

added to his stirring words on Byron's giants the remark: 'and Capt. Wallis also met them afterwards, though he seems rather to lower the account of the commodore; yet they both establish the certainty of the existence of a race of men of a greater height than is known in any other part of the world'.

Philosophers also found ways of accepting the apparently conflicting evidence of the two voyages as being of equal validity. This was made possible by Byron's assertion that the Patagonians whom he had seen in 1764 were not the same people as those encountered on the second voyage: a conclusion based on the fact that officers who had sailed on both voyages were said to have denied that they had seen any of the objects which Byron distributed.[1] This was alleged despite the fact that Wallis noticed 'beads similar to those I gave them, and two had pieces of Red Baise, which makes me think that some among them were seen by Commodore Byron two years ago, only their Bulk does not answer the discription'.[2] Thus Pennant made a vigorous defence of the theory of the existence of the giants. The people described by Carteret and Wallis were placed in his 'second class' of Patagonian: people who exceeded the common height of Europeans by only a few inches or perhaps the head. As Bougainville's report on the size of the Patagonians supported the evidence of Carteret and Wallis, he suggested that Bougainville had met the same people. The Tierra del Fuegans belonged to the first class of Patagonian, men of ordinary size, and the giants to the third class, those 'whose height is so extraordinary as to occasion so great a disbelief . . . yet they are indisputable an existent people'.[3] These were the people who had been seen by Magellan and six other expeditions in the sixteenth century and by two if not three expeditions in the eighteenth century. Pennant was not deterred from invoking the Jesuit Father Falkner as a further authority for the giants, although during thirty-eight years of residence with the Patagonians Falkner claimed to have heard no report of the 'gigantic race', and had himself met only one exceptionally tall Patagonian.[4] In defence of

---

[1] Byron's memorandum in Pennant (1788), 16.
[2] Wallis's log, P.R.O., Adm. 55/35, 17 December 1766. (See also Hawkesworth, I, 375.) 'Their Bulk' evidently refers to the Patagonians' size.
[3] Pennant (1788), 13–14.   [4] Falkner, 26.

those who had given credence to the existence of the giants—notably Dr Maty—Pennant censured as illiberal and prejudiced the authorities who considered that the reports of Carteret, Wallis and Bougainville had invalidated the reports of Byron and Clerke. Two years later, Lord Monboddo was to claim with equal assurance that Hawkesworth 'has fairly stated the evidence on both sides; by which I think it is proved, as much as a fact of that kind can well be, unless we shall set mere negative evidence against positive, that men of such a size are to be found in the southern parts of the South continent of America'.[1]

It is easier to understand the unwillingness of natural philosophers at home to surrender their belief in the giants than to explain how the reports of the giants came to be made by apparently reliable witnesses in the first place. The explanation, as Gould suggests, seems to be simply that the average height of the Patagonians at six feet or a little more, is considerably above that of any other people. Estimates made without measuring rods would give rise to an exaggeration of their height on account of their large stature: 'What makes them appear gigantic, are their prodigious broad shoulders, the size of their heads, and the thickness of all their limbs,' Bougainville concluded from his encounter in December 1767,[2] thus confirming the impression made on his previous visit of 'ces Patagons si décriés, & que nous n'avons trouvés ni plus grands, ni même aussi mechans, que les autres hommes'.[3] Calling the Patagonians 'these mis-named giants',[4] Darwin wrote (in 1834): 'Their height appears greater than it really is, from their large guanaco mantles, their long flowing hair and general figure.'[5] Fitz-Roy pointed out that when seated they would look taller than they really were because of the disproportionate

[1] J. B. Monboddo, *Of the Origin & Progress of Language*, 2nd ed., 1 (1774), 267–8, n.
[2] Bougainville (1773), 142.
[3] Bougainville's letter of 26 August 1765 to Dom Pernetty, published by Pernetty in *Journal historique d'un Voyage fait aux Iles Malouines en 1763 & 1764* . . . (1769), II, 651–2. Bougainville's conclusion did not win Pernetty from his firm belief in the 'Patagons-Géans' (as he listed them in his index). Like other philosophers, he preferred the more spectacular evidence of Byron and Cumming, and of Bougainville's officers, Duclos-Guyot and Chenard de la Giraudais. (I, v– xii; II, 660–1.)
[4] 30 January 1834: *The Beagle Diary* (1933), 207.
[5] Darwin, *Voyage of the Beagle* (1906; reprint 1955), 221.

size of the upper parts of their bodies.[1] The fact that they wore their capes loose (as Byron notes)[2] would also make them look larger. As most of Byron's men saw the Patagonians at a distance, and seated for much of the time, all these factors would contribute to the exaggerated impressions received. It is even possible that the men watching from the ship thought some of the Patagonians who were on horseback were on foot. The over-estimate of their size by Byron and Cumming, the only men to meet the Patagonians at close quarters, can be explained by the fact that most people over-estimate the height of anyone considerably larger than they are. When unusually large men are also unusually strong (unlike freak giants),[3] this effect must be heightened, as in the following incident, described by Molyneux: 'The Master of the Prince Frederick is a fatt Lusty man But one of the Indians lifted him off the Ground with one Hand with Pleasure'.[4] A natural instinct to improve on a good story would be enough to do the rest. The Government on their side undoubtedly made political capital out of the giants, in the hope of distracting the attention of the French and Spanish governments from more serious issues.

That these are the true explanations of the legend of the giants, and in particular of Byron's giants, is clear from the confession finally obtained from one of the chief figures in Byron's drama, Lieutenant James Cumming. Questioned on the subject, he 'evinced some reluctance to enter on the discussion; but at length it was partly gathered and partly extorted from him, that had the occurrence taken place any where else than at Patagonia, they should have set them down as good sturdy savages, and thought no farther about them'.[5]

Carteret's letter to Maty on the Patagonians was read to the

---

[1] Fitz-Roy, I, 100.

[2] See his letter, Document No. 1.

[3] Gould (p. 25) explains that a man's weight varies roughly as the cube of his height, but his strength as the square. Thus the circus dwarf is usually much stronger in proportion to his size than the circus giant.

[4] Molyneux's Log, 17 December 1766 (British Museum, Add. MS 47, 106).

[5] *An historical account of the circumnavigation of the globe* [Edinburgh Cabinet Library, XXI (1836)], 201. The anecdote first appeared in an edition of Byron's *Narrative* of 1812. The statement was made to the uncle of Sir Walter Scott, Captain Scott of Rosebank. I am indebted to Mr G. P. B. Naish for the reference.

Royal Society on 25 January 1770 and appeared in the *Philosophical Transactions* of the following year.[1] As a reasoned scientific account of the supposed giants it must have helped to restore the reputations of Maty and the Royal Society. Maty had not only presented Byron's report on the giants to scholars in England and France, but he had also (in his letter to M. de La Lande) used it to support a general theory of natural history in opposition to M. de Buffon's: 'L'existence des Géants est donc confirmée: on en a vu & *manié* plusieurs centaines. Le terroir de l'Amérique peut donc produire des colosses, & la puissance génératrice n'y est point dans l'enfance'.[2] When taken to task by La Condamine, he had answered all the points with new arguments of his own, denying the accusation that the news was an 'artifice of government, to conceal the true object of the expedition'. 'Can it be believed', he wrote (as Coyer reports), 'that so many persons should combine to impose on us, by affirming that on the East side of South America, they saw a company of four or five hundred men, women, and children, taller by two or three feet than us Europeans.' He also cited a letter by Byron[3] as authenticating the facts, and an eye-witness account.[4] This enthusiastic support for the giants provoked other scholars besides La Condamine to criticize—and to ridicule—the scholarship of Maty and the Royal Society. Coyer's satirical essay, *Lettre au Docteur Maty . . . sur les Géants Patagons*, appeared in 1767;[5] and in 1768–9 the memorialist M. de Pxxx (Corneille de Pauw) in his *Recherches Philosophiques sur les Americains*, which set out all the evidence against the giants, including slighting references to Dr Maty, 'si connu par sa petite taille & son Journal

[1] *Philosophical Transactions* LX (1771), 20–6. Printed in Wallis, *Carteret* (1963), Document No. 39, with an appendix by the editor.

[2] Quoted by M. de P[auw] in his *Recherches Philosophiques sur les Americains* (Berlin, 1771), I, 307. Both La Condamine and Coyer refer to the letter from Maty. See Coyer, *Letter* (1767), 24.

[3] Presumably similar to Byron's memorandum to Pennant (1771). See above, p. 189, n. 2.

[4] Coyer, *Letter*, 26–9. The eye-witness account was presumably Clerke's; printed below, pp. 210–13.

[5] See above, p. 187, n. 1. The essay ends with an account of a Patagonian Utopia, and like other critics, Coyer could not resist some personal sallies against Maty himself: 'D'ailleurs y-a-t-il tant de mal à tenir un peu aux Géants? Ils valent peut-être mieux que les petits hommes qui ne sauroient vivre en paix.' *Lettre*, 1–2.

Britannique'.[1] Although Dr Maty was defended by other controversialists, such as Dom Pernetty in his critique of M. de Pauw's memoir,[2] Carteret's reasoned scientific report to the Royal Society may have been a more compelling corrective. Many details from Carteret's report, for example, were included in Pennant's essay;[3] but in defending Maty, Pennant himself was on the side of the giants.[4] Carteret thus helped to silence one of the last echoes of Mandeville's medieval fables. Even so, the giants in a slightly less exaggerated form still made occasional appearances. A Captain Coleman in 1793 saw between 400 and 500 Patagonians, 'whose stature has given rise to so much altercation and debate. They are from seven and an half to eight feet high, remarkably stout, and very affable . . .', as the *Naval Chronicle* reported in 1799.[5] A final postscript comes from the pen of Byron's grandson, the poet, in a letter of 20 August 1819 from Bologna to John Cam Hobhouse: 'and now what do you think of doing? I have two notions: one to visit England in the Spring, the other to go to South America. Europe is grown decrepit. . . . Besides, I am enamoured of General Paer, who has proved that my grandfather spoke truth about the Patagonians, with his gigantic cavalry'.[6]

[1] *Recherches Philosophiques*, I, 306–7. This is beyond doubt the memoir which Pennant criticizes so vigorously for its attacks on Maty, naming the author as M. de Premontal (sometimes Premontel). Pennant was probably led into this false identification by the fact that Andre-Pierre Le Guay de Premontval (1716–1764) was an Academician of Berlin and a noted controversialist; and that the *Recherches* by 'M. de Pxxx' were first published in Berlin by the Royal Printer.

[2] Dom Pernetty: *Dissertation sur l'Amérique et les Américains, contre les Recherches Philosophiques* (1770), 65–6. This was answered by De Pauw in his *Défense des Recherches Philosophiaues* (1770–71), which was answered in turn by the *Examen des Recherches Philosophiques . . . et de la défense de cet ouvrage* (1771).

[3] Pennant's essay was originally written in 1771, in the form of a letter to Daines Barrington, and was occasioned by a recent visit of Pennant to Father Falkner. It was privately printed with additions (such as references to Hawkesworth's *Voyages*) in 1788, and was reprinted in Pennant's *Literary Life* (1793) as Appendix No. 1, pp. 47–69.

[4] I am much indebted to Dr Jean Paul Faivre of Paris for his help in the elucidation of many obscure points in the controversy over the Patagonian giants.

[5] *Naval Chronicle*, I (1799), 126.

[6] Peter Quennell (ed.), *Byron. A Self-Portrait. Letters and diaries 1798 to 1824*, II (1950), 483. 'Paer' [sic] is José Antonio Paez, the Venezuelan patriot general whose cowboy *llaneros* defeated the Spaniards in 1819.

2. *Appendix to* A Voyage round the World, in . . . the *Dolphin* . . . By an Officer (*1767*)

As the discovery of the gigantic race of Patagonians is one of the most curious and extraordinary particulars of this voyage, the editor imagines it will be proper here to lay before the reader, what has been said by the authors of former voyages on this subject, with some remarks. Indeed, one important consequence of this voyage, is the putting an end to the dispute, which for two centuries and a half has subsisted between geographers, in relation to the reality of their being a nation of people of such an amazing stature, of which the concurrent testimony of all on board the Dolphin and Tamer can now leave no room for doubt.

These were seen by Magellan, whose ship was the first which visited that coast, and who in 1519, discovered the streights that bear his name: but the writer of that voyage has mingled with his description of them circumstances that are equally fabulous and absurd, and that are only calculated to disguise truth in the habit of fiction. Speaking of one of these people who came on board, he says, 'his bulk and stature were such, as would easily allow him the character of a giant: the head of one of our middle-sized men reached but to his waist, and he was proportionably big.' So far was without doubt strictly true; but he proceeds, 'His body was formidably painted, especially his face, a stag's horn being drawn upon each cheek, and great circles about his eyes: his colour was otherwise mostly yellow, only his hair was white. For his apparel he had the skin of a beast clumsily sewed together; but a beast as strange as he that wore it, neither mule, horse, nor camel; but something of each, the ears of the first, the tail of the second, and the shape and body of the last. It was an entire suit, all of one piece from head to foot. The arms he brought with him were a stout bow and arrows; the string of the former was a gut or sinew of that monstrous beast, and the latter, instead of iron heads, were tipped with sharp stones. The Admiral made him eat and drink, and he

197

seemed to enjoy himself very comfortably, till casting his eyes on a great looking-glass, he was in such a fright, that starting back, he threw a couple of men that stood by him to the ground: however, he fared so well, that we had soon the company of more, and the Admiral, being desirous of making some of these gigantic people prisoners, his crew filled their hands with toys that pleased them, and in the mean time put iron shackles on their legs, which they thought were very fine play things, and were pleased with their jingling sound, till they found how they were hampered and betrayed: but then they fell a bellowing like bulls, and in that extremity implored the help of Setebos. One alone tried the utmost force of nine men that were employed to master him, and though they had him down, and bound his hands tightly, yet he freed himself from his bonds, and got loose, in spite of all their endeavours to hold him. Their appetite is proportionable to their strength; for one of them eat up a whole basket of ship biscuit at a meal, and they eat their flesh raw. They have no fixed habitations, but certain moveable cottages.' We are here to remark, that it was impossible the author should know their language, and yet he asserts, that they report strange things of horrid forms and appearances frequently seen amongst them; of horned dæmons with long shaggy hair, throwing out fire both before and behind. Their pretended practice of physic is equally absurd and ridiculous: this he represents as consisting only of bleeding and vomiting, the former by giving a good chop with an edge tool in the part affected, whether the leg, arm, or face; and that to procure a vomit, they thrust an arrow a foot and a half down their throats. Which circumstances must undoubtedly destroy the credit of his narration, though in other particulars it was true and accurate.

These people are afterwards mentioned by Sir Thomas Cavendish, who seems to have seen them only at a distance, and to have judged of their stature by the print of their feet in the sand; for having observed, that they killed two of his people with their arrows, he says, they seemed of a gigantic race, the measure of one of their feet being eighteen inches in length. Hence he gave this country the name of Patagonia, by which he meant to signify, that the people were five cubits and a half high.

The public were afterwards informed by the writer of Admiral

Van Noort's voyage made in 1598, that they learned from an Indian boy, whom they carried away with them from the streights of Magellan, and taught him Dutch, that the country was inhabited by four tribes, three of which were of the ordinary size, but the fourth were ten or twelve feet high. This is indeed only the testimony of a boy; but in the account of a voyage made the same year by the Dutch captain Sebald de Weert, this boy's testimony was confirmed; for that captain, says he found seven canoes in the streights of Magellan, in which were savages of a reddish colour and long hair, who appeared to be ten or eleven feet high.

Those people were likewise mentioned by Admiral Spelbergen, who sailed through the streights of Magellan in the year 1614, and observes, that they one day saw a man on shore who first climbed one hill, and then another, to look at the fleet, and at last came to the sea-side for the same purpose, so that he was seen by all on board, who unanimously concluded, that he was taller than these people had been represented by the author of Magellan's voyage.

The last author who mentions these Patagonians is captain Shelvock, who, in his account of his voyage round the world in 1719, describing the island of Chiloe, which is opposite the coast of Chili, in the forty-third degree south latitude, says, 'the generality of the people are of the ordinary stature; but that according to Mons. Frazier, in the inland part of the continent, there is a race of an extraordinary size, and that he was credibly informed by several who had been eye-witnesses, that some were about nine or ten feet high.'

In short, this voyage has effectually established the testimony of these authors with respect to the size of the Patagonians, which we would consider separately from the other circumstances they have mentioned, that appear to be merely fanciful. What use Divines may make of this, we know not; but it certainly proves what is recorded in scripture, and even in heathen authors, that there was, (and still is) a race of giants.

3. *An Account of the Giants lately discovered;*
In a Letter to a Friend in the Country[1]

First printed in 1766

Dear Will,

Though people in the country are enough disposed to believe
wonders, yet are they prudently apt to suspend giving credit to all
that are sent from London, except of a political cast. You good folks
still believe in an uninterrupted generation of Patriots; and, though
they so seldom come to years of maturity, you trust in them as fast
as they are produced in St. Stephen's Chapel. For other monstrous
births, you are fonder of them, the farther they come. Ghosts and
Witches are entirely of your own growth. Excepting the famous
Ghost of a Sound in Cock Lane, from which the Methodists
expected such a rich harvest (for what might not a rising Church
promise itself from such well-imagined nonsense as the Apparition
of a Noise?); I think many, many years have elapsed, since the
Capital could boast of having regenerated a Spirit. Your sagacity
will therefore incline you to doubt the marvellous account I am
going to give you of a new-discovered race of Giants.

Perhaps you will take the relation for some political allegory, or
think it a new-vamped edition of Swift's Brobdignags. My good
Friend, it is neither the one nor the other; though, I must own, a
political mystery, and a wonderful one too, for it is really kept a
secret.—The very crew of the ship, who saw five hundred of these
lofty personages, did not utter a word of the matter for a whole
year; and even now, that a general idea has taken wind, can scarce
be brought to give any particulars to their most intimate friends.

All that the public can yet learn is, that Captain Byron and his
men have seen on the coast of Patagonia five hundred Giants on
horseback. Giants! you will cry; what do you call Giants? Why, my
Friend, not men of fifty or an hundred feet high; yet still very

[1] *The Repository . . . of Wit and Humor*, I (London, 1783), 101–20.

personable Giants, and much taller than any individual ever exhibited at Charing Cross. Come, what do you think of nine or ten feet high? and what do you think of five hundred such? Will Mrs. ——— cry, 'Pish! That is no Giant; it is only a well-made Man!'

I am told, for I am no reader of Travels, that this Gigantic nation was known to exist as early as the discovery of that continent: that Sir John Narborough mentions them; and of late years, Maupertuis. The Spaniards assert, that they have long been acquainted with their existence—So *they*, you see, can keep a secret too. But the reasons given why we know so little of the matter are, that few ships ever touch on that coast, standing more out to sea, in order to double the Cape; and that these Giants are a roving nation, and seldom come down to the coast, and then, I suppose, only *to bob for Whales*.

You will be eager to know a great deal more than I can tell you; but thus much, I think, is allowed. That Captain Byron, being on that coast, saw a body of men at a distance, on very small horses; as they approached, he perceived that the horses were common-sized horses, but that the riders were enormously tall, though I do not hear that their legs trailed much on the ground. This was fine game for a man sent on discoveries. The Captain and part of his crew immediately landed; on which Messieurs the Giants as quickly retreated. Whether this timidity was owing to the terror which the English arms have struck into all parts of the known, and, I conclude, unknown world; whether they took Captain Byron for Mr. Pitt; whether they took our men for Spaniards, whose name must be in horror to all Americans; or whether they had any apprehensions of fire-arms; I cannot tell. Be that as it may, the more the Captain and his men advanced, the faster the Giants kept trotting off. Seeing this, the Captain took a bold and sensible resolution: he ordered his men to lay down their arms and remain stock-still, himself alone advancing. I doubt much whether Homer would have cared to venture his Jupiter alone against five hundred Titans.

Captain Byron's Titans had more of the *sçavoir vivre*; and, seeing him advance alone, stopped. He came up with them, and addressed them in all the languages he knew, and that they did not. They replied in the Giant-tongue, which, I am told, a very reverend Critic, upon the strength of one syllable which the Captain remembered, affirms is plainly Phœnician. The Captain, not being master of that exceedingly useful and obsolete language, had the misfortune of not comprehending a word they said. Had he been a deep Scholar, he would undoubtedly have had recourse to Hieroglyphics; which, the Learned tell us, was the first way of conveying instruction: but I must beg leave to observe, that it was very lucky the Captain had not so much erudition. I do not know whether he can *draw* or not; but most probably, if he can, he had not his implements with him. At most, perhaps, a black-lead pencil, or a pen and ink, and the cover of a letter. He could not with such tools have asked many questions; and, as the Giants are probably not better Painters than the Egyptians, he would have understood their answers as little as the Learned do the figures on obelisks. Thus he would have lost his time, and got no information; or, what is worse to every man but a Critic, have made a thousand absurd guesses. The Captain having a great deal more sense, and the savages some, they naturally fell into that *succedaneum* to language, Signs. Yet I do not hear that either side gained much information.

The first thing, or rather first sign, he said to them in this dilemma, was, *sit down*; which he explained by sitting down on the ground himself. The poor good Giants understood him, dismounted, and sat down too. It is said, but far be it from me to affirm it, that when the Captain (who I am told is upwards of six feet) rose again, the nearest Giant to him, though sitting, was taller than he.

An hour or two was spent in fruitlessly endeavouring to understand one another: all, I hear, the Captain comprehended was, that the Giants invited him very civilly to go with them into the woods, where, I suppose, Gigantopolis stands, and their king resides, who, no doubt, is at least two feet taller than the tallest of his grenadiers. The Captain declined the offer; at which these polite savages expressed much concern, but never once, as any still more polite people would have done, attempted to force him.

When he took his leave, they remained motionless; and continued so, as he observed by his glasses, till the ship was out of their sight.

Very few other particulars are come to my knowledge, except that they were cloathed in skins of beasts, and had their eyes painted of different colours; that they had no weapons, but spears pointed with fish-bones; that they devour fish raw; and that they shewed great repugnance to taste any liquids offered to them by the Captain; and that, though they were too polite absolutely to refuse his toast, they spit the liquor out of their mouths again; whether from apprehension of intoxication or poison, is not certain: however, it looks as if they had some notion of such European arts. What is more remarkable; the weather being very severe at that season, the whole Colossal troop seemed as sensible of the cold, and shivered like us little delicate mortals of six feet high. They had a few Giantesses with them; but, as the Captain did not survey them with the small end of his spying-glass, I do not hear that he was much struck with their charms.

This, my dear Friend, is all the satisfaction I can give you. However, I am proud to be the first who has communicated this important discovery to Europe.

The speculations it has already occasioned, and will occasion, are infinite. The Wolf of the Gevaudan, that terror of the French Monarchy, is already forgotten. Naturalists, Politicians, Divines, and Writers of Romance, have a new field opened to them. The scale of Being ascends; we mount from the Pigmies of Lapland to the Giants of Patagonia.

You will ask, but I cannot answer you, Whether the scale of the country is in proportion to such inhabitants? whether their oaks are half as lofty again as the British; and such is your zeal for England, you will already figure a fleet built of their timber. How large is the grain of their Corn? of what size their Sheep, Cows, and Poultry? Do not go and compute by Gulliver's measures, and tell me that a populous nation of such dimensions would devour the products of such a country as Great Tartary in half a year. Giants there are; but what proportionable food they have, except Elephants and Leviathans, is more than I can tell. They probably do not live upon Bantam Chicken.

As you are still more of a Politician than a Naturalist, you will be impatient to know if Captain Byron took possession of the country for the Crown of England; and to have his Majesty's style run, GEORGE the Third, by the Grace of GOD, King of *Great-Britain, France, Ireland, and the Giants!* You will ask, why some of their women were not brought away to mend our breed, which, all good Patriots assert, has been dwindling for some hundreds of years; and whether there is any gold or diamonds in the country? Mr. Whitfield wants to know the same thing; and, it is said, intends a visit, for the conversion of these poor blinded Savages.

As soon as they are properly civilized, that is, enslaved, due care will undoubtedly be taken to specify in their Charter, that these Giants shall be subject to the Parliament of Great Britain, and shall not wear a sheep's skin that is not legally stamped. A riot of Giants would be very unpleasant to an infant Colony. But experience, I hope, will teach us, that the invaluable liberties of Englishmen are not to be wantonly scattered all over the globe. Let us enjoy them ourselves; but they are too sacred to be communicated. If Giants once get an idea of freedom, they will soon be our masters instead of our slaves. But what pretensions can they have to freedom? They are as distinct from the common species as Blacks, and, by being larger, may be more useful: I would advise our prudent Merchants to employ them in the Sugar trade; they are capable of more labour; but even then they must be worse treated, if possible, than our Black Slaves are; they must be lamed and maimed, and have their spirits well-broken, or they may become dangerous. This too will give a little respite to Africa, where we have half exhausted the human, I mean, the Black breed, by that wise maxim of our Planters, that, if a Slave lives four years, he has earned his purchase-money, consequently you may afford to work him to death in that time.

The Mother Country is not only the first, but ought to be the sole, object of our political considerations. If we once begin to extend the idea of the love of our Country, it will embrace the Universe, and consequently annihilate all notion of our Country. The Romans, so much the object of modern admiration, were with difficulty persuaded to admit even the rest of Italy to be their Countrymen. The true Patriots never regarded any thing without the walls of Rome, except their own *villas*, as their Country. Every thing was done for immortal Rome; and it was immortal Rome that did every thing. Conquered nations, which to them answered to discovered nations with us, for they conquered as fast as they discovered, were always treated accordingly; and it is remarkable, that two men equally famous for their eloquence have been the only Two that ever had the weakness to think that conquered Countries were entitled to all the Blessings of the Mother Country. Cicero treated Sicily and Cilicia as tenderly as the district of Arpinum; and I doubt it was the folly of that example that misled his too exact Imitator on a late occasion. However, the Giants must be impressed with other ideas. Bless us! if, like that pigmy old Oliver, they should come to think the Speaker's mace a bawble!

What have we to do with America, but to conquer, enslave, and make it tend to the advantage of our commerce? Shall the noblest rivers in the World roll for Savages? shall mines teem with gold for the natives of the soil? and shall the world produce any thing but for England, France, and Spain? It is enough that the overflowings of riches in those three countries are every ten years wasted in Germany.

Still, my political Friend, I am not for occupying Patagonia, as we did Virginia, Carolina, &c. Such might be the politics of Queen Elizabeth's days. But modern improvements are wiser. If the Giants in question are masters of a rich and flourishing Empire, I think they ought to be put under their Majesties, a West-Indian Company; the Directors of which may retail out a small portion of their imperial revenues to the Proprietors, under the name of a DIVIDEND. This is an excellent scheme of Government, totally unknown to the Ancients. I can but think how poor Livy, or Tacitus, would have been hampered, in giving an account of such an *imperium in imperio*. Cassimirus Alius Caunus (for they Latinized every proper name, instead of delivering it as uncouthly pronounced by their soldiers and sailors) would have sounded well enough: but Dividends, Discounts, India Bonds, &c. were not made for the majesty of History. But I am wandering from my subject; though, while I am talking of the Stocks and Funds, I could chalk out a very pretty new South-Sea scheme, *à propos* to the Patagonians. It would not ruin above half the nation; and would make the fortunes of such industrious gentlemen as, during the want of a war in Germany, cannot turn Commissaries.

Command is the object of every man's ambition; but, by the impolitic assent of ages and nations to Hereditary Monarchy, you must be begotten on a Queen, or are for ever excluded from wearing a diadem; except in a very few instances; as in Poland, where the Throne is elective; in Corsica, where they will not acknowledge Hereditary Right, in the Republic of Genoa; in Russia, where a Soldier's Trull succeeded her Husband the Czar, and where there are other ways of succeeding a Husband; in Peru, where they are tired of exchanging their Gold for Tyrants; and in Paraguay, where the Outcasts of the Earth, and the Inventors of the Oath of Obedience, have thrown off all submission to their Prince, and, having mounted the Throne, will probably renounce the Oath of Chastity too. But it is to England that persons of the lowest birth are indebted for the invention and facility of weilding at least part of a scepter. Buy but an India Bond, and you have a property in the Kingdom of Bengal. Rise to be a Director, and the Mogul has not more power of appointing and displacing Nabobs. Indian Sovereigns may now be born in Threadneedle-street.

What the Government means, by pocketing a whole nation of Giants, is not to be conceived. It ought again to draw down the vengeance of their antagonists on the present Ministers. I am sure, they have done nothing worse. Who knows but at this instant they may be preparing to pour in forty or fifty thousand Giants upon us? Their love of liberty, their tenderness for the constitution, their lenity, mildness, and disinterestedness, their attention to the merchants, in short, all their virtues, may be affected, and only calculated to lull us asleep, until the fatal blow is struck. I own, my apprehensions are gloomy; yet, thank GOD, we have a pretty *tall* Opposition, who will not suffer us to be enslaved by any thing higher than themselves.

In the mean time, till we know something of the matter, it is to be hoped that all speculative Authors, who are so kind as to govern and reform the world through the channel of the News-papers, will turn their thoughts to plans for settling this new-acquired country. I call it new-acquired, because whoever finds a country though nobody has lost it, is from that instant intitled to take possession of it, for himself or his Sovereign. Europe has no other title to America; except force and murder, which are rather the executive parts of Government, than a right. Though Spain pretends a knowledge of our Giants, she has forfeited all pretensions to their allegiance by concealing the discovery; as is plain from the decision of the Canon Law, tit. 'De novis Regionibus non abscondendis'.

The first thought that will occur to every good Christian is, that this race of Giants ought to be exterminated, and their country colonized; but I have already mentioned the great utility that may be drawn from them in the light of Slaves. I have also said, that a moderate importation might be tolerated, for the sake of mending our breed; but I would by no means come into a project I have heard dropped, and in which propagation would not be concerned; I mean, the scheme of bringing over a number of Giants for second husbands to Dowagers. Ireland is already kept in a state of humiliation. We check their trade, and do not allow them to avail themselves of the best-situated harbours in the world. Matrimony is their only branch of commerce unrestricted; and it would be a most crying injustice to clog that too.

In truth, we are not sufficiently acquainted with these Goliahs, to decide peremptorily on their properties. No account of them has been yet transmitted to the Royal Society*: but it would be exceedingly adviseable, that a Jury of Matrons should be sent in the next embarkation, to make a report; and, old Women for old Women, I would trust to the analysis of the Matrons, in preference to that of the Philosophers.

I will now, my Friend, drop the political part of this discussion, and inform you what effect this phænomenon has had on another set of men. It has started an obvious and very perplexing question, viz. whether these Giants are *Aborigines*; if they are not, from which of the sons of Noah are they descended, and in that case how we shall account for this extraordinary increase of stature?

The modern Philosophers are peremptory that these Giants are *Aborigines*; that is, that their country has been inhabited by Giants from the creation of the world. The Scriptures, say those gentlemen, mention Giants, but never posterior to the Flood; whence

* An account of these formidable men appeared, soon after, in the Philosophical Transactions, vol. LVII. p. 75. dated *Nov.* 3, 1766; which bordered so nearly on the marvellous, that it was deemed by many an imposition on that respectable Society.

we ought to believe that they perished in the general deluge. Neither, add they, are we told that any son of Noah was of stature supereminent to his brethren. Yet we will suppose, say they, that some of their descendants might have shot-up to an extraordinary height, without notice being taken of it in Sacred Writ. Nay, they allow that this increase of stature might not have appeared till after the date of Holy Writ. Yet is it credible, say they, that a race of Giants should have been formed, and remain unknown to all ages, all nations, all history? Did these Monsters pass unobserved from the most Eastern part of the continent (the supposed communication by which America was peopled) to the Northern parts of the other world, and migrate down that whole continent to the most Southern point of it, without leaving any trace, even by tradition, in the memory of mankind? Or are we to believe, that tribes of Giants sailed from Africa to America? What vessels wafted them? Was Navigation so perfected in the infant-ages of the world, that fleets, enormously larger than any now existing, were constructed for the transporation of a race of Polyphemes? or, to come to the third point, is it the climate that has ripened them (as Jamaica swells Oranges to Shadocks) to this stupendous volume? But North and South of them are men of the ordinary size; nor has the same latitudes produced any thing similar, Natural Philosophers cannot account for it, therefore Divines certainly can; and, when this people shall be better known, I do not doubt but the mystery will be cleared up; for, as these Giants have indubitably remained unmixed longer than any other people, we shall probably discover stronger traces of their Jewish origin. Their cult is in all likelihood less corrupted from that of the sons of Noah, than is to be found elsewhere; their language possibly the genuine Hebrew, not Phœnicnan; and, if I might hazard a conjecture, these Giants are probably the descendants of the *ten tribes* so long lost, and so fruitlessly sought by the Learned; and, having deviated less from the true Religion of their forefathers, may have been restored to, or preserved in, their primitive stature and vigour. I offer this opinion with much modesty, though I think it more reasonable than any hypothesis I have yet heard on the subject.

Whatever their Religion shall appear to be, it will be matter of great curiosity. We scarce know of any people, except the

Hottentots, or the Heroes who lived in the days of Fingal, among whom no traces of any Religious notions or worship have been discovered.

If they are not Jews, but Idolaters, the statues of their Divinities, their sacrificing-instruments, or whatever are the trinkets of their devotion, will be great rarities, and worthy of a place in any Museum.

Their Poetry will be another object of inquiry; and, if their minds are at all in proportion to their bodies, must abound in the most lofty images, in the true sublime. Oh! if we could come at an Heroic Poem penned by a Giant! We should see other images than our puny Writers of Romance have conceived; and a little different from the cold tale of a late notable Author,* who did not know better what to do with his Giant than to make him grow till he shook his own castle about his own ears.

In short, my good Friend, here is ample room for speculation: but I hope we shall go calmly and systematically to work; that we shall not exterminate these poor Monsters, till we are fully acquainted with their History, Laws, Opinions, Police, &c.; that we shall not convert them to Christianity, only to cut their throats afterwards; that nobody will beg a million of acres of Giant-land, till we have determined what to do with the present occupiers: and that we shall not throw away fifteen or twenty thousand men in conquering their country, as we did at the Havannah, only to restore it to the Spaniards!   Yours,

July 1, 1766.   *S. T.*[1]

* The Author here alluded to is certainly the Gentleman who some time before gave to the Publick that very pleasing Romance, intituled, 'The Castle of Otranto.' Perhaps a careful perusal of the present performance, and an attentive comparison thereof with other pieces of humour known to be written by the same hand, will lead to a very probable conjecture concerning the Author of this excellent and humourous 'Account of the Giants'.

[1] I.e. Horace Walpole. See above p. 188, n.1.

4. *Letter from Charles Clerke to the Royal Society, 13 November 1766*[1]

'An account of the very tall Men, seen near the Streights of Magellan, in the Year 1764, by the Equipage of the Dolphin Man of War, under the Command of the Hon. Commodore Byron; in a Letter from Mr. Charles Clarke [*sic*], Officer on board the said Ship, to M. Maty, M. D. Sec. R. S.'

Weathersfield, November 3, 1766

Sir,

Read Feb. 12, 1767.

I Had the pleasure of seeing my friend Mr. M—— a few days ago, when he made me acquainted with your desire of a particular account of the Patagonians, which I most readily undertake to give, as it will make me extremely happy if I can render it in the least amusing or agreeable to you. I wish I could embellish it with language more worthy your perusal; however, I will give it the embellishment of truth, and rely on your goodness to excuse a tar's dialect.

We had not got above ten or twelve leagues into the streights of Magellan, from the Atlantic ocean, before we saw several people, some on horseback and some on foot, upon the north shore (continent), and with the help of our glasses could perceive them beckoning to us to come on shore, and at the same time observed to each other that they seemed of an extraordinary size; however we continued to stand on, and should have passed without taking the least farther notice of them, could we have proceeded, but our breeze dying away, and the tide making against us, we were obliged to anchor, when the commodore ordered his boat of twelve oars and another of six to be hoisted out, manned and armed. In the first went the commodore, in the other Mr. Cummings our first lieutenant and myself. At our first leaving the ship, their number

[1] From *Philosophical Transactions, Giving Some Account of the Present Undertakings, Studies, and Labours, of the Ingenious, in Many Considerable Parts of the World*, LVII (London, 1768), 75-9.

did not exceed forty; but as we approached the shore, we perceived them pouring down from all quarters, some galloping, others running, all making use of their utmost expedition. They collected themselves in a body, just at the place we steered for. When we had got within twelve or fourteen yards of the beach, we found it a disagreeable flat shore with very large stones, which we apprehended would injure the boat; so looked at two or three different places, to find the most convenient for landing. They supposed we deferred coming on shore, through apprehensions of danger from them, upon which they all threw open the skins which were over their shoulders, which was the only cloathing they had, and consequently the only thing they could secret any kind of arms with, and many of them laid down close to the water's edge. The commodore made a motion for them to go a little way from the water, that we might have room to land, which they immediately complied with, and withdrew thirty or forty yards; we then landed, and formed each man with his musquet, in case any violence should be offered. As soon as we were formed, the commodore went from us to them, then at about twenty yards distance; they seemed vastly happy at his going among them, immediately gathered round him, and made a rude kind of noise, which I believe was their method of singing, as their countenances bespoke it a species of jollity. The commodore then made a motion to them to sit down, which they did in a circle with him in the middle, when Mr. Byron took some beads and ribbons, which he had brought for that purpose, and tied about the women's necks, &c. with which they seemed infinitely pleased. We were struck with the greatest astonishment at the sight of people of such gigantic stature, notwithstanding our previous notice with our glasses from the ship; their number was increased by the time we got on shore to about five hundred, men, women, and children. The men and women both rid in the same manner; the women had a kind of belt to close their skin round the waist, which the men had not, as theirs were only flung over their shoulders, and tied with two little slips (cut from the skin) round the neck. At the time of the commodore's motion for them to retire farther up the beach, they all dismounted, and turned their horses loose, which were gentle and stood very quietly. The commodore, having disposed of all his presents and satisfied his curiosity, thought proper to retire, but they were vastly anxious to have him go up into the country to eat with them; (that they wanted him to go with them to eat, we could very well understand by their motion, but their language was wholly unintelligible to us.) There was a very great smoke to which they pointed, about a mile from us, where there must have been several fires; but some intervening hills prevented our seeing any thing but the smoke. The commodore returned the compliment, by inviting them on board the ship, but they would not favour him with their company, so we embarked and returned to the ship. We were with them near two hours at noon day, within a very few yards, though none had the honour of shaking hands but Mr. Byron and Mr. Cummings; however, we were near enough and long enough with them to convince our senses so far as not to be caviled out of the very existence of those senses at that time, which some of our countrymen and friends would absolutely attempt to do. They are of a copper colour, with long black hair, and some of them are certainly nine feet if they don't exceed it. The commodore, who is very near six foot, could but just reach the top of one of their heads, which he attempted, on tip toes, and there were several taller than him on whom the experiment was tried. They are prodigious stout, and as well and proportionally made as ever I saw people in my life. That they have some kind of arms among them is, I think, indisputable, from their taking methods to convince us they had none at that time about them. The women, I think, bear much the same proportion to the men as our Europeans do; there was hardly a man less than eight feet, most of them considerably more; the women, I believe, run from $7\frac{1}{2}$ to 8. Their horses were stout and bony, but not remarkably tall; they are in my opinion from 15 to $15\frac{1}{2}$ hands. They had a great number of dogs, about the size of a middling pointer, with a fox nose. They continued upon the beach till we got under way, which was two hours after we got on board; I believe, they had some expectations of our returning again; but as soon as they saw us getting off, they betook themselves to the country.

The country of Patagonia is rather hilly, though not remarkably so. You have here and there a ridge of hills, but no very high ones. We lay some time at Port Desire, which is not a great way to the northward of the streights, where we traversed the country many miles round; we found firebrands in different places, which convinced us there had been people, and we suppose them to have been the Patagonians. The soil is sandy, produces nothing but a coarse harsh grass, and a few small shrubs, of which Sir John Narborough remarked, he could not find one of size enough to make the helve of a hatchet, which observation we found very just. It was some time in december we made this visit to our gigantic friends. I am debarred being so particular as I could wish, from the loss of my journals, which were demanded by their lordships of the admiralty, immediately upon our return; but if any article is omitted which you are desirous of being acquainted with, I beg you will take some means of letting me know it, for I will most readily communicate every circumstance of the matter, that fell under my observation, as it is with the greatest pleasure and respect that I subscribe myself,

Sir,

Your very humble servant,
Charles Clarke.

INDEX